THE JAPANESE KITCHEN

THE JAPANESE KITCHEN

250 RECIPES IN A TRADITIONAL SPIRIT

Hiroko Shimbo

ILLUSTRATIONS BY RODICA PRATO

THE HARVARD COMMON PRESS

Boston, Massachusetts

The Harvard Common Press
535 Albany Street
Boston, Massachusetts 02118

Printed in the United States of America

Printed on acid-free paper

Library of Congress Cataloging-in-Publication Data

Shimbo-Beitchman, Hiroko.
The Japanese kitchen : 250 recipes in a traditional spirit /
Hiroko Shimbo ; illustrations by Rodica Prato.
p. cm.
Includes index.
ISBN 1-55832-176-4 (hc : alk. paper) — ISBN 1-55832-177-2 (pbk. : alk. paper)
1. Cookery, Japanese. I. Title.

TX724.5.J3 S5192 2000
641.5952—dc21
00-033505

Special bulk-order discounts are available on this and other
Harvard Common Press books. Companies and organizations may purchase books
for premiums or resale, or may arrange a custom edition, by contacting
the Marketing Director at the address above.

Cover photograph by Ellen Silverman

Cover design by Suzanne Heiser

Text design by Barbara M. Bachman

Illustrations by Rodica Prato

10 9 8 7 6 5 4 3 2 1

ACKNOWLEDGMENTS

I was blessed with the help of so many people who contributed their time and knowledge to this book.

My deepest appreciation is for my mother, who has been my mentor in creating *The Japanese Kitchen*.

My sincere thanks go also to the many people at each of the food production companies that I have visited over the years. The knowledge they shared is the basis of this book. Special thanks to Tsuyoshi Iio, Kazuhiko Morita, Akihiro Nemoto, Toshio Sumiya, and Ken'ichi Kotani, each of whom maintains in his own special way the culinary heritage of Japan.

Linda Ziedrich, my editor, who from our first acquaintance expressed her devoted interest in and deep understanding of Japanese cuisine and my manuscript, polished the book with her attentive professionalism. Without her patience and close assistance, the book would not be in the useful and accessible form in which it now exists.

Special thanks to Ellen Silverman, who took the cover photograph, and, for her generous help, to Christopher Hirsheimer, and executive editor and photographer at *Saveur* magazine.

Another special, heartfelt thank-you to Rodica Prato. Her charming and precise illustrations turned my book into a very attractive and useful one.

I would also like to extend heartfelt thanks to Dan Rosenberg, Bruce Shaw, Christine Alaimo, Debra Hudak, Skye Stewart, Jodi Marchowsky, and Jamie MacLachlan of the Harvard Common Press, for their confidence and their intensive, attentive professional support in all areas in producing *The Japanese Kitchen*.

Finally, this book could not be born without years of encouragement and devoted assistance from Buzz, my husband, best friend, and charming lover. Like my mother, Buzz cares about food with a love of all cuisines and joy in discovering new dining experiences. His experience of living in Japan for nearly fifteen years taught him much about Japanese culture, traditions, and history. He has been the principal critic of my cooking and recipes since we married, and he repeatedly edited my manuscript as I rewrote it many times over many years. Certainly this book is a child of ours, and we look forward to watching it grow by opening windows to a new world for you, the readers.

C O N T E N T S

...

PART I • THE JAPANESE KITCHEN • 7

FOREWORD

BY MING TSAI

The first time that I stepped into the kitchen of Hiroko Shimbo, I knew that I was in store for an exceptional treat. Her kitchen emitted a welcoming feeling that was matched only by Hiroko herself. Fresh, enticing aromas wafted from the simple, uncluttered, cooking space. Such smells were a true foreshadow of the exquisite dishes that I would soon have the opportunity to experience.

Hiroko's strong belief in traditionalism and purity of cuisine is manifested through her words and her cooking. It seems a bit odd, in fact, that she selected me to contribute to her book. As a chef who practices East-meets-West cooking, I am far from a traditionalist. But that is not to say that I do not respect and admire purist cooking. I feel that one must understand the authentic techniques and ingredients of each cuisine before beginning to create and blend new flavors.

Besides, Japanese cooking is not completely untouched. At the turn of the twentieth century, Japan underwent its own internal mixing of cuisines when its borders were opened to the outside world. French influences are apparent in *omu raisu* (rice-filled omelette), while German flavors inspired *tonkatsu* (pork cutlet), a twist on *Wiener schnitzel*. Both dishes found a permanent position in native Japanese cuisine.

The Japanese Kitchen is the culmination of Hiroko's life work, through which she hopes to bring her authentic cuisine to cooks at all levels. Her aim is to demystify Japanese cuisine by systematically describing the major ingredients and techniques. Hailing from Kanazawa and Tokyo, she explores the diverse tastes and specialties of the many regions of Japan. One of her goals is to illustrate that Japanese cooking reaches far beyond the ubiquitous California roll. Her book guides the reader through the preparation of more familiar dishes like miso soup and sushi, and also highlights the incredible diversity of the cuisine through many hot dishes. *Satsuma-age* (golden brown fish cakes), *suzuki no sake-mushi* (steamed ginger-flavored sea bass), and *gyuniku no misozuke* (pan-fried miso-marinated beef) are just a sampling of the recipes that compose the far-reaching Japanese repertoire.

To Hiroko, Japanese food is a way of life, one that she hopes to make accessible to those who enjoy the world of food. She stresses that the freshness and quality of ingredients are the key elements in creating a tasteful finished dish. As people become more health-conscious, they are seeking out foods that will contribute to a healthy diet. Japanese cuisine can fill this need. Ingredients that are natural and pure produce dishes that are inherently healthy.

It is an honor to help bring Hiroko's great knowledge to the public realm. *The Japanese Kitchen* is a tool that should hold a place in the library of every cook. From beginners to seasoned chefs, all will learn a great deal from Hiroko. Her concise and insightful writing combines with her warm and sincere personality to create an inviting guide to the world of Japanese cuisine.

Ming Tsai

PREFACE

In the past, Japanese cuisine was generally regarded as a very special culinary art, separate and distinct from the world's other cuisines and with limited appeal beyond the borders of Japan. Only in the past 30 years has this view begun to change.

Perhaps the first widely disseminated influence of Japanese cooking occurred in the 1970s, with the emergence of French nouvelle cuisine. This style adopted the look, but not the ingredients, techniques, or preparations of Japanese cooking. Nouvelle cuisine attempted to capture the visual beauty of Japanese presentations, but without any Japanese content.

The real explosion in the spread of Japanese cooking came with the international popularization of sushi in the 1980s and nineties. Indeed, I know of intersections in New York where there is a sushi shop on every corner. My husband and I have seen sushi restaurants in small American towns, in Moscow, in Johannesburg, in Caracas, in Sydney, and in every major city—and many not-so-major cities—in Europe.

At the same time as the sushi craze came "fusion," in which creative restaurant chefs tried, with widely varying degrees of success, to integrate Japanese ingredients into Western cooking. Tuna tartare, and its nearly Japanese cousins made with wasabi, *shoyu* (soy sauce), *mirin* (sweet cooking wine), and other Japanese materials, found its way onto menus in sophisticated restaurants around the globe. Unfortunately, many times a poor understanding of the materials and their proper uses resulted more in confusion than fusion.

But now the stage has been set for the introduction of Japanese cuisine to a broad audience of non-Japanese amateur and professional cooks. Through the spread of information about Japanese food, the public is becoming aware of the health and nutritional benefits of Japanese cooking, and of the wonderful variety of tastes, aromas, and textures provided by this unique cuisine. It is time for Japanese food to appear on the dining tables of Western homes and non-Japanese restaurants alike. The ingredients and techniques of Japanese cooking can now be presented without mystery for preparation in ordinary Western kitchens by cooks without specialized training. This is the purpose of my book.

I began teaching Japanese cooking twelve years ago to non-Japanese students in Tokyo. I entered this challenging business as a natural result of my upbringing. I was born into a doctor's family, as were both my father and mother. Just as my mother had, I grew up with a kitchen always full of cooking aromas and a huge variety of ingredients. This is because our home in Tokyo also served as my father's clinic. My father, a surgeon, performed minor operations at his clinic, so it included a hospital with a half-dozen beds. Since there were always several patients staying with us, my mother and an assistant cook worked in the kitchen from morning till night to prepare three daily meals for the patients as well as for the family.

The meals for the patients were typically bland hospital food—very plain, and rather tasteless and colorless. Little salt, oil, or other condiments were included, and the vegetables were usually cooked a long time, so that the patients could consume and digest them easily. In contrast, our family dinners were always flavorful, varied, and plentiful. As was customary in Japan, my father's patients often sent him thank-you gifts of fresh fish and shellfish and the best seasonal vegetables and fruits from all over the country. Western-style sausages and hams, and basic ingredients such as *shoyu* (soy sauce), sugar, and oil, were delivered to our door by messenger services all the year around. With these plentiful but disparate ingredients in the kitchen, my mother, who was bored by cooking bland food for the patients, devoted her love and labor to creating delicious and attractive meals for us. This is how I, as a child, came to know and enjoy good foods of all kinds. It is my mother's enthusiasm for good cooking that I wish to pass on to you, the readers of this book.

When I first began teaching, I was unprepared for many of my students' questions: How is this product made? How is that ingredient connected to the culture and history of Japan? What is the shelf life of this product? Where can I buy these products, and how can I identify them? What is the effect of cooking this ingredient? What is the nutritional value of this product? And so on. These are questions I had never pondered, since I grew up so close to these foods. I began to realize how limited my own knowledge was. This inspired me to visit food producers across the country to gather thorough and accurate information about the food products of Japan, through personal experience rather than just from a book or advertising materials. I visited small, artisanal food producers who still used traditional methods and materials without artificial ingredients. After I acquired in-depth knowledge of each ingredient from these studies, suddenly the materials that I had simply used as my mother did became very easy to handle in the kitchen. With my new knowledge, I could confidently prepare classic Japanese dishes and create new dishes with Japanese materials.

When I passed this new knowledge on to my students, they began to exhibit a new attitude toward Japanese cooking. No longer intimidated by unfamiliar ingredients, the students were able to handle them confidently and to use them in producing wonderful Japanese dishes. Many students became so comfortable with Japanese ingredients and preparation techniques that they were able to integrate them into their everyday culinary repertoire.

This experience has encouraged me to write this book. Today, at a time of growing interest in Japanese cuisine, this book offers the easiest path to understanding Japanese ingredients, preparation techniques, presentation techniques, and Western kitchens around the world. I hope you will enjoy these dishes both as part of traditional Japanese meals and as delicious components of meals prepared in any style.

Hiroko Shimbo
June 1998
London

INTRODUCTION

Hiroko's Kitchen, Your Kitchen

With the increasing interest throughout the West in Japanese food and its preparation, this book was written to demystify the world of Japanese cooking, by providing simple, clear instructions and explanations grounded in basic food science. Once you understand, for example, why tempura batter is prepared in a particular way, why and when fish is salted before grilling, what the salt content of miso is, and exactly what *shoyu* (soy sauce) is composed of and how it should be treated in cooking, there are no hidden secrets and no barriers to mastering Japanese cooking. Such knowledge allows cooks, with minimal practice, not only to prepare Japanese dishes, but also to successfully incorporate Japanese ingredients and techniques into their own cooking in modern Western kitchens. The result is delicious, nutritious, and attractive Japanese dishes and "borderless" preparations that enlarge the cook's and the diners' sphere of culinary experience.

This book is divided into two parts. In Part I you will find all of the essential information regarding traditional Japanese ingredients and cooking techniques. For most of the ingredients, simple and appealing recipes are also provided. Not only do these recipes produce wonderful results, but they also teach the basic characteristics of the ingredients and the necessary preparation techniques. In addition, Part I tells where to buy these ingredients, how to select them, and how to store them.

In Part II you will find a collection of carefully chosen recipes for delicious Japanese dishes from traditional to modern. These recipes reflect Japanese culinary history. Japanese cuisine has passed through several major transitions as Japan has encountered new ingredients and cooking techniques from the outside world. By adopting these new elements, the Japanese have created numerous dishes, some of which have been polished and finally assimilated into Japanese cuisine to the extent that their origins are not at all obvious. Throughout Part II, you will find such foreign-influenced dishes from China, Portugal, France, England, America, and, most recently, Southeast Asia. The Chinese food culture came first, as early as the sixth century A.D., along with Chinese Buddhism. The Portuguese were the first Western visitors to Japan, in the sixteenth century. With them they brought not only their cooking traditions, resulting in Japanese tempura and many other dishes, but also New World fruits and vegetables previously unknown in Japan. The English, the French, and other Europeans arrived after the opening of Japan in the late nineteenth and early twentieth centuries. Their influence brought beefsteak, croquettes, cutlets, omelettes, stew, and curry into Japanese cuisine. And in the late twentieth century came hamburgers, fried chicken, pizza, and all the rest from you-know-where.

In the text accompanying the recipes I have included fascinating information on the origins and transformations of many dishes. Here and there, I have also added my touches to some traditional recipes to increase their appeal to today's international diners.

In Part II, the recipes are categorized in chapters headed "Appetizers," "Soups," "Vegetable Dishes," "Sushi," "Rice and Noodle Dishes," "Main Dishes," and "Desserts."

"Appetizers" is a collection of dishes that are outstanding starters for a Western or Japanese meal. These dishes can also serve as excellent party foods.

"Soups" includes traditional Japanese preparations and others with a modern touch. Any of the soups can be served as part of either a Japanese or a Western meal. One reminder: Soup portions in a Japanese dinner are generally smaller than those served in Western meals. When serving larger portions than suggested in the recipes, you should reduce the salt content somewhat, generally by adjusting the amount of miso.

In "Vegetable Dishes," the recipes are varied. They include very traditional dishes that should be served in small portions as side dishes. Some of the dishes, however, can be served as complete main courses.

Sushi is a curious subject. Many varieties are prepared and eaten in Japan, and a sampling of these are found in the chapter headed "Sushi." Preparing sushi, however, is not an everyday practice in a Japanese home kitchen. At home, the Japanese do occasionally make *makizushi* (rolled sushi), *inarizushi* (sushi stuffed in a tofu pocket), or *oshizushi* (boxed sushi) for a lunch box or a picnic basket. *Gomoku chirashizushi* (tossed sushi) is made at home for special festive occasions. However, when it comes to *nigirizushi*, a slice of raw fish or another ingredient (such as shrimp, omelette, or grilled eel) placed on a small portion of sushi rice, the Japanese all go to a favorite sushi restaurant and watch the chef prepare fresh sushi to order in front of them. I recommend that you do the same, since raw fish for sushi must be very fresh, barely handled, and served immediately after preparation. But do try the sushi dishes in this book, especially for a party. They will bring you great enjoyment both in preparation and eating.

"Rice and Noodles Dishes" offers a large selection of preparations, from simple, old-fashioned Japanese dishes to Chinese-influenced one-bowl meals to modern creations.

"Main Dishes" includes fish, shellfish, fowl, pork, beef, and my own lamb stew. A larger number of Japanese meat dishes may be found in this book than in previously published Japanese cookbooks.

In "Desserts," finally, are both traditional and modern sweets that are usually served in Japan at teatime, with a cup of brown or green Japanese tea. But these recipes are carefully selected to also serve as perfect endings for full-course Western-style meals.

THE JAPANESE DINNER AND DINING ETIQUETTE

I encourage you to make Japanese ingredients and preparations a regular part of your ordinary dining experience. Indeed, many of the dishes in this book are excellent as part of a Western meal in a Western setting. Nonetheless, you will want to understand the style and process of true Japanese dining, if only because the contrasts between Japanese and Western customs are so fascinating. Besides, you may find yourself at some time in a "real" Japanese dining experience, at a formal Japanese restaurant or, perhaps, in Japan. The information provided here will give you comfort if you ever have the opportunity to dine Japanese-style.

A typical Japanese dinner consists of a bowl of rice, a bowl of soup, a plate of a protein dish such as grilled fish, and several vegetable side dishes, including a small plate of pickled vegetables. In a Japanese meal, none of these dishes is considered the "main dish." Each complements the other to create a meal that is balanced in flavor, texture, color, fragrance, and nutrients.

A Japanese meal is usually a simultaneous rather than a sequential event—that is, nearly all of the dishes are set in front of the diners at one time. Only in the most formal restaurants do the dishes follow one after the other. In such a dinner, the soup and rice are usually the last course before dessert.

In any Japanese dinner, a pair of lacquered chopsticks, *hashi*, is set horizontally in front of each each diner. The chopsticks usually rest on a holder, *hashioki*, especially in a more formal dinner. For a right-hander the chopsticks are placed with the thicker ends on the right; for a left-hander the thicker ends are on the left.

After a diner picks up the chopsticks, with which dish to begin to meal seems to be a big concern and mystery to many non-Japanese people. The only rule of etiquette concerning this matter is that you do not finish one dish before moving on to another. Rather, you eat a little from each dish and then move from dish to dish. Starting with a small sip of soup may wet your mouth and stomach and prepare you to enjoy the dinner, and a mouthful of plain cooked rice eaten after several bites from highly flavored dishes will certainly refresh your palate. Custom does not, however, prescribe these sequences. (I must disclose that my husband, who mastered the art of eating the Japanese way during his fifteen-year residence in Japan, still tends to finish the soup at the beginning of the dinner, despite my silent disapproval.)

For many Japanese diners, from all walks of life, properly attacking a meal at a high-class French restaurant is still a nightmarish mission. How to hold the wine glass properly, how to drink the soup without holding or lifting the soup bowl, how to eat soup or noodles without making a slurping noise, which spoon and fork should be used first when several of them are at each place on the table—these are perplexing problems. But there is good news for you who are already familiar with this complex etiquette. Mastering Japanese dining table etiquette is very pleasant and relaxed, because you can forget all those prohibitions that your mother taught you. During a Japanese dinner, you must pick up your bowl of rice, your bowl of soup, and some of the other small bowls and plates, and move them close to your mouth. In this way you avoid dropping the food held between the chopsticks on the table or your lap, and making a mess. No spoon is served with the soup, so you must sip it directly from the bowl. It is impolite, however, to shovel the food with chopsticks from the bowl or plate directly into your mouth.

Other rules of Japanese dining etiquette are related to handling the chopsticks. Do not stand chopsticks in a bowl of rice; do not lick chopsticks; do not point them at people; and do not pick up food by spearing it.

With few exceptions, the entire Japanese meal is eaten with chopsticks. Therefore, the foods are always cut into bite-sized pieces or strips so that they are easy to pick up. Occasionally, you may encounter food that you need to "cut" with chopsticks—for example, a grilled fish fillet, or a small block of simmered meat, vegetable, or tofu. If you find it difficult to break the food into smaller pieces with chopsticks held in one hand, simply pick up the whole piece with your chopsticks, have a bite, and return the rest to the plate.

When food is served on a communal platter or in a large communal bowl, a pair of serving chopsticks or a serving spoon may or may not be provided. If not, use your own chopsticks, but reverse them so that the parts that have been in your mouth do not touch the food in the communal dish.

During a Japanese dinner, no tea or water is consumed. The beverage served with meals may be beer, *sake* (rice wine), *shochu* (a high-proof distilled liquor), or, nowadays, wine. Among these, beer is first in popularity for dinner served at home, probably because it is inexpensive and a good complement to many different types of Japanese foods.

Finally, a Japanese dinner concludes not with a rich dessert but, usually, with carefully selected seasonal, peeled, seeded, and cut fruit, typically in small portions. For example, a few grapes—usually *kyoho*, a very sweet and juicy, rich purple variety with fruits more than 1 inch in diameter—may be served neatly peeled and seeded as the entire dessert.

Tea, without milk, sugar, or lemon, is the beverage that concludes a Japanese meal. Tea refreshes the palate and aids digestion. *Bancha*, brown twig tea, is served on informal occasions, and *ryokucha*, green leaf tea, at more formal meals.

A Japanese meal begins and ends with formal expressions of appreciation and respect. Before eating, every diner says, *"Itadakimasu,"* "We are going to receive the meal"—the Japanese counterpart of *"Bon appétit!"* *Itadakimasu* implies great respect for everyone from the farmer to the truck driver to the shopkeeper and the cook who helped to make the meal happen. At the end of the meal, everyone says, *"Gochisosama,"* "I have feasted."

No matter by which language I express my appreciation of foods, I feel the happiest when I can enjoy meals prepared with fresh, seasonal ingredients, using appropriate preparation techniques and with family and friends to share in the appreciation. I hope this book inspires you to do the same, at every opportunity, whether you are preparing an all-Japanese dinner, combining Japanese dishes with some from another cuisine, or incorporating Japanese elements into dishes of your own creation.

THE JAPANESE KITCHEN

You can cook Japanese food with the ordinary equipment of a typical Western kitchen. Japanese implements, however, do some jobs more efficiently and better than Western substitutes. If you have the means and opportunity to obtain some of these utensils, I recommend that you do so. With your new tools, you may find that preparation times are shorter, cooking tasks are easier, and the dishes you produce look much better. You will find these tools very valuable for preparing non-Japanese foods, too.

DONABE • Earthenware Casserole
TETSUNABE • Iron Pot

These large pots are indispensable for *nabemono*—hot-pot—preparations, such as sukiyaki (beef and vegetables quickly braised in sweetened *shoyu* or soy sauce, broth), *shabu-shabu* (beef slices blanched in boiling water), and *torinabe* (chicken and vegetables cooked in flavored stock or water).

Earthenware donabe, *iron* tetsunabe, *and tabletop gas stove*

An earthenware casserole, the *donabe*, is made from special clay and fired at a high temperature so that it can withstand a direct flame. The casserole comes with a heavy earthenware lid with a tiny hole from which steam can escape during cooking. A *donabe* is perfect for any type of hot-pot preparations except sukiyaki. The most frequently used size is about 12 inches in diameter and $3^1/_2$ inches in depth; a smaller casserole is available for preparing fewer servings.

Here are several tips for using a *donabe*: Heat it and cool it gradually, because sudden changes in temperature can cause it to crack. Never place it on a direct flame when the pot has no liquid in it. A traditional *donabe* casserole should not be put into the oven, although modern versions may be oven-safe (check the instructions). A heavy enameled pot can be substituted for a *donabe*.

The second type of large cooking pot is a *tetsunabe*, a heavy iron pot used for making sukiyaki. Round, shallow, flat-bottomed, and about 10 inches in diameter, a *tetsunabe* comes without a lid. Because iron rusts when not treated properly, the pot should be dried immediately and completely after each washing. A deep iron skillet may be substituted for a *tetsunabe*.

FUKIN • Cotton Kitchen Cloth

A *fukin* is a thin, rectangular cotton cloth from 12 to 16 inches in length and about 10 inches in width. Like cheesecloth, a *fukin* is used for a variety of purposes, including wrapping and forming cooked rice into shapes, lining a colander before straining stock, and squeezing excess water from tofu. Cheesecloth is too loosely woven to substitute for a *fukin*, however, and a terrycloth towel is too thick. Tightly woven unbleached muslin makes a good substitute.

HANGIRI • Wooden Sushi Tub

A *hangiri* is a flat-bottomed wooden tub, as large as 16 inches in diameter, that resembles a baby's bathtub. This tub is used primarily in the preparation of sushi rice. In the tub, steaming piping-hot cooked rice is tossed with dressing—a mixture of rice vinegar, sugar, and salt. The wood quickly absorbs a portion of the moisture and, at the same time, retains some of the heat. Also, the large surface area of the tub helps moisture to evaporate quickly. So the rice, which is very moist from cooking, does not become watery or lumpy when it is tossed with additional liquid and stored in the tub. A substitute for a *hangiri* is a large, deep, unfinished wooden salad bowl.

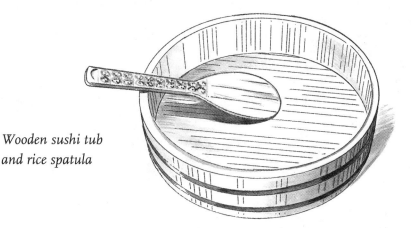

*Wooden sushi tub
and rice spatula*

HOCHO • Japanese Knives

Many people are amazed when they see my collection of knives and how well they cut. I carry these high-quality knives with me wherever in the world I am teaching. I also spend considerable time and effort caring for them, sharpening them frequently and storing them properly. If you have a variety of good, sharp Western knives in your kitchen, you can use them in preparing all types of Japanese foods.

Japanese knives are easily distinguished from their Western counterparts. Except in the case of vegetable knives (*nakkiri bocho*) and all-purpose knives (*bunka bocho*), only one side of the Japanese blade is ground to form the cutting edge. Also, on a Japanese knife the cutting edge is straight, not curved. Because of these characteristics, Japanese knives make cleaner, quicker cuts.

Most Japanese knife blades are made either entirely of carbon steel or of soft iron and carbon steel hammered together. The latter type is more widely used today, because mixing iron and steel produces blades that are both much more durable and less costly. The all-carbon blade is vulnerable to extreme shock and needs more care in handling and sharpening. Both types rust quickly, so they must be cleaned, rinsed, and wiped completely dry with a towel after each use.

Recent technological advances have produced new types of Japanese knife blades. Some blades are made from a new carbon-steel material that does not rust easily. There are also the new ceramic knives. Made of a mixture of materials, the ceramic blades are very thin and white, and remain sharp a long time. The drawbacks of ceramic knives are that they are vulnerable to shock and need professional sharpening.

No matter which type of knife you choose, never wash it in the dishwasher. After using it, rinse it with hot water and wipe it completely dry before putting it away.

Following are common types of Japanese knives.

Deba Bocho (Heavy-Duty Knife)

This knife has a thicker blade than most others. It is used to chop off fish heads, fillet fish, and cut chicken including the bones. About 7 inches in length, the *deba bocho* has a pointed tip, to do delicate jobs such as cutting open a fish belly.

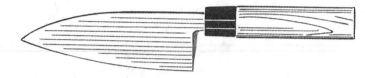

Sashimi Bocho (Fish Slicer)

This knife has a long, thin blade, about 10 inches in length and a little more than an inch in width. *Sashimi bocho* is used to cut filleted fish for sushi and sashimi. With a single, continuous stroke, the long, thin blade produces a clean slice of fish. Prepared foods are also cut with this fine knife before serving.

Nakkiri Bocho (Vegetable Knife)

This knife has a broad, rectangular blade (about $6^1/_2$ inches long and almost 2 inches wide). Unlike other Japanese knives, this one has a cutting edge formed by grinding both sides of the blade. The broad, thin blade is perfect for making symmetrical cuts on either side of an item. *Nakkiri bocho* is one of the most frequently used knives in the home kitchen.

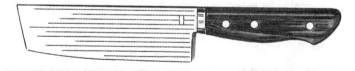

Bunka Bocho (All-Purpose Knife)

In the past, every home was equipped with a *nakkiri bocho* (vegetable knife) and a *deba bocho* (heavy-duty knife). Since few home cooks today fillet fish and bone chicken, *deba bocho* knives are disappearing from home kitchens. Cooks' demand for a new type of *nakkiri bocho* that does some of the work of a *deba bocho* created a knife called *bunka bocho*. The blade of this knife has a pointed tip and cutting edges on either side, like a *nakkiri bocho*.

Today many young Japanese home cooks handle all preparations using only this knife.

To sharpen Japanese knives, a moistened rectangular whetstone is used. A Japanese whetstone sharpens Western knives as well, and much more thoroughly than a steel. I recommend sharpening your knives at the end of the day, as a last chore in the kitchen. Knives that are sharpened just before use transfer a metallic flavor to the prepared dishes.

KUSHI • Bamboo Skewers

Kushi, bamboo skewers, are used for preparing some grilled Japanese dishes, such as *yakitori*—chicken pieces threaded onto bamboo skewers and grilled while being frequently basted with sweet, rich soy sauce–based sauce. The cook continually turns the skewers so that the meat is evenly cooked and basted. For this reason, bamboo skewers are essential; steel skewers would become too hot to handle. The skewers are soaked in water for 30 minutes before use so that they won't burn during cooking. Supermarkets as well as Japanese and Chinese food stores sell bamboo skewers.

MUSHIKI • Steamer

Two types of steamers are used in Japan, bamboo and metal. The bamboo steamer is of Chinese origin, and the metal steamer is Western. I prefer to use the Chinese type. I place it on top of a deep pot, which can hold sufficient water for producing copious steam. The steam escapes through the spaces in the woven bamboo lid instead of dripping on the steaming food.

If you want to buy a bamboo steamer, choose one that will just fit over the rim of the deep pot you plan to use with it.

Bamboo steamer
(lid not shown)

Metal steamer

If you use a metal steamer, line the underside of the lid with a finely woven cotton cloth to absorb moisture, and set the lid ajar to allow some of the steam to escape.

OROSHIGANE • Steel Grater
OROSHIKI • Porcelain Grater

Oroshigane, a steel grater with very fine spikes, is useful for grating wasabi, ginger, and daikon radish. But graters called *oroshiki*, which are made of porcelain, are better than the metal type because they do not impart any metallic flavor to the food. They are also safer for your hands; you need not worry about scraping and injuring your skin, as can easily happen with sharp steel spikes.

There are two kinds of porcelain graters, one with larger spikes set widely apart on the grating surface and another with smaller, more closely spaced spikes. The former is good for coarsely grating daikon, lotus root, and mountain yam. The latter, for producing finer results, is good for grating *shoga* ginger, wasabi, and garlic. Western graters cannot perform these precision jobs satisfactorily, which is why so many students have asked me how to produce a teaspoon of grated ginger or ginger juice.

If you want to grate ginger fine and juicy and you do not have a Japanese grater, try this technique: Place a layer of sturdy plastic wrap over your ordinary steel grater, on the side with the smallest, most closely placed spikes. Grate the ginger over the plastic wrap.

I recently found a new Western grater that does a good job of grating a large daikon root fine and juicy. Called a Microplane, this grater has small spikes on an 8-inch-long steel plate, which is topped by a black grip.

OSHIZUSHI NO KATA • Wooden Sushi Mold

Oshizushi no kata is a rectangular wooden mold used in the preparation of *oshizushi*, pressed or boxed sushi. This style of sushi is popular in the Kansai region, which includes Osaka and Kyoto. In Tokyo, the familiar handmade *nigirizushi* are more popular. But using the wooden sushi mold is a much easier way to make sushi. With it, the novice can produce perfect sushi every time.

The mold is a rectangular wooden frame, about 4 by 7 inches and $1^3/_4$ inches in depth, with a separate lid and bottom board. The lid is slightly smaller than the frame so it can slide down inside.

To prepare *oshizushi*, first soak the frame and lid in cold water for 30 minutes. Fit the frame over the bottom board, and pack sushi rice in the mold. Lay sliced fish over the rice.

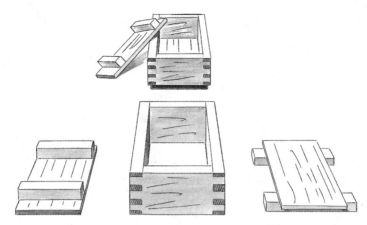

Place the lid on top and firmly press down. Remove the lid and frame, and cut the sushi into bite-sized pieces.

After using your *oshizushi no kata*, soak the mold in cold water for 20 minutes, and remove the rice residue with a hard brush. Dry the mold completely before storing it.

RYORIBASHI • Cooking Chopsticks

When I teach cooking classes in the West, students are amazed to see me perform nearly all kitchen tasks using a pair of long cooking chopsticks. Cooking chopsticks are 14 inches in length. Once you learn how to manipulate them, you will find that with them you can do nearly everything—beating, picking up, stirring, turning, cutting, and more. There is no better kitchen utensil than cooking chopsticks.

A pair of cooking chopsticks is always tied together with a short cotton string at the upper end, to prevent the loss of one member of the pair—a simple and clever invention

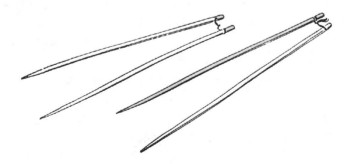

that spread because so many single chopsticks were lost in the homes and professional kitchens of Japan!

SHAMOJI • Wooden or Bamboo Rice Spatula

The *shamoji* is used to mix cooked rice and to transfer the rice into individual bowls. The standard *shamoji* is about 9 inches in length, and a larger size is about 12 inches in length. The larger size is used with a wooden sushi tub, *hangiri*, in preparing sushi rice. With it you can fold the vinegar dressing into the cooked rice without crushing the cooked grains.

SOKUSEKI TSUKEMONO-KI • Japanese Pickling Pot

For making small quantities of quick pickled vegetables, Japanese food stores sell special pickling pots. These rectangular or round containers hold only 1 to 2 quarts, to fit into typically small Japanese refrigerators.

A pickling pot comes with a large screw in the center, connected to a plastic inner lid. When you screw down the inner lid, it presses the vegetables to the bottom of the container, leaving no air space. The lid takes the place of the stone or other heavy weight traditionally used for salt pickling.

Two drawbacks of the pickling pot are that, first, it is small, and, second, the screw may partially unwind when you put a large quantity of vegetables into the container.

SUIHANKI • Electric Rice Cooker

Today the electric rice cooker is equipped with many functions. It cooks polished rice as well as unpolished brown rice, and then keeps the cooked rice warm for quite a long time. Some advanced machines have memory functions so that you can set the cooker to start cooking at any convenient time. For example, you set the clock before going to bed, and the next morning rice is cooked just in time for your breakfast. Another advanced type is equipped with so-called fuzzy technology. This type of rice cooker automatically selects the best cooking time depending on the condition of the rice—from year-old, dry rice to newly harvested rice with a high water content.

A substitute for this modern electronic miracle is, of course, a simple, heavy-bottomed deep pot with a heavy lid, and a skillful cook.

The Japanese mortar and pestle are a unique set of grinding instruments. The ceramic mortar, with a rough, combed pattern in its unglazed interior, comes in various sizes, from 5 to 12 inches. The *surikogi* is a wooden pestle about 10 inches in length. To use it, you hold the thinner end firmly and, with the thicker end, press and scrape the contents down the inner surface of the mortar.

Most *surikogi* pestles are made of Japanese cypress wood. More expensive ones, easily recognized by their bumpy, bark-covered upper surface, are made from the wood of the *sansho* pepper tree, whose edible berries and young leaves are treasured for their pungent, delicious flavor and fragrant aroma. It is said that a pestle made from this tree imparts some flavor to the ground materials. My own experience indicates that such flavor enhancement, if it exists at all, is quite negligible.

The *suribachi* and *surikogi* have many uses in Japanese cooking. Freshly toasted sesame seeds are ground immediately before use into a creamy, oily paste with these utensils, although today many cooks prefer to use commercially available sesame paste. Many different Japanese dressings are made with a mortar and pestle, using ingredients such as tofu, miso, sesame seeds, rice vinegar, walnuts, and *shoyu* (soy sauce). No matter what foods you grind with a Japanese mortar and pestle—sesame seeds, walnuts, fish, shellfish, or meat—a well-pasted product always results.

When using a Japanese mortar, place it on top of a moist cloth so that the bowl does not move during grinding. Afterward, clean the bowl with a hard brush and a little detergent to remove any residue from the comb pattern. Rinse the pestle, and wipe it dry.

COOKING IMPLEMENTS •

TAKUJO KONRO • Portable Cookstove

A *takujo konro* is a portable gas stove for use at the dining table. A large pot such as a *don-abe* (earthenware casserole) or *tetsunabe* (iron pot) is placed on top of the stove, and the cooking is done at the table. The stove is fitted with a small, replaceable can of compressed propane gas; each can contains enough gas for three to four hot-pot meals. The stoves are available at Japanese and Chinese stores for a fairly low price, about fifty dollars. If you cannot find a Japanese portable gas stove, use any portable gas cookstove approved for indoor use.

TAMAGOYAKI-KI • Rectangular Omelette Pan

A Japanese omelette is formed from multiple thin layers of cooked beaten egg rolled into a thick cylinder. To make a Japanese omelette, you need a rectangular skillet, about 6 by 7 inches, called a *tamagoyaki-ki*. The skillet is usually made of iron or heavy aluminum. Today nonstick versions are also available, and many professional chefs use a heavy copper skillet that is coated with tin. A good substitute for a Japanese omelette pan is an 8-inch nonstick skillet.

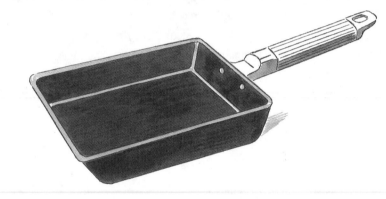

WOK

For stir-frying, the Japanese long ago adopted the traditional, round-bottomed Chinese wok. The most useful size is 14 inches in diameter, and the preferred source of heat is a large gas flame. A real Chinese wok, made of thin iron, is the best buy, although you can substitute a large skillet or a modern, flat-bottomed Chinese skillet, with gas, electric, or another heat source.

When using an iron wok for the first time, you need to season it, to remove the chemical coating from the inside and to prevent the wok from rusting:

- Place the wok over high heat, and heat it until the entire inner surface changes from dark grey to light bluish grey.
- Rinse the wok under cold tap water and using a hard brush with a little powdered detergent remove the burnt chemicals.
- Fill the wok with water, bring the water to a boil, and discard it. Wipe the wok dry with a paper towel.
- Add $1/3$ cup vegetable oil. Heat the oil until it is almost smoking. Gently swirl the wok to coat the entire inner surface with oil. Be careful not to let the oil catch fire. Discard the oil.
- Fill the wok with water again, and bring it to a boil. Discard the water. Repeat this process two more times. Wipe the wok dry with a paper towel.
- Add 3 tablespoons fresh vegetable oil to the wok, spread the oil over the entire inner surface, and wipe off the excess. Now the wok is ready to use.

After using the wok, clean it with detergent, and rinse it with hot water. Wipe it completely dry with a paper towel before putting it away.

ZARU • Bamboo Baskets

Steaming, simmering, and grilling techniques are dominant in the Japanese kitchen. To drain off cooking liquid and rinse the cooked foods, a large sieve is indispensable.

The Japanese strainer or sieve, *zaru*, is a shallow basket made of woven bamboo. The traditional Japanese kitchen contains baskets in various sizes, depths, and shapes, to suit various culinary purposes.

After using a *zaru*, brush off any food residue under running water, and clean the basket with a little detergent. Let the basket dry completely before storing it.

Western strainers and colanders can of course serve as substitutes for bamboo baskets.

AGERU • Deep-Frying

The first cooking oil used in Japan was probably sesame oil, *goma abura*, introduced by the Chinese during the eighth century (see page 99). Although sesame oil is still popular, the Japanese today use mainly refined, flavorless vegetables oils for deep-frying. As in the United States, *sarada abura*, "salad oil," can be canola, soybean, cottonseed, corn, safflower, or sunflower oil, or a combination of two or more of these.

Because sunflower and safflower oils, when heated to frying temperature, are easily oxidized and take on a bitter taste, these light oils are best used in preparing dressings. For deep-frying as well as sautéing and stir-frying, the more heat-stable oils—canola, soybean, corn, and sesame—are preferable.

The rules for successful deep-frying are universal:

- Maintain a constant proper temperature to produce the best results—a crisp outside and a juicy inside. Because it can easily maintain a constant temperature, a large, heavy, flat-bottomed iron pot is ideal for deep-frying.
- Do not crowd pieces of food in the oil, or they will absorb moisture from each other's steam and become soggy. It is ideal to leave two-thirds of the surface unoccupied by frying foods.
- While frying, continually skim the oil to remove burnt batter or other bits of food. This prevents the frying foods from taking on a bitter flavor and burnt color.
- After foods are fried, drain them on a steel rack or paper towel. Never pile or even overlap them, or the steam they emit will make them soggy.
- Be sure your oil is fresh. Keep it in a tightly capped container in a dark, cool, and dry place. Once the container is opened, use the oil as soon as possible.

To check the temperature of frying oil, use a thermometer if the oil is deep enough. If the oil is only 1 to 2 inches deep, or if you have no thermometer handy, you can substitute either of one or two methods, using cooking chopsticks or batter.

To check the oil temperature with cooking chopsticks, submerge their tips in the oil. When the temperature reaches 320 degrees F (low frying temperature), tiny bubbles will start emerging from the tips of the chopsticks. When the temperature reaches 340 degrees F (medium frying temperature), larger, brisker bubbles will rise from the chopsticks. At 360 degrees F (high frying temperature), the bubbles will be slightly larger still and *very* brisk.

To use the batter method, drop a very small amount of tempura or other flour-water batter into the heated oil. At 320 degrees F, the batter will sink to the bottom, and then float to the surface after a few seconds. At 340 degrees F, the batter will sink to the bottom but rise more quickly. At 360 degrees F, the batter will not sink at all, but will break up and scatter over the surface of the oil.

You can reuse frying oil, but it's best to do so only once, and not at all if you have used the oil to fry fish. If you have used the oil to fry chicken or meat, use it only to fry the same foods later. And avoid mixing used oil with new oil, or the new oil will be oxidized by the old.

To be sure used oil is fresh enough to use again, heat it in a skillet over medium heat. If bubbles continously emerge, the oil contains too much oxidized material and moisture.

Do not discard used oil in the sink. Place shredded newspaper in a plastic bag, and let the paper absorb the used oil.

TAMAGO NO TOKIKATA • Beating Eggs

For many Japanese preparations, the cook must beat eggs without creating foam. To do this, use a pair of cooking chopsticks. Beat gently and break up the thick part of the egg white by continually lifting the mixture with the chopsticks.

To make a Japanese thick rolled omelette, do not beat the eggs thoroughly; the mixture should look uneven. This results in a less dense omelette.

If you have trouble beating eggs with chopsticks, use a fork rather than a whisk.

DAIKON OROSHI • Grated Daikon

MOMIJI OROSHI • Spicy Grated Daikon

Fried dishes, including tempura, and grilled or broiled oily fish are almost always served with grated daikon. To produce the best grated daikon or *daikon oroshi*, choose a radish that is heavy for its size, so it will be juicy. Grate only the top part, which is sweeter than the lower part. For a very fine grate, use a porcelain grater (see page 14).

Let the grated daikon rest on a sieve 2 to 5 seconds to remove excess juice, but do not let the daikon become dry. It should be not watery, but quite moist.

Momiji, which literally means "autumn leaf color," is so named because its pleasant reddish color reminds diners of autumn leaves. To prepare *momiji oroshi*, use a cooking chopstick to make two deep holes on the cut surface of a disk of daikon. Insert one *akatogarashi* (Japanese dried red chile) into each hole. Grate the daikon and chile together. This produces a slightly red, spicy *oroshi*.

HIYA-GOHAN • Day-old Rice

When rice becomes cold, its grains are no longer sticky, because of a structural change in the glucose chain. This makes the rice perfect for use in stir-frying or rice soup. Day-old rice tends to become lumpy, so you may have to break it up with your hands before using it. Rinsing freshly cooked rice in cold water also reduces stickiness.

KAI NO SUNA NO HAKASE-KATA • Desanding Clams

To remove sand from clams, the following technique works well: Place the clams in a colander and hang it over a bowl. Add salt water (1 tablespoon salt to 1 quart water) until the clams are barely submerged. Leave the clams in the bowl in a cool and dark place for 2 to 3 hours. Drain the clams, and rinse them under cold tap water.

The key to this technique is that the clams are suspended in the middle of the bowl of water and not placed on the bottom. This prevents them from taking in the ejected sand and other ejected material that collects on the bottom of the bowl.

KARATSUKI EBI NO SEWATA NO TORI-KATA
Deveining Shrimp in Their Shells

To do this you need a toothpick or bamboo skewer. Insert the toothpick or skewer in the space between the first and second joints from the top of the tail, $1/3$ inch deep in the flesh beneath the shell. Pull the vein out gently, so as not to break it. When the shrimp is fresh this operation is easier.

Deveining shrimp

ITAMERU • Stir-Frying

For stir-frying, every ingredient should be cut into small and uniform pieces. Vegetables that need longer cooking, such as broccoli and root vegetables, should be precooked in boiling water or in oil. In either case, shake off any excess water or oil before stir-frying.

The proper vessel for stir-frying is a Chinese wok or large skillet (see page 18), and the preferred source of heat is a large gas flame. First heat the wok or skillet until it is very hot but not smoking. Coat the entire surface of the wok or skillet with oil, and add the stir-frying ingredients. If the wok or skillet is not heated enough or not coated well with oil, the ingredients will stick to the surface.

Before adding other ingredients, stir-fry ginger, garlic, or scallions to flavor the oil. These ingredients can burn instantly, creating a burnt, bitter flavor, so hold the wok or skillet away from the heat (you need not lower the flame). With just 20 to 30 seconds of cooking, these ingredients will give up their delicious flavors to the oil.

While you are stir-frying, move your spatula constantly, tossing and turning the ingredients so they are evenly heated through. This won't take long, since vegetables that need longer cooking should have been precooked. In stir-frying, you are reheating the vegetables and preparing them to be flavored with seasonings such as sugar, salt, and soy sauce.

When adding soy sauce, pour it directly onto the hot surface of the wok or skillet, not over the vegetables. This instant burning gives a wonderful aroma and flavor to the stir-fried dish. After adding soy sauce, toss and cook the ingredients for only a few seconds more.

ITAZURI • Rolling Cucumber in Salt

Before a cucumber is used in a salad, it is rolled over a little salt, about $1/4$ teaspoon. This stabilizes the chlorophyl, preserving the green color, and softens the skin. Cucumber treated this way is then cut into thin slices or strips.

MIZUKIRI • Removing Excess Water

This operation is often applied to fresh tofu to remove excess water before the tofu is used in a salad or other preparation. To learn to do *mizukiri* for tofu, see page 134.

Mizukiri is also applied to cooked vegetables. Excess water is usually removed by shaking the vegetables in a bamboo tray or basket or squeezing them by hand. But sometimes a special *mizukiri* technique is applied to spinach. In Japan spinach is sold with roots attached, and, after cleaning, it is boiled whole. After the spinach is drained and cooled, the roots are collected together at one end, and *mizukiri* is done by rolling and squeezing the spinach in a *makisu* (bamboo mat). Only then is the root cut off. The spinach bunch is divided in two, and the one portion is placed with its leafy top over the stems of the other portion, so the stack is uniformly thick. The spinach is rolled again in a bamboo mat, to shape it into a perfect cylinder, and then it is cut into 2-inch lengths. This produces very neat and attractive spinach disks.

 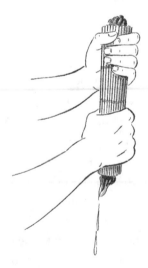

Rolling spinach in a bamboo mat

Although spinach with its roots is thoroughly washed by the producers, a final rinsing at home is necessary. Have a large bowl of cold water in the sink. Hold the middle part of the spinach stems, submerge the roots, and vigorously swish-swash them in the water. Once you're sure that no soil is entering the water, discard the dirty water, and rinse the spinach thoroughly under cold tap water.

You can treat whole spinach bunches this way even if the roots have been cut off. But if you can find only loose spinach leaves, boil them loose, drain them, and cool them in cold water. Then pile them evenly on a bamboo mat, and follow the same rolling, squeezing, and shaping process as described for spinach with roots.

MUSU • Steaming

I have been using a Chinese bamboo steamer for years, and I prefer it to a metal steamer. The woven bamboo lid allows some steam to escape during cooking, so the ideal amount of steam is retained. Also, the bamboo body doesn't heat up as much as the body of a metal steamer, which tends to distribute heat unevenly.

To steam foods, put plenty of water into a deep steamer pot, and bring the water to a rolling boil over high heat, for maximum steam production, before putting any food into the steamer. Bring more water to a boil in another pot, so if additional water is required in the steamer pot you can add boiling water, not cold water. If you are using a metal steamer, cover the underside of the lid with a tightly woven thin cotton cloth to prevent condensed steam from dripping onto the steaming foods. When you open the steamer lid, be careful not to burn yourself in the very hot condensed steam.

Fish, rice, and dumplings are always steamed at high heat. To steam egg mixtures, though, the proper temperature is about 195 degrees F. To obtain this temperature, use high heat for about 2 minutes and then reduce the heat to medium. If the temperature is higher, the egg protein coagulates before steam condensed in the cool liquid egg evaporates. This produces a rough-textured custard.

NIRU • Simmering

Vegetables, chicken, and fish are often simmered in the Japanese kitchen. Except for small fish, which are simmered whole, these ingredients are always cut into pieces that are manageable with chopsticks before they are simmered. The base of the broth can be *dashi* (fish stock), *kombu dashi* (kelp stock), water, or *sake* (rice wine). After simmering, the broth is flavored with sweet and salty condiments such as sugar, *mirin* (sweet cooking wine), and *shoyu* (soy sauce).

A special lid called *otoshibuta*, or "drop-lid," is frequently used in simmering. This wooden lid comes in various sizes; the right size is about 1 inch smaller in diameter than the pot with which it is used. The lid is placed directly on the simmering foods, which have been barely covered with broth. During the cooking, the broth boils up to the lid, hits it, and continuously falls back on the simmering foods. This technique ensures even flavor, color, and cooking.

A lightweight pot lid, 1 inch smaller in diameter than the pot, can be a good substitute for an *otoshibuta*. Or cut a circle of aluminum foil a little bigger around than the pot, and fold in the edge to make a disk about 1 inch smaller in diameter than the pot.

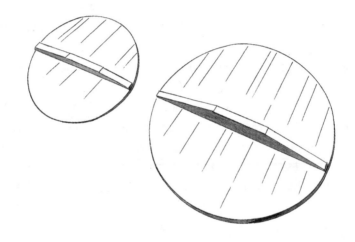

YASAI NO KIRIKATA • Special Cutting Techniques

Shiraga negi

Literally "grey-hair long onion," *shiraga negi* is the white part of Japanese long onion (*naganegi*), cut into very thin strips, like human hair. The white stem of the onion is first cut into 2-inch lengths. Each piece is slit open lengthwise, and the inner, tubular part of the onion is removed. The remaining thin layers of onion are cut into narrow strips. These strips are then soaked in ice water to make them crisp and a little curly. *Shiraga negi* make a very refreshing and attractive garnish.

Hana ninjin • Floral-Cut Carrot

To cut a carrot into floral shapes, take a short length of carrot, about 2 inches, and cut five small wedges, equally spaced, from the outside. Cut the carrot piece into half-inch slices crosswise. Slope each "petal" by trimming it diagonally. Trim the corners to round them.

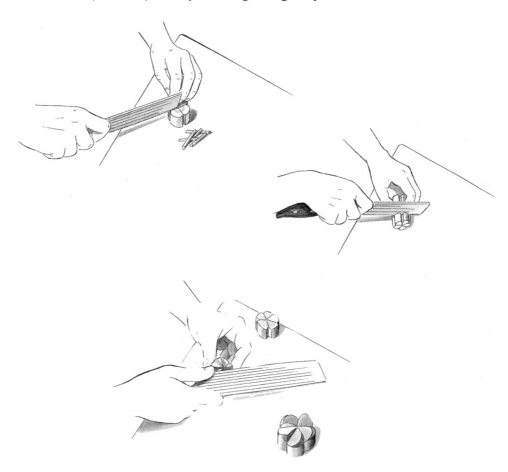

Katsura muki

Daikon, cucumber, and carrot are prepared using this technique. First cut the vegetable crosswise into cylinders about 3 inches long, and peel off the skin by holding the knife along the length of each cylinder and rotating the cylinder. Then, in the same way, cut the flesh into a continuous paper-thin sheet.

Usually a sheet of *katsura muki* is later cut into thin strips. The julienned daikon on which sashimi traditionally rests is prepared in this way.

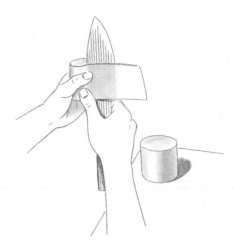

You may notice that during slack time at a sushi bar the chef works on preparing *katsura muki*. You will be amazed by the thin, continuous sheet the chef will produce. It takes a bit of practice to "unroll" a daikon, but the technique is easily mastered.

Rangiri

Literally "disordered cut," this technique is usually applied to cylindrically shaped vegetables, such as carrot, *gobo* (burdock), lotus root, and other vegetables such as eggplant and cucumber. The cut vegetables are used in simmered dishes.

To make a *rangiri* cut, hold the knife diagonally to the vegetable, and, keeping the angle fixed, rotate the vegetable a quarter turn before making each cut. In this way, each piece will have a large surface area, which facilitates quicker, even cooking.

Sengiri

In Japanese preparations, both root vegetables and leafy vegetables are often cut into thin julienne strips by a method called *sengiri*. *Sengiri* literally means "cut into thin, linelike strips."

To do *sengiri* with root vegetables, first cut them into 2- to 3-inch lengths crosswise. Then cut each piece into very thin lengthwise slices. Make a small pile of these slices, and cut them lengthwise into very thin, narrow strips.

For celery or fennel, cut thin slices with the grain.

Before cutting a plump cucumber *sengiri*-style, scrape out the seed cavity. This isn't necessary for Japanese cucumbers.

To make *sengiri* strips from leafy vegetables, cut them into 2- to 3-inch lengths, pile the leaves together, and cut them into thin lengthwise strips.

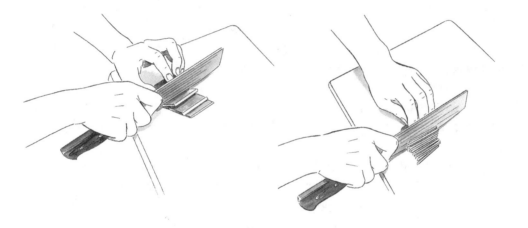

SUMIZU • Vinegared Water to Prevent Discoloration

Because *gobo* (burdock) immediately discolors when it is peeled and comes in contact with air, this vegetable is always soaked in vinegared water (1 teaspoon vinegar to 1 cup water) from the time it is peeled or cut until it is cooked. Burdock can also be cooked in vinegared water to whiten it. Lotus root undergoes a slower and milder discoloration, but the same technique is advised.

Pickles once played an important roll in the Japanese dinner. Most of the daily nutritional needs of the Japanese population were met by a bowl of rice; miso soup with a protein food such as tofu, chicken, or pork and seasonal fresh vegetables; and pickled vegetables on the side. In the past, *tsukemono* was the method of preserving fresh produce so that people could enjoy a variety of vegetables even through the cold winter months.

Traditional Japanese pickling does not employ vinegar. In Japan, vegetables are pickled in plain salt, *sake* lees, rice-bran mash, mustard paste, and miso. When I was young, home pickling in rice-bran mash, *nukamiso*, was very popular in Japan. Rich in B vitamins, rice bran is an excellent pickling medium. My mother made wonderful *nukamiso* pickles with seasonal vegetables such as eggplant, daikon, cabbage, and carrot. Her recipe for the pickling mash includes rice bran, salt, *kombu* (kelp), soybeans, mustard powder, and Japanese red chile pepper. Every guest who came to our house claimed that my mother's *nukamiso* pickles were the best in town, and we were really proud of them. Every night, she added fresh vegetables to the mash for the next day's consumption. Before placing the vegetables in the pickling pot, she tossed the strong-smelling mash hundreds of times with her hands, lifting it from the bottom of the pot to the top to provide oxygen and prevent the mash from becoming moldy. Unfortunately, the tradition of making *nukamiso* pickles, which requires hard work and constant watching, has nearly disappeared from the Japanese home kitchen. I myself no longer make *nukamiso* pickles at home.

A still popular home method of *tsukemono* production is salt pickling. In the past, large quantities of salt were used in brine pickling, for the purpose was long-term preservation. Today we make pickles for consumption within hours, or a few days at most. This requires a quantity of salt equal to only 2 percent of the weight of the vegetables. For example, if you are using about 7 ounces of vegetables, you need 1 teaspoon salt to make pickles that will be consumed within a few hours. To make pickles that will be ready for consumption after two to three days requires 4 percent salt by weight; the 7 ounces of vegetables require 2 teaspoons salt.

In salt pickling, a weight is normally placed on the vegetables to help extract water from them, so that they form their own brine. You can use two or more unopened cans of food together, or go outside and find one or more stones, weighing altogether around 2 pounds. Or you can use a Japanese pickling pot, a plastic container with an inner lid that is screwed down to apply proper pressure to the vegetables (see page 16).

Basic salt grilling, *shioyaki*, and cleaning and salting fish before grilling, are discussed on page 364. Marinated fish or fowl can burn easily during grilling or broiling. To prevent burning, increase the space between the heat and the food, if you can, and watch carefully. If you can't raise the grill or lower the broiling pan, you may need to cover the food with aluminum foil for a portion of the cooking time.

In *teriyaki* grilling or broiling, fish or fowl is basted frequently while it cooks. Before applying basting sauce, remove the food from the grill or broiler. The hot fish or fowl will be covered with oil and juice exuded during cooking; if you were to apply basting sauce over these liquids it would simply run off. Instead, let the fish or fowl cool and dry for 20 seconds. Then apply the basting sauce and return the food to the broiler or grill, where the heat will dry the surface. Repeat this process until the surface is covered with a glossy layer of basting sauce.

YUDERU • Blanching and Parboiling

In Japanese cooking, leafy greens and vegetables such as asparagus and broccoli are often blanched—that is, plunged very briefly into boiling water to soften the surface and remove excess water from the vegetables. Or they are parboiled—cooked in boiling water until heated through but still firm.

Water for blanching or parboiling—or *yuderu*, in Japanese—is salted (using 2 percent salt by volume, or $1\frac{1}{3}$ tablespoons per quart) to raise the boiling point of the water. This reduces the cooking time and thus helps to preserve both color and nutrients.

After the vegetables are parboiled or blanched, they should be drained quickly and bathed in ice water to stop the cooking. Change the cooling water several times, until it remains cool. Then quickly drain the vegetables, and squeeze excess water from them. Do not let the cooked vegetables soak in water for longer than 2 minutes, lest they absorb water and their texture become soggy.

When root vegetables such as *gobo* (burdock) or lotus root are blanched or parboiled, vinegar is added to the water (1 teaspoon of vinegar to 1 cup water). The vinegar prevents these vegetables from turning brown from oxidation.

Fish and shellfish are occasionally treated with a technique called *shimofuri*, meaning "frost-covered." Fish or shellfish are briefly blanched in boiling water, just until the outside becomes white. This eliminates excess oil and strong flavors and readies the fish or shell-fish for further preparations

Sashimi fish fillets, especially if they are from the thin belly of the fish, where the skin is hard to remove, are frequently treated with *shimofuri*. This cooks the skin and makes it easy to chew, while the flesh remains nearly raw. A few seconds after the fish is treated with boiling water, it should be plunged into ice water to stop further cooking. As soon as the fish has cooled—within 2 minutes—it should be drained and wiped dry.

Most of the vegetables and fruits used in Japanese cooking originated in other countries. Many vegetables and fruits reached Japan from the eighth through the tenth centuries, by way of China and Korea. Vegetables from the New World traveled to Japan through Southeast Asia in the 1500s.

Over the centuries, these imported vegetables and fruits have become adapted to the soil and climate of Japan, and also to the tastes of the Japanese people. Customary preparation techniques and seasonings influenced the development of Japanese cultivars that differed from the originals in flavor, texture, and size. Eggplant grown in the soil of Japan, for example, no longer tastes quite like eggplant grown in its native India.

In this chapter, I have included only those vegetables that are popular in Japan and available, but less familiar, in the West. Other vegetables common in Japan, such as green beans, asparagus, broccoli, and carrots, are stored and prepared in ways familiar to Western cooks. I have excluded vegetables that are used in Japan but are unavailable elsewhere.

Three fruits are introduced in this chapter. One of them, *yuzu* (citron), originated in Japan. Another, *ume* (Japanese green plum), is at this writing unavailable outside Japan, except in its pickled form (*umeboshi*; see page 142). *Kaki*, persimmon, is widely available in the United States.

DAIKON Radish

Often thought of as a signature Japanese vegetable, daikon originated in China and the Mediterranean region. A large white radish, it is juicy, crisp, and refreshing. In Japan, the shape and length of daikon varies, from the slender, three-foot-long Moriguchi variety to the plump, twenty-pound Sakurajima variety. The most common variety in Japan is a thick, foot-long root $2^1/_2$ to 3 inches in diameter. In the United States, the average root is a little thinner and shorter than its Japanese counterpart.

Daikon is available year-round, but it becomes sweeter during the cold season. The top green leaves, which unfortunately are frequently cut off before sale, are rich in vitamin A. They may be stir-fried, simmered, or used in miso soup. The whole root is rich in digestive enzymes, such as amylase, as well as in vitamin C.

The flavor of daikon differs slightly depending on the part of the root that is used. The upper part is sweeter and without bitterness. It is perfect for *daikon oroshi* (peeled and grated daikon, page 22), which accompanies deep-fried foods such as tempura and grilled oily fish and meat. The top part is also suitable for use in salads.

The bottom half of the root has a mild and pleasant bitter taste. This part is usually simmered for a long time in water, until it becomes so soft that it can be broken with chopsticks. Simmered daikon (*furofuki daikon*, page 253) is served piping hot, topped with a flavored miso sauce. This is a hearty winter dish in Japan.

SOURCES: Daikon is available at most supermarkets as well as at Japanese and other Asian food stores.

WHAT TO LOOK FOR: Choose a crisp, moist root. It should be without cracks, heavy for its size, and unwrinkled.

STORAGE: Keep uncut daikon in a plastic bag in a warmer part of the refrigerator. After cutting the root, wrap it in plastic wrap. Use daikon within five days of purchase.

EDAMAME • Green Soybeans

Heralding the arrival of summer, *edamame* are one of the most celebrated delicacies of that season in Japan. It is almost impossible for the Japanese to endure the long hot and humid summer without these delicious green beans. Boiled green soybeans with a glass of ice-cold beer is a summertime treat throughout the country.

Edamame are fresh green soybeans. Two or three beans, each about $1/2$ inch in diameter, are packed into each 2-inch-long pod, whose outer skin is covered with downy fuzz. Soybeans originated in China and are today cultivated all over the world. However, soybeans are most often dried and used to produce oil and vegetable protein products. The practice of eating the fresh green beans, which have a sweet and nutty flavor, seems to be limited to the Japanese population. *Edamame* are rich in protein, vitamin A and B vitamins, and calcium. They also contain a substantial amount of vitamin C, which is lost in the dried beans.

To prepare *edamame*, first rub the pods with a little salt in your palms. This removes the downy fuzz. Then parboil the pods in salted boiling water for 3 to 5 minutes. Drain the pods, and spread them in a wide, flat-bottomed colander so they dry quickly. While the beans are still hot, toss them with a generous amount of salt. Serve them as they are, in their pods.

At bars and restaurants in Japan, *edamame* tend to be quite salty. This, of course, is a trick to make customers thirstier as they snack on the delicious beans. Salted peanuts play exactly the same role in an American bar.

Getting the green beans out of the tough pods and into your mouth is simple and amusing. Pick up a pod, bring it close to your mouth, and squeeze the bottom of the pod. The beans inside will pop out into your mouth.

Once you discover the flavor of young soybeans, you will become addicted. Cooked without oil and eaten immediately, they are much healthier to munch than salty snack nuts.

SOURCES: At this writing fresh *edamame* may be difficult to obtain in the United States. Frozen *edamame*, parboiled and packed in plastic bags, can be found in freezer cases at Japanese food stores. Cook the frozen beans in boiling salted water for 2 to 3 minutes, then drain and salt them as you would the fresh beans.

WHAT TO LOOK FOR: The pods should be plump and heavy for their size.

STORAGE: Store *edamame* in a breathable bag at room temperature. Use them within two days of purchase.

ENOKITAKE Mushrooms

These pale yellow mushrooms have long, slender stems and tiny caps, both of which are edible. *Enokitake* mushrooms have a faint but distinctive flavor. When they are eaten raw, they have a pleasant, crisp bite; briefly cooked they have a chewy texture.

Enokitake are traditionally harvested in the wild from late autumn through spring. Today, however, *enokitake* cultivated in sawdust beds are available throughout the year.

Enokitake mushrooms are suitable for all methods of cooking as well as for eating raw. They may be deep-fried, stir-fried, simmered, or steamed. Avoid overcooking them.

SOURCES: *Enokitake* mushrooms are available at Japanese food stores and at large supermarkets.

WHAT TO LOOK FOR: Choose mushrooms that are firm and unbrowned.

STORAGE: Refrigerate *enokitake* in a paper bag, and use them within two days of purchase.

GINNAN • Gingko Nuts

When I was small, there were large gingko trees in the park near our house. In October the trees dropped many mature fruits. When the ripe fruit hits the ground, its golden yellow skin breaks, and the fruit becomes mushy and unattractive. It also gives off an awful smell. My mother always warned me not to pick up the fruits, because they irritate the skin. Based on this description, no one would think that within this fruit is a delicious nut that has been used in Japanese and Chinese cooking for centuries, and is reputed to have powerful medicinal properties.

Vegetable stores and supermarkets in Japan carry this autumn delicacy, gingko nuts, from October through November. When the nuts reach the stores, the smelly flesh has already been removed, and the nuts have been rinsed.

Before cooking the nuts, you must crack the hard shells, by hitting them with a heavy object such as the back edge of a heavy knife. After breaking the shell, remove the soft inner pale yellow nut.

Cook the nuts in salted boiling water. While they cook, rub the nuts with the back of a flat, perforated spatula to remove the thin skins. After only a brief time in boiling water, the color of the nuts changes to bright green.

After removing the skins, drain the nuts, and refresh them in cold water. Then they may be stir-fried, deep-fried, or added to simmered or steamed dishes or soups. Including only a few bright green gingko nuts in a dish during autumn surely heightens the sense of season for the diners.

SOURCES: Look for unshelled gingko nuts in the autumn in Japanese food stores. When gingko nuts are not available in their shells, buy cooked, peeled nuts in a can in a Japanese or other Asian food store. Canned nuts are yellow, unfortunately, and their flavor is not as good as that of fresh-shelled nuts.

WHAT TO LOOK FOR: Fresh gingko nuts are sold in their hard, camel-colored shells.

STORAGE: Keep in a breathable bag and place it in a cool, dark place. Use nuts while they are heavy and fresh.

GOBO • Burdock

Introduced to Japan from China as a medicine before the tenth century, *gobo* has over the years gained popularity as a table vegetable. This slender, brown-skinned root vegetable may grow to more than 2 feet in length under ideal soil conditions. Often sold with soil still attached, *gobo* is unappealing to people who see this vegetable for the first time or know burdock only as a weed. But the cultivated variety, unlike the wild type, is tight-fleshed and sweet-flavored. *Gobo* is highly praised in Japan for its nutty flavor and pleasant, crunchy texture after brief cooking. In addition, the root is very rich in dietary fiber.

If you can't find a source for *gobo* in your area, you might substitute salsify, a similar root vegetable that is a little more widely available. Salsify, however, has a rough texture and a less sweet flavor.

When preparing fresh burdock or salsify, prevent discoloration by soaking the peeled and cut root is a mild vinegar solution (see page 29).

Gobo is suitable for cooking in many ways, but it is not normally eaten raw.

SOURCES: Gobo, burdock, is available at Japanese food stores. It is also easy to grow from seeds, which are readily available from mail-order seed companies.

WHAT TO LOOK FOR: Choose a root that looks plump and feels heavy for its size. Try to find one with soil still clinging to it.

Avoid purchasing *gobo* that has been rinsed, partially skinned, and perhaps even cut into julienne strips before being packed in a plastic bag. When the root is exposed to air by skinning or cutting, it quickly discolors. To prevent this discoloration, the supplier may treat the *gobo* products with chemicals. Therefore, these products are best avoided.

STORAGE: Wrap the root in paper and keep it in a cool, dark place. Refrigeration is not necessary. Use the root within five days, while it is fresh and juicy.

HAKUSAI • Chinese Cabbage

Unlike other vegetables of Chinese origin, *hakusai*, Chinese cabbage, did not reach Japan until the late nineteenth century. It is one of a limited number of winter vegetables produced in China, where it is frequently sold from big roadside piles with no other vegetables. Chinese cabbage heads are about 10 inches in length and 6 inches across at the base. The lower parts of the leaves are white and quite thick. The upper parts are light green, thin, and wrinkled.

In Japan as in China, Chinese cabbage is a favorite vegetable for pickling. My mother pickled Chinese cabbage every December. She filled a wooden barrel with whole cabbage leaves and brine, weighted down the cabbage with a large, heavy stone, and left the barrel outside for fermentation. After three to four weeks, a delightful, tart smell began to permeate the cold air. This was the time for the entire family to indulge and enjoy the crisp pickled cabbage.

Besides making an excellent pickle, Chinese cabbage also plays an important role in *nabemono* (hot-pot) preparations. Since this vegetable does not have a strong flavor of its own, it is perfect for cooking with richly flavored stocks. Briefly cooked, Chinese cabbage has a wonderful, crisp texture.

Chinese cabbage can be stir-fried or quickly braised as well. Modern Japanese even serve it with cream or béchamel sauce.

SOURCES: Hakusai, Chinese cabbage, is available at most supermarkets as well as at Japanese and other Asian food stores.

WHAT TO LOOK FOR: Look for heads that are tightly closed and unwilted.

STORAGE: Wrapped whole in paper and stored in an unheated cellar or outbuilding during the cold winter months, Chinese cabbage keeps for one to two weeks. Once a head is cut, it should be refrigerated and used within four days.

KABOCHA • Japanese Squash

Shaped like a pumpkin and about 6 to 7 inches in diameter, this winter squash has a thick, tough, dark green skin. Cutting a *kabocha* with a heavy-duty knife reveals the bright, deep orange flesh, which is rich in vitamins and minerals. When this flesh is cooked, it becomes very sweet and creamy.

Kabocha is at its best in summer, just after harvest. Uncut, the vegetable can be stored through the following winter. Because of this, in the past *kabocha* was an indispensable vegetable to be consumed during the winter months, when other vegetables were scarce.

Like other winter squashes, *kabocha* is a versatile vegetable. Simmered *kabocha* in fish stock, sugar, and soy sauce (*kabocha no umani*, page 247) is one of the most popular home-style dishes of Japan. *Kabocha* is also wonderful in soup and Western-style pumpkin pie. Deep-frying is another excellent way to cook this vegetable.

If you can't find *kabocha*, substitute pumpkin or buttercup squash, an American variety that is similar in texture and flavor.

SOURCES : *Kabocha* is available at Japanese and other Asian food stores and at some large supermarkets.

WHAT TO LOOK FOR: Choose a *kabocha* that is firm and heavy for its size.

STORAGE: Once cut, *kabocha* should be stored in a plastic bag in the refrigerator. Use it within four days.

KAIWARE • Daikon Sprouts

The thin, white, 4-inch-long stem of a daikon sprout is topped with two tiny heart-shaped deep-green leaves. If you remember your high school biology, you will recognize that these delicate leave are not those of the mature plant, but are the cotyledons—the first leaves that come from the newly sprouted seeds. The tiny sprouts, *kaiware*, have a pleasantly bitter, refreshing taste.

Kaiware are eaten raw. To use the sprouts, cut off their roots, rinse the sprouts, and add them to salads or roll them into sushi. Or use them as a condiment for sashimi (sliced raw fish) or noodle dishes.

SOURCES: *Kaiware*, daikon sprouts, are available at Japanese foods stores and some large supermarkets. They are sold along with other sprouts, such as alfalfa.

WHAT TO LOOK FOR: *Kaiware* are available year-round, but they taste best from spring through early autumn. Choose fresh, unwilted sprouts.

STORAGE: Fresh *kaiware* will keep in a plastic bag in the refrigerator for two to three days.

KAKI • Persimmon

Until I began to teach outside Japan, I never expected that a store would sell a persimmon so astringent that I would have to spit it out. This happened in Spain a few years ago, when I found a plump, ink-brush-shaped, deep orange persimmon. Now I have also learned that persimmon is not a favorite fruit in America. The orange, ripe-looking fruits most often sold in the United States are also a very astringent variety. These persimmons must be left until they become very soft, almost like jam. This texture clearly puts off many consumers.

When I was young, a relative who lived far from our Tokyo home sent us a large box of tree-ripened persimmons every autumn. While our housemaid was separating the good persimmons from the ones that were overripe or had been mashed during transport, I always sat next to her and watched. I grabbed the discarded, crushed, jamlike persimmons and enjoyed their very sweet flavor, eating as many as I could, until my mother came and took me away from them. She always warned me, "Persimmons cool your body. Do not eat so many. Overeating persimmons slows down your bowels!" No matter how many times my mother warned me, every autumn I could hardly wait to taste the very sweet, crushed persimmons. And, frankly, I never did suffer any ill effects from the experience.

Persimmons, *kaki*, originated in Asia and have been cultivated in Japan for centuries. Both sweet and astringent varieties are grown in Japan. Sweet *kaki* also contains the chemicals, called tannins, that produce the astringency in unripe persimmons. The ripening process inactivates the tannins, so the astringency disappears. Fuyu, Nishimura-wase, and Jiro are popular varieties of sweet *kaki*. These sweet varieties have a round and slightly flatter shape. Astringent *kaki*, shaped like an acorn, becomes less astringent when the fruit is left to become very soft and mushy. These varieties are perfect for drying, since the drying process also removes astringency. *Kaki* are rich in vitamin A, vitamin C, and potassium.

SOURCES: Kaki, persimmons, are available in the late autumn at Japanese food stores and supermarkets.

WHAT TO LOOK FOR: Choose sweet *kaki* fruits, of the Fuyu, Nishimura-wase, or Jiro variety, that are neither very firm nor very soft.

If the persimmons are acorn-shaped, they are an astringent variety. Let them stand until they become *very* soft. At this stage, you can eat them, use them in baking, or make them into a delightful persimmon jam.

STORAGE: Store ripe persimmons in the refrigerator, and eat them within three days.

KYURI • Japanese Cucumber

Originally from the Himalayan region, cucumbers have over the years emerged in many varieties, because of different soil and climatic conditions and hybridization. Japanese cucumbers are slender and long, about 8 inches. Unlike American slicing cucumbers, which have smooth skins, Japanese cucumbers have tiny bumps all over. Their skins are deep green, thicker than the skins of American cucumbers, and *very* crispy to the bite. Inside, Japanese cucumbers have fewer seeds than the American type, so seeding is unnecessary. One of the best and simplest ways to enjoy a Japanese cucumber is to cut it into large sticks, spread some brown miso on it, and eat it as is.

If you are interested in nutrition, there is a curious fact you should know about this vegetable: Cut or grated cucumber produces an enzyme that destroys vitamin C. To inactivate this enzyme, toss cut or grated cucumber with some rice vinegar before combining the cucumber with other ingredients.

One of the few vegetables that are indigenous to Japan, mizuna has been cultivated in and around Kyoto for many centuries. Recently the vegetable has gained popularity in large cities in the United States. It has become a standard constituent in mesclun, a combination of young salad leaves.

A member of the mustard family, mizuna grows in bunches. A big bunch can have more than five hundred thin, snow white stalks with light green leaves. Each leaf is about the size of an arugula leaf, but is deeply serrated.

Mizuna got its name, which means "water greens," because this vegetable is grown in fields that are shallowly flooded with water. In Japan, mizuna is also known by another name, *kyona*, or "greens from the Kyoto region," where the cool climate produces tender, flavorful leaves. In this region, mizuna is a preferred pickling vegetable because, despite its tender appearance, it has a firm, crisp texture. Mizuna is also eaten raw in salads, stir-fried, simmered, and used in hot-pot dishes.

SOURCES: Mizuna is sold at Japanese food stores and many large supermarkets and natural-food stores. It is easy to grow from seeds, which are available from many mail-order seed companies.

WHAT TO LOOK FOR: Choose mizuna with firm, unwilted leaves.

STORAGE: Store mizuna in a plastic bag in the refrigerator. Use it within three days.

MOYASHI · Bean Sprouts

Sprouts grown from many different kinds of legume seeds—soybeans, mung beans, azuki beans, alfalfa, peas, and lentils—are generally known as *moyashi*. All of these sprouts are rich in vitamins, minerals, and protein. Until recently, *moyashi* used for cooking in Japan were predominantly soybean sprouts. Mung-bean sprouts are now sold next to the soybean variety. Soybean sprouts have yellow heads and thick, snow white stems. Mung-bean sprouts have small green heads and thinner, longer stems.

Neither soybean nor mung-bean sprouts have a particularly distinctive flavor, but their crisp texture and low cost makes them very popular in Japan. Bean sprouts are used in soups and stir-fried and simmered preparations. Heating sprouts can quickly soften their flesh, so they should be cooked for only a very short time. Generally they are added at the very last step of cooking.

Try bean sprouts in miso soup with sliced *abura-age* (fried thin tofu). The crisp, refreshing bean sprouts are a perfect complement to the rich flavor and the soft texture of *abura-age*.

SOURCES: Both soybean and mung-bean sprouts are sold at Japanese and other Asian food stores, large supermarkets, and natural-food stores.

WHAT TO LOOK FOR: Purchase sprouts that have snow white stems and no brown spots on their heads.

STORAGE: Store bean sprouts in a plastic bag in the refrigerator. Use them within two days of purchase.

NAGANEGI • Long Onion

Naganegi literally means "long onion," and this is a fitting description for this non-bulbing onion. A *naganegi* onion is about 12 to 16 inches long and, at the base, about 1 inch in diameter. The top third of the onion is composed of green tubular blades, and the rest is tight white stem. The white part is lengthened by the heaping of soil around the stem.

Both the white and green parts of the onion are used in cooking. The green blades, which are rich in carotene and vitamin C, are sliced thin and used as a garnish in soup and noodle dishes. The white stem, which has a strong onion flavor when it is eaten raw, becomes very mild and sweet when it is cooked. It is grilled and used in simmered dishes.

If *naganegi* are not available, scallions or spring onions are usually a good substitute, because of their similar flavor and texture. But, the thickness of *naganegi* is necessary in some preparations.

NASU • Japanese Eggplant

Eggplant originated in the Old World and traveled to Japan from India by way of China during the eighth century. Today Japanese eggplant varieties are distinctive. They are short—about 4 to 5 inches—and slender. They are less seedy than other eggplant varieties, and when they are cooked they become creamier than the large American eggplants do.

Japanese eggplant is prepared in many ways—pickled, stir-fried, deep-fried, steamed, grilled, or simmered. Available year-round in Japan, Japanese eggplant tastes the best in autumn, when the flesh becomes even less seedy, much creamier, and milder in flavor. There is a saying in Japan, "Do not treat your daughter-in-law to (delicious) autumn eggplant" (*Akinasu wa yomeni kuwasuna*). Some people say this shows the ill nature of mothers-in-law, who think that autumn eggplant is too good for their daughters-in-law. Another, less harsh interpretation is that giving a daughter-in-law a seedless eggplant is bad luck—it might keep her from getting pregnant.

There is another popular type of eggplant, *kamonasu,* that is used in Japan. After peeling or slicing eggplant, soak it in cold water to prevent it from discoloring.

SOURCES: Japanese eggplant is sold at Japanese food stores, and it has recently become available at large supermarkets, along with other slender varieties that are labeled Italian. These slender eggplants are a good substitute for Japanese varieties.

WHAT TO LOOK FOR: Purchase eggplant that is dark purple, glossy, and firm to the touch. Refrigerate the eggplant in a plastic bag, and use it within three days after purchase.

NIRA • Chinese Chives

Also called garlic chives, for their mixed flavor of garlic and chive, Chinese chives have long (up to 1 foot), flat, thin, dark green leaves. They are rich in vitamins A, B, and C, as well as in minerals such as calcium.

Chinese chives are used in a wide variety of Japanese dishes. A popular miso soup ingredient, they go very well with *abura-age* (fried thin tofu) slices and bean sprouts. Briefly blanched, still crisp Chinese chives can be dressed with any of several Japanese dressings, such as *shoyu* dressing (page 92), ponzu dressing (page 73), and *ohitashi* dressing (page 237). Quickly stir-fried, this vegetable gives a bright green color, crisp texture, and garlicky flavor to any stir-fried dish.

When Chinese chives are not available, the green part of a scallion makes a good substitute. Scallion, however, lacks the distinctive flavor and crisp texture of Chinese chives, and has too strong an onion flavor.

SOURCES: Available throughout the year at Japanese and other Asian food stores, Chinese chives are also easy to grow from seeds, which are available from many mail-order seed companies.

WHAT TO LOOK FOR: Chinese chives are most tender in early spring. Purchase a bunch with leaves that are firm, erect, and free of brown spots.

STORAGE: Refrigerate Chinese chives in a plastic bag, and use them within two days after purchase.

RENKON • Lotus Root

Renkon is the root of the lotus or water lily plant, *hasu*, which was introduced to Japan from India by way of China almost two thousand years ago. The plant produces pretty white, pink, and purple flowers as it grows from the muddy bottom of a pond or lake. The root, which grows in sausagelike links, has longitudinal tubular channels, usually ten. When the root is cut crosswise, the cut surface displays an attractive flowerlike pattern.

The flavor of lotus root is not strong, but, when it is briefly cooked, it has a pleasant crunchy texture; overcooking makes the flesh soft and mushy. Sliced thin and cooked briefly in vinegared boiling water, then pickled in a sweet vinegar marinade, lotus root makes a delicious side dish.

SOURCES: Lotus root is available at Japanese and other Asian food stores.

WHAT TO LOOK FOR: Purchase a root that has smooth skin, looks plump, and is heavy for its size. Check the inner surfaces of the root tubes, if they are visible; they should be snow white. These surfaces become brown as the root grows older.

STORAGE: Refrigerate lotus root in a plastic bag, and use the root within three days after purchase.

SATO-IMO • Taro

Known as taro in the United States, *sato-imo* is the root of a perennial plant that is found everywhere in tropical Asia. There are many varieties of taro; the shape varies from small and round to long and sticklike. The cut surface displays a snow white flesh.

Taro has no distinctive flavor, but it has a pleasant, soft texture and is a good source of starch and potassium. In traditional preparations, taro is simmered in flavored broth, stewed together with meat or fowl, or added to soups. As a solid constituent that absorbs the flavor of the broth, taro is a useful ingredient in soups and stews.

Before further preparation, taro is washed, peeled, and parboiled. First rinse the root thoroughly to remove any soil residue, and wipe it completely dry with a paper towel. Then peel the taro with a knife. When the flesh contacts water, it develops a slightly slimy texture. Cooking taro in water makes it more slimy. To reduce the sliminess, cook taro briefly once or twice in new water and discard the water before proceeding with further preparations.

46

SOURCES: Sato-imo, taro, is available at Japanese and other Asian food stores and at some large supermarkets.

WHAT TO LOOK FOR: Choose roots that look moist and are heavy for their size, and whose cut surfaces are white, not brown.

STORAGE: Store taro in a paper bag in a cool, dark place.

Originally from Central and South America, sweet potatoes were introduced by Spanish conquistadores to the Philippines, from whence they reached China. They were introduced to Japan from China in the seventeenth century.

Japanese improvements in quality over the years have produced a very sweet and creamy sweet potato—as sweet and creamy as cooked sweet chestnuts, some Japanese boast. The skin of the Japanese sweet potato is a bright, reddish purple. The inside is creamy white when raw, bright yellow when cooked.

Sweet potatoes are delicious baked, simmered, or fried. They are often simmered in *dashi* (fish stock) flavored with *shoyu* (soy sauce) and sugar. Sliced thin and fried, they are also a favorite tempura ingredient.

During the wintertime in Japan, on the streets of small towns and big cities alike, you can spot vendors selling baked sweet potatoes from their small wooden carts (or, these days, pickup trucks). Each vendor chants his distinctive sales cry (or plays it on a recorded tape) as the sweet smell of baked sweet potatoes permeates the area. On each cart or truck, potatoes are baked by being immersed in tiny heated pebbles over a wood or charcoal fire. The baked sweet potatoes are known as *yaki-imo* (baked potato).

American sweet potatoes are less sweet and creamy and, when cooked, more watery than the Japanese variety. In simmered dishes, Japanese sweet potatoes hold their shape much better. When they are unavailable, the orange-fleshed American sweet potatoes called yams are a better substitute than the paler-fleshed, less sweet varieties. But not even the sweetest American varieties are as sweet and creamy as Japanese sweet potatoes. To compensate for the lack of sweetness, you may need to add sugar or another sweetener to the dish.

SOURCES: *Satsuma-imo*, Japanese sweet potatoes, are available at Japanese food stores.

WHAT TO LOOK FOR: Purchase sweet potatoes that are firm, smooth, and without brown spots.

STORAGE: Store sweet potatoes in a cool, dark, dry place—not the refrigerator. Use them within five days after purchase.

47

SHIMEJI Mushrooms

Shimeji mushrooms have white, short, plump stems topped with little brown caps. About 2 to 3 inches in height, the mushrooms naturally grow in clumps from stumps. Most of the *shimeji* sold in markets have been cultivated in sawdust beds, however, so the mushrooms are available year-round.

Shimeji mushrooms have a delicate flavor and fragrance. They are delicious when quickly sautéed, simmered, or deep-fried.

SOURCES: *Shimeji* mushrooms are available at Japanese food stores and some supermarkets.

WHAT TO LOOK FOR: Look for mushrooms with a firm, plump appearance.

STORAGE: Refrigerate *shimeji* mushrooms in a paper bag, and use them within two days after purchase.

SHISHITOGARASHI • Small Green Pepper

Shishitogarashi, literally "Chinese lion pepper," got its name because this 3-inch-long green pepper resembles a miniature Chinese lion head. Although you might expect a pepper by this name to be extremely hot, most *shishitogarashi* are quite mild, although an occasional rebel may surprise you with its hotness.

Shishitogarashi is a uniquely Japanese pepper variety. When the Portuguese introduced the chile pepper to Japan from South America during the sixteenth century, the Japanese found this vegetable too hot for their tastes. So, over the years, the Japanese hybridized the chile pepper until it completely lost its fiery spiciness and became the mild pepper called *shishitogarashi*.

Shishitogarashi peppers taste best when stir-fried or deep-fried. In either preparation, the cooking time should be very short. To keep a pepper from exploding in hot oil, prick it all over with a toothpick before frying it.

Like hot peppers, *shishitogarashi* are rich in vitamins A and C. Unlike hot peppers, though, *shishitogarashi* can be eaten in large quantity, so are an excellent source of these nutrients.

When *shishitogarashi* are not available, substitute green bell peppers.

SOURCES: *Shishitogarashi* peppers are sold at Japanese food stores. Look for them during the summer, when they are in season.

WHAT TO LOOK FOR: Choose peppers that are bright green, firm, and glossy.

STORAGE: Refrigerate the peppers in a plastic bag, and use them within three days after purchase.

SHUNGIKU • Chrysanthemum Leaves

Edible chrysanthemum leaves appear in the market during the cold months in Japan. The leaves resemble those of the flowering chrysanthemum, but the edible chrysanthemum is cultivated for its own purpose.

The slightly bitter leaves can be used either raw or cooked. They are included in all hot-pot dishes, such as sukiyaki (beef and vegetables quickly braised in a sweetened broth with soy sauce, page 462), *shabu-shabu* (beef slices blanched in boiling water, page 451), and *torinabe* (chicken and vegetables cooked in flavored broth or water, page 426). Parboiled chrysanthemum leaves, which retain their crispness and bright green color, make a delicious Japanese salad when served with tofu dressing (page 138), sesame dressing (page 103), or with a mixture of fish stock and soy sauce (*ohitashi* dressing, page 237). Uncooked leaves, especially young and tender ones, are excellent additions to a Western salad.

Good substitutes for chrysanthemum leaves are spinach, turnip greens, and mustard greens.

SOURCES: Shungiku, chrysanthemum leaves, are available in Japanese food stores.

WHAT TO LOOK FOR: Choose a bunch of leaves that do not look wilted.

STORAGE: Refrigerate chrysanthemum leaves in a plastic bag, and use them within three days after purchase.

TAKENOKO • Bamboo Shoots

Spring is the time when bamboo sends forth its amazing shoots, which nearly burst from the ground, growing up to a foot in a single night. The fresh, raw shoots, 6 to 10 inches tall, are sold still covered with layers of brown husk. The shoots must be cooked very soon after harvest, or they will develop a bitter and harsh taste, and the flesh will become dry and hard.

In Japan, bamboo shoots that have shown just their tips above ground are dug out and served raw in sashimi style, with wasabi and *shoyu* (soy sauce). These shoots are so tender, sweet, and juicy that there is no need to cook them.

But most bamboo shoots sold in stores are harvested when they are 5 to 7 inches above ground. They appear in retail stores only a day later, when they have already grown tough and astringent. At this stage they are boiled in their husks for three hours, in water to which rice bran and a few dried red chile peppers have been added (see page 54). Freshly prepared, these shoots have a delicate, sweet flavor and crisp texture that canned bamboo shoots cannot match.

Trimming a bamboo shoot

SOURCES: Fresh bamboo shoots are sold in the spring at Japanese and Chinese food stores and at a few large supermarkets.

Parboiled bamboo shoots are available year-round, in sealed plastic bags or cans. But these have little flavor compared with fresh harvested and cooked bamboo shoots.

WHAT TO LOOK FOR: The bamboo shoots sold in Japan are of the *Mosochiku* variety. Fresh shoots sold in the United States may be of another, smaller variety. If you find whole bamboo shoots, make sure they are young and fresh. The bottom of the stem should appear moist.

STORAGE: Store fresh bamboo shoots at room temperature, and use them within a day of purchase.

UME • Japanese Green Plum

In Japan, *ume* blossoms herald the very beginning of spring, even when snow is still about. The elegant shape and fragrant smell of the blossoms are highly praised by the Japanese.

After the blossoms fall, the trees begin to bear tiny fruit, and by the end of May they are studded with many beautiful, plump green *ume*. The "plums," which actually belong to the same genus as apricots, are so attractive that you may think to pick one and taste it. Unfortunately, fresh *ume* are inedible. They are very astringent and contain a little of a poisonous substance. So the Japanese created several delicious ways to prepare and enjoy them.

The favorite way to use the plums is to pickle them (see page 142). They are also the basis for three more delicious preserves: *umejusu* (plum juice, page 487), plum jelly, and, most important, *umeshu* (plum wine, page 488).

SOURCES: Fresh *ume*, Japanese green plums, are unfortunately still hard to find outside Japan. But you may be able to find them at a large Japanese supermarket in late May or early June.

WHAT TO LOOK FOR: As *ume* ripen, their color changes to yellow. Choose plums that are still firm and green.

STORAGE: Store *ume* in a breathable plastic bag in a dark place at cool room temperature.

YAMA-IMO • Mountain Yam

Yama-imo is the tuberous root of a climbing vine. Different varieties of this plant produce roots of different shapes, from the long, straight *naga-imo* to the larger, thicker, triangular-headed *icho-imo* and the round *tsukune-imo*. All types are rich in carbohydrates, potassium, and the digestive enzyme amylase.

Mountain yams are usually grated before they are used. Grated yam is white and has a slippery, gluey texture, which varies in thickness from one type of yam to another. Grated yam is added uncooked to salad or sauce. It is also used as a binder in dishes such as tofu dumplings and Japanese pancakes, *okonomiyaki*. *Naga-imo*, which contains the most water and is the least gluey, is served julienned in salad.

Before using mountain yams, remove their thick peels. To prevent the inner surfaces from discoloring upon exposure to oxygen, soak peeled or cut yam in rice vinegar or in water with vinegar added.

SOURCES: *Yama-imo*, mountain yam, is available at Japanese food stores and at Chinese vegetable markets.

W H A T   T O   L O O K   F O R : Choose a yam that has no dark, soft spots and that is heavy for its size.

S T O R A G E : Store a mountain yam in a breathable plastic bag in the warmest part of the refrigerator. Use the yam within three days of purchase.

YUZU Citron

Yuzu is a tangerine-size variety of citron, a species of citrus fruit with a thick, bumpy rind. Bright green in summer, *yuzu* turns yellow in autumn, when it is ripe. Like lemon, *yuzu* is valued for its rind, which has a pleasant tart and bitter flavor, as well as for its juice.

Yuzu is used to enhance the flavor of prepared dishes and sauces. A hint of *yuzu* juice and rind reminds diners of the approaching winter season in Japan. *Yuzu* juice is an important ingredient in ponzu dressing (page 73), which also contains *komezu* (rice vinegar), *dashi* (fish stock), *shoyu* (soy sauce), and *mirin* (sweet cooking wine). Today, *yuzu* juice and rind are also used to make an extremely refreshing sherbet.

Many recipes in this book call for a garnish of julienned *yuzu* rind. To julienne the rind, use a zester, or use a vegetable peeler and then cut the strips into thinner ones. Or peel the yellow rind with a knife, leaving the inner, white part of the skin behind, then cut the rind into thin strips.

Yuzu can be difficult to find, so substitutions are sometimes necessary. For *yuzu* rind, substitute lime or lemon rind. For *yuzu* juice, a good substitute is usually equal parts lime juice and orange or grapefruit juice.

S O U R C E S : Yuzu citron is available in winter at Japanese food stores.

W H A T   T O   L O O K   F O R : Choose fruits that are firm and heavy for their size.

S T O R A G E : Store *yuzu* in the refrigerator.

VEGETABLES AND FRUITS

SPICES AND HERBS

For centuries, spices and herbs have been used in nearly every cuisine, to help preserve foods, to hide strong odors, and to enhance the flavor of prepared dishes. Compared with most other cuisines, however, Japanese cooking employs a small variety and quantity of spices and herbs. The reasons for this are geographic, climatic, and historical. Stretching from latitude 30 degrees north to 45 degrees north, with a long coastline, Japan is neither very chilly nor tropical. The four distinct seasons provide many varieties of fresh fish and shellfish, vegetables, fruits, fowl, and meat throughout the year. The continuous availability of fresh foods has minimized the need to use spices and herbs as preservatives. And, since Japan is situated far from Western countries and early trade routes, the country never became a crossroads in the spice trade. Over the centuries, Japan's isolation and the country's abundant food sources have shaped a cuisine with little reliance on herbs and spices.

A few herbs and spices have been popular in Japan since ancient times. Early Japanese history books (*Kojiki* of 712 A.D. and *Nihonshoki* of 720 A.D.) describe the use of ginger. Other spices, such as garlic, *myoga* ginger (see page 56), *sansho* pepper (see page 57), and *tade* (a plant belonging to the smartweed family whose stems and leaves have a peppery, bitter flavor and a distinctive aroma), have also been used in Japan for centuries. Europeans brought cardamom, cinnamon, cloves, nutmeg, mustard, fennel, caraway seeds, and black pepper, but until the end of the nineteenth century these were mainly used as medicines. The chile pepper, which was brought by the Portuguese from Central America, has managed to become one of the indispensable spices of Japanese cooking today, although it has had an even stronger influence on Chinese, Korean, and Southeast Asian cuisine.

Listed here are spices and herbs common in today's Japanese kitchen.

AKATOGARASHI • Japanese Dried Red Chile Pepper
SHICHIMI TOGARASHI • Seven-Spice Powder
TOBAN JIANG • Chile-Bean Paste

Akatogarashi (Japanese Dried Red Chile Pepper)

This dried, whole, small hot red chile, between 1 and 2 inches long, is one of the hottest chile varieties in the world. It is also sold in a powdered form, called *ichimi togarashi*. Whole or powdered, this chile is used in modest amounts in Japanese preparations, including pickled dishes, dipping sauces and marinades, dressings, and stir-fried dishes.

If you can't find *akatogarashi*, use the little dried red chiles called *japonés*, which are sold in Mexican food stores and the Mexican sections of large supermarkets. For *ichimi togarashi*, substitute cayenne or other powdered red chile.

Shichimi Togarashi (Seven-Spice Powder)

During the Edo Era (1600 to 1868), the Japanese created this blended spice mixture, which is also called simply *shichimi*. It is a combination of seven spices: *akatogarashi*, *sansho* pepper (see page 57), poppy seeds, sesame seeds, hemp seeds, dried orange peel, and nori (see page 128). *Shichimi togarashi* is a popular condiment used to enhance the flavor of noodle, hot-pot, and stir-fried dishes. At noodle restaurants in Japan, a small glass or wooden jar of seven-spice powder appears on every table.

Toban Jiang (Chile-Bean Sauce)

Another popular chile-based condiment, *toban jiang*, or "chile-bean sauce," is frequently used in Japanized Chinese dishes. The sauce is made of crushed chiles, salt, and fermented broad beans. *Toban jiang* is very hot and at the same time quite salty. You can see the bits of chopped chiles in the red paste.

SOURCES: *Akatogarashi* (whole dried red chiles), *ichimi togarashi* (ground dried red chiles), *shichimi togarashi* (seven-spice powder), and *toban jiang* (chile-bean sauce) are sold at Japanese and other Asian food stores and some large supermarkets.

WHAT TO LOOK FOR: Choose *akatogarashi* chiles whose color is an intense red and whose entire skin surface is shiny. As the color fades to brown over time, the flavor and heat also fade. *Ichimi togarashi* and *shichimi togarashi* are sold in small plastic bags or glass jars. Choose one that has been packed recently. *Toban jiang* is sold in small glass jars with red caps.

KARASHI • Mustard

Karashi is the general word for *mustard*; *wa-garashi* is the expression for Japanese mustard, which is hotter than its Western counterpart, *yo-garashi*. *Wa-garashi* has a dark yellow color and a pleasant bitter flavor. It is always sold in powdered form, called *konakarashi*. The paste form of mustard, *nerigarashi*, is simply mustard powder mixed with water.

Paste mustard is served as a condiment for dishes such as *oden* (a hot stew of assorted fish cakes), *gyoza* (pot-stickers or pan-fried dumplings, *jiaoji*), simmered vegetable and meat dishes, and miso soups. Mustard is also used in dressings.

If you can't find Japanese mustard, substitute Chinese mustard powder or Colman's English mustard. These, like the Japanese type, are made from a hot, yellow variety of mustard seed.

To make mustard paste, vigorously stir equal parts of mustard powder and lukewarm water (heated to about 105 degrees F), until the paste becomes pungent. One teaspoon of mustard powder produces 1 teaspoon of the paste form. Sometimes I call for thin mustard paste; in these cases, use $1^1/_2$ teaspoons water for each teaspoon mustard powder. Because the pungency of mustard paste declines quickly with exposure to air, cover the paste with plastic wrap until you are ready to use it.

SOURCES: Japanese and other Asian food stores sell hot mustard powder and paste. Colman's English mustard is available in supermarkets.

WHAT TO LOOK FOR: Japanese mustard powder is packed in a mustard-colored can. The paste form comes in a plastic tube with a yellow cap.

STORAGE: After opening the container, refrigerate mustard powder or paste. Use the paste type within ten days.

MITSUBA Greens

Indigenous to Japan, China, and Korea, this herb has a pale green, slender stalk, 6 to 8 inches long, topped with a green leaf composed of three flat, deeply cut leaflets. Because the Japanese word *mitsuba* literally means "three leaves," the name for this herb is often translated as "trefoil." *Mitsuba* is related to parsley and celery, and its flavor is like a mixture of these two relatives, only milder and much more fragrant. The herb is used in soups, egg custards, hot stews, and salads.

SOURCES: *Mitsuba* is sold at Japanese food stores.

WHAT TO LOOK FOR: *Mitsuba* is cultivated year-round, so it can be found at any time. However, *mitsuba* harvested in spring has more delicate leaves and a better aroma. Choose a bunch with crisp leaves and stems.

STORAGE: Refrigerate *mitsuba* in a plastic bag, and use it within two days after purchase.

MYOGA Ginger

Myoga is the small, young bud of a mountain plant, which shoots out of the ground in spring through early summer. A member of the ginger family, *myoga* has a sharp, bitter, refreshing, flavor, like ginger but a little milder. Thin-sliced *myoga* is used as a condiment for soups, noodle dishes, salads, and sashimi. *Myoga* is also pickled in brine or in sweetened vinegar.

SOURCES: Japanese food stores sell fresh *myoga*.

WHAT TO LOOK FOR: Choose buds that are tightly closed and firm to the touch.

STORAGE: Refrigerate *myoga* in a plastic bag, and use it within two days after purchase.

SANSHO Pepper

I call these berries "pepper" because of their sharp, mintlike, slightly bitter flavor, but *sansho* is not related to black pepper. The berries are from the Japanese prickly ash shrub, which is related to Chinese fagara, the source of Szechuan pepper. But *sansho* and Szechuan pepper each have their own distinctive aroma and flavor. While Szechuan pepper has a clovelike smell and a strong anise flavor, *sansho* has an aroma and flavor similar to mint and citrus. This makes it impossible to substitute Szechuan pepper for *sansho*, or *sansho* for Szechuan pepper.

The husks and berries of Szechuan pepper are dried and used together, but *sansho* husks are dried without their berries. The pretty, light green husks are ground to a powder before they can turn brown, as they otherwise would. Powdered *sansho* is an indispensable condiment for certain Japanese dishes, such as *unagi no kabayaki* (grilled, flavored eel, page 287). The pleasant, sharp bitterness and citruslike flavor of *sansho* refresh the palate after a bite of rich, oily eel.

The young leaves of the *sansho* tree, which appear in early spring, are called *kinome*. Harvested when they are only $1^1/_2$ inches long, they are each composed of fifteen to seventeen tiny leaflets attached symmetrically to one thin stalk. *Kinome* has a sharp, refreshing aroma that is slightly different from that of *sansho*. In early spring, *kinome* is used as a garnish, or chopped or ground and mixed into sauce or dressing (see page 261), to remind the diner of the season.

SOURCES: Japanese food stores sell powdered *sansho* and sometimes whole dried *sansho* berry husks. Unfortunately, *kinome* is not yet widely available outside Japan.

WHAT TO LOOK FOR: *Sansho* in both whole and powdered form is packed in small glass jars or plastic bags. The lid or package is always green, a reminder of the color of *sansho*.

STORAGE: For best flavor, refrigerate an opened jar or package of whole or powdered *sansho*, and use it within two months. Wrap *kinome* in plastic wrap, and store it in the refrigerator. Use it within two days.

SHISO

An annual herb that originated in southern China, shiso, sometimes called perilla, has been cultivated in Japan since the eighth century. There are two types of shiso, green and red.

Green shiso, the type called for in recipes in this book, has a sharp, refreshing mintlike flavor. The dark green leaf is dentate, round, and up to 3 inches in length. Green shiso is rich in carotene and is said to have antiseptic and other medicinal properties. This is why sashimi (sliced raw fish) has been served with shiso leaves for many centuries.

In addition to the green variety, there is a reddish-purple shiso, *akajiso*. *Akajiso* is used in making *umeboshi* (pickled plums). The red pigment in the *akajiso* leaf dyes the green plums a pretty reddish-purple.

SOURCES: Japanese food stores sell fresh shiso.

WHAT TO LOOK FOR: Ten to twenty leaves are usually tied together at the stem with a tiny rubber band and placed in a Styrofoam case, which is covered with plastic wrap. Choose shiso that has no brown spots or wrinkles.

STORAGE: The fresh leaves wither quickly. Refrigerate them in their package, and use them within two days after purchase.

SHOGA • Ginger

Shoga, ginger, is one of the oldest seasonings in Japan. Originally from tropical Asia, it was brought to Japan from China. With its pleasant, sharp bite and fragrant bouquet, ginger promotes a good appetite. It also suppresses undesirable odors from other foods. Because of its antiseptic properties, ginger has always been an important condiment for sashimi and sushi. Folk medicine uses ginger to fight against colds and coughing, and also for stomachache and diarrhea. Finely grated fresh ginger appears as a condiment with many prepared dishes, such as grilled fish or meat, chilled fresh tofu cubes, deep-fried vegetables, deep-fried tofu, grilled vegetables, and cold udon noodles.

It is easiest to grate ginger with a fine-spiked Japanese porcelain grater, which won't tear your skin or impart a metallic flavor (see page 14).

Some recipes in this book call for ginger juice. To extract ginger juice, simply squeeze some finely grated ginger in your hand. Two tablespoons grated ginger makes 1 to 2 teaspoons ginger juice, depending on how fresh and juicy the ginger is.

Japanese food stores sell pickled ginger in two varieties. *Benishoga* is brine-pickled ginger that is tinted bright red. *Shoga amazu-zuke*—or *gari*, as it is known in sushi restaurants—is thin-sliced young ginger that is pickled in sugar and vinegar; the vinegar turns the

ginger a faint pink color. You can make your own *gari* to accompany your sushi by following the recipe on page 292.

SOURCES: Japanese and other Asian food stores and general supermarkets carry fresh
shoga, ginger. Young ginger for pickling is sometimes available at Asian markets.

WHAT TO LOOK FOR: Choose a root that is heavy for its size, unwrinkled, and moist-
looking. Young ginger has a very thin skin and a creamy white color with pinkish knobs.

STORAGE: Wrap the root in plastic wrap, and store it in the warmest part of the refrigerator. Whole, chopped, or grated ginger freezes well, with little change in quality. Use fresh
ginger within a week or so of purchase.

WASABI

Although wasabi is similar to horseradish in taste and culinary function, the two pungent-
flavored roots are unrelated. Unlike horseradish, which grows in soil, wasabi is a water
plant. It grows in shallow, cold, clean water, reaching its green root about 6 inches into the
soil of a stream bed.

Like ginger, wasabi has antiseptic properties, so it has traditionally been served with
sushi and sashimi dishes. Wasabi also helps to promote digestion.

Fresh wasabi root should be grated immediately before consumption. Cut off the top
part of the root and the thick skin, and grate the root from the top down in a very slow, even
motion. Using a fine grater is important; restaurants use a grating surface made of real shark
skin. Slow grinding produces a more pungent paste, and the upper part of the root is more
pungent than the bottom part. Since the spiciness of freshly grated wasabi quickly fades,
you should grate no more than is immediately needed.

Fresh wasabi can be hard to find, so you may need to substitute powdered or paste wasabi. Both of these are more pungent than the freshly grated root, but they are also less fragrant and flavorful.

Powdered wasabi, *konawasabi*, is a mixture of wasabi and horseradish powders. To increase the pungency, mustard powder is frequently added to the mixture, and an artificial green color is added to simulate real wasabi.

To make a paste from powdered wasabi, vigorously stir equal parts of the powder and water in a small cup until the paste develops a pungent aroma. Cover the cup with plastic wrap, and let the paste stand for 5 minutes to allow the flavor and pungency to develop. One tablespoon of wasabi powder produces 1 tablespoon of wasabi paste.

The paste form of wasabi, called *neriwasabi*, comes packed in a small tube, like toothpaste.

Many people love wasabi so much that they overuse it with sashimi or sushi. Do not let wasabi clean out your sinuses or make you cry. Too much wasabi masks the delicate flavor of fish and other foods.

SOURCES: Japanese and Asian food stores and large supermarkets carry powdered wasabi. Recently the paste type, *neriwasabi*, has become available at many of these stores.

Fresh wasabi root is available at some Japanese stores in large cities, and can be purchased by direct mail from farmers in the Northwest. Check food magazines or the Internet for suppliers.

WHAT TO LOOK FOR: Wasabi powder is packed in a small green can; wasabi paste comes in a plastic tube with a green cap. Purchase a can or tube with the most recent manufacturing date.

Fresh wasabi root should be thick, green, and moist-looking. The tiny bumps on the skin should be close together.

STORAGE: Refrigerate an opened can of wasabi powder or a plastic tube of wasabi paste, tightly closed. For the best flavor, use the paste within ten days, the powder within two months.

KOMBU • Kelp
KATSUOBUSHI • Bonito Flakes for *Dashi* (Stock)

A clear and non-oily fish stock, *dashi* is the foundation of many Japanese dishes, including soups, simmered dishes, salad dressings, and marinades. *Dashi* provides subtle but delicious flavor to these dishes and valuable nutrients for the body.

Many non-Japanese cooks misunderstand *dashi*. They believe it is just a broth made of fishy stuff, which makes prepared dishes taste fishy. Even some Japanese cooks never realize the true flavor and nutritious value of *dashi* in Japanese preparations. The result is a huge consumption of synthetically processed fish stock powders and liquid concentrates. These products have poor flavor and little nutritional value, and many are laden with chemicals.

In this section, you will learn how to make your own fresh *dashi*. Not only is homemade *dashi* good for Japanese preparations, but it can also be used as a base for many Western dishes. It is a healthy substitute for meat- or fowl-based stocks.

The ingredients used to make *dashi* depend on the type of dish in which the stock is to be used. *Dashi* can be based on kelp (*kombu*), dried bonito (*katsuobushi*), dried baby sardines (*niboshi*), dried shiitake mushrooms, or a combination of two or three of these ingredients. In this book we'll use the most common combination, kelp and dried bonito.

Kombu (Kelp)

This tall, leafy plant grows from the sea floor in shallow water. The dark olive green leaves may reach lengths of three feet or so, and their width ranges from 2 to 13 inches. In Japan, kelp is harvested between July and September and dried in the sun. Used as a food since the beginning of Japanese civilization, kelp provides important minerals, including iodine, vitamins, protein, and dietary fiber.

Recent scientific studies show that kelp also contains chemicals that can fight against high cholesterol, high blood pressure, and even some forms of cancer. To extract these constituents, soak kelp in a small amount of water overnight. The next day you will find that the water has developed a somewhat slimy texture. This liquid contains beneficial chemicals that lower blood pressure and the risk of certain diseases. According to Japanese folk medicine, people suffering from high blood pressure should drink a little kelp water every day. This liquid is also effective against constipation.

At the beginning of the twentieth century, a Japanese researcher studied stock made with kelp to determine the key chemical that both provides a delicious flavor and enhances the flavors of other ingredients. His investigation revealed the presence in kelp of natural glutamic acid, and led eventually to the production of synthetic monosodium glutamate (MSG) as a flavor enhancer. Unfortunately, this synthetic product does not provide the other natural nutrients of kelp and may cause allergic symptoms in some people.

Katsuobushi (Bonito Flakes)

Although kelp and water alone produce a delicious vegetarian stock (shojin dashi), adding one more ingredient, dried bonito fish (katsuobushi), which is also rich in minerals, vitamins, and protein, creates an even more flavorful and nutritious stock. Katsuobushi has been used as a stock base in Japan since at least the early eighth century. Bonito fish (katsuo) is filleted, boned, boiled, smoked, and dried in the sun to make a hard, woodlike block with a concentrated, rich, and smoky flavor.

In the past, dried bonito fish was sold only in this hard block form. To make dashi, people shaved flakes from the block with a special tool, katsuobushi kezuri, that resembles a carpenter's plane. When I was a child, my mother shaved katsuobushi before each meal. I still can hear the vigorous sound of shaving and smell the fragrant aroma of freshly shaved dried bonito. Today shaved katsuobushi, packed in an airtight plastic bag, has become a mainstream product, and the tradition of shaving dried fish has unfortunately disappeared from nearly all home kitchens.

It was about twenty-five years ago that my mother switched to dried bonito flakes. At that time I was happy to see her domestic workload reduced, and I did not even care about the big change in flavor. But after years passed and I married, I rediscovered the true flavor and nutrients of *katsuobushi*. I asked my mother whether she could give me her charming bonito shaver, so that I could revive the old tradition and enjoy the true flavor of dried bonito. Unfortunately, she had thrown the shaver away quite some time before, and I could not turn back the clock. Today both *katsuobushi* blocks and *katsuobushi* shavers are very rare.

Today tuna (*maguro*), mackerel (*saba*), and horse mackerel (*aji*) are used as well as bonito to produce dried fish flakes. Flakes from these other fish are frequently mixed and packed with bonito flakes, and sold under the same name, although these other fish have a stronger flavor. Check the package label carefully to see if flakes from other fish have been added.

One attractive feature of *dashi* is its ease of preparation. Unlike Western stocks—chicken, beef, seafood, or vegetable—*dashi* is simple and quick to make. In only 10 minutes you can prepare one or two quarts, which you can keep in a clean container with a tightly fitting lid in the refrigerator for up to four days without major changes in quality. Freshly made *dashi* also freezes well. Freeze it in an ice cube tray, and then transfer the frozen cubes to a plastic bag. These little cubes often come in handy, because many traditional Japanese recipes call for only a few tablespoons of *dashi*.

Kelp and dried bonito, both of which seem frugal products, once played important roles as good-luck gifts in Japanese society, because of clever wordplay on their names. In the military society of the Japanese civil war period, in the fourteenth through the sixteenth centuries, members of the warrior class fought each other to expand their spheres of power. *Katsuobushi* means "dried bonito fish," but the word can also be interpreted in a very different way: *Katsu* means "to win," *o* means "man," and *bushi* means "warrior." So dried bonito fish was regarded as a food that could bring a soldier good luck. Kelp has also been treated as a good-luck food, because *kombu*, in regions where the *m* is not pronounced, is part of the Japanese word *yorokobu*, which means "to congratulate."

Dried Japanese *kombu* (kelp) and *katsuobushi* (bonito flakes) are found at Japanese and Asian food stores and health- and natural-food stores. Health- and natural-food stores also sell American kelp, which, although different, is a good substitute for Japanese *kombu*. Instant concentrated forms of *dashi*, either liquid or powdered, are not recommended, but can be used if *kombu* and *katsuobushi* are unavailable. The best concentrates may be found at health- and natural-food stores.

WHAT TO LOOK FOR: Dried *kombu* leaves are packed in clear plastic bags. The surface of each leaf is naturally coated with a thin layer of white powder. This is not mold or an indication of age or poor quality. Choose leaves that are thick, wide, very dark green, and glossy-looking.

Shaved *katsuobushi* (dried bonito) resembles wood shavings. The flakes are packed in a clear, airtight bag that looks like a bag of pink chips. The flakes vary in size; the large ones are for making fish stock, whereas the smaller flakes, which always come in a smaller packet, are used to garnish prepared dishes. If you order spinach *ohitashi* (parboiled spinach salad) at a Japanese restaurant, you will probably find the cooked spinach garnished with these small flakes.

STORAGE: Keep *kombu* in a cool, dry place. It will retain its quality for about one year. Opened bags of *katsuobushi* flakes should be tightly closed and stored in the refrigerator. Use up an opened bag as soon as possible, within three weeks, Otherwise the fish oil will oxidize and make your *dashi* taste bitter and fishy.

BASIC RECIPES

FISH AND KELP STOCKS

Ichiban, Niban, and *Kombu Dashi*

Once you have experienced the fragrant flavor of freshly made *dashi*, and the healthfulness of dishes made with it, you may find yourself preparing it often.

If *katsuobushi*, bonito flakes, are unavailable, simply prepare *dashi* with *kombu*, kelp, alone. *Kombu dashi* is also called *shojin dashi*, vegetarian stock. In all of the recipes in this book that call for *dashi*, *kombu dashi* can be substituted for *ichiban dashi* or *niban dashi*, both of which are made with bonito flakes.

Here are two tips for preparing excellent *dashi*: First, before using *kombu* do not rinse it, lest the white powder be removed. This powder is a source of rich flavor and important nutrients. Second, do not cook the *kombu* and dried fish longer than specified in the recipe. If overcooked, the stock develops a bitter, strong flavor and becomes cloudy.

Once *kombu* and *katsuobushi* are cooked, they spoil quickly, so always make *niban dashi* immediately after *ichiban dashi*.

Ichiban Dashi (First Fish Stock) and *Kombu Dashi* (Kelp Stock)

Ichiban Dashi, "first fish stock," extracts the best flavor and nutrients from *kombu* (kelp) and *katsuobushi* (bonito flakes). The very short cooking time prevents the stock from becoming strongly flavored or yellowish. *Ichiban dashi* is used in preparations for which refined flavor and weak color are required.

> *2 quarts water*
> *Five 6-inch squares* kombu *(kelp)*
> *1 cup tightly packed* katsuobushi *(bonito fish flakes)*

Wipe the *kombu* with a damp cotton cloth or paper towel. In a large pot, bring the water and *kombu* almost to a boil over medium heat. This should take about 10 minutes. Immediately before the water reaches a boil, remove the *kombu*, and either discard it or save it for preparing "second fish stock." Use the liquid *(kombu dashi)* as a vegetarian stock, or follow the remaining instructions to make **ichiban dashi** ("first fish stock").

Immediately after removing the kelp, add the *katsuobushi* (bonito flakes) all at once. Wait 10 seconds or until the liquid comes to a boil. Then turn off the heat, skim off any foam, and let the mixture stand for 2 minutes.

Strain the stock through a sieve lined with a tightly woven cotton cloth. Discard the bonito flakes, or save them with the *kombu* to make second fish stock.

Refrigerate the stock, tightly covered, for up to four days, or freeze it into cubes in an ice tray.

- *Yields 2 quarts stock*

Niban Dashi (Second Fish Stock)

Niban Dashi, "second fish stock," is obtained by simmering the kelp and dried bonito flakes used in preparing *ichiban dashi* in the same volume of fresh water. A longer cooking time extracts the remaining flavor and fragrance from the used ingredients. With a less refined flavor and a cloudy appearance, *niban dashi* is good in everyday miso soups and in simmered dishes, where strong-flavored condiments or ingredients such as fish, chicken, or meat are employed.

> 2 quarts water
> Kombu (kelp) and katsuobushi (bonito flakes)
> remaining from the preparation of ichiban dashi

In a large pot, combine the water, *kombu*, and bonito flakes. Cook the mixture over low heat for 10 minutes. Strain the stock through a sieve lined with tightly woven cotton cloth, and discard the bonito flakes and *kombu*. Refrigerate the stock, tightly covered, for up to four days, or freeze it into cubes in an ice tray.

- *Yields 2 quarts stock*

BASIC RECIPES

BROTH FOR HOT NOODLES, TEMPURA DIPPING SAUCE, AND COLD DIPPING SAUCE FOR NOODLES

Kakejiru, Tentsuyu, Tsukejiru

Kakejiru (Broth for Hot Noodles)

A "broth to pour over (ingredients)," *kakejiru* is a mild-flavored broth to be poured hot over udon (cooked thick wheat noodles) or soba (buckwheat noodles).

> 1 quart ichiban **dashi**
> 1^1/$_2$ tablespoons sugar
> 1^1/$_2$ teaspoons salt
> 1 tablespoon shoyu (soy sauce)
> 1^1/$_2$ teaspoons usukuchi shoyu (light-colored soy sauce),
> preferably, or regular shoyu

In a medium pot, bring all the ingredients to a slow boil over low to medium heat. Use the broth immediately, or refrigerate it, covered, for up to four days.

- *Yields 1 quart broth*

Tentsuyu (Tempura Dipping Sauce)

Tentsuyu is a dipping sauce that is served with piping-hot fried foods, such as tempura. Dipping hot foods in *tentsuyu* cools them a little, and at the same time provides extra flavor. This sauce is served at room temperature.

3 tablespoons mirin *(sweet cooking wine)*
2 cups ichiban dashi *(first fish stock)*
5 tablespoons usukuchi shoyu *(light-colored soy sauce)*
1½ tablespoons shoyu *(soy sauce)*
1½ tablespoons sugar

In a medium pot, bring all the ingredients to a boil. Remove the pot from the heat, and let the sauce cool to room temperature.

You can refrigerate the sauce for up to three days, covered. Before using it, heat it through and let it cool to room temperature.

- *Yields 2⅔ cups sauce*

Tsukejiru (Noodle-Dipping Sauce)

Tsukejiru is more strongly flavored than *kakejiru,* since more salt and sugar are added to the fish stock. Cooked, cooled noodles are dipped in this sauce before they are eaten.

At noodle restaurants, *tsukejiru* preparation begins with the making of a base, **kaeshi**. *Kaeshi* is refrigerated for a week to let the flavor mature, then cooked with fish stock and additional dried bonito flakes to produce *tsukejiru. Kaeshi* improves the flavor of the dipping sauce. To save time and trouble at home, however, you can cook all the ingredients for *kaeshi* and *tsukejiru* in one pot at one time, although the most perfectionist Japanese noodle connoisseur might not approve.

6 tablespoons shoyu *(soy sauce)*
2 teaspoons tamari
1 tablespoon sugar

3 cups ichiban dashi *(first fish stock)*
½ cup kaeshi *(base for dipping sauce)*
½ cup katsuobushi *(dried bonito fish flakes)*

To make the *kaeshi*, in a small saucepan, heat the two soy sauces over low heat until the mixture is hot. Add the sugar, and cook, stirring, until it is dissolved. Turn off the heat, and let the mixture cool. Refrigerate it, covered, for a week before using it to make *tsukejiru*.

• *Yields about $^1/_2$ cup sauce base*

To make the *tsukejiru*, in a medium pot, bring the *dashi* and *kaeshi* to a boil over moderate heat. Add the fish flakes, and immediately remove the pot from the heat. Strain the mixture through a sieve lined with a tightly woven cotton cloth. Let the sauce cool, then refrigerate it, covered, for up to three days.

• *Yields 3 cups sauce*

KOMEZU • Rice Vinegar

Iio-san, Mr. Iio, is the president and owner of a family-run company that makes *komezu*, rice vinegar. I first met him five years ago at his factory in Kyoto Prefecture, when I was researching traditionally manufactured rice vinegar. For one hundred years this family business has been brewing rice vinegar by traditional methods, using "real" ingredients—organically grown rice and spring water.

I told Mr. Iio that Japanese rice vinegar is known outside Japan as one of the weakest in flavor and the least interesting vinegars for use in cooking. He blamed the taste of modern Japanese consumers for this poor reputation. Mass demand forced the manufacturers to change from traditional richly flavored vinegar to today's bland mass-produced products.

Immediately after tasting Mr. Iio's rice vinegar, which has a sharp, robust flavor, I realized that his product did not follow this trend. With his vinegar, I could solve a problem that I had borne for many years. I had always been unhappy with the sushi rice that I prepared using mass-produced rice vinegar; the rice vinegar did not impart a rich, sharp flavor to the prepared rice. Mr Iio and I laughed together, concluding that in Japan any strong characteristic, whether of human beings or of rice vinegar, will be "hammered down" and eventually forced to disappear from conformist Japanese society.

Yet now Mr. Iio and producers like him are trying to change the image of rice vinegar by reintroducing the public to the real thing. Whether this effort will succeed in today's changing Japanese society remains to be seen.

At Mr. Iio's factory, *komezu* production takes place in two totally separate processes, many kilometers apart. One factory produces alcohol from rice, while the other one converts the alcohol into vinegar. This physical separation is absolutely necessary, because both processes involve biological transformations. If the yeast and bacteria contaminated each other's domain, disaster would result.

The process of producing alcohol to make rice vinegar is very similar to that of making *sake*, rice wine, except that the rice used in vinegar production contains more protein than the rice used in making *sake*. The rice is also less thoroughly hulled for vinegar production than it would be for *sake* production. Therefore, brewed alcohol that is going to be converted to vinegar contains a large amount of amino acids, which determine the flavor and nutrients of the rice vinegar.

At the alcohol-producing factory, partially hulled and soaked rice is first steamed in a large pressure cooker for an hour. A portion of this steamed rice is inoculated with *koji* mold (*Aspergillus oryzae*), then left for three full days to become *koji* rice. When I visited the factory, the rice had just been steamed. It was a very chilly morning in February, and skin-tearing cold gusts were blowing in through the open factory door from the nearby Japan Sea. The elderly employees, who wore thin short-sleeved shirts, were shoveling the steaming rice out of the large rice cooker into a wooden bin. For a minute or so the steam made the interior of the factory invisible. Then the cold, blowing air quickly subdued the steam. The workers deftly sprinkled and tossed the rice with green *koji* powder, whose color reminded me of the mold found in blue cheese. They moved the inoculated rice to a temperature-controlled room, where the *koji* mold would multiply for three days. The cultured rice, or *koji* rice, would then be mixed with spring water, more steamed rice, and yeast. This mixture would be transferred to a large fermentation tank, where more steamed rice, *koji* rice, and spring water would be added.

The brew produced during vinegar making is not called *sake* but *sumoto moromi*, "a *sake* base for vinegar." *Sumoto moromi* has a very rough, complex flavor with strong characteristics never found in ordinary rice wine.

During our cross-town journey from the alcohol-producing factory to the second facility, where the *sumoto moromi* is converted to rice vinegar, Mr. Iio told me an interesting story. His family has been producing rice vinegar, and in the process *sumoto moromi*, for more than one hundred years. But only two years previously, the local government complained for the first time that the factory was producing rice wine without a license. Of course, such a license would require a fee. At this writing, the case is still under consideration. What an absurd way the government is handling this matter!

At the second factory, *sumoto moromi* and spring water are combined in large tanks. Each tank is heated, and then a small portion of an active acetic-acid-forming bacterial culture, *sakusankin*, is added. The liquid is left in the tank for three to four months. During this time, a white bacterial film grows, eventually covering the entire surface of the liquid in the tank. The bacteria convert alcohol into vinegar, filling every corner of the factory with a strong, sharp, tart smell. The finished vinegar is then transferred to a concrete vat in a second room. Here the vinegar matures for four months longer. By this traditional method, the production of rice vinegar takes nine to twelve months.

In addition to rice vinegar from hulled rice, Mr. Iio's factory produces vinegar from unpolished, brown rice. This vinegar, called *genmaizu*, has an even more robust flavor, a darker, golden brown color, and more nutrients than vinegar produced from white rice.

Mr. Iio's rice vinegars are exceptional. Rice vinegar produced in larger, more modern factories lacks complex flavors. This is frequently because the *sumoto moromi* is made from inferior ingredients, such as rice powder (a by-product of the rice-hulling process in *sake* manufacturing), other starches, or sugarcane. The production process is also automated and shortened to about two months.

Komezu has numerous merits other than providing tart flavor to prepared dishes. The various amino acids and organic acids present in rice vinegar help to improve the diner's appetite and promote good digestion. Because of its strong acidity, rice vinegar, whose pH (measure of acidity) is 2.8 to 3.1, slows the multiplication of harmful food-borne bacteria. This is why sushi rice, which is often left at room temperature even during warm weather, keeps several days without spoilage. Medical researchers have also proved that rice vinegar has an ability to improve the ratio of "good" cholesterol, HDL, to "bad" cholesterol, LDL, in people who routinely consume the vinegar. And if you want to prevent a hangover from drinking *sake*, take Mr. Iio's advice: Before the banquet, drink a small cup of diluted rice vinegar (one part vinegar to five or six parts water).

Here are some useful tips to remember about using rice vinegar in the kitchen:

- Adding a little rice vinegar to grated daikon slows the destruction of vitamin C.
- Soaking *gobo* (burdock) and lotus root in water with a little rice vinegar added prevents the vegetables from discoloring.
- Green vegetables should not be simmered in a liquid with rice vinegar, because the acid will alter the green pigment, chlorophyl, and discolor the vegetables. But rice vinegar brings out the pigment anthocyanin. This is why sweet pickled, sliced ginger, *shoga amazuzuke* or *gari*, which is served with sushi and sashimi dishes, has a pleasant pink color.

Because the main constituent of rice vinegar, acetic acid, dissolves calcium, deep-fried whole small fish that are marinated in rice-vinegar sauce, and whole small fish cooked in broth and rice vinegar, are wonderful sources of digestible calcium.

SOURCES: *Komezu* from large-scale manufacturers is sold in Japanese and Asian food stores and large supermarkets. Health- and natural-food stores carry better-quality *komezu* and also *genmaizu*, brown rice vinegar.

WHAT TO LOOK FOR: *Komezu* is sold in glass bottles. Good *komezu* has a rich golden color. *Genmaizu* has a darker color than regular rice vinegar. For Japanese preparations, it is best to avoid rice vinegar made in other Asian countries, where different materials and manufacturing processes produce vinegar that is different in taste and color.

Some stores carry prepared rice-vinegar products, especially *sushizu* (sushi vinegar). *Sushizu* is a mixture of rice vinegar, sugar, and salt. You may prefer to make your own, since bottled *sushizu* may contain too much sugar or salt or other chemical ingredients. At some Japanese food stores you may also find ponzu and *tosazu*, two other rice-vinegar products, recipes for which follow.

STORAGE: Unopened, *komezu* keeps about a year and half after the date of manufacture. To enjoy the best flavor, store an opened bottle in the refrigerator or another cool, dark place, and use up the vinegar within a month or so.

BASIC RECIPES

KOMEZU-BASED DRESSINGS

Amazu, Kimizu, Nihaizu, Ponzu, Sanbaizu, Tosazu

Amazu (Sweet Rice Vinegar Dressing)

Amazu is a sweet vinegar dressing. It is good for pickling vegetables such as daikon, carrot, lotus root, turnip, Chinese cabbage, and cucumber.

> *5 tablespoons* komezu *(rice vinegar)*
> *2 tablespoons sugar*
> *1 teaspoon salt*

In a small saucepan, combine all the ingredients, and bring them to a boil over medium heat. Turn off the heat, let the mixture cool. Store it in a covered container in the refrigerator for up to a week.

- *Yield $^1/_3$ cup dressing*

Kimizu (Egg-Vinegar Sauce)

Kimizu is a glossy golden yellow sauce made from egg yolk, rice vinegar, salt, and sugar. The refined flavor of this sauce compliments delicate foods such as shellfish, white fish, and chicken.

> *3 egg yolks*
> *$^1/_3$ teaspoon salt*
> *2 tablespoons sugar*
> *3 tablespoons* komezu *(rice vinegar)*

Have at hand a bowl of cold water and ice cubes. Bring a medium pot of water to a simmer.

Put the egg yolks into a mortar or a bowl, and purée the yolks with a *surikogi* (pestle) or beat them with a whisk. Beat in the salt and sugar, then the *komezu*.

Transfer the egg mixture to a medium bowl that will fit into the pot of simmering water, and float the bowl on the hot water. Cook the egg mixture in the bowl over low heat, stirring with a wooden spoon all the time, until the mixture thickens. Do not allow the egg to coagulate.

When the sauce has thickened, transfer the bowl to the ice water. Stir until the sauce is cool.

- *Yields about $^1/_3$ cup sauce*

Nihaizu (Rice Vinegar and Soy Sauce Dressing)

Nihaizu is a combination of *komezu* and *shoyu* (soy sauce). No sugar is added to this dressing, which is used for tossing with raw or cooked fish, shellfish (oysters or crabmeat), and vegetables. *Nihaizu* is also good sprinkled over grilled fish or meat.

> $^1/_4$ *cup* komezu *(rice vinegar)*
> *2 tablespoons* shoyu *(soy sauce)*

In a small saucepan, combine both ingredients, and bring to a boil over medium heat. Turn off the heat, and let the mixture cool. Store the dressing in the refrigerator for up to a week.

- *Yields $^1/_2$ cup dressing*

Ponzu (Rice Vinegar and *Yuzu* Dressing)

Ponzu is made with the juice of a kind of citron, *yuzu*. This fruit has its own unique, refreshing citrus aroma and flavor that might best be described as a mixture of lemon, lime, and grapefruit. When *yuzu* is unavailable, it may be best to replace it in this recipe with additional good-quality *komezu*.

Ponzu makes a delicious dressing or sauce for grilled, pan-fried, or deep-fried fish, meat, or vegetables.

> *3 tablespoons* komezu *(rice vinegar)*
> *2$^1/_2$ tablespoons* mirin *(sweet cooking wine)*
> *2 tablespoons* yuzu *citron juice*
> *5 tablespoons* shoyu *(soy sauce)*
> *6 tablespoons* dashi *(fish stock)*

In a small saucepan, combine all the ingredients, and bring them to a boil over medium heat. Turn off the heat, and let the mixture cool. Store it in the refrigerator in a covered container for up to a week.

- *Yields $^1/_2$ cup dressing*

Sanbaizu (Sweet Rice Vinegar and Soy Sauce Dressing)

Sanbaizu is a slightly sweetened version of *nihaizu*. It is used for tossing with raw or cooked fish, shellfish, and vegetables. Because *sanbaizu* contains sugar, it is best for foods that lack any natural sweetness or are high in acidity. *Sanbaizu* also makes a perfect oil-free salad dressing.

> $^1/_2$ *cup* komezu *(rice vinegar)*
> 2 *tablespoons* mirin *(sweet cooking wine)*
> $^1/_2$ *teaspoon* shoyu *(soy sauce)*
> $^1/_2$ *teaspoon salt*
> 2 *tablespoons sugar*

In a small saucepan combine all the ingredients, and bring them to a boil over medium heat. Turn off the heat, and let the mixture cool. Store it in a covered container in the refrigerator for up to a week.

- *Yields $^3/_4$ cup dressing*

Tosazu (Bonito-Flavored Rice Vinegar Dressing)

Tosazu is a rice vinegar dressing with bonito flakes added for a robust flavor. This dressing is used to coat seasonal fresh fish, shellfish, sea vegetables, and fresh or cooked vegetables.

> $2^1/_2$ *tablespoons* komezu *(rice vinegar)*
> 1 *tablespoon sugar*
> $^1/_4$ *cup* shoyu *(soy sauce)*
> $^1/_2$ *cup* katsuobushi *(bonito flakes)*

In a small saucepan, combine all the ingredients, and bring them almost to a boil over medium heat. Turn off the heat, and let the mixture stand for 1 minute. Then strain the liquid through a colander lined with a tightly woven cotton cloth, and discard the bonito flakes. Let the dressing cool. Store it in the refrigerator in a covered container for up to a week. Heat the dressing through before using it.

- *Yields 10 tablespoons dressing*

True *mirin* is a golden yellow, sweet, rich-textured rice wine with an alcohol content of about 14 percent. It is traditionally made by mixing *koji*-cultured rice, glutinous rice, and distilled alcohol. This sweet rice wine was once drunk as an alcoholic beverage.

To discover more about authentic *mirin* I visited a family-owned company that has been manufacturing it for over a century. The Sumiya Bunjiro Shoten factory is situated in a small country town near Mikawa Bay in Aichi Prefecture, a 30-minute express train ride from Nagoya. Mr. Sumiya, the president of the company, told me the history of *mirin*.

Sweet rice wine was first produced very early in Japan's history, using glutinous rice and ordinary rice wine, or *sake*. By the fifteenth century the technology for distilling alcohol had reached Japan, and production of *shochu*, a distilled clear alcohol, began. This distilled alcohol soon replaced *sake* in sweet rice wine production, because with *shochu* the end product was much sweeter and more richly flavored. This was the beginning of modern *mirin* production. Because sugar was still scarce and expensive in Japan, *mirin* soon began to be used as a sweetener in cooking.

Mr. Sumiya asked me whether I drink *toso* at the new year. *Toso* is a sweet drink made by infusing several kinds of Chinese medicinal herbs in *mirin*. For centuries *toso* has been customarily drunk at new year's celebrations as part of a prayer for perfect health. I was ashamed to tell Mr. Sumiya that my family has been preparing *toso* with *sake*, regular rice wine, since it is difficult to find good, drinkable *mirin.* With a big sigh, he lamented that real *mirin* almost disappeared from the market around the time of World War II, and was replaced by synthetically mass-processed, inexpensive *mirin*, which can be used only in cooking.

Today the word *mirin* generally refers to this synthetic product, not to traditional sweet rice wine. The synthetic type has poor flavor, a low alcohol content, and a chemical taste, which make it unpalatable to drink as an alcoholic beverage.

Why has synthetic *mirin* replaced the authentic version? During and for some years after the war, Japan had a severe shortage of rice. This forced *mirin* producers to search for substitute sources of starch. During this time the government also imposed heavy taxes on authentic *mirin*, which contained enough alcohol that it was regarded as an alcoholic beverage. By 1955, the tax on *mirin* had risen to 230 percent. Because of this, the sales of authentic *mirin* plunged, and manufacturers had no choice but to produce an inexpensive synthetic type using other materials.

These unfortunate old days are now over, Mr. Sumiya says, but most large manufacturers continue to produce the same poor-quality synthetic *mirin*. He emphasized that the time has come to return to authentic *mirin* production and let consumers know and appreciate the true flavor, texture, and cooking merits of this traditional product.

At the Sumiya Bunjiro factory, *mirin* is produced by a traditional two-step method. The first step is the production of a distilled liquor, which contains about 40 percent alcohol. The second step is allowing *koji*-cultured rice and glutinous rice to ferment in the distilled liquor for 60 to 90 days. During this period, starch converts to sugar, while the high alcohol content prevents the sugar from being converted to alcohol, so a very sweet liquid is produced. At the same time, protein in the rice breaks down into numerous kinds of amino acids. These processes together are responsible for the complex, rich, sweet flavor, thick texture, and golden yellow color of *mirin*. The matured *mirin* is then pressed to separate it from the mash, and left to mature in a large tank for another 200 days. The mash is not thrown away, but is used as a delicious pickling base for vegetables.

At the end of the factory tour, Mr. Sumiya gave me a taste of his *mirin*. It was a delicious alcoholic beverage, whose flavor reminded me of sweet sherry.

The sugar in *mirin* is composed of both glucose and maltose. This combination provides a more refined sweetness to the palate than ordinary sugar, which is a combination of fructose and glucose. The alcohol and sugars of *mirin* have an important effect on foods. I performed an experiment in which I placed one piece of meat in *mirin* and another in water. I let the meat stand overnight in the refrigerator. The next day I found that the water was cloudy with meat juices, and the meat in the water was swollen and flaccid-looking. But the *mirin* in which the other piece of meat soaked showed no significant change in its clarity, and the meat held its shape and looked firm. This demonstrates that *mirin* causes meat to retain its natural juices while flavoring it.

When *mirin* is used in cooking, it is frequently heated to cook off the alcohol before other flavoring ingredients are added. This technique is called *nikirimirin*. *Nikirimirin* improves prepared dishes by adding flavors created by the chemical reactions between the sugars and the amino acids in *mirin*.

Not only does it contribute a rich, delicious flavor to foods, but it can also give them an attractive, glossy brown appearance. One of the most popular Japanese basting sauces, *tare*, which is frequently applied during grilling or broiling, uses a large amount of *mirin*. Grilled eel basted with *tare* (*unagi no kabayaki*) and grilled chicken pieces basted with *tare* (*yakitori*) are two of the most popular *tare*-basted dishes.

When *mirin* is not available, an acceptable substitute can be made with a combination of *sake* (regular rice wine) and sugar. In place of 1 tablespoon of *mirin*, use 1 tablespoon *sake* plus 2 teaspoons sugar.

SOURCES: *Mirin* is sold at Japanese and Asian food stores and some large supermarket chains. Virtually all of the *mirin* sold at these stores is the synthetically produced type. Authentic *mirin* can be found at health- and natural-food stores.

WHAT TO LOOK FOR: Synthetic *mirin* is sold under such names as *mirin-fū chomiryo* ("a kind of *mirin*"), *aji-mirin* ("*mirin* taste"), or *hon-mirin* ("real *mirin*"). These types have a low alcohol content, less than 10 percent, compared to the 14 percent in authentic *mirin*.

STORAGE: After opening a bottle of *mirin*, whether real or synthetic, store it in a dry, cool, and dark place. Use the *mirin* within two months after opening the bottle.

BASIC RECIPE

TERIYAKI SAUCE

Teriyaki no Tare

It seems everyone who lives outside Japan today has heard the word *teriyaki*, but most people still do not know exactly what it means. In any large American supermarket, finding a bottle of something called teriyaki sauce is as easy as locating a bottle of *shoyu* (soy sauce). I've studied many labels on these teriyaki sauce bottles, and have always found inauthentic recipes. Now you can learn to make real, basic teriyaki sauce, with *mirin*, and enjoy this delicious cooking style.

Teriyaki is a name for a special grilling technique (*teri* means "glossy"; *yaki* means "grilling"). This technique requires a basting sauce, called *tare*. Continual basting with *tare* imparts a deep, rich, caramelized flavor to the grilled food, and at the same time gives it an attractive, glossy brown appearance. The original *teriyaki no tare* (teriyaki basting sauce) recipe employs only *shoyu* (soy sauce), *mirin* (sweet cooking wine), and sometimes sugar. Adding other seasonings—honey, grated ginger, grated garlic, chopped scallions, fruit juice, fresh or dried chile or *toban jiang* (chili-bean sauce)—produces any number of teriyaki sauce variations. After mastering the authentic basting sauce, create your own, so that you no longer need to buy a bottle of prepared sauce at the store.

> $^1/_2$ *cup* mirin *(sweet cooking wine)*
> $^1/_4$ *cup* sake *(rice wine)*
> $^1/_4$ *cup* shoyu *(soy sauce)*
> 2 *tablespoons sugar*

In a small saucepan, heat the *mirin* and *sake* over low to medium heat for 5 minutes. Add the *shoyu* and sugar, and stir until the sugar is dissolved. Cook the mixture over low heat for 25 minutes. Let the sauce cool, and then store it in the refrigerator for up to a week.

• *Yields about $^1/_2$ cup sauce*

QUICK PICKLED DAIKON AND CARROT

Daikon to Ninjin no Tsukemono

A small plate of *tsukemono*, pickled vegetables, is an important component of a complete informal or formal Japanese meal. Popular vegetables for pickling are daikon, carrot, cabbage, cucumber, eggplant, Chinese cabbage, mustard greens, and turnip. The flavor, texture, and color of the vegetables vary according to the type of pickling agent used—brine, *sake* lee mash, *mirin*, miso marinade, salted rice bran mash, vinegar, or mustard—and the length of pickling time. Homemade pickles made with this recipe will be less salty than commercially prepared pickles. The reduced salt may shorten the storage life of pickled vegetables, but do not worry. They disappear very quickly when I prepare them for my family. Daikon is available at large supermarkets and every Asian food market. If it is not available, use turnips with their green leaves.

KEY INGREDIENTS

78

> Top 4 inches of a daikon *(about 3 inches in diameter),*
> *quartered lengthwise*
> 1 medium carrot, *halved lengthwise*
> 1 teaspoon salt
> $^1/_4$ cup mirin *(sweet cooking wine)*
> 5 tablespoons komezu *(rice vinegar)*
> 1 tablespoon sugar

In a medium bowl, toss the vegetables with the salt. Cover the vegetables with plastic wrap, place a plate on top, and weight the plate (a suitable weight might be a 1-quart Pyrex measuring cup two-thirds full of water). Let the vegetables stand for 5 to 6 hours at room temperature.

Remove the vegetables from the bowl, and put them into a sealable plastic bag with the *mirin*, *komezu*, and sugar. Leave the vegetables in the plastic bag at room temperature for three to four hours, shaking the bag several times to distribute the pickling liquid evenly.

Refrigerate the vegetables in the plastic bag overnight or for as long as 3 days.

Cut the pickles into $\frac{1}{5}$-inch crosswise slices, and serve them drizzled with a little soy sauce, if you like.

• *Yields 4 to 6 servings*

MISO • Soybean Paste

Miso is a salty, fermented soybean paste that resembles nut butters in texture but is not oily. One of the most representative, everyday Japanese dishes, *misoshiru*, or miso soup, is made by combining this paste with *dashi*, fish stock. Many Westerners can't imagine breakfast without coffee; miso soup plays a similar role in the Japanese diet, although the actual consumption of this soup at breakfast has declined as people have come to prefer a quick Western-style meal. However, the fragrant aroma of freshly made miso soup from the kitchen at any time of day announces to diners that "the meal is ready!"

What makes miso so integral to Japanese life? The answer is its deep, rich flavor and exceptional nutritional value. The use of miso in Japanese cuisine is not limited to soup, but is very diverse. Miso is used to create delicious marinades, dressings, and sauces, and to provide a unique taste in stir-fried and simmered dishes. Recently, many creative chefs outside Japan have begun to adopt miso into their Western preparations.

Let's discover miso by examining its traditional production at a family-owned hundred-year-old factory, Yamaki Jozo, in Saitama Prefecture, 80 kilometers northwest of Tokyo. The president of Yamaki Jozo, Mr. Kitani, is known as the mentor and sponsor of organic farmers in his region. His factory makes *akamiso* (brown miso) from organically grown soybeans and grains, sea salt, and spring water.

First, rice or barley is steamed in a huge steel pressure cooker, and a fermentation starter, *koji* mold, is applied. The mixture is then left for the *koji* to multiply. Soybeans are also soaked and steamed in the pressure cooker. The grain and beans are then mashed together, and mixed with sea salt and spring water. This mixture is then left in a wooden barrel to ferment for 12 months. The fermentation, which is largely carried out by *koji* but is assisted by hundreds of kinds of bacteria living in the wooden staves of the barrel, produces peptides and amino acids, organic acids, and other nutrients. These chemicals account for the wonderful flavor and nutritional value of miso.

At the end of the manufacturing process, the paste is usually heat-treated to stop fermentation and prevent further changes in quality. But in non-heat-treated miso, or *namamiso*, the natural enzymes remain functioning, and fermentation continues during storage. Therefore, non-heat-treated miso is packed in a plastic bag with a tiny hole through which the miso can emit carbon dioxide during continuing fermentation. The best miso is alive, says Mr. Kitani of the Yamaki Jozo factory.

Miso was once made in many households in Japan. When I was a child, my mother's distant relatives living in the country still made homemade miso, and they frequently sent us a portion. I remember that it was a very salty miso. Such individual variations in flavor were a source of great pride for each home, and the expression *Temae miso desu, ga* ("I do not want to boast about my miso, but. . .") was born from this pride. This expression, a very Japanese kind of metaphoric apology, is still used as a preface when people discuss their own or a family member's success or accomplishment. "I do not want to brag about my miso," a parent might say, "but my daughter was just accepted by Harvard University."

Today, most of the miso consumed in Japan is produced in large factories by shortened methods. As people get less and less chance to savor the wonderful flavor of homemade miso, the use of the delightful expression *Temae miso desu, ga* is falling out of favor.

The different types of grains used in the production process yield three different kinds of miso. They are *komemiso* (rice miso), *mugimiso* (barley miso), and *mamemiso* (soybean miso). *Komemiso* is made of rice and soybeans, *mugimiso* of barley and soybeans, *mamemiso* nearly entirely of soybeans.

About 80 percent of the miso produced and marketed in Japan is rice miso. A recent health-food boom has encouraged the manufacturers to produce rice miso using unpolished brown rice, *genmai*. *Genmaimiso*, brown rice miso, has more flavor and nutrients than regular rice miso.

Barley miso and soybean miso are regional products. Barley miso is found mostly in the southern part of the country, including the southern part of Honshu and the Chugoku regions of the main island of Japan, and the islands of Kyushu and Shikoku.

Soybean miso is produced only in the three prefectures of Aichi, Mie, and Gifu, where tamari is also made. One of the most representative brands of *mamemiso* is Hatcho miso, from Aichi Prefecture. Unlike the other two kinds of miso, soybean miso has a strong, distinctive color, like chocolate, a bean-rich flavor, and a firm texture.

Miso can be also classified according to its color and saltiness. Salty-flavored *akamiso*, brown miso, can be made from either rice or barley. Brown miso contains about 13 percent salt by volume, or about $1/2$ teaspoon salt per tablespoon miso.

Shiromiso, white miso, has a pale yellow color, a sweet flavor, and a salt content that varies from 5 to 10 percent. The sweetest and most refined *shiromiso* is Saikyo miso, from Kyoto Prefecture. This type has a salt content of only 5 percent. Saikyo miso production differs greatly from that of salty brown miso. The former employs a larger proportion of rice, a smaller proportion of soybeans, and a weaker brine. Brown miso ferments for a year, but the production of Saikyo miso requires only a week or so.

Most white miso produced in other prefectures has a higher salt content, about 10 percent, and lacks the sweetness of Saikyo miso. In this book, I refer to Saikyo miso as "sweet white miso." If you cannot find this product, use ordinary white miso, but reduce the quantity by half and add some extra sugar or *mirin* (sweet cooking wine) to compensate for the lack of sweetness. You'll need to add $2/3$ to 1 tablespoon sugar or 2 tablespoons *mirin* to each tablespoon of the substitute miso to achieve the sweetness of Saikyo miso.

The three types of miso are used in different preparations. For marinating delicate-flavored fish and shellfish, sweet white miso is used. Because of its robust flavor, brown miso is best for marinating red meat, but the marinating period must be short, no longer than overnight, or the high salt content in the miso will remove much of the natural juice from the meat, change the texture, and harm the flavor. Brown miso and soybean miso are well suited for simmered dishes of oily fish or red meat. For better-flavored miso soups, brown miso, white miso, sweet white miso, and soybean miso are frequently mixed together, in varying proportions. Sweet white miso is favored over the other types in the Kansai region, including Kyoto, for soups, dressings, and other preparations.

Miso of every type has outstanding nutritional value. The major ingredient of miso, soybeans, is the only vegetable whose protein content is so high that it provides almost as many essential amino acids as milk. The process of fermenting soybeans to make miso breaks down soy protein into peptides and amino acids, forms that can be effectively and quickly absorbed in our bodies. Soybeans consumed along with grains, such as rice, wheat, barley, or oats, are an excellent source of protein. This may be why a frugal traditional Japanese diet—a bowl of brown rice, a bowl of miso soup, and a plate of vegetables pickled in rice-bran mash—could have provided a minimally sufficient diet for the Japanese population over the centuries. Recently chemists and medical professionals have learned more about soy protein: It improves the flexibility of blood vessels, it helps to lower blood cholesterol, and it alkalizes the blood. And chemicals produced during miso fermentation, we now know, have anticarcinogenic properties and give strength to the body's immune system. Miso is mighty!

SOURCES: *Akamiso* (brown miso), *mamemiso* (soybean miso), and *shiromiso* (white miso, either Saikyo miso or a saltier type) are sold at Japanese and Asian food stores. Some large supermarkets also carry brown miso, soybean miso, or a saltier type of white miso. Health- and natural-food stores frequently sell miso made with organic materials and by traditional production methods, in Japan or in the United States. Some of these misos are non-heat-treated. These products are displayed in the refrigerator case.

WHAT TO LOOK FOR: Miso is packed in plastic bags or plastic containers. To distinguish brown miso, white miso, and soybean miso, study the color and texture. Also check the salt content, which is usually displayed on the package label.

STORAGE: After opening a package of miso, store it in the refrigerator, covered. Brown miso keeps for three to four months after opening without significant quality changes, soybean miso for twelve months. Saikyo miso, sweet white miso, is best consumed within three weeks after the package is opened. Beyond these periods miso will not spoil, but its flavor and nutritional value will diminish greatly. Soybean miso, which contains less water becomes hard after long months of storage.

BASIC RECIPE

MISO SOUP WITH TOFU, *WAKAME* SEA VEGETABLE, AND SCALLION

Miso-shiru

Among all the world's soups, miso soup is the simplest and quickest to prepare. It is also very versatile: The ingredients can vary among seasonal garden vegetables, sea vegetables, tofu and tofu products, fish, shellfish, chicken, and pork. Depending on the ingredients and preparation techniques you choose, you can make your miso soup simple and lean or rich and smooth.

The only important point to remember in preparing miso soup is that miso requires only a very short cooking time. Overcooking miso destroys the natural fragrant flavor, and the texture of the soup becomes rough to the tongue. Cook the vegetables and other ingredients in fish stock first, then, just before serving, add the miso and stir until it dissolves.

In a Japanese family-style meal, miso soup is served in wooden bowls and consumed together with other dishes, which can include rice, a protein dish such as grilled fish, and several vegetable side dishes. But a simple miso soup goes well with any kind of dish, at any meal. You can serve miso soup in a small bowl or mug to accompany your informal Western meal.

After miso soup stands for a few minutes, the miso separates from the clear stock. This does not indicate that the soup is no longer edible. Simply stir the soup with chopsticks before taking a mouthful.

In this recipe, tofu, *wakame* sea vegetable, and scallions are combined to make one of the most popular versions of miso soup. If you like, replace part of the Saikyo miso (sweet white miso) with brown miso or soybean miso to create your own favorite flavor.

> *1 tablespoon instant-form* wakame *sea vegetable, soaked in cold water for 2 minutes, then drained*
> *2¹/₂ cups* dashi *(fish stock)*
> *3 to 4 tablespoons* Saikyo miso *(sweet white miso)*
> *7 ounces (¹/₂ block) firm or soft tofu, cut into ¹/₃-inch cubes*
> *3 tablespoons thin scallion disks, both green and white parts*

Just before serving time, bring the fish stock to a boil in a medium pot. Reduce the heat to moderate, add the miso, and stir until it dissolves. Add the tofu, and cook for 30 seconds. Add the *wakame* and scallions, and cook for 30 seconds more. Remove the pot from the heat, and serve the soup immediately.

• *Yields 3 to 4 servings*

MISO-AND-EGG SAUCE

Tama-miso

Made from egg yolk and Saikyo miso (sweet white miso), *tama-miso* is used as a topping or basting sauce for grilled foods, and a base for dressings. You will find recipes that call for *tama-miso* in Part II.

Tama-miso is prepared in a Japanese mortar, a *suribachi*, with a wooden pestle, a *surikogi*. If you do not have these utensils, use a bowl and a sturdy plastic spatula.

> *2 tablespoons* sake *(rice wine)*
> *3¹/₂ ounces (about 5 tablespoons)* Saikyo miso *(sweet white miso)*

1 tablespoon sugar

1 large egg yolk

About ¹/₈ teaspoon usukuchi shoyu *(light-colored*

soy sauce), preferably, or regular shoyu

In a small cup, mix the *sake* with 2 tablespoons water. In a *suribachi* or other mortar, grind the miso, sugar, and egg yolk to a smooth paste. Add the rice wine and water mixture little by little, grinding all the time. Season to taste with *shoyu*.

Have at hand a bowl half-filled with cold water and ice cubes. Transfer the sauce to the top of a double-boiler, and cook the sauce over simmering water, stirring constantly and thoroughly so you do not scramble the egg, until the sauce becomes thicker, about 6 to 8 minutes.

Set the bowl of sauce in the bowl of cold water and ice cubes to cool. *Tama-miso* may be stored in the refrigerator, covered, for three days. Heat the sauce through before using it.

• *Yields ²/₃ cup sauce*

SAKE • Rice Wine

Mr. Nemoto is the son of a *sake*-producing family in a small town in Ibaragi Prefecture, 100 kilometers northeast of Tokyo. His family has been running a traditional rice-wine brewery for more than three hundred years. Having finished his studies in biology at a university in Tokyo, Mr. Nemoto has returned to his hometown to take up and manage the family business. He is the sixteenth generation in his family to join the *sake*-making tradition.

Mr. Nemoto showed me around the brewery and introduced me to every one of the detailed steps of rice-wine production. It was in this factory that I for the first time tasted freshly filtered *sake*, which was neither treated by heat nor diluted with water. When people describe fine grape wine, they use the term *bouquet*. The *sake* I tasted had a wonderful, fruity bouquet, which I never expected to find in a wine made only from rice.

The rice used to make *sake* is slightly different from that which is eaten. A grain of rice for rice-wine production is slightly larger than a grain of table rice and contains a higher proportion of starch.

The first step in *sake* production is the hulling of the rice. Hulling removes the protein and oil that reside in the outer part of rice grain; they would cause off flavors in the finished *sake*. The more the rice is hulled, the better the *sake*. For example, to make ordinary-grade *sake*, 30 percent of the grain mass is removed, but for a premier grade, up to 70 percent is ground away. At the brewery of my young Japanese friend, a large rice-hulling machine runs continuously, around the clock, for several days during the chilly *sake* production season, which extends from November to April.

After rice, next in importance to *sake* production is water quality. Many Japanese *sake* breweries either have a source of natural spring water within their factory compounds or withdraw clean spring water from a nearby source. These waters are considered divine; in fact, they are called *goshinsui*, "god water." According to Mr. Nemoto, one night his ancestor who founded the family business had a very sacred dream. In his dream, a god appeared and instructed him to draw water from a nearby spring and to use it for *sake* production. The brewery still uses the same spring to this day.

The water to make good *sake* must have several important characteristics. It must be clean, with minimal bacteria; it must contain certain desirable minerals; and its iron and manganese content must be low because these minerals would hinder the fermentation process and result in poor-quality *sake*.

The traditional *sake* production process is scrupulously followed at Mr. Nemoto's brewery and at hundreds of other small breweries across Japan. Itinerant professional *sake* makers, called *toji*, travel to *sake*-producing regions during the cold months of *sake* production. *Toji* supervise almost the entire production process. First, hulled rice is rinsed, soaked in spring water, and then steamed in a large steel steamer. Part of the steamed rice is inoculated with a fermentation starter, *koji* mold (*Aspergillus oryzae*), and is then transferred to a special room, the *kojimuro*, whose temperature is maintained at 82 degrees F. Here the rice is left for the *koji* to multiply. In the *kojimuro* the starch breaks down to glucose, and the microorganisms multiply to create a snow white fuzz with a strong, sweet fragrance.

This *koji* rice is then mixed with the remaining steamed rice, spring water, and yeast to make a seed mash. During the next two weeks, lactic acids and other organic acids are produced. This creates ideal conditions for the final fermentation process.

The seed mash is mixed with additional spring water and steamed rice and left in a huge vat to ferment. During this final fermentation, carbon dioxide gas is emitted in volumes sufficient to asphyxiate any worker who mistakenly falls into the tank. Fortunately, such accidents happen only occasionally. But outside the tanks the carbon dioxide–laden vapor is not only harmless but magically fragrant.

When the process reaches the right stage, distilled alcohol is usually added to stop the fermentation and create a softer, refined taste. The added alcohol also functions as a preservative. The *sake* is then filtered and stored in a large tank. At this point, the *sake* has a pale golden color, a somewhat acidic smell, and an alcohol content of about 18 to 20 percent. When Mr. Nemoto finished my guided tour of his brewery, he offered me a glass of freshly brewed and clarified *sake*. It tasted like heaven—a very robust, but fruity and slightly *koji*-flavored *sake*.

Before bottling, the stored *sake* is filtered through active carbon again, resulting in a clear liquid, and spring water is added to reduce the alcohol content to around 15 percent. Finally, most *sake* is heat-treated to prevent microbial growth. Today advanced technology makes it possible to store and distribute freshly unpasteurized *sake*, called *namazake*, in Japan, but only during the cold *sake*-producing months. When it can be found, *namazake* is a particularly delicious treat.

Today large breweries produce *sake* by automated and shortened methods year-round. However, there are still hundreds of good, small breweries across the country. They continue to follow the traditional preparation methods and work tirelessly to improve the quality of *sake*.

Sake plays an important role in Japanese cooking. The addition of *sake* improves the flavor of many prepared dishes. It also accelerates protein coagulation during cooking. In steaming a delicate-flavored white-fleshed fish, for example, *sake* is an indispensable ingredient. Not only does it firm the flesh of the fish, but it also helps to retain the fish's delicate flavor.

As Westerners have inexpensive "cooking wine," Japanese have "cooking *sake*." This type of *sake* does not have a true, rich flavor. Its alcohol content is low, and it may contain unnecessary sugar, salt, and chemical ingredients. Therefore, you cannot expect good results when cooking with this product. Avoid it, if possible, and instead use moderately priced drinking *sake* in your cooking.

SOURCES: *Sake* is sold at stores that are licensed to sell it. Which stores are licensed varies, of course, from one government jurisdiction to another. Most Japanese and Asian food stores carry *sake*. Liquor and wine stores are expanding their *sake* selections. In some states, supermarkets sell *sake* along with other wines.

WHAT TO LOOK FOR: Unfortunately, outside Japan the *sake* selection is still very limited. This is changing, however, since some large Japanese breweries have begun producing reasonably good *sake* in the United States. If you find a store that carries several kinds of *sake*, look at the label to identify the type and grade.

Sake is classified into two major types, according to the production process employed. One type, *jozo-shu*, has added alcohol; pure rice *sake*, or *junmaishu*, does not.

Each type of *sake* is made in different grades, from ordinary to superior (*ginjoshu*) and premier (*dai-ginjoshu*). They differ in the materials used, the amount of labor required, and how much of the production process is traditional. The grade usually appears on the bottle label, written in Japanese characters if not in letters. If you wish to select the best *sake* for your table and kitchen, it is worth the effort to become familiar with these designations.

Jozo-shu, alcohol-added *sake*, comes in these grades:

1. *Futsu-shu,* ordinary table *sake*, is the most widely consumed grade. The bottle may be labeled either *futsu-shu* or simply *seishu*. *Seishu*, "pure *sake*," is a generic term for all kinds of *sake*. *Futsu-shu* has no distinguishing characteristics. It is made of ordinary grades of rice, *koji*, spring water, and distilled alcohol. The added alcohol may be made from rice, sugarcane, potato, barley, or another grain. The amount of alcohol added is more than twice the volume of that which is actually produced during the *sake* fermentation process. This *sake* is best consumed warm, at about 105 to 125 degrees F. It is also perfect for use in cooking.

2. *Honjozo-shu* is a higher grade of *jozo-shu*, alcohol-added *sake*. It is made with a better grade of rice, *koji*, spring water, and distilled alcohol. A higher proportion of the alcohol is produced during *sake* fermentation; only about one-quarter of the total alcohol is added. The quality of *honjozo-shu* can vary depending on the source and the quality of the added alcohol.

Honjozo-shu has a lighter, milder, rounder flavor than *futsu-shu*. This grade is suitable for consuming either warmed or cooled.

3. *Honjozo-ginjoshu*, superior grade, and *honjozo-dai-ginjoshu*, premier grade, are the highest grades of alcohol-added *sake*. The rice used to produce these grades is of the highest quality. Also, more care is taken throughout the production process. For example, 50 and 70 percent of its volume is ground away, respectively, and it ferments for a little longer and at a lower temperature than it does for lower grades of *sake*. This process produces a very refined, delicate, distinctive and slightly fruity beverage.

Honjozo-ginjoshu and *honjozo-dai-ginjoshu* are best consumed cooled, to avoid cooking away their delicate fragrance.

Junmai-shu comes in these grades:

1. Ordinary *junmai-shu* is made with a grade of rice similar to that used in *honjozo-shu* production, *koji*, and spring water. The flavor of *junmai-shu* is strong, rougher, and richer than that of *jozu-shu* because there is no added alcohol to soften the flavor. *Junmai-shu* once almost disappeared from Japan, since during and after World War II rice was in short supply. Now, with the growing popularity of stronger, richer *sake*, many smaller breweries like Nemoto Shuzo have begun to produce traditional *junmai-shu*.

Junmai-shu is best consumed cooled, like a white wine.

2. *Junmai-ginjoshu*, superior grade, and *junmai-daiginjoshu*, premier grade, are the highest grades of *junmai-shu*, pure rice *sake*. Just as for the highest grades of alcohol-added *sake*, the rice used to produce these grades of *sake* is of the highest quality. More care is

taken throughout the production process: 50 to 70 percent of the rice is ground away, respectively, and it ferments for a little longer and at a lower temperature than it does for other types of *sake*.

Junmai-ginjoshu, and *junmai-daiginjoshu* are best consumed chilled.

Consider also whether you'd prefer dry or sweet *sake*. Whether *sake* is dry or sweet depends on several variables in the manufacturing process. Stopping fermentation at an earlier stage makes *sake* taste sweeter, because some of the glucose is left unconverted to alcohol. Also, *sake* tastes drier when its acidity is higher. Some *sake* producers indicate acidity on the bottle label. Look for this information.

STORAGE: Unlike vintage wine, *sake* is seldom stored for a long period of time before drinking. *Namazake* (unpasteurized *sake*) does not travel well, requires refrigeration at all times, and should be consumed very soon after it is produced. *Ginjoshu*, superior grade, and *dai-ginjoshu*, premier grade, should be kept in a cool, dark, and dry place or in the refrigerator to prevent a decline in quality. Once opened they should be consumed as soon as possible. They will not become undrinkable for some time, but oxidation diminishes their flavor and quality.

BASIC RECIPE

HOW TO WARM *SAKE*

Okan

Sake may be served warmed or chilled. During the heat of summer, *sake* is most pleasant chilled. In any season, the refined, delicate flavor and bouquet of some of the premier class might be best enjoyed when the *sake* is chilled. *Namazake*, unpasteurized *sake*, is always consumed chilled. For best flavor, remove the bottle from the refrigerator 10 to 20 minutes before drinking. With these exceptions, though, *sake* is well suited to be warmed before serving. When it is warmed, it tastes sweeter.

Since days of old, *sake* has been traditionally consumed warm. This tradition is closely related to other features of Japanese culture. Warming and serving *sake* have always been a woman's job, while the men have had the pleasure of enjoying the warm drink. When I was young and we had male guests, my mother would spend the entire meal busily going back and forth between the kitchen and the dining room to warm *sake*. This custom continues to this day, for the concept of sexual equality in *sake* consumption has not yet come to Japan. I recommend that the person who does the warming receive an equal share of this delicious drink.

To warm *sake*, put it into a *tokkuri*, a small, uncapped ceramic bottle, or into a heat-resistant glass bottle that holds about one cup. Hold the bottle in a pot of simmering water, keeping its base from touching the bottom of the pot, and warm the *sake* to between 105 and 120 degrees F. This temperature is called *hitohada*, or "warm skin." To check the temperature of warmed *sake* without pouring it into a cup, lift the bottle from the simmering water, wait a few seconds, and then place your fingertips on the bottom of the bottle. When the bottle feels warm, the *sake* is ready. Although some people prefer their *sake* hot, or *atsukan*, overheated *sake* loses its fragrance and flavor and develops an unpleasant aroma.

Serve warmed *sake* in *ochoko*, a small cup made for the purpose.

SHOYU • Soy Sauce

One of the most important seasonings in Asian kitchens, soy sauce can be spotted in most Western home kitchens today as well. The Japanese especially treasure their soy sauce, or *shoyu*. Because of differences in proportions of ingredients and production processes, Japanese soy sauce tastes, smells, and feels (in the diner's mouth) different from its counterparts elsewhere in Asia. Comments like the following are often made by Japanese people, regardless of age, sex, or occupation, upon returning from an overseas trip: "After eating meal after meal cooked with butter and oil, and flavored with salt and other Western condiments, what I missed the most was the flavor and aroma of *shoyu*." Today, while the Japanese are eager to adopt new Western-style dishes into our diet, we also create many "Japanized" dishes, in which *shoyu* is a major flavor ingredient. Consider, for example, teriyaki chicken pizza. In this dish you will find grilled cubed chicken flavored with *shoyu* sprinkled over pizza crust along with the usual tomato sauce and melted cheese.

According to connoisseurs, the *shoyu* bouquet has more than two hundred constituents, which result from the lengthy, complex fermentation process. For the sauce to acquire this complexity takes 12 to 24 months by traditional production methods. The basic ingredients used are soybeans, wheat, spring water, *koji*, and sea salt. The wheat is first roasted and cracked. The soybeans are soaked in water and steamed. Both are then mixed together, and the whole is inoculated with *koji* mold, a fermentation starter. Over the next 40 hours, the *koji* multiply in the mixture. The sweet-smelling brew is then combined with salted spring water and left to ferment in a wooden barrel for up to one year. While the high salt content prevents unwanted bacteria from growing in the barrel, proteins are broken down into amino acids, and starch into sugars, alcohol, and organic acids. These give *shoyu* its rich flavor and hundreds of aromatic compounds. Fermentation also increases the nutritional benefits of *shoyu*. The bacteria synthesize enzymes and vitamins, including vitamin B_{12}, and create a more usable amino-acid balance.

After fermentation and aging, the mixture is pressed to separate the liquid, *shoyu*, from the mash. The *shoyu* is filtered and then heat-treated, to stop fermentation, sterilize the *shoyu*, and add an extra flavor component—a sort of caramelized flavor. Today advanced refrigeration and transportation technologies in Japan allow the producers to distribute non-heat-treated *shoyu*, called *kijoyu* or *namashoyu*, which is still biologically active. Unpasteurized *shoyu* has a distinctive robust, natural flavor that some people prefer.

Much of the *shoyu* made by large manufacturers is produced in a shortened, more automated way. Fermentation is done in temperature-controlled tanks, so production time can be reduced to only four to five months. This results in *shoyu* with less flavor than traditionally made soy sauce.

A Japanese kitchen uses three types of *shoyu*, which differ in color, flavor, and degree of saltiness. The most widely available, both in Japan and overseas, is **koikuchi shoyu**. This type is also called simply *shoyu*, the name I use in this book. *Koikuchi shoyu* has a dark brown color, rich flavor, and complex aroma. The salt content of *koikuchi shoyu* is 17 to 18 percent; that is, 1 tablespoon contains over $1/2$ teaspoon salt. *Koikuchi shoyu* is used with all types of ingredients—poultry, meat, fish, and vegetables—and in all types of preparations—sauces, soups, and braised and stir-fried dishes. *Koikuchi shoyu* gives foods a dark brown color and rich flavor.

The second type of Japanese soy sauce is **usukuchi shoyu**, "light-colored soy sauce." To produce light-colored *shoyu*, the wheat is more lightly roasted, and more salt is added to slow the fermentation. A small amount of *mirin*, sweet rice wine, may also be added. The resulting *shoyu* is lighter in color, less strongly flavored, and slightly higher in salt content than regular *shoyu*, about 19 percent. Because of these characteristics, *usukuchi shoyu* is used in recipes where a refined color and weak flavor are required.

The third kind of soy sauce, **tamari**, is traditionally produced in only three Japanese prefectures, Aichi, Gifu, and Mie. Tamari is made nearly entirely from soybeans, and only a very small amount of water is added to the fermenting mixture. After about 20 months of fermentation, tamari is thicker than the other types, dark brown in color, rich in bean flavor, and about as salty as regular *shoyu*. Unlike the two other types of *shoyu*, tamari is preferred as a condiment or flavor enhancer rather than as a basic cooking ingredient. Tamari may also be added to dishes at the end of the cooking process.

The key point to keep in mind when cooking with *shoyu* is that it should generally be cooked for only a short time. Brief cooking preserves its natural fragrance, flavor, and color. Because of its high salt content, *shoyu* should be added to a simmered dish toward the end of cooking, to prevent the foods from losing too much of their juices. In stir-frying, *shoyu* is also added at the end of cooking, by running it over the heated inside wall of the wok or skillet. This quick burning adds a nice caramelized flavor to the dish.

Shoyu is a wonderful pickling and marinade ingredient. It has a high salt content, mild acidity (its pH is about 4.8), and a low alcohol content. All of these characteristics make it useful in food preservation.

SOURCES: Regular soy sauce—*koikuchi shoyu*, or simply *shoyu*—and tamari are easily found in large supermarkets as well as at Japanese and Asian food stores. Health- and natural-food stores carry *shoyu* made from organically grown rice and soybeans and produced by traditional processes. *Usukuchi shoyu*, light-colored soy sauce, can be found only at Japanese food stores. But please note that it is almost always interchangeable with *koikuchi shoyu*, although dishes made with *koikuchi shoyu* will have a stronger color and more *shoyu* flavor.

WHAT TO LOOK FOR: *Shoyu* is sold in glass or plastic bottles. A glass bottle is better, because it transmits less oxygen and thus slows oxidation.

I do not recommend buying reduced-salt *shoyu*, which is often labeled *gen'en shoyu* or "lite" soy sauce, unless you are on a strict salt-reduced diet. Low-salt *shoyu* usually has preservatives and other additives to take the place of the salt.

Good *shoyu* may be made in the United States or Japan. But avoid soy sauce made in China, which has a different flavor and texture. Check the label to ascertain the ingredients and place of manufacture.

STORAGE: Unopened, *shoyu* keeps for about one and a half years. Opened bottles should be kept covered in a cool, dry, dark place or in the refrigerator. As time goes by, oxidation darkens *shoyu* and diminishes its flavor and nutritional value. So it is best to purchase small bottles and use them up within a month or two after opening.

SOY SAUCE–MUSTARD DRESSING

Karashi-joyu

This traditional oil-free dressing is a mixture of *shoyu* (soy sauce), *dashi* (fish stock), salt, *mirin* (sweet cooking wine), and *nerigarashi* (mustard paste). Japanese mustard has a pleasant bitter-spicy flavor. *Karashi-joyu* goes well with briefly boiled vegetables, such as spinach, watercress, mustard leaf, cabbage, broccoli, asparagus, and bean sprouts.

> $1^{1}/_{2}$ *teaspoons* usukuchi shoyu *(light-colored soy sauce)*
> or regular shoyu *(soy sauce)*
> 1 *tablespoon* mirin *(sweet cooking wine)*
> $^{1}/_{2}$ *cup* dashi *(fish stock)*
> $^{1}/_{4}$ *teaspoon salt*
> 1 *teaspoon hot mustard paste (see page 55)*

In a medium bowl, combine all the ingredients except the mustard paste. Add the mustard paste little by little, stirring. Taste the dressing when you've added half the mustard paste, and either stop or continue adding it, to suit your taste. Toss the dressing with about 9 ounces briefly boiled and cooled vegetables, and serve.

• *Yields* $^{1}/_{2}$ *cup dressing*

SOY SAUCE DRESSING

Shoyu Doressingu

Since the day I first began teaching Japanese cooking classes in Tokyo, nine out of ten students have asked me how to make "that delicious *shoyu* dressing" they had at some restaurant or other. I instantly know what they are describing. This soy sauce dressing, characterized by the pleasant, nutty flavor of sesame oil and often served with raw vegetables, is quite a new addition to the Japanese repertoire. In fact, the entire concept of a raw-vegetable salad with dressing is a very recent import from the West. Because the dressing is new, there is no set recipe; proportions vary from one restaurant to another, and one home to another. But the ingredients generally include *shoyu*; sesame oil; vegetable oil; *komezu* (rice vinegar); grated vegetables such as onion and carrot; and sugar, sesame seeds, or both.

Here is my recipe for *shoyu* dressing. Try it when you want a change from "French" or "Italian"—the same vegetables will taste different. If you love spice, sprinkle a little *shichimi togarashi*, seven-spice powder, into the finished dressing.

1 teaspoon smooth French mustard
1 small garlic clove, halved
$^1/_4$ cup komezu (rice vinegar)
2 tablespoons finely grated carrot
$1^1/_2$ teaspoons finely grated onion
$^1/_4$ to 1 teaspoon ginger juice (see page 58), to taste
$1^1/_2$ teaspoons shoyu (soy sauce)
$^1/_2$ teaspoon salt
1 teaspoon tamari
1 tablespoon sugar
$1^1/_2$ teaspoons white sesame seeds, toasted (see page 100)
$^1/_4$ cup vegetable oil
1 teaspoon sesame oil

In a large bowl, combine all the ingredients except the sesame oil, and mix well. Refrigerate the dressing, covered, for 30 minutes.

Remove the garlic from the dressing. To serve, coat the vegetables of your choice, either raw or briefly boiled, with the sesame oil, and then toss them with a generous amount of the dressing.

• *Yields about $^3/_4$ cup dressing*

PORK CUTLET SAUCE

Tonkatsu Sôsu

A combination of *shoyu* and Western ingredients, *tonkatsu* sauce was invented at the beginning of the twentieth century along with many other fusion dishes, such as *tonkatsu* (fried pork cutlet, page 432), *korokke* (potato and beef croquette, page 455), and *ebifurai* (fried shrimp, page 388).

This thick, brown, spicy sauce is not just for pork cutlets, but is very versatile. In this cookbook the following recipes call for *tonkatsu* sauce: *kushikatsu* (pork and long onion on skewers, page 432), *chikin-katsu* (chicken cutlet, page 417), *Miso-katsu* (pork cutlet flavored with soybean miso, page 429), *korokke* (potato and beef croquette, page 455), *kakifurai* (fried oysters, page 386), *ebifurai sando* (fried shrimp with two sauces in a sandwich, page 389), *unagi baagaa* (eel burger, page 398), and *kurimu korokke* (creamy croquette, page 396). You may find other uses in your kitchen for this delightful sauce.

> $^1/_2$ *cup* Worcestershire sauce
> $^1/_4$ *cup sugar*
> $^1/_4$ *cup* shoyu *(soy sauce)*
> $^1/_4$ *cup tomato ketchup*
> 1 *tablespoon smooth French mustard*
> $^1/_4$ *teaspoon ground allspice*

In a small saucepan, combine the Worcestershire sauce, sugar, *shoyu*, and ketchup. Cook the mixture over low heat, stirring, until the volume is reduced by 20 percent.

Add the mustard and allspice, stirring. Remove the pan from the heat, and let the sauce cool to room temperature.

The sauce will keep for one week, refrigerated in a sterilized bottle with a tight-fitting lid.

• *Yields 1 cup sauce*

AZUKI • Dried Azuki Beans
DAIZU • Soybeans

Azuki (Dried Azuki Beans)

Because of their intense color, these tiny reddish-purple beans have always been treated as a festive ingredient in Japanese food preparations. In ancient times, the imperial court made *mochi*, glutinous rice cakes, with azuki beans. After small but steady sugar imports began during the Muromachi Era (1336 to 1573), azuki beans became an indispensable ingredient in the preparation of Japanese sweets.

Today, almost 90 percent of Japanese sweets contain azuki beans. Even some Western-looking buns, cakes, and pies are filled with sweetened azuki bean paste, or *anko*. With its faint chestnutlike flavor, *anko* seems to be an acquired taste for many Westerners. Perhaps its dark purple-brown color reminds people of chocolate, so the flavor seems wrong at first. But you may grow to love *anko*'s distinctive, sweet, mild flavor and appealing consistency, like marzipan but a little more moist.

If you stroll in any city or town in Japan, you will find traditional Japanese sweets stores in every shopping district, as you will find a patisserie on many street corners of France. The traditional sweets sold in Japanese stores appear different depending on the time of year. They are shaped into various flowers, fruits, birds, fish, and scenery to give a strong sense of each season. But only the forms and colors of these sweets change, not their tastes.

These sweets usually consist of two parts. Sweetened azuki beans, either whole or in paste form, are used as filling. Rice flour, wheat flour, soba (buckwheat) flour, or sweet potato purée is used to make the outer dough. Most of these traditional sweets are prepared by steaming, which cooks the dough into a soft and spongy cake or to a soft, sticky, chewy texture.

Other than for sweets, azuki beans have many uses in Japanese cooking. *Sekihan* is a rice dish in which azuki beans are cooked with polished white rice, either regular or glutinous. The azuki beans tint the cooked rice pink. Because of its festive color, *sekihan* is served at celebrations such as birthday parties and weddings. But the azuki beans do more than color the rice. Because they are rich in thiamine, protein, iron, potassium, and dietary fiber, azuki beans compensate for the lack of vitamins and minerals in the polished white rice.

When cooking azuki beans, avoid using an iron pot. The pigment in the beans, anthocyanin, becomes dark brown when it contacts iron. During cooking, scoop azuki beans out of their liquid several times to expose them to air. This makes the beans and their cooking liquid a striking, bright purple-red.

Daizu (Dried Soybeans)

Japanese cuisine could not survive without *daizu*, soybeans. *Daizu* are used in producing many basic Japanese foods, such as *shoyu* (soy sauce), miso, tofu, tofu products, *natto* (fermented soybeans), roasted soybean flour, and vegetable oil.

Soybeans are very important in Japanese culture. On February 3 or 4 each year is a festival called Setsubun, which literally means "to divide the seasons." This is the day to welcome spring, or the new year, according to the old lunar calendar. On the eve of Setsubun, dry-toasted soybeans are thrown into every room and corner of Japanese houses to drive away devils and welcome good fortune and health into the home for the new year. People, young and old, shout loudly and joyfully while throwing *daizu*, *"Fuku wa uchi, oni wa soto"* ("Devils out, good fortune in!"). After the bean throwing, each person eats one roasted *daizu* for each year he or she has lived. Eating dry, tough, rough soybeans is not pleasant, but it is said to bring health and longevity.

Although today most of the soybeans consumed in Japan are imported from the United States, Canada, or China, several varieties are still cultivated in Japan. Soybeans come in five colors—yellow, green, black, red, and brown. The yellow variety is the most common; it is used in the production of miso, *shoyu* (soy sauce), tofu, and *natto* (fermented soybeans). Black, red, and brown soybeans are used in cooking. The green variety, when toasted and ground into flour (*kinako*), is mixed with sugar and used to coat moist or sticky Japanese sweets. During the summertime, fresh green soybeans, called *edamame*, are eaten fresh (see page 34).

S O U R C E S : Dried azuki beans and *daizu*, soybeans, are sold at Japanese food stores, Asian food stores, and health- and natural-food stores.

W H A T   T O   L O O K   F O R : Dried azuki beans and soybeans are packed in clear plastic bags. Choose beans that are glossy, plump, and uniform in size and color. Discard any that float on the surface of the water when you soak them.

S T O R A G E : Keep the beans in a dry, cool, and dark place. Dried beans keep for up to a year, but for the best flavor you should use them as soon as possible.

BASIC RECIPE

FESTIVE PINK AZUKI RICE

Sekihan

Unlike other dried beans, azuki do not require presoaking. The older the beans are, though, the longer they will take to cook.

Azuki rice is served garnished with *gomashio*, a combination of toasted black sesame seeds and a little salt, for additional color, flavor, and nutrients. Black sesame seeds are available at Japanese and Chinese food stores, but if you can't find them you can substitute white sesame seeds.

> *³/₄ cup azuki beans*
> *3³/₄ cups (5 rice-cooker cups) white short-grain Japanese or*
> *medium-grain California rice*
> *1¹/₃ teaspoons salt*
> *3 tablespoons black sesame seeds, toasted (see page 100)*

Rinse the rice as described on page 152. Cover it with fresh cold water, and soak it for one hour.

In a small saucepan, bring the azuki beans and 4 cups water to a boil. Discard the water, reserving the beans, and add 4 cups fresh water. Bring the mixture to a boil. Reduce the heat to medium to low, and cook the beans, uncovered, for 15 minutes. During the cooking, scoop up the cooking liquid several times to expose the beans to air. This helps to intensify their purple color.

Drain the beans, reserving the cooking liquid, and return the beans to the saucepan. Add 4 cups fresh water to the saucepan, and cook the beans until they are tender, about 50 to 60 minutes.

Drain the beans, discarding the cooking liquid. Drain the rice and put it into a rice cooker or heavy-bottomed pot, put the drained rice. Measure the reserved bean liquid, and add water to make 4$^1/_2$ cups (6 rice-cooker cups). Add the measured liquid, the cooked azuki beans, and 1 teaspoon salt to the rice cooker or pot. Cook the rice; if you're using the stove top, follow the method on page 151.

In a small cup, combine the black sesame seeds and the remaining $^1/_3$ teaspoon salt.

Let the cooked rice stand, covered, for 10 minutes. Then toss the rice thoroughly with the beans. Serve the rice, garnished with the mixture of black sesame seeds and salt, in small bowls.

- *Yields 8 servings as a side dish*

BASIC RECIPE

SOYBEAN LOVER'S SOYBEAN RICE

Daizu Gohan

After the jolly Setsubun bean-throwing and bean-eating ritual, I always end up with a plastic bag of leftover tough, dry-roasted *daizu*, soybeans. A friend suggested that I cook them with rice. The result was a delicious success. I now buy soybeans without waiting for Setsubun, toast them in a skillet, and prepare this dish.

> $^1/_4$ *cup dried soybeans*
> 1$^1/_2$ *cups (2 rice-cooker cups) short- or*
> *medium-grain brown rice*
> 2 *tablespoons* sake *(rice wine)*
> 1$^1/_2$ *teaspoons* mirin *(sweet cooking wine)*
> 1$^1/_2$ *tablespoons* usukuchi shoyu *(light-colored soy sauce)*
> 1 *tablespoon minced* shiso *leaves, preferably, or parsley*

Put the soybeans into a medium bowl, and cover them with cold water. Soak them overnight.

Rinse and soak the rice as described on page 152.

Drain the soybeans, wipe them dry in a paper towel, and dry-toast them in a skillet over low heat, shaking continuously, until they turn slightly golden, 4 to 5 minutes.

In a rice cooker or heavy-bottomed pot, combine the rice, water, *sake*, *mirin*, and *shoyu*. Put the toasted soybeans on top of the rice, and cook. If you're using the stove top, follow the method on page 151.

Let the cooked rice and beans stand, covered, for 15 minutes. Add the minced shiso or parsley, and toss thoroughly.

- *Yields 4 servings as a side dish*

GOMA • Sesame Seeds
GOMA ABURA • Sesame Oil

When I first saw the tiny, humble white sesame flower, which is shaped like a small church bell, I could not believe that this ordinary-looking blossom produces such wonderful seeds, full of rich nutrients and flavor. *Goma*, sesame seeds, have been an indispensable staple in Japanese cuisine since the dawn of history. Oil from these tiny seeds was already popular in Japan by the eighth or ninth century A.D.

Goma (Sesame Seeds)

Sesame seeds are found in two colors, white and black, and both types of sesame seeds are available in several forms. White sesame seeds contain more oil than black ones and are used to produce sesame oil. Black sesame seeds have a stronger, nuttier flavor than the white variety. In Japan, sesame seeds are used unhulled or hulled. Sesame seeds are sold in several forms: untoasted, toasted, toasted and roughly ground, and toasted and ground to a smooth paste, with a little oil from the seeds floating on top. Japanese sesame paste made from white sesame seeds is similar to Middle Eastern tahini. This paste is a favorite ingredient in various Japanese dressings and sauces.

In the past, sesame paste for dressings was made by hand: Toasted sesame seeds were ground in a Japanese grinding bowl, *suribachi*, with a wooden pestle, *surikogi*, until oil was produced and the seeds became creamy in texture. Because this was quite hard work, a colloquial expression was born from the practice, *goma-suri*, or "grinding sesame seeds." This phrase indicates flattery to gain someone's favor, especially flattery of a superior, such as one's boss. The relationship between grinding sesame seeds and flattery may seem obscure, but the image of exerting great physical effort to pulverize tiny seeds does suggest, like flattery, doing too much.

The simplest way to enjoy sesame seeds, either black or white, is to toast them briefly, then grind them roughly. **To toast sesame seeds,** heat a skillet over low to medium heat. When it is hot, add the seeds and cook them, shaking the skillet occasionally, until the seeds are heated through and plump-looking, about 1 to 2 minutes. Roughly grind the seeds in a *suribachi* or smooth-walled ceramic or marble mortar, but you will have to work much harder to crush the seeds. Then sprinkle the seeds over plain cooked rice, or mix them with miso and spread the mixture over slices of hot toast. I believe that consuming a small portion of sesame seeds every day, whether with rice or with bread, contributes greatly to my health.

Goma Abura (Sesame Oil)

Introduced to Japan from China during the eighth century, sesame oil was first used in preparing Chinese-style dinners at the Imperial court. Today two types of sesame oil are available, one made from toasted seeds and the other from raw seeds. While the latter type is clear and mild-flavored, the former type, which is more widely used in Japan, has a pleasing golden brown color and a rich, nutty flavor. This is the type I am referring to when I call for sesame oil in my recipes.

The Japanese have also adopted chile-flavored sesame oil, a favorite condiment in the Chinese kitchen. Called *rayu* in Japan, chile oil is now a popular ingredient in Japanese and adapted Chinese preparations.

Although little oil is used in Japanese preparations, several popular expressions illustrate the cultural importance of edible oil in Japan:

- *Abura ga noru*, "a fish in season contains much more oil than an out-of-season fish, and therefore is tasty," describes the height of a person's private and professional status.
- *Mizu to abura no naka*, "a relationship of water and oil" describes bad relationships between two parties. Oil and water don't mix!
- *Abura o shiboru*, "squeeze the oil out of seeds," means to scold someone for poor achievement or misdemeanors, to give a "dressing down."
- *Abura o uru* literally means "to sell oil." In the past, peddlers sold cooking oil out of large buckets carried on their shoulders. With a wooden measuring cup, the peddler scooped the oil out of the bucket and poured it into a container that the customer supplied. Since the viscous oil flowed slowly and stuck to the cup, the oil peddler had a lot of time to spend gossiping with his customers. Hence, this expression means "to spend time idly."

SOURCES: Sesame seeds and sesame oil are sold at Japanese and Asian food stores, at health- and natural-food stores, and in the Asian food sections of large supermarkets. Roughly ground sesame seeds, *surigoma*, are sold at Japanese food stores. *Nerigoma*, sesame paste, can be found at Japanese food stores, Asian food stores, large supermarkets, Middle Eastern food stores, and natural-food stores.

WHAT TO LOOK FOR: For Japanese preparations, make sure the sesame seeds you buy are unhulled. Unhulled white sesame seeds are actually a buff color. At Japanese food stores, both white and black sesame seeds come untoasted (*araigoma*) and toasted (*irigoma*). Once sesame seeds are toasted their oil begins to oxidize, so it is best to purchase untoasted seeds and toast them before using them. Even already toasted seeds improve in aroma and flavor when they are retoasted in a skillet.

Sesame paste sold at Asian food stores and Middle Eastern food stores tends to be priced lower than that sold at Japanese food stores. But Chinese sesame paste is usually darker in color and rougher in texture, and it often contains unnecessary ingredients such as salt and sugar. Tahini is made from hulled sesame seeds, toasted or not. If you must substitute tahini for Japanese sesame paste, make sure the tahini is made from toasted seeds.

Health- and natural-food stores and Japanese food stores carry a product called *gomashio*. This mixture of dry-toasted black sesame seeds and sea salt is used as a condiment for plain cooked white rice. You can easily make your own *gomashio*; see below.

You can tell by the color whether sesame oil is made from raw or toasted seeds. For the recipes in this book, choose the latter. Check the date of processing, and buy the freshest oil available. By the time oil is a year old, it is partially spoiled by oxidation.

STORAGE: Refrigerate opened packages of either toasted or untoasted sesame seeds. Store opened jars of sesame paste in a dry, cool, dark place or in the refrigerator. Refrigerated sesame paste becomes very stiff, but softens after standing for a while at room temperature. After opening a jar of sesame paste, use it up within a month or so or by the date suggested on the package. Keep sesame oil in a tightly capped container in a dark, cool, and dry place.

BASIC RECIPE

BLACK SESAME SEEDS WITH SALT

Gomashio

This condiment is always served with *okowa*, steamed glutinous rice. It is also delicious with plain cooked white or brown rice.

> *3 tablespoons black sesame seeds*
> *2 teaspoons salt*

In a small skillet, toast the black sesame seeds over low heat until each seed is heated through and plump. In a *suribachi* mortar, lightly grind the sesame seeds—or, if you prefer, leave them whole. Add the salt to the sesame seeds, and let the mixture cool to room temperature. Store it in a bottle with a tight-fitting lid. It will keep one month in the refrigerator.

• *Yields 6 servings*

CLASSIC CREAMY SESAME-VINEGAR DRESSING WITH BROCCOLI

Burokkori no Gomazu-ae

This is one of the most popular salad dressings of Japan. In this recipe I use purchased sesame paste to save time and labor. However, I also include freshly toasted and ground sesame seeds to add a nuttier flavor and pleasant, coarse texture. The dressing is made in a Japanese mortar, a *suribachi*. If you don't have one, you can use a smooth-walled mortar, but it will be more work to crush the seeds.

Any kind of briefly boiled vegetables are suitable for tossing with this dressing.

> *1 tablespoon white sesame seeds, toasted*
> *(see page 100)*
> *3 tablespoons Japanese sesame paste, preferably, or tahini*
> *1½ teaspoons* shoyu *(soy sauce)*
> *1 tablespoon* mirin *(sweet cooking wine)*
> *1 tablespoon sugar*
> *1 tablespoon* komezu *(rice vinegar)*
> *Dashi (fish stock)*
> *1 small broccoli head*

In a *suribachi* mortar, preferably, or another mortar, grind the toasted sesame seeds fine. Add the sesame paste, and continue grinding until it is thoroughly mixed with the seeds. Add the *shoyu, mirin*, sugar, and *komezu* one at a time, grinding continuously. Loosen the mixture with *dashi*; the dressing should be a little looser than Middle Eastern hummus. Taste, and, if you like, add more *shoyu, mirin*, sugar, or *komezu*. If you won't be using the dressing immediately, store it for up to a day in the refrigerator, covered.

Break the broccoli heads into small flowerets. In a medium pot of boiling water, boil the broccoli with a little salt for 1 minute. Drain the broccoli, and plunge it into cold water to stop the cooking. Spin-dry the broccoli, or pat it dry in a paper towel.

Let it cool to room temperature. Immediately before serving, cover the broccoli with the sesame-vinegar dressing.

• *Yields 4 servings as a side dish*

Until I introduced this black-colored sea vegetable to Westerners in my Japanese cooking classes, I did not realize that the color of food matters in determining whether or not a food is appetizing. It is true that I lose my appetite when I see something—a sweet or a drink—that is obviously artificially colored and looks too red, yellow, pink, or blue. However, I never expected that a food that is naturally black in color could be somewhat threatening to people who are not familiar with black food. I tried to learn if there are any Western foods that are black. Yes, there are. Risotto or spaghetti with squid and squid ink is one. Aside from the squid-ink dishes, there are black olives, black caviar, black truffles, and licorice candy. If you were not raised to appreciate these ingredients, please try to conquer your bias, if you have any, and make *hijiki* sea vegetable a delicious and nutritious addition to your daily diet.

When it is fresh, *hijiki* is actually reddish brown. After harvesting, it is steamed and then dried completely, which causes it to take on an intense black color. In dried form, *hijiki* resembles Chinese black tea leaves.

Like the sea vegetables *wakame* and *kombu* (kelp), *hijiki* is rich in vegetable protein and minerals. *Hijiki* has especially high levels of calcium and iron: $3^1/_2$ ounces of *hijiki* contains 1,400 milligrams of calcium and 55 milligrams of iron. In addition, over 9 percent of dried *hijiki* is dietary fiber, which aids bowel function and helps lower blood cholesterol.

Hijiki is the basis for one of the most popular traditional home-style Japanese dishes. Called *hijiki no nitsuke*, it is made from *hijiki* and *abura-age*, fried thin tofu, simmered together. This dish frequently appears on the lunch and dinner menus at company cafeterias, as well as in lunch boxes. It is also found in the take-out section of every supermarket and department store. Today young married gentlemen lament that their beautiful wives, while eager to learn to make French or other Western dishes rich in butter and cream, do not know how to prepare this simple, traditional dish "the way Okā-san [Mother] used to make it." You will find the recipe on page 105. And the day may come when you have a chance to teach *hijiki no nitsuke* to a young Japanese friend, man or woman. If you do, I will say bravo!

Before using it in any preparations, *hijiki* must be soaked in cold water for 20 minutes. Do not soak it longer, lest the texture become unpleasantly soft and some nutrients be lost in the water. During reconstitution, the volume of the sea vegetable increases about five to six times. Reconstituted *hijiki* has a pleasant, faint fragrance of the sea, and improves in flavor and texture when it is cooked in a little oil before being used in further preparations. Avoid cooking *hijiki* so long that it becomes mushy.

SOURCES: Hijiki sea vegetable is sold at Japanese and some Asian food stores. Health- and natural-food stores also carry *hijiki*.

WHAT TO LOOK FOR: At Japanese food stores you can find two kinds of *hijiki*, *nagahijiki* and *mehijiki*. *Nagahijiki*, "long *hijiki*," comes from the stem of the plant. Each piece is longer and tougher in texture than a piece of *mehijiki*. *Mehijiki*, "bud of *hijiki*," is the leaf of the plant. It is therefore softer and, according to many people, better tasting. However, I prefer *nagahijiki*, because its texture remains pleasantly firm even after fairly long cooking. Either type should be glossy, sheer, and black.

STORAGE: Hijiki sea vegetable keeps for two years in a sealed container in a dry, cool, and dark place.

BASIC RECIPE

CLASSIC *HIJIKI* AND *ABURA-AGE* IN A SWEET *SHOYU* BROTH

Hijiki no Nitsuke

The flavor of this dish varies from home to home and from restaurant to restaurant, depending on the proportions of the ingredients. I use less sugar and less soy sauce than my mother did. I also spice up this dish by adding *shichimi togarashi*, seven-spice powder. Served with a bowl of miso soup with seasonal vegetables, and plain cooked rice or a piece of toast, *hijiki no nitsuke* makes a light, nutritious lunch.

> $^3/_4$ *ounce* ($^1/_2$ *cup*) hijiki *sea vegetable, soaked in cold*
> *water for 20 minutes*
> 2 *sheets* abura-age *(fried thin tofu)*
> 2 *tablespoons sesame oil*
> $^1/_2$ *cup* dashi *(fish stock)*
> 2 *tablespoons sugar*
> 1 *tablespoon plus 2 teaspoons* shoyu *(soy sauce)*
> 2 *tablespoons white sesame seeds, toasted*
> *(see page 100)*
> Shichimi togarashi *(seven-spice powder)*

Drain the *hijiki*, and set it aside. Rinse the *abura-age* with boiling water to remove excess oil. Drain the tofu, squeeze it to remove excess water, cut it in half lengthwise, and then cut it into thin strips crosswise.

Set a wok or a large skillet over medium heat, and heat it until it is hot but not smoking. Add the sesame oil and, when the oil is hot, add the *hijiki*. Cook, stirring, for 1 to 2 minutes.

Add the *abura-age*, and give several more stirs. Reduce the heat to low to medium, add the *dashi* and sugar, and cook, stirring, until the liquid is almost absorbed.

Add the *shoyu*, and cook, stirring, until it is absorbed, about 10 to 20 seconds. Turn off the heat, add the sesame seeds and *shichimi togarashi,* and toss thoroughly. You can serve the dish right away, but the taste will mature if you let the dish sit for an hour after preparation.

• *Yields 4 servings as a side dish*

HOSHI SHIITAKE • Dried Shiitake Mushrooms

When I was small, my mother kept several two-foot-long logs on the ground next to our bathroom. It seemed miraculous to me to see tiny mushrooms one day suddenly pop up from the bare brown wood. Later I learned how this miracle happened. The logs were moistened with water in which rice had been rinsed; several shallow cuts were made on the surface of the logs; and the cuts were inoculated with spores. The logs were then covered with straw mats and left until one of our family made an exciting discovery: Shiitake mushrooms had appeared!

Shiitake mushrooms are native to Japan. For centuries they were harvested only in the wild, from the trunks of several kinds of Japanese oak and chestnut trees. Cultivation was first attempted during the seventeenth century. Cut logs, their bark scraped and roughened to catch the naturally airborne mushroom spores, were left on the ground in dark, moist places. Today the logs may be made of molded sawdust, and they are always inoculated with spores.

Since fresh mushrooms spoil quickly, it has been the custom to dry most freshly picked shiitake mushrooms in the sun. The drying process, while removing water from the mushrooms, concentrates their flavors and nutrients. Dried, the mushrooms have a richer, sweeter flavor and more intense fragrance than they do when they are fresh. The drying process also changes the texture of the mushrooms. Fresh shiitake mushrooms are tender, break easily, and quickly soften with cooking, but the reconstituted dried mushrooms have a pleasantly firm and chewy texture even after long hours of cooking. Drying the mushrooms in the sun also increases their nutritional value, by converting one of the chemicals in the mushrooms to vitamin D. (This conversion does not occur when the mushrooms are dried by machine, unless they are left in the sun for at least two hours.)

Students frequently ask me which type of shiitake mushrooms—dried or fresh—I prefer to use in cooking. The answer is both, but each has unique characteristics.

Fresh mushrooms taste best grilled, stir-fried, simmered, and deep-fried. The cooking time for these preparations should be short; otherwise too much juice is removed from the flesh, and the mushrooms shrink and lose most of their flavor.

Reconstituted dried shiitake mushrooms can be cooked in a number of ways, including simmering, steaming, deep-frying, and stir-frying. They require soaking in cold water prior to cooking, from 15 minutes to one hour, depending on the quality and variety of shiitake.

The water in which dried shiitake mushrooms are steeped has a wonderful flavor and contains water-soluble nutrients. This liquid is often used to prepare basic stock for soups and simmered dishes.

SOURCES: Shiitake mushrooms, dried and fresh, are sold at Japanese and Asian food stores, health- and natural-food stores, and large supermarkets.

WHAT TO LOOK FOR: At Japanese food stores, you may find three different kinds of dried shiitake mushrooms:

- *Donko* shiitake mushrooms are easy to distinguish because of their thick, plump caps, patterned like a turtle shell, and thick stems. This type has the best flavor and texture of the three.
- *Koshin* shiitake mushrooms are the variety most widely available and the most frequently consumed in Japan, because of their moderate price. They have flatter, thinner caps and thinner stems than do the *donko*.
- *Koko* shiitake mushrooms are a hybrid newly developed to meet consumers' demand for a mushroom with good quality and a price between that of the *donko* and the *koshin*.

STORAGE: Dried shiitake mushrooms keep for many months if they are stored properly. After opening the bag, transfer the mushrooms to a sealable plastic bag or other airtight container, and keep them in a cool, dry, and dark place or in the refrigerator. Dried mushrooms are vulnerable to insects, and they easily get moldy when they are exposed to moisture. If they become moist, which often happens in Japan during the rainy season of June through

July, take the mushrooms out of the container or package on a sunny day and dry them in the sun for a few hours. Let the mushrooms cool to room temperature, then return them to the airtight container, and store them in the refrigerator or a cool, dry, dark place once again.

SWEET SIMMERED DRIED SHIITAKE MUSHROOMS

Hoshi Shiitake no Umani

This is the traditional way of cooking dried shiitake mushrooms. The mushrooms are cooked in their soaking liquid, seasoned with *sake*, *shoyu*, and sugar. The cooked mushrooms can be served along with other simmered vegetables, sliced and used as a noodle topping, or minced and tossed with plain cooked rice or sushi rice along with chopped shiso or parsley and freshly toasted white sesame seeds. The cooked mushrooms freeze well for later use.

6 to 7 large dried shiitake mushrooms, soaked in
cold water for 20 minutes
1 tablespoon sake
2 tablespoons sugar
1¹/₂ tablespoons usukuchi shoyu (light-colored
soy sauce) or shoyu (soy sauce)
Pinch of salt

Drain the mushrooms, preserving their soaking liquid. Cut away and discard their stems.

In a small saucepan, combine the mushroom caps and the reserved soaking liquid. Add enough additional water to barely cover the mushroom caps. Add the *sake* and bring the mixture to a boil over medium heat. Reduce the heat to low, and cook the mushrooms, covered with a drop lid (see page 26), for 10 minutes.

Add the sugar, and cook for 5 minutes.

Add the soy sauce and salt, and cook until almost all the liquid is absorbed. Let the mushrooms cool to room temperature before serving.

• *Yields 6 to 7 simmered shiitake mushrooms*

If you buy an assortment of *hosomaki,* thin-rolled sushi, from a sushi take-out shop, you are likely to get some rolls made with green cucumber strips, some with yellow pickled daikon, and others with brown, sweet simmered *kanpyo*, dried gourd.

Kanpyo is the dried form of a gourd called *fukube*. A *fukube* is round, light green in color, and an average of 12 pounds in weight. It is harvested in the glittering heat of summer, from the beginning of July through the end of August. Farmers harvest the gourds early in the morning to avoid the hottest part of the day, and carry them back to their small home processing plants. A machine peels the skin and cuts the flesh into $1^1/_2$-inch-wide strips. The strips are then dried in the sun for two days. If you travel through Tochigi Prefecture, north of Tokyo, in the summer, you will observe a sea of white gourd strips, hung on poles but seeming to swim in the air under the brilliant sun. The drying process concentrates the flesh and gives the *kanpyo* a special sweet flavor.

Before they are cooked, *kanpyo* strips are rubbed with a little salt to remove any foreign substances. They are then soaked in cold water for 15 minutes to soften. The softened gourd strips are first cooked in plain water, and then further cooked with seasonings. Cooked *kanpyo* strips have a pleasant elastic texture. Because they are long and thin, the strips are used in certain dishes as edible string, to tie other ingredients together.

SOURCES: *Kanpyo*, dried gourd, is found at Japanese food stores, and health- and natural-food stores.

WHAT TO LOOK FOR: *Kanpyo* is packed in flat plastic bags. The long creamy white strips may remind you of shoelaces or cotton ribbon. As time goes by, the color darkens, becoming brownish. This makes it easy to distinguish fresh *kanpyo* from old. However, if the strips are snow white, bleach has been used in their processing. Avoid them.

STORAGE: *Kanpyo* keeps for one to two years. Store unopened packages in a cool, dry, and dark place. After opening, refrigerate *kanpyo* in a sealed container with the desiccant that comes in the package. *Kanpyo* strips quickly absorb moisture, so watch for mold.

SWEET SIMMERED DRIED GOURD STRIPS

Kanpyo no Umani

Prepare *kanpyo* this way for your next sushi party. Roll the whole gourd strips in sushi rice, or mince them and toss them with the rice. Cooked *kanpyo* freezes well for later use.

> *1 ounce (thirty 8-inch strips)* kanpyo *(dried gourd)*
> *1 teaspoon salt*
> *2 tablespoons sugar*
> *2 tablespoons* sake *(rice wine)*
> *2 tablespoons* shoyu *(soy sauce)*

Rub the *kanpyo* with the salt. Rinse off the *kanpyo* under cold running water. In a medium bowl of cold water, soak the gourd strips until they are softened, about 15 minutes.

Drain the gourd strips, and transfer them to a medium pot. Add enough water to barely cover them, and bring the mixture to a boil over medium heat. Cook them, covered with a drop lid (see page 26), for 10 minutes.

Add the sugar and *sake*, and cook, covered, for 5 minutes.

Add the soy sauce and cook uncovered until nearly all the liquid is absorbed, turning them several times so they color evenly.

Transfer the gourd strips to a colander, and let them cool to room temperature before using them.

• *Yields 1¹/₂ cups cooked* kanpyo

KANTEN • Agar-Agar

Kanten—or agar-agar, a Malay word—is a dried form of a mass of red algae. When *kanten* is cooked with liquid and cooled, it forms a gel that is very stable at relatively high temperatures. Because of this characteristic, *kanten* has traditionally been used to prepare special dishes in Japan. Today, because it is both more stable than conventional gelatin and very healthful, agar-agar is a popular thickening and gelling agent used worldwide in many products, such as dressings, ice creams, jellies, and sweets.

Cooked with water and made into a gelatin without adding sugar, *kanten* is called *tokoroten*. *Tokoroten* was originally made from fresh algae. With its delicate, faint sea-vegetable flavor, *tokoroten* has for centuries been a favorite chilled summertime dish, served with a refreshing sauce of *shoyu* (soy sauce) and *komezu* (rice vinegar) as a side dish, or with syrup as a snack.

Kanten is said to have been invented by mistake in the middle of the seventeenth century. A powerful feudal ruler, Lord Shimazu, stayed at an inn in Kyoto during some freezing winter nights. Treating the lord with most deferential hospitality, the owner of the inn served *tokoroten* during a formal dinner. That night, the leftover *tokoroten* was thrown away in the backyard of the inn. The next morning, it was frozen solid. During the day, the sun thawed the frozen *tokoroten* and evaporated the water from it. The innkeeper later cooked this freeze-dried *tokoroten* with water, and found that not only did it still have gelling power, but it produced a gelatin that was much smoother than the original. Freeze-dried *tokoroten* became known as *kanten*, which literally means "dried in the cold air."

Today, people seeking healthier ways of eating are finding in *kanten* a substitute for animal-based gelatin. *Kanten* and conventional gelatin are interchangeable gelling agents in many preparations. But note the following differences: Like other sea vegetables, such as *wakame* and *hijiki*, *kanten* is rich in minerals, vegetable protein, and dietary fiber, and it has no calories. When it sets, *kanten* is opaque and firm, which sometimes puts off Westerners raised with wobbly animal gelatin. Whereas conventional gelatin must be refrigerated to set, *kanten* sets at a temperature of around 85 to 100 degrees F, depending on the thickness of the liquid and how much *kanten* is added to it. Once *kanten* gelatin sets, it won't melt until it reaches a temperature of around 176 degrees F; animal gelatin melts at a much lower temperature. And whereas conventional gelatin tends to adhere to a mold, you can easily slide *kanten* gelatin out of a mold by simply pushing the edge to make a space between the gelatin and the mold.

In the past, *kanten* was always sold in the form of a thick stick, *bō kanten*, or long strings, *ito kanten*. Stick *kanten* was the dominant form sold in Japan and at Japanese food stores outside the country. Today, a more convenient powdered form of *kanten* has been replacing the old stick form. Among these three products, I prefer *ito kanten*, which preferably should be soaked overnight in cold water before cooking. *Ito kanten* produces gelatin with the softest texture. *Bo kanten*, which needs only a short soaking, about 5 minutes, produces a firmer gelatin. The most convenient, powdered type of *kanten* needs no soaking and has the shortest cooking time, but produces a gelatin that is much more opaque than the ones made from the other two forms of the product. You can take your choice among these three products.

To make *kanten* gelatin, use $1^3/_4$ to 2 cups water for one stick *bo kanten*, about $^1/_4$ ounce (7.5 grams) *ito kanten*, or 2 teaspoons powdered *kanten*. More water produces a softer gelatin. Cook the *kanten* in the water until the *kanten* is dissolved, stirring continuously lest the *kanten* sink to the bottom of the pot and stick to it. Add sugar, cook until it is dissolved, and then leave the gelatin to set.

Part of the water can be replaced with milk, wine, or fruit juice. When using milk or wine, add it with the sugar. When using fruit juice, the juice should be at room temperature. Cook the *kanten* liquid for 3 to 5 minutes over low heat after the sugar is dissolved. Transfer the *kanten* liquid to a bowl, and let the liquid cool almost to room temperature. Before the gelatin sets, stir in the fruit juice.

Kanten is a favorite ingredient in Japanese cold sweets. The simplest example is *kanten* cooked with sugar, set in a traditional square stainless-steel mold, cut into small cubes, and served chilled in a brown-sugar syrup. Another popular sweet is made of *kanten* liquid mixed with sweet azuki bean paste. The chilled gelatin is cut into small squares and served on a bright green cherry leaf. Nothing is more refreshing than this azuki gelatin, called *mizu yokan* (see page 474), on a sweltering summer day.

SOURCES: *Bo* (stick) *kanten* and powdered *kanten* are sold at Japanese and Asian food stores, and health- and natural-food stores. *Ito* (string) *kanten* is sold at many Asian food stores, but *not* at Japanese food stores.

WHAT TO LOOK FOR: *Bo kanten* sticks are sold in long plastic bags, each of which usually contains two sticks. The translucent white sticks are about 10 inches long and weigh practically nothing. They look like shriveled sticks of plastic.

Translucent *ito kanten* strings are bundled and packed in 14-inch-long plastic bags.

Powdered *kanten* comes packed in small plastic bags inside a small cardboard box or a larger plastic bag. Each small bag contains $^1/_7$ ounce (1 teaspoon) *kanten* powder.

STORAGE: *Kanten* in any of the three forms keeps for a long time. Store it in a cool, dry, and dark place.

CLASSIC AGAR-AGAR GELATIN IN SYRUP

Mitsumame

A traditional summertime sweet, *mitsumame* brings back childhood memories of a hot and humid August day in Tokyo—bright blue sky, dazzling sunshine, continuous singing of cicadas, a cotton sundress, a straw hat, plastic sandals, and a bowl of chilled *mitsumame*.

Even though the dominant ingredient used in this sweet is cubes of agar-agar gelatin, *mitsumame* literally means "peas in sugar syrup." The peas are a red variety with a naturally sweet and nutty flavor. Cooked red peas, packed in a small can, can be found at Japanese food stores. Ask the shop owner about them, or leave the peas out.

To make the gelatin, you will need a 6-by-6-inch square steel, glass, or plastic mold.

> 1 bo kanten *(agar-agar stick)* or 1 package *(4 grams)*
> kanten *(agar-agar) powder*
> 1³/₄ cups sugar, divided
> ¹/₄ pound dried apricots
> 2 cups combined cubed fresh fruit, such as
> cantaloupe, kiwi, peach, berries,
> watermelon, and banana
> 1 can red peas *(optional)*
> 4 scoops vanilla ice cream

If you're using an agar-agar stick, tear it into quarters, and soak the pieces in a medium bowl of cold water for 5 minutes. Drain the pieces, and squeeze them to remove excess water.

In a medium pot, combine the agar-agar pieces or powder and 1³/₄ cups water, and bring the mixture to a boil over medium heat. Cook the mixture, stirring all the time, until the agar-agar fibers are completely dissolved, about 6 to 8 minutes for the stick form and 2 to 3 minutes for the powdered form. Add ¹/₂ cup of the sugar to the gelatin liquid, and cook, stirring, until the sugar is dissolved.

Strain the mixture through a sieve. Wet the inside of a 6-by-6-inch mold with water, and pour in the gelatin liquid. Let it stand at room temperature to cool, then chill it, covered.

In a small saucepan, combine 1 cup water and 1 cup of the sugar, and bring the mixture to a boil over medium heat. Cook, stirring, until the sugar is dissolved. Transfer the syrup to a bowl, let the syrup cool to room temperature, and then chill it, covered.

Into a clean small saucepan, add the apricots and enough water to cover them. Stir in the remaining 1/4 cup sugar, and cook the apricots until they are plump and tender but not mushy, about 2 to 3 minutes. Let the apricots cool in their syrup at room temperature, and later chill them, covered.

Unmold the gelatin (there is no need to warm the mold), and cut it into 1/2-inch cubes. In a large bowl, combine the gelatin, apricots, fruit cubes, and peas, if you're using them. Pour the syrup over the mixture. Toss it gently, and refrigerate it, covered, for 1 hour.

Serve the mixture in individual dessert bowls topped with scoops of ice cream.

• *Yields 4 servings*

KATAKURIKO • Potato Starch
KUZUKO • Arrowroot Starch
KŌN STĀCHI • Cornstarch

Potato starch is used in Japanese cooking to coat foods to be boiled or fried. In boiled preparations, the starch provides a soft and slightly chewy texture, while protecting the foods from direct contact with heat. In fried preparations, the starch protects the food from direct contact with the cooking oil and adds a crisp texture and extra flavor.

Potato starch is also used as a thickening agent, to give a silky smooth texture to soups and broths.

Two other starches are used in the Japanese kitchen, although not as frequently as potato starch. They are arrowroot starch and cornstarch. The different characteristics of these starches can be understood by performing the following experiment: Put 2 tablespoons of each starch into separate small saucepans, and add 1 cup water to each saucepan. Bring the mixtures to a boil, and cook them over medium heat until each thickens. Continue cooking the mixtures, for 3 more minutes.

Each starch will develop a gluey texture, but the mixtures will differ. Arrowroot starch produces the clearest, stickiest mixture. Potato starch produces a less sticky mixture with a frosty color. Cornstarch produces the most liquid mixture among the three, and its color is whitish, not clear. These three starches are interchangeable in cooking if you are aware of their characteristics and consider how much to increase or decrease the amount of starch when making a substitution.

Another important tip to remember when using these starches is that acid breaks down the tightly knit net of cooked starch. Recipes for soups, sauces, and broth containing highly acidic ingredients, therefore, usually call for a little extra starch. The acidic ingredient—vinegar or lemon juice, for example—should be added at the end of cooking, after the soup base, sauce, or broth has been thickened.

KIKURAGE • Wood-Ear Fungus

Kikurage is an edible fungus that grows on dead or fallen trees such as mulberry, elm, willow, and pomegranate. The Chinese written characters describe this fungus as "wood ear," because its shape resembles the human ear. But the Japanese use a different set of characters, which mean "wood jellyfish." Because of its crunchy texture, *kikurage* reminds the Japanese of the popular edible jellyfish.

Kikurage is sold dried and looks like chips of wrinkled bark. It comes in two colors, black and pale gold. Black *kikurage* is more abundant and less expensive and, therefore, more popular than the pale gold variety. The pale gold *kikurage*, which is softer and more digestible than its black counterpart, has for centuries been treasured by the Chinese for its curative properties. But in the Japanese kitchen, the black type is predominantly used, in many ways—stir-fried, steamed, simmered, and in soups.

Before using black *kikurage*, soak it in lukewarm water until it is soft, about 20 minutes. It will swell five to eight times its original size. Unlike shiitake mushrooms, which develop a strong, sweet flavor and fragrance through drying, dried *kikurage* fungus has very little flavor or fragrance. This is good news for the cook, since *kikurage* can be added to any dish without conflicting with the flavors of other ingredients. However, the pleasant crunchiness of *kikurage* is a wonderful addition to many dishes.

Despite its weak flavor, *kikurage* is rich in nutrients, including B vitamins, vitamin E, calcium, iron, and potassium.

SOURCES: Black *kikurage* is sold at Japanese and Asian food stores and the Asian sections of large supermarkets.

WHAT TO LOOK FOR: Black *kikurage* comes packed in small plastic bags. The size of the pieces varies from about $1/2$ inch to about 2 inches. At Japanese stores, the pieces tend to be larger and thicker than those sold at Chinese food stores, and are two-toned, dark brown on one side and white on the other side. At Chinese stores, the *kikurage* resembles large dried tea leaves and is only one color, light brown, on both sides.

STORAGE: The dried *kikurage* keeps indefinitely. Store it in a cool, dark, and dry place.

STIR-FRIED RICE WITH BLACK KIKURAGE

Black *Kikurage Cha-han*

Stir-fried rice is a preparation borrowed from the Chinese kitchen. It is said that a Chinese chef who did not want to waste leftover plain cooked rice stored it overnight and stir-fried it the next day with several other ingredients. He produced a delicious new dish.

As this story indicates, the cooked rice used in stir-fried rice is preferably day-old. Since cold day-old rice grains are no longer sticky, they remain firm and separated in the finished dish. But rice becomes lumpy when left in the refrigerator overnight, so you must break up the lumps into separate grains with your hands before stir-frying the rice. You can substitute freshly cooked rice if you rinse it in a sieve under cold running water until the rice is cool. This removes the surface starch and separates the grains. Drain the rinsed rice completely before stir-frying it.

This recipe uses *chozume*, Chinese pork sausage, which comes in firm links about $^3/_4$ inch thick and 6 inches long. Available at Chinese food stores, *chozume* contains a lot of fat, but it gives a rich flavor to dishes like stir-fried rice.

In this recipe, black *kikurage* provides a crunchy texture, an appealing color contrast, and valuable nutrients to the mixture of white rice, yellow egg, and green scallion.

1 large (2-inch) dried black kikurage

$^1/_3$ cup fresh or frozen green peas

3 tablespoons vegetable oil, divided

2 eggs, lightly beaten

1 tablespoon sesame oil

1$^3/_4$ ounces chozume *(Chinese sausage) or
      other firm sausage, cubed*

1 garlic clove, minced

*1 scallion (both green and white parts),
      cut into thin disks*

*2$^1/_2$ cups day-old cooked short-grain or
      medium-grain rice, broken up by hand*

About $^3/_4$ teaspoon salt

About $^1/_4$ teaspoon tamari

About $^1/_2$ teaspoon ground white pepper

In a medium bowl of lukewarm water, soak the dried *kikurage* until it is softened, about 20 minutes. Drain it, cut off and discard the tough stem, and cut the remainder of the fungus into thin strips.

In a small saucepan of boiling water, cook the green peas for 3 minutes if they're fresh, or 1 minute if they're frozen. Drain them, and let them stand in lukewarm water until you're ready to use them.

Heat a wok or large skillet over moderately high heat, and add 2 tablespoons of the vegetable oil. When the oil is hot, add the eggs. Cook the eggs until they are 80 percent done, giving several large stirs during the cooking. Transfer the eggs to a plate.

Reduce the heat to medium, and add the remaining vegetable oil and the sesame oil to the wok or skillet. Add the sausage, and cook it, stirring occasionally, until it is crisp. Add the garlic, and cook, stirring, for 30 seconds. Drain the peas, and add them with the *kikurage* and scallions. Cook for 1 minute, stirring over high heat. Add the rice, and cook it until it is heated through, stirring thoroughly. Return the cooked egg to the wok or skillet, break it into small pieces with your spatula, and toss it thoroughly with the other ingredients. Season the mixture to taste with salt, tamari, and ground white pepper, and serve.

• *Yields 2 servings as a light main dish*

KONNYAKU • Taro Gelatin

Konnyaku is a humble-looking firm gelatin-like, opaque cake. It is made from a plant in the taro family called *konnyaku imo.* When you touch taro gelatin, you will find it more elastic and much firmer than conventional gelatin, and, when you eat it, it will seem almost flavorless. So, every student asks me, what is the purpose and merit of eating taro gelatin? For the answer, please continue to read!

Konnyaku imo, konnyaku taro, was first introduced to Japan from China as a medicine, perhaps as early as 200 B.C. It is said that taro gelatin originally came from the region of the present Vietnam. By the Kamakura Era (1192 to 1333), *konnyaku* taro was a popular vegetarian food among the priests at Zen temples, and, by the middle of the Edo Era (1600 to 1868), the commoners were using *konnyaku* taro in its present gelatinized form in many preparations. One of the most interesting uses was in a particular miso soup called *tanuki-jiru*, "racoon soup." Racoon meat had been frequently used in this soup as well as in other preparations since olden days. But in the Edo Era, with the spread of vegetarian cuisine among the commoners, someone came up with the idea of replacing racoon meat with taro gelatin, because of its dark color and chewy, meatlike texture (its flavor, of course, is not like that of a racoon). "Racoon miso soup" still remains popular; however, these days it is never made with racoon meat but always with taro gelatin.

Konnyaku *gelatin cake and* shirataki *noodles*

Konnyaku taro grows on well-drained slopes in the high mountains, where there is abundant rainfall and a large temperature variation between the day and night. When it is three to five years old, the plant bears a large trumpet-shaped flower. The root is usually dug up after three years, when it is on average 6 inches in diameter and weighs up to 5 pounds. The root is then rinsed, peeled, sliced, dried, and ground to a powder. The powder is combined with water to form a weak natural gelatin. A coagulating agent, hydrated calcium, is added to make the gelatin into a firm cake. The set gelatin is then cooked in boiling water and cooled in cold water. Today most of these production processes are automated.

Taro gelatin has no calories but is rich in dietary fiber, so it helps to lower blood cholesterol and relieve constipation.

Taro gelatin is available in several varieties and colors. Whole blocks can be found in several colors: white, made from peeled roots; dark brown, made from unpeeled roots, with or without added sea vegetable flakes; and red, made from peeled roots with red chile pepper flakes added. The gelatin also comes in the form of thin noodles, called *shirataki*, an indispensable ingredient in hot-pot dishes such as sukiyaki. All of these types of taro gelatin require cooking before eating.

One type of taro gelatin requires no cooking. *Sashimi konnyaku*, or sashimi-style taro gelatin, can be eaten as is, with a little wasabi paste and *shoyu* (soy sauce) or sweet miso sauce. The flavor is, of course, that of wasabi and *shoyu*, or miso. But this is a very refreshing side dish. The elastic texture of the chilled *konnyaku* is enjoyable on hot summer days.

SOURCES: *Konnyaku*, taro gelatin, is sold at Japanese food stores in the refrigerator case.

Square blocks of *konnyaku*, packed in clear plastic bags with water, are sometimes sold as "yam cakes." Thin taro gelatin noodles, *shirataki*, are sold in round bundles packed in water in plastic bags. *Shirataki* may be mistakenly labeled as "yam noodles." *Sashimi konnyaku* comes as a whole square cake or already cut into thin slices. A tiny package of sweet miso sauce is frequently included as a condiment.

STORAGE: Sealed in its package, *konnyaku* of all types keeps in the refrigerator for two months after the date of manufacture. Once the package is opened, *konnyaku* should be consumed within a few days.

BASIC RECIPE

"RACOON" MISO SOUP, OR MISO SOUP WITH TARO GELATIN

Tanuki-jiru

Konnyaku, taro gelatin, takes the place of the racoon meat that was once used in this traditional soup.

   Konnyaku is always cooked in boiling water or sautéed in oil to remove excess water before further use. For this soup, after parboiling the taro gelatin I fry it in a little oil, until the outside turns firm and golden and blisters. This gives the gelatin a pleasant, crusty texture.

   You can make *tanuki-jiru* as miso soup with only taro gelatin added, or you can prepare the soup as my mother does, with vegetables such as burdock, daikon, and dried shiitake mushrooms. My mother often calls this soup "a cleaning agent for the digestive system."

> 1 konnyaku *(taro gelatin) cake*
> 2¹/₂ *tablespoons sesame oil, divided*
> ¹/₂ *cup 2-by-¹/₄-by-¹/₄-inch strips of gobo*
>   *(burdock) or turnip*
> ¹/₂ *cup 2-by-¹/₄-inch strips of daikon*
> ¹/₂ *cup 2-by-¹/₄-by-¹/₄-inch strips of carrot*
> 3 *cups dashi (fish stock)*
> 2 *scallions, the white part cut into 1-inch lengths,*
>   *and the green part into thin rings*

2 *tablespoons* akamiso *(brown miso)*
¹/₂ tablespoon shiromiso *(white miso)*
Sansho *pepper or ground black pepper*

In a medium pot of boiling water, parboil the taro gelatin for 2 minutes. Drain it, wipe it dry with a paper towel, and cut it into 2-by-¹/₄-by-¹/₄-inch strips.

Heat a small skillet over medium heat. Add 2 tablespoons of the sesame oil and the taro gelatin, and cook the gelatin, stirring occasionally, until the outside turns golden and blisters, 5 minutes. Remove the skillet from the heat.

In a medium pot, put the remaining ¹/₂ tablespoon of sesame oil, and when the oil is hot, add the burdock, daikon, and carrot. Cook, stirring, for 1 minute. Add the *dashi*, the taro gelatin, and the white part of the scallion, and bring the mixture to a boil. Reduce the heat to low, and cook for 10 minutes.

Add the miso and stir until it dissolves. Add the green part of the scallion, give a few stirs, and turn off the heat.

Serve the soup sprinkled with a little *sansho* pepper or black pepper.

• *Yields 3 servings*

KOYADOFU • Freeze-Dried Tofu

Tofu has been made and sold fresh for many centuries. The dried form of tofu, *koyadofu*, was invented by accident around the twelfth century, when, it is said, a priest at Mt. Koya Temple left freshly made tofu as an offering on the altar one snowy cold night. The next morning the tofu was frozen, so he threw it away in the back garden. During the day, the sun melted the tofu and evaporated some of the water from it. After several sunny days, the tofu was found completely dried. Later it was learned that the dried form keeps for a long time and, after being reconstituted, has many uses in cooking. Ever since, freeze-dried tofu has been called *koyadofu*, after the mountain temple at which it was created. *Koyadofu* is also called *koridofu*, "frozen tofu."

Koyadofu comes in flat, creamy white squares. Each square weighs virtually nothing. When it is soaked in warm water, it absorbs a large amount of liquid and takes on a slightly spongy character and mild but distinctive sweet flavor. Reconstituted dried tofu bears no resemblance to soft, creamy-textured freshly made tofu. One would never suspect they are basically the same material.

To reconstitute freeze-dried tofu, soak it in warm water (heated to 140 degrees F) for about 2 minutes. Drain the tofu, rinse it, and gently squeeze out most of the water. Reconstituted dried tofu has many uses. Although it does not have a strong flavor, it absorbs

OTHER FOOD PRODUCTS

• 120

flavors from other ingredients. It can be stir-fried, simmered, or deep-fried. Because it is rich in protein, freeze-dried tofu is an ideal vegetarian food. Minced, reconstituted tofu can be used in place of minced meat—or how about in a curry sauce?

SOURCES: Japanese food stores and health- and natural-food stores carry *koyadofu*, freeze-dried tofu.

WHAT TO LOOK FOR: Freeze-dried tofu comes in squares, about 2 inches by 2³/₄ inches, and in 3-inch cubes. It is sold in a plastic bag which may be packed in a small box. Choose a brand that feels smooth through the plastic and is a creamy yellow color.

STORAGE: Freeze-dried tofu keeps for six months after the date of manufacture. Keep it in a cool, dry, and dark place before opening the package, and in the refrigerator afterward.

BASIC RECIPE

STIR-FRIED FREEZE-DRIED TOFU

Koyadofu Itame

In this preparation, freeze-dried tofu is first simmered in chicken broth to absorb its rich flavor. The tofu is then stir-fried with red and green bell peppers in a sauce spiced with a very popular adopted Chinese condiment, *toban jiang*, chile-bean sauce. Use red chile pepper flakes if chile-bean sauce is not available.

> ¹/₄ *cup dried black* kikurage, *soaked in cold water*
> *for 20 minutes*
> 2 koyadofu *(freeze-dried tofu) cakes*
> 1 red bell pepper, *stem, seeds, and ribs removed*
> 1 green bell pepper, *stem, seeds, and ribs removed*
> 2 cups chicken broth
> 2 tablespoons plus 2 teaspoons sesame oil, divided
> 1 thumb-size piece of ginger, peeled and julienned
> ¹/₂ to 1 teaspoon toban jiang *(chile-bean sauce)*
> 1 tablespoon sake *(rice wine)*
> 1 tablespoon sugar
> 2 teaspoons shoyu *(soy sauce)*

Drain the *kikurage,* cut off and discard the tough stems, and cut the remainder into thin strips.

In a medium bowl of warm water, soak the freeze-dried tofu until it is softened, 2 minutes. Drain it, and squeeze it to remove excess water.

In a medium pot of boiling water, blanch the red and green bell peppers for 30 seconds, then plunge them into cold water to stop the cooking. Drain them, spin them or wipe them dry, and cut them into thick 2-inch-long strips.

In a small saucepan, bring 2 cups chicken broth to a boil over medium heat. Reduce the heat to low, add the freeze-dried tofu, and cook the tofu in the broth, partially covered, for 10 minutes.

Drain the tofu, reserving the cooking broth. Cut the tofu cakes in half lengthwise, then cut each piece crosswise into $3/8$-inch-thick slices. Heat a wok or large skillet over high heat. Add 2 tablespoons of the sesame oil, and, when the oil is hot, add the ginger. Cook, stirring, for 30 seconds. Add the chile-bean sauce, and cook, stirring, for 10 seconds. Add the *kikurage,* bell peppers, and freeze-dried tofu, and cook, stirring, for 2 minutes. Reduce the heat to medium, add $1/4$ cup of the reserved chicken broth (save the rest for soup), the *sake*, and the sugar, and cook for 2 minutes. Add the *shoyu*, and cook, stirring, for 2 minutes. Sprinkle in the remaining 2 teaspoons sesame oil, and serve.

• *Yields 2 servings as a light main dish or 4 servings as a side dish*

NATTO • Fermented Soybeans

There are several food-related questions that Japanese frequently ask Westerners, not only to measure how deeply foreigners understand Japan, but also to reassure themselves that the Japanese people are unique. Such questions include "Do you eat raw fish?" and "Can you use chopsticks?" and "Do you eat *natto*?" Just as the Japanese tend to think that non-Japanese people cannot master speaking Japanese, they are certain that foreigners do not like *natto*.

Natto is a fermented product. It has a sticky texture and a slight ammonia-like smell. Its production employs only two materials—soybeans and the fermentation starter *natto kin*.

It is said that the invention of *natto* involves an interesting coincidence. There are several similar stories of this invention, of which some originated as early as the tenth century. Farmers or warriors threw away leftover, still warm, cooked soybeans on top of discarded rice straw. Later they found that the beans had fermented in the straw and were transformed into a food with a distinctive flavor and texture. Certain bacteria that reside in rice straw had performed the miracle of creating a new food, rather than spoiled waste. In 1905 a Jap-

anese researcher succeeded in isolating the *natto* bacteria from other varieties in rice straw. By 1919 cultured *natto* bacteria were introduced to the *natto* industry, and *natto* production became safer, more stable, and prosperous. When I was small, *natto* was sold in rice-straw wrappers, which always reminded me of the story of *natto*'s invention. Today a small Styrofoam tray or paper cup has replaced the traditional straw container, and this piece of interesting culinary history is almost forgotten.

To make *natto*, soaked soybeans are cooked until tender, about four to five hours. In the past they were then wrapped in rice straw and left in a warm, moist place to ferment. Today cooked soybeans are inoculated with *natto* bacteria, and left in a temperature-controlled fermentation room. The initial temperature of 100 degrees F is raised to about 124 degrees F during the 20 hours of fermentation. The finished product is cooled to room temperature, packed in small Styrofoam trays or paper cups, and stored in the refrigerator overnight to mature. Next morning, the freshly made *natto* is distributed to stores. *Natto* tastes the best on the third or fourth day after leaving the fermentation room.

When you open a package of whole-bean *natto*, you will find very dry-looking, pale camel-colored beans. Stirring makes the beans slimy and moist. Because of its distinctive texture and strong smell, even some Japanese avoid this food. Until recently it was unpopular in the Kansai region, which includes Kyoto, Osaka, and their surroundings.

But the recent demand for healthy food has greatly contributed to increased sales of *natto* in the Kansai region as well as elsewhere. This is because *natto* is rich in minerals, such as calcium and potassium, and easily digestible protein. Also, fermentation improves the quality of B vitamins in soybeans and produces vitamin B_{12}.

For many non-Japanese, this specialty-food product is an acquired taste, but the delicious nutty flavor and nutritional value of *natto* make it very appealing, especially in some of the recipes presented here. Please try it—with an open mind! After you have learned to love this unique Japanese treat, find an opportunity to tell a Japanese friend how much you like *natto*. Watch the reaction!

The simplest way to enjoy *natto* is to stir it with a little *shoyu* (soy sauce) and Japanese hot mustard paste, and pour it over steaming-hot cooked rice. Or make a hearty *natto* miso soup: Chop the fermented beans roughly, cook them in *dashi* (fish stock), and flavor the soup with brown miso to produce one of the most healthy and satisfying soups.

S O U R C E S : *Natto*, fermented soybeans, is sold at Japanese food stores in the refrigerator or freezer case.

W H A T   T O   L O O K   F O R : *Natto* is sold in small Styrofoam trays or in small paper cups. On the label there is the term *otsubu* (large beans), *kotsubu* (small beans), or *hikiwari natto* (chopped beans). The large, small, or chopped beans are interchangeable in most dishes. Inside a container of *natto*, you will find a tiny bag of mustard paste and, sometimes, another tiny bag of sauce. The sauce is a mixture of *dashi* (fish stock), *shoyu* (soy sauce), sugar, and some other flavorings. The mustard paste and sauce are condiments for the fermented beans.

S T O R A G E : In the refrigerator, *natto* keeps for about four days after the manufacturing date. *Natto* freezes well.

BASIC RECIPE

MISO SOUP WITH FERMENTED SOYBEANS

Natto Miso-shiru

Not everyone appreciates the sticky texture of *natto*, fermented soybeans, but the stickiness disappears in this soup, which therefore provides a good introduction to this very nourishing food product. Serve the soup with a small drop of thin Japanese hot mustard paste.

1 package (1³/₄ ounces) natto *(fermented soybeans)*
2¹/₂ cups dashi *(fish stock)*
1 scallion (green and white parts), cut into thin disks
2 tablespoons akamiso *(brown miso)*
¹/₂ teaspoon thin hot mustard paste (see page 55)

Put the fermented soybeans into a colander, rinse them with warm water, and drain them well. This removes their stickiness. Unless you are using *hikiwari* (chopped) *natto*, chop the soybeans coarsely.

In a medium pot, bring the *dashi* to a boil over medium heat. Add the fermented soybeans, reduce the heat to low, and cook for 2 minutes. Add the scallion, and cook for 1 minute. Add the miso to the soup, and stir until the miso dissolves.

Serve the soup immediately, in individual soup bowls, garnished with a little hot mustard paste in the center.

• *Yields 3 servings*

NERIMONO • Fish Cake

Nerimono is a processed marine product with a pleasantly smooth, slightly resilient texture. An example is imitation crabmeat sticks—the latest version of *nerimono* in Japan, and one that has gained popularity elsewhere. Ingredients used to produce such products are minced fish such as cod and pollock, starch, sugar, salt, and egg white. Some *nerimono* products also contain flavoring and coloring chemicals. All are quite salty.

Nerimono manufacture makes it easy to eat fish that have many hairlike bones, which, along with the flesh are pounded into a paste. The present form of *nerimono* production began as early as the Muromachi Era (1393 to 1573).

Nerimono is a regional product. In different parts of Japan, different preparation methods produce fish cakes of different shapes and slightly different colors, textures, and tastes. Kanagawa Prefecture, next to metropolitan Tokyo, produces a fine fish cake called *kamaboko*. To prepare *kamaboko*, salted fish paste (*surimi*) is first mounded on a wooden board into a half-cylinder shape, and then steamed. Miyagi Prefecture, in the northern part of Japan, is known for its *sasa-kamaboko*, and Osaka Prefecture for its *yaki-kamaboko*. Both types are prepared by broiling the fish paste after it has been steamed. *Sasa-kamaboko* is shaped like a bamboo leaf (*sasa*), and *yaki-kamaboko* is formed on a wooden board into a half-cylinder shape. Kagoshima Prefecture, on Kyushu Island in the southern part of Japan, is famous for its deep-fried fish cakes, small, flat disks with a distinctive, rich flavor. Fried fish cakes are called *satsuma-age* because during the Edo Era (1600 to 1868) Satsuma was the provincial name for present-day Kagoshima Prefecture. Because of its location, Satsuma was a crossroads of culture and trade between Japan and foreign countries. The method of deep-frying the fish paste was an adaptation of Portuguese, Spanish, and Chinese techniques.

Regular *kamaboko*, steamed fish cake, is delicious simply sliced and eaten with a little *shoyu* (soy sauce), and wasabi. It is a popular lunch box food. Grilled *kamaboko* (*sasa-* and *yaki-kamaboko*) and deep-fried fish cakes (*satsuma-age*) taste best when reheated and then served with Japanese hot mustard paste and *shoyu*.

Following are other *nerimono* varieties:

- *Chikuwa*, "bamboo ring." Ground fish paste is formed on a bamboo stick, and then broiled. Later the bamboo stick is removed. The resulting fish cake is shaped like a long stick with a hole down the center. *Chikuwa* is eaten with *shoyu* and wasabi or used in simmered dishes.

- *Narutomaki*. *Naruto* means "whirlpool," and *maki* means "circle." As the name implies, when this long stick of fish cake is cut crosswise, every slice shows a pink swirl pattern. When you order any of certain kinds of hot noodle dishes, you will always find a few disks of *narutomaki*, along with other toppings, floating beautifully on the hot broth.

- *Hanpen*. To make this soft and fluffy snow white cake, puréed fish is mixed with grated Japanese mountain yam and whipped to add air bubbles. The mixture is then placed in a mold and simmered. Biting into *hanpen* is like biting into a soft meringue. *Hanpen* is eaten as is in soups, or it is broiled or simmered in a richly flavored stock.

SOURCES: *Nerimono*, fish cake, products are sold at Japanese food stores and some Asian food stores. Imitation crabmeat sticks, *kani-kamaboko*, can be found at large supermarket chains. All of these products are kept in refrigerator or freezer cases.

WHAT TO LOOK FOR: *Nerimono* products are packed in clear plastic wrap or bags. Regular steamed fish cakes, *kamaboko*, should not have a slimy outer surface. Sliminess is a sign that the product is old. Deep-fried fish cakes should appear freshly fried, and should not have a glittering appearance.

STORAGE: All types of *nerimono*, fish cake, have a rather short shelf life. Steamed or broiled *kamaboko* keeps in the refrigerator for 12 days from the date of manufacture; fried fish cakes, imitation crabmeat sticks, and *hanpen* around 5 days; and *narutomaki* and *chikuwa* about 10 days. Opened packages should be used within a few days. All of these products freeze well.

HOT STEW WITH ASSORTED FISH CAKES

Oden

Oden, hot stew with assorted fish cakes, is a favorite winter hot-pot dish. An assortment of fish cakes is cooked in a large pot with other ingredients, such as daikon, *konnyaku* (taro gelatin), and potato, in *kombu* (kelp) or chicken stock. Cooking many ingredients together in one pot for several hours creates a delicious harmony of blended flavors.

Oden-ya are restaurants in which *oden* is served as a main dish along with small seasonal side dishes and alcoholic drinks, such as *sake* (rice wine) and beer. These informal eateries are popular hangouts for businesspeople after their long, stressful hours in the office or factory.

My mother prepared *oden* on many cold winter nights and served it piping hot from a large pot on a portable gas stove on the table. My sisters and I frequently fought over our favorite items in the pot.

When Japanese *nerimono* (prepared fish cakes) are not available, you may find similar marine products—steamed, broiled, or deep-fried—at Asian food stores.

Serve this wholesome one-pot meal with plain cooked white or brown rice.

1 pound daikon, *peeled, halved lengthwise, then cross-wise into 1-inch-thick half moons*

³/₄ pound (6 to 8) small potatoes

1 konnyaku *(taro gelatin) cake*

8 to 10 satsuma-age *(fried fish cakes) the size of Ping Pong balls*

2 hanpen *(simmered fish cakes), quartered into triangle shapes*

1 kamaboko *(steamed fish cake), cut into ¹/₃-inch slices*

7 cups kombu dashi *(kelp stock, page 65)*

¹/₄ cup usukuchi shoyu *(light-colored soy sauce)*

¹/₄ cup shoyu *(soy sauce)*
¹/₄ cup mirin *(sweet cooking wine)*
1 tablespoon sugar
4 hard-boiled eggs, shelled
Hot mustard paste (see page 55)

Put the daikon into a medium pot, and add water to cover the daikon by 2 inches. Place the pot over moderate heat, bring the water to a boil, and cook for 15 minutes. Drain the daikon and set it aside.

Put the potatoes into a medium pot, cover them with cold water, and cook them until they are done but still firm. Drain them, and cut them into halves.

Put the taro gelatin into a medium pot of boiling water, and boil the gelatin for 1 minute. Drain it, and cut it into four triangles.

To remove excess oil from the fried fish cakes, put them in a colander and rinse them with boiling water.

In a large stew pot, bring the kelp stock, *usukuchi* and regular *shoyu*, *mirin*, and sugar to a boil over high heat. Reduce the heat to low, and add all the fish cakes and the par-boiled ingredients including the eggs. Cook, partially covered for 3 hours. Add water as necessary to keep the broth from reducing to less than half of its original quantity. Taste the broth and add a little more *shoyu*, *mirin*, or sugar, if you like.

Bring the hot pot to the table. If possible, keep the stew hot on a portable stove. Let the diners help themselves, choosing the ingredients they prefer and transferring them to individual bowls along with some broth and mustard paste.

• *Yields 4 to 6 servings*

NORI • Sea Vegetable

Like *wakame* and *kombu* (kelp), nori is a popular sea vegetable in Japan. Also sometimes called laver, it is becoming increasingly popular outside Japan mainly because it is used in *makizushi*, rolled sushi.

Unlike *wakame*, *kombu*, and *hijiki*, which are sold in the form of individual leaves, nori is sold as a sheet made from small, soft, dark brown algae, which have been cultivated in bays and lagoons since the middle of the Edo Era (1600 to 1868). The technique of drying the collected algae on wooden frames was borrowed from the famous Japanese paper-making industry.

A small daily portion of nori can be an important part of one's diet. The delicious taste of this sea vegetable is due to its high level of glutamic acid, one of the amino acids. Nori is rich in many other important nutrients, including protein, minerals, and vitamins. Nori exceeds all of the other sea vegetables in vitamin A content; in fact, five nori sheets contain as much vitamin A as does *one pound* of butter.

Small squares of nori frequently appear at a traditional Japanese breakfast. A bowl of plain cooked white rice is served with a pile of toasted nori sheets. If you stay at a traditional Japanese inn, a *ryokan*, you will still be welcomed with this hearty, healthy breakfast (although, like me, you may find yourself craving a good cup of coffee at the end). To enjoy this breakfast, first pick up one small sheet of nori with chopsticks, and wet one side with *shoyu* (soy sauce), which is always served with nori. Next, place the nori, *shoyu*-soaked side down, on top of the rice. Wrap some rice in it with your chopsticks, and eat the stuffed nori in one or two bites. The crispy toasted nori provides a wonderful textural contrast to the soft cooked rice.

Another popular rice snack that uses nori is *onigiri*. *Onigiri* is a stuffed rice ball wrapped in a nori sheet. This traditional Japanese fast food is available at every convenience store in Japan for people on the go. *Onigiri* also comes—only in Japan—in the form of an ingenious kit that allows the consumer to wrap the rice in the crisp nori immediately before eating, without touching the rice. Stuffing ingredients vary from *umeboshi* (pickled plum) to cubes of grilled salted salmon or cod roe. Less traditional stuffings include tempura shrimp and cooked vegetables. As with rolled sushi, nori prevents the cooked rice from drying out before it is eaten and from sticking to the fingers while it is eaten.

Shredded nori scattered over plain hot or cold noodle dishes is a popular condiment.

In the past, nori sheets were sold only untoasted. Before they were eaten, they were toasted over an open flame. Today almost all of the nori sold is already *yakinori*, toasted nori. However, even *yakinori* has better flavor and texture if it is toasted over an open flame just before it is eaten. To toast nori, place two whole sheets together, shiny sides facing each other, and hold them by one end. Quickly pass the nori over a high flame. Then hold the other end, and, in a second quick pass through the flame, toast the area missed on the first pass. Be careful not to burn your fingers or the nori. Overtoasted nori deforms and blackens.

Some recipes call for shredded nori. The shredding is easiest to do with scissors.

In addition to plain nori, there is a flavored type on the market. It is basted with a mixture of *shoyu*, *mirin* (sweet cooking wine), and other condiments. This type, called *ajinori*, is always sold in small squares, one-eighth of a whole sheet. *Ajinori* is the type frequently served with a bowl of plain cooked rice at breakfast.

SOURCES: Nori is sold at Japanese and Asian food stores, health- and natural-food stores, and some large supermarkets. *Ajinori*, flavored nori, can be found at Japanese food stores.

WHAT TO LOOK FOR: Nori sheets come in the standard size of 8.2 by 7 inches. Ten sheets are packed in a plastic bag, which usually displays a picture of *makizushi*, rolled sushi. The price of nori varies greatly. In general, the higher the price, the better the quality, but a medium-priced package is usually a good buy. Good nori sheets are thick, with an evenly smooth and shiny surface and no holes or tears. The sheets are dark green and have a good fragrance. The best nori melts smoothly in one's mouth yet is crisp when bitten.

STORAGE: Nori stays fresh about nine months after the date of manufacture. An opened bag should be stored in an airtight container or refrigerated in a sealed plastic bag. Once opened, nori should be used as quickly as possible. If stored improperly, nori easily absorbs moisture and loses both its crispy texture and its fragrant flavor. The sheets also deform badly over time. Retoasting will not bring a moist, deformed sheet back to the original flat, crispy form.

BASIC RECIPE

RICE BALLS IN CRISP NORI

Onigiri

Making *onigiri*, rice balls, brings back pleasant memories of my childhood days. We three sisters often asked our mother to teach us how to make rice balls. Although she knew what a mess we always made during these lessons, my mother enjoyed teaching us to make rice balls in various shapes—round, barrel-shaped, and triangular—each with a different stuffing. By the time we finished battling with the hot, steamy, sticky rice in an attempt to shape it into the proper form, we found ourselves, the kitchen counter, and the floor all covered with rice grains and as sticky as glue! Recently I have been surprised to learn that few young Japanese people today know how to make proper rice balls. I feel sorry that they are missing the great adventure that I experienced in my childhood.

The stuffing ingredients in this preparation are smoked salmon, Japanese pickled vegetables, and *umeboshi* (pickled plums). Create your own special rice balls by using whatever stuffing strikes your fancy.

2¹/₄ cups (3 rice-cooker cups) white short-grain Japanese
rice or medium-grain California rice
3 ounces smoked salmon
2 umeboshi (pickled plums), pitted and chopped fine
¹/₃ cup tsukemono (Japanese pickled vegetables,
page 78), diced fine
1 tablespoon white sesame seeds, toasted (see page 100)
3 or 6 nori sheets
1 teaspoon salt

Rinse, soak, and cook the rice as described on page 152.

While the rice is cooking, place the smoked salmon slices on lightly greased aluminum foil, and broil them close to the heat source until the surface is lightly charred here and there. Cut the smoked salmon into ¹/₂-inch squares.

In a bowl, combine the chopped plums and pickled vegetables and the toasted sesame seeds.

Retoast the nori over high heat as described on page 129. Cut each sheet in half cross-wise.

Have a small bowl of 1 cup water mixed with 1 teaspoon salt and a teacup at hand. As soon as the rice has finished cooking (it must be very hot), divide it into thirds, and put one-quarter of the rice from that portion into the teacup. Press the rice in the center to make a deep depression. Place half of the smoked salmon in the depression, and cover it with another quarter portion of hot rice.

Lightly moisten your palms with the salt water to prevent the rice grains from sticking to your hands. Now transfer all the stuffed rice in the teacup to your palm, and shape the rice, squeezing it into a firm, round ball. Wrap the rice ball with a half-sheet of nori. Then, if you like, cover it completely with another half sheet.

Make a second rice ball with smoked salmon. Make two with pickled vegetables, and make two more with a mixture of pickled plums and sesame seeds.

- *Yields 6 rice balls, 2 each of 3 flavors, for 3 servings as a light lunch or 6 servings as a snack*

TOFU
TONYU • Soy Milk
OKARA • Soybean Pulp

Tofu

When I was small, every community in Japan had its own mom-and-pop tofu store, the *tofu-ya*, where fresh tofu was made every day, starting in the very early morning. My mother often sent me to buy a block of tofu from one of these small operations. The owners of the *tofu-ya* in my neighborhood, a middle-aged couple wearing crisp white cotton uniforms with large, heavy rubber aprons and rubber boots, worked hard all day long. When I passed the store early in the morning on my way to school, the windows of this *tofu-ya* were always cloudy with steam, and the sweet smell of cooked soybeans permeated the area. I liked to go to the store to purchase tofu and observe the sales ritual. When the wife saw me running to her store with a large steel bowl in my hands, she always greeted me with a big smile. After receiving my order, she very carefully lifted up the end of a large piece of freshly made tofu in its tub of water. She then cut the tofu directly on her hand into smaller squares, about 10 ounces each, with a large aluminum knife shaped like a Chinese cleaver. She gently pushed the uncut piece back into the water, then quickly wrapped the cut tofu in *kyogi*, a very thin sheet of cedar or cypress wood, and carefully placed it in the bowl that I was holding. Her sodden, wrinkled hands, which showed the years of hard work and the continual immersion in hot and cold water, always impressed me. When I paid her, I always felt sorry, because the very low price of the tofu did not seem to compensate for all of the hard work she and her husband did.

Tofu peddlers also bicycled around my neighborhood selling freshly made tofu from a locker mounted on the bike. The peddler announced his arrival in the neighborhood by blowing a small trumpetlike horn. This tradition survives in some areas, but it is quickly disappearing today, as is delicious tofu made in mom-and-pop shops. Many of these tofu makers were forced to close their operations because they had no successors to take over their small family businesses.

And so mass-produced tofu has become the norm. To buy this type, you go to the supermarket. The tofu is already packed in a white plastic case with water and sealed with clear plastic wrap on top. Unfortunately, there is no steam, no smell of cooked soybeans, and no lasting memories coming from those white blocks in plastic containers.

In Okinawa Prefecture, the southernmost island of Japan, the population is known for having the greatest longevity and a low incidence of cardiovascular diseases. When their diet was studied, it was found that Okinawan people consume twice as much tofu as other

Japanese. Their cuisine also includes large quantities of sea vegetables, seasonal vegetables, and pork. Tofu is, of course, not the only contributor to their longevity and lower rate of certain diseases, but their high intake of tofu does seem to have a great effect on their health.

Tofu was brought to Japan along with Buddhism from China by way of the Korean Peninsula around the twelfth century. Tofu was first prepared and used in cooking by priests at Buddhist temples. By the seventeenth century, tofu had finally reached the commoners' kitchens, and it became a very popular ingredient in vegetarian dishes. This popularity led to the publication of two tofu cookbooks in the middle of the eighteenth century. Together, these two cookbooks contain 238 recipes. Some of these preparations remain popular today.

Tofu is available in two different styles: a firm, rough type and a soft, silky type. Different production processes create these differences in texture as well as variations in flavor and nutrients. The ingredients employed in tofu production are dried whole soybeans, spring water, and a natural coagulant, *nigari*, which is a mineral extract from seawater. *Nigari* contains such chemicals as magnesium chloride and calcium sulfate. At large tofu factories today, this natural coagulating agent may be replaced by chemically synthesized agents.

Let's observe the traditional tofu production process. Dried soybeans are first soaked in water overnight. Then the beans are ground with water until they are thoroughly mashed. In the past this process was done in a large stone mortar; today a machine is used. The mashed soybeans are transferred to a pot with water, and cooked. Cooking eliminates unpleasant aromas and flavors found in raw soybeans, and also dissolves the water-soluble protein, vitamins, starch, and minerals in the cooking liquid. The mixture is then pressed through a colander lined with a cotton cloth, and is thereby separated into *tonyu*, soy milk, and *okara*, soybean mash. The coagulating agent is then stirred into the soy milk.

To make firm tofu, the mixture is poured into a cotton-lined square wooden box whose bottom has many holes. Another piece of cotton cloth is placed on top of the mixture, a weight is placed on top, and the tofu is then left for a while. During this period, excess water is pressed out of the tofu. When removed from the box, the finished, firm tofu block has distinctive imprints on all sides from the *momen*, or cotton cloth. So this type of tofu is named *momen dofu*, "cotton tofu."

The soft type of tofu, which is called *kinu dofu*, "silk tofu," is made without the cloth and the weight, and thus contains more water and has a softer and smoother texture, like silk, *kinu*. Soft tofu has a lighter, less concentrated soybean flavor and slightly less protein and fat than firm tofu. Soft tofu is also slightly higher in water-soluble vitamins and minerals than its firmer cousin.

In Japan tofu is often enjoyed in a very simple way. Freshly made tofu, either firm or soft, is eaten uncooked, chilled and served with several condiments and a little *shoyu* (soy sauce) regardless of the season. This dish is called *hiya-yakko*. Popular condiments are grated fresh ginger, chopped scallion, bonito fish flakes, spicy salted cod roe, or seasonal herbs such as shiso leaves and *myoga* ginger. You may also enjoy chilled fresh tofu in salads.

In miso soup, either type of tofu is suitable.

For stir-frying and deep-frying preparations, firm tofu is more suitable since it contains less water.

Tofu is also used in sauces and dressings, after creaming it in a *suribachi* or other mortar. You can instead break up tofu in a bowl with a fork, and then finish creaming the tofu with a sturdy spatula. But don't blend tofu in a food processor—it would produce an unpalatable, overly smooth texture.

Before using tofu in stir-fried or deep-fried preparations or salad dressings, always remove some of the water from the tofu. This process is called *mizukiri*, "to cut out excess water." If the tofu is later to be creamed, simply squeeze it in a tightly woven, clean cotton cloth. If you want to maintain the shape of the tofu block, wrap the block in a clean cotton cloth and place it between heavy dinner plates or small chopping boards at a slight incline, and let it stand for a while. The water will drain away from the tofu. How much water should be removed depends on the character of each brand of tofu. To judge when water removal is complete, break off a corner of the block, and press the tofu between your fingers. If the process is complete, water will no longer exude.

In the West even today, tofu still seems to be favored only by health-conscious people. Ironically, its low price makes people feel uncomfortable about using tofu for special occasions. It is time to overcome prejudice against tofu and to enjoy it fully and frequently.

SOURCES: Fresh tofu is sold in refrigerator cases at Japanese and Asian food stores and in most supermarkets. Health- and natural-food stores carry tofu made with a natural coagulating agent. Some Asian stores carry fresh tofu in bulk, in a large, water-filled display case. When purchasing this type of tofu, you should make sure the water is clean and cold. Long-keeping tofu, packed in an aseptic foil pouch, can be found at Japanese and Asian stores and in some large supermarkets, unrefrigerated.

WHAT TO LOOK FOR: One block of tofu weighs between $10\frac{1}{2}$ and 16 ounces. It is better to purchase tofu packed in a sealed water-filled container rather than in bulk, so that you can be assured that the water in which the tofu is packed is clean. Tofu is also sold in vacuum-sealed plastic bags without water in refrigerator cases. Personally, I am not keen about long-keeping tofu, since it does not have a rich tofu flavor.

STORAGE: Tofu in an aseptic package, before it is opened, keeps one year without refrigeration.

Plan to use fresh tofu within two to three days after the date of manufacture, or check the label for a suggested usage date. Refrigerate fresh tofu in its original package. After opening the package, transfer leftover tofu to a container and cover it with clean, cold water, and change the water every day.

Tonyu (Soy Milk)

Soy milk is sold in bottles or cartons in the refrigerator case. Fresh bottled soy milk should be consumed on the day of purchase. Long-keeping soy milk is packed in aseptic foil-lined cartons. Refrigerate an opened carton, and consume the soy milk within three days or before the suggested usage date. Most soy milk sold in the United States contains additives, such as corn syrup, salt, and other flavorings. Check the label to be sure you are buying pure soy milk.

Soy milk is a good substitute for milk or cream in soups and other preparations. When you use soy milk in cooking, do not overheat it, or the protein will curdle and take on an undesirable texture and appearance.

Okara (Soybean Pulp)

This, wet, pale yellow, fluffy mash is left over when soy milk is extracted from soybeans. Soybean pulp contains a substantial amount of protein, calcium, and dietary fiber, and it is very inexpensive. It is used to make one of the most popular and delicious Japanese home dishes, *unohana*, in which dry-roasted *okara* is cooked in a little sesame oil, *shoyu* (soy sauce), and *mirin* (sweet cooking wine) with julienned vegetables such as carrot, burdock, and dried shiitake mushrooms. The combination produces a delightful, nutritious side dish. Soybean pulp can also be used as a nutritious replacement for part of the flour in baked goods.

Unfortunately, this side product from tofu manufacturing is hard to find outside Japan and very perishable. But if you can locate a tofu manufacturer in your area, you may be able to obtain some pulp from that source. Try a little detective work to see if you can find this wonderful food.

FIRM TOFU FROM SCRATCH

Tezukuri Momen-dofu

Today natural-food stores have begun to sell *nigari*, the coagulating agent used in making fresh tofu. So it is now possible for many cooks to make their own tofu from scratch. The process of making tofu is very simple, but requires a bit of patience. Homemade tofu has a sweet soybean aroma and flavor that is not often found in commercial versions. Try making your own!

Superior tofu is made with three important ingredients: superior-quality soybeans, which contain less fat than the beans raised to produce oil; clean spring water; and natural *nigari,* rather than a chemical coagulating agent. You can find these materials at natural-food stores.

7 ounces (about 1¹/₃ cups) dried soybeans
2 teaspoons nigari (coagulant)

Soak the soybeans in 4¹/₂ cups water (preferably spring water) for 8 hours in warm weather, or 20 hours in winter.

Dissolve the *nigari* in 6 tablespoons lukewarm spring water.

In a food processor, grind the soybeans with their soaking water for 2 minutes or until the beans are ground fine. In a large pot, bring 5 cups spring water to a boil. Add the ground soybeans to the pot, and bring the mixture almost to a boil over medium heat, stirring continuously with a wooden spatula. Immediately before the mixture comes to a boil, reduce the heat to low. Cook the beans for 8 minutes, stirring.

Strain the hot mixture through a strainer lined with finely woven cotton cloth. You may wish to wear clean rubber gloves for protection from the heat. Reserve the very nutritious pulp, called *okara*, for other preparations, but remember that you must use the pulp the same day, because it does not keep. Transfer the soy milk to the pot, and cook the soy milk over low heat, stirring continuously with the wooden spatula. When the temperature registers between 150 to 155 degrees F, remove the pot from the heat.

Add half of the *nigari* mixture to the soy milk, stirring with the spatula in a whirlpool pattern. Add the remaining *nigari* mixture, and this time stir gently, making a figure eight. Soon you will notice that the soy milk is beginning to coagulate. Cover the pot, and let it stand for 15 minutes.

Line a colander with a tightly woven cotton cloth, and set the colander over a bowl that can support it. With a soup ladle, gently transfer the coagulated soy milk to the cloth-lined colander. Fold the cloth over the top of the coagulated soy milk, and place a weight of about $1\frac{1}{2}$ pounds on top. Let the tofu stand for 15 minutes. This process removes excess water and makes the tofu firm.

Place a large bowl in the sink, and fill it with cold water. Remove the weight from the tofu, unfold the cotton cloth, and gently transfer the tofu to the cold water. Gently run cold water from the tap into the bowl for 15 minutes, without letting the water hit the tofu directly.

Serve the tofu immediately as *hiya-yakko*, or store it in fresh cold water in the refrigerator.

- *Yields about 14 ounces firm tofu*

BASIC RECIPE

FRESH TOFU WITH GINGER, SCALLIONS, AND TAMARI

Hiya-yakko

When you have made your own tofu or purchased it fresh from a really good source, this is the best way to enjoy its delightful flavor.

> 1 block fresh soft or firm tofu (11 to 14 ounces), chilled
> 2 tablespoons finely grated ginger, with its juice
> 2 scallions, white and green parts, cut into thin disks
> 1 teaspoon white sesame seeds, toasted (see page 100)
> Tamari

Cut the chilled tofu into bite-sized pieces, about $1\frac{1}{2}$ inches on each side. Arrange the tofu cubes on a large serving platter. Top each square with a portion of the ginger, scallions, and sesame seeds.

Each diner should transfer some of the tofu squares to an individual plate and pour about $\frac{1}{4}$ teaspoon tamari over each square.

- *Yields 2 servings*

ASPARAGUS, MANGO, AND APPLE IN A CREAMY TOFU DRESSING

Shira-ae

Shira-ae literally means "dressed in white." As the name implies, this salad is tossed with a creamy white dressing, which is made from firm tofu and ground white sesame seeds. Traditional ingredients in the salad include flavored and simmered carrot, *hijiki* sea vegetable, spinach, and chrysanthemum leaves. Here I use asparagus and fresh fruit.

In the past, all the sesame seeds for this dressing were freshly toasted and then ground to a fine paste in a *suribachi* or other mortar. Today commercial sesame paste is used. However, adding a small amount of freshly ground white sesame seeds to the sesame paste greatly improves the flavor of this dressing. If Japanese sesame paste is not available, use tahini, or Chinese sesame paste without added ingredients.

Before tossing the vegetables and fruit with the dressing, please be sure to spin or wipe them dry, so that the dressing is not diluted with water.

¹/₂ block (about 7 ounces) firm tofu

2 tablespoons white sesame seeds, toasted (see page 100)

3 tablespoons sesame paste, preferably Japanese

1 tablespoon usukuchi shoyu *(light-colored soy sauce),*
       preferably, or regular shoyu

1 tablespoon mirin *(sweet cooking wine)*

Salt

9 ounces asparagus, tough ends and tips removed

¹/₂ mango, pitted, peeled, and cut into ¹/₂-inch cubes

1 crisp, tart apple, cored, cut into ¹/₂-inch cubes,
       and tossed with lemon juice

Set the tofu in a basket or colander that will fit inside a medium pot. In the pot, bring plenty of water to a boil. Blanch the tofu for 20 seconds. Drain it, place it on a tightly woven cotton cloth, and squeeze it to remove excess water.

In a *suribachi* mortar, preferably, or in another mortar, grind the toasted sesame seeds fine. Add the sesame paste, and grind until the mixture is well combined. Add the tofu, and grind until the mixture is creamy and fluffy. Mix in the *shoyu*, the *mirin*, and a little salt. The dressing may be stored in the refrigerator, covered, for use later in the day.

In a medium pot of boiling water, parboil the asparagus for 1 minute. Drain it, plunge it into cold water to stop the cooking, and wipe it dry in a paper towel. Cut the asparagus into $1/_2$-inch pieces.

Immediately before serving, toss salad ingredients with tofu dressing. Serve the salad in small individual bowls or place it next to broiled fish or meat on a dinner plate.

- *Yields 4 to 6 servings as a side dish*

TOFU SEIHIN • Cooked Tofu Products

At Japanese stores you can find a variety of tofu products, usually next to fresh tofu in the display case. These tofu products are not to be confused with tempeh, a fermented soybean product of Indonesian origin.

Abura-age (Fried Thin Tofu)

Abura-age, fried thin tofu, is prepared by cutting tofu into thin sheets, about 1/4 inch thick, and then cooking the sheets in oil. The cooked sheets are golden brown and look rather like cloth. One of the most popular tofu products, *abura-age* is used in many preparations, such as miso soups, noodle dishes, simmered dishes, and stir-fried dishes. Try it simply grilled or broiled until crisp, cut into strips, and served with blanched spinach and a little *tosazu* dressing (page 74).

One type of *abura-age*, called *sushi-age*, is sold specially for the preparation of *inarizushi*, small barrel-shaped, brown sushi. *Sushi-age* comes slit to make a pocket into which sushi rice can be stuffed.

In one of the Japanese folk religions, foxes are believed to act as mediators between the people and the God of the Harvest, that is, the God who ensures good business. Foxes, so the story goes, love *abura-age*. Therefore at shrines for the God of the Harvest, Inari, stone statues of foxes stand as guardians inside the red shrine gate, and worshipers customarily make offerings of *abura-age* or *inarizushi* to these guardians. Inari shrines are found everywhere in Japan—even at busy, urban street corners and on the roofs of large office buildings in the center of Tokyo.

Before using *abura-age* in any preparation, rinse it with boiling water to remove excess oil. This technique is called *aburakiri*. After rinsing it, squeeze it gently but thoroughly to remove excess water.

Atsuage (Fried Tofu)

Atsuage, also known as *nama-age,* is sometimes sold in the United States as "tofu cutlet." It is prepared by cooking a whole block of tofu in oil until the outside is golden brown. When cut, *atsuage* displays its snow-white interior. This fried tofu is a popular ingredient in simmered dishes, because the outer layer absorbs flavors more easily than fresh tofu does. Fried tofu also imparts an extra-rich flavor to the simmering broth, and maintains its texture while being simmered. *Atsuage* is ideal for stir-frying as well, and produces delicious vegetarian dishes.

Like *abura-age*, *atsuage* needs to be rinsed in boiling water to remove excess oil— before further preparation.

Ganmodoki (Fried Tofu Dumplings)

These "false wild goose" dumplings are made by mixing mashed tofu, julienned vegetables, and some sea vegetables, forming small balls of the mixture, and then deep-frying them. *Ganmodoki* was invented by poor people who could not afford wild goose meat for their dumplings.

Ganmodoki are used in traditional simmered preparations. Like *atsuage*, the dumplings have a skin that absorbs all of the good flavors from the broth in which they are cooked. Homemade piping hot *ganmodoki* served with a tempura dipping sauce, *ganmodoki* is a delicious side dish.

Before using store-purchased cold *ganmodoki,* rinse the dumplings with boiling water to remove excess oil.

Yakidofu (Lightly Broiled Tofu)

Yakidofu is a broiled tofu block, whose surface shows charring here and there. Together with thinly sliced beef, *nananegi* long onion, chrysanthemum leaves, and *shirataki* (taro gelatin noodles), *yakidofu* is a usual ingredient in *sukiyaki.* Broiled tofu is also used in other hot-pot preparations.

Yuba (Soy Milk Sheet)

When cow's milk is heated, a thin film begins to cover the surface. *Yuba* is the film that forms in the same way on the top of heated soy milk. Because freshly collected *yuba* is soft and fragile, many sheets may be piled together and rolled into a 1-inch-thick stick. The stick is chilled, cut into bite-sized pieces, and eaten with a little *shoyu* (soy sauce) and grated wasabi. Fresh *yuba* has a wonderful creamy texture and a sweet, nutty taste.

Because fresh *yuba* is very perishable, most *yuba* found at stores is in the form of a dried sheet. Before using a dried sheet of *yuba*, reconstitute it in water. After it has regained its flexibility and silky texture, it makes an ideal wrapper for meat and vegetables in fried and simmered dishes.

SOURCES: *Abura-age* (fried thin tofu), *atsuage* (fried tofu), *yakidofu* (broiled tofu), *gan-modoki* (fried tofu dumplings), and dried *yuba* (soy milk sheet), are sold at Japanese food stores and some Asian food stores. At Asian stores you may find similar but non-Japanese products; these may have a different appearance, taste, and texture than their Japanese counterparts. Except for dried *yuba,* all of the products are sold in refrigerator cases. *Abura-age* freezes well, so you may find it in freezer cases as well.

WHAT TO LOOK FOR: *Abura-age* (fried thin tofu) comes in rectangular sheets, two of which are packed together in a clear plastic bag. Each sheet weighs around $^3/_4$ ounce.

Atsuage (fried tofu), comes in blocks the size of fresh tofu blocks and is packed in clear bags or placed on trays and wrapped in plastic.

Ganmodoki (fried tofu dumplings), are sold as small, deflated-looking balls, from golf-ball to tennis-ball size. Several come packed in a plastic bag.

Because of its charred appearance, *yakidofu* (broiled tofu), is easily distinguished from other tofu products. It is packed in the same manner as fresh tofu.

Dried *yuba* (soy milk sheet), comes in various dimensions. The sheets are paper-thin and very fragile, and their color varies from creamy yellow to mustard yellow. The sheets come packed in plastic bags.

STORAGE: Except for dried *yuba* (soy milk sheet), all of these products should be refrigerated in sealed containers and used within 3 days. Fresh *yuba* keeps only one day. Dried *yuba* keeps more than a year if it is stored in a cool, dark, and dry place. After reconstituting dried *yuba*, use it immediately. *Abura-age* (fried thin tofu) freezes very well, but the other products do not.

GRILLED CHEESE-STUFFED FRIED THIN TOFU

Abura-age no Fukuro-yaki

This is a simple, pleasant new way to enjoy the flavor and texture of *abura-age* (fried thin tofu).

> *2 sheets* abura-age *(fried thin tofu)*
> *6 slices cheddar cheese, 2 inches square and* $^1/_4$ *inch thick*
> *2 tablespoons green sliced scallion*
> *Tamari*
> *Grated daikon*

Rinse the tofu with boiling water to remove excess oil, and then squeeze it to remove excess water. Carefully cut open one end of each tofu piece to make a pocket. Stuff half the cheddar cheese and scallion into each pocket. Close the open ends with toothpicks.

Grill or broil the tofu close to the heat source until the outside is crisp and the cheese inside is melted. Cut each pocket into four pieces, sprinkle a little tamari over them, and serve them with the daikon on the side.

• *Yields 2 servings as an appetizer*

UMEBOSHI • Pickled Plums

Umeboshi, pickled plums, are made from *ume*, Japanese green plums (see page 50). The reddish color of *umeboshi* is obtained by employing a purple shiso (*akajiso*) leaf in the pickling process. In the past, *ume* were pickled in many homes, especially in the country. Today the tradition of pickling *ume* at home barely survives, because the preparation requires long hours of labor, patience, and experience. Homemade *umeboshi* have been nearly completely replaced by commercially prepared products, which are available everywhere.

Umeboshi look like deflated, wrinkled, small balls. Hence the phrase *umeboshi (o)bāsan*, "an old lady whose skin is shriveled like the skin of an *umeboshi*," was born. In Japan this phrase does not carry a bad connotation, but is used in a pleasant way. However, I wonder why nobody says *umeboshi (o)jīsan* ("*umeboshi* old gentleman")!

The pickling begins in early June, during the rainy season. Named in honor of the ubiquitous green plums, *tsuyu*, or the "plum rain season," stretches to the end of July. During this season, wet green plums hang on the trees in the quietly falling rain.

To make *umeboshi*, the picked plums are first soaked in water overnight. They are then drained, wiped dry, and layered with salt in a porcelain pot. After several days, the plums become covered with their own tart juices. They are left as they are until the purple shiso plant bears its mature leaves. Shiso leaves are then added to the brine, which quickly turns a bright crimson hue. When the weather becomes stable, by the beginning of August, the plums are taken out of the liquid and transferred to a bamboo tray. The tray with the plums is then placed on top of the pot with the plum liquid, and the two together are left in the sun for a day, during which the plums cure and the liquid concentrates. At night the plums are returned to the brine, and for two more days the process is repeated. After three days and nights of drying and soaking, the plums begin to exhibit deep wrinkles and a covering of salt grains. The finished pickled plums are then packed in a storage container.

The pickled plums are eaten with many dishes. *Umeboshi* and plain cooked white rice have been good partners for years. *Onigiri*, rice balls, are stuffed with pitted pickled plums. Plain cooked white rice packed in an *obento* lunch box is almost always decorated with a pickled plum in the center. The tiny red *umeboshi* brightens up the plain white rice and provides a very appetizing tart, salty flavor. And because the *umeboshi* has antiseptic properties, it slows the spoilage of the rice with which it is packed. This lunch was once called Hinomaru *bento*, Japanese flag lunch box, because of its resemblance to the Japanese flag, the Hinomaru.

Pickled plums are healthful. Although they are tart, *umeboshi* alkalize the blood and help in restoring energy.

SOURCES: *Umeboshi* (pickled plums) are sold at Japanese food stores, some Asian food stores, and health- and natural-food stores. Asian food stores carry pickled plums made in other Asian countries, which are very different from the Japanese product.

WHAT TO LOOK FOR: *Umeboshi* are sold in a glass jar, a small plastic container, or a plastic bag. The plums look deflated, and their skins are shriveled. Some plums, especially the traditional types, look drier than others, because they have undergone a lengthy drying process and are much saltier. A recent health-food boom gave birth to moderately salted, quickly pickled plums, called *shio-hikaeme umeboshi*. These plums are much juicier. A paste made of pickled plums, called *neri-ume*, is also available. Plum paste is spread over foods and mixed into dressings and sauces.

STORAGE: Traditional *umeboshi* keep one year at room temperature, but as time goes by the plums get drier and lose their rich flavor. *Neri-ume*, plum paste, also keeps about a year at room temperature. Refrigerate low-salt pickled plums, covered, and consume by the suggested usage date.

BASIC RECIPE

UMEBOSHI WITH COOKED RICE

1¹/₂ *cups (2 rice-cooker cups) hot freshly cooked white rice*
2 *umeboshi (pickled plums), pitted and chopped fine*
1 *tablespoon minced parsley*
1 *tablespoon white sesame seeds, toasted (see page 100)*
1 *teaspoon virgin olive oil (optional)*

Toss the hot rice with all the other ingredients. The olive oil gives an extra gloss and smoothness to the rice.

• *Yields 2 servings*

BASIC RECIPE

UMEBOSHI DRESSING

1 *umeboshi (pickled plum), pitted and chopped*
2 *tablespoons* komezu *(rice vinegar)*
2 *teaspoons sugar*
2 *tablespoons virgin olive oil*
Tamari

Grind the *umeboshi* in a *suribachi* or other mortar to make a smooth purée. Loosen the purée with the *komezu*, blend in the sugar, and, while grinding, slowly drizzle in the olive oil. Blend in a little tamari, and serve the dressing over mixed salad greens.

• *Yields about ¹/₃ cup dressing*

WAKAME • Sea Vegetable

Wakame is one of the most popular sea vegetables in the Japanese diet. It appears in miso soups, noodle dishes, salads, sashimi, and simmered dishes. Manuscripts from the ninth century show that the ancient Japanese already knew the nutritional importance of *wakame*.

Wakame can be written in Japanese *kanji* characters in either of two combinations: as the characters for *young* and *woman*, or as the characters for *young* and *bud*. Both of these are pronounced *waka-me*. As the characters convey, *wakame* has always been regarded as a healthful food that prevents our bodies from aging.

Wakame sea vegetable was once harvested from the wild in Japanese waters, from the northernmost island of Hokkaido to the southernmost island of Okinawa. Cultivation began during the 1960s. Today most of the *wakame* consumed in Japan is cultivated. Differences in water temperature and other conditions produce differences in quality, so that cultivated *wakame* may be soft or hard, and thick or thin. I prefer *wakame* from Iwate Prefecture, on the Pacific Ocean side of the main Japanese island of Honshu, 300 kilometers north of Tokyo. This *wakame* has a thicker leaf and a crunchier texture than others.

Laboratory studies have proved *wakame's* immense nutritional value. Chemicals in the water-soluble fibers of the sea vegetable remove excess sodium from the body, reduce blood cholesterol, and work as an anticoagulating agent in the blood. These chemicals also bind up toxic minerals such as cadmium, mercury, and lead, and remove them from the body. The dietary fiber abundant in this sea vegetable helps prevent constipation and thereby ultimately reduces the risk of colon cancer. *Wakame* is an excellent source of calcium, especially when consumed along with foods rich in protein and vitamin C, which, some studies show, cause the absorption of calcium from *wakame* to triple. The iron content of *wakame* is moderately high, and *wakame* is rich in vitamins A and B_2, iodine, and other trace minerals. Furthermore, it is a no-calorie food. To get the most benefit from *wakame*, consume a small portion every day as part of a healthy diet.

Cultivated *wakame* sea vegetable is harvested from January to April. In the past, the only way of preserving freshly harvested *wakame* was by coating it with ash and drying it in the sun. Today the most popular storage method starts with parboiling *wakame* in boiling salt water for 30 to 50 seconds. The naturally brown sea vegetable becomes a bright, dark green. The *wakame* is then brine-pickled. Later, the brined sea vegetable is partially freeze-dried, leaving the leaves with a shiny, wet appearance. This final product is called *yutoshi shiozo wakame*.

Before using *yutoshi shiozo wakame*, soak it in water for about 10 minutes, and then rinse it thoroughly to remove excess salt. After rinsing, have a little bite. Rinse the *wakame* further if it still tastes salty.

Recent technology has allowed the introduction of a new, convenient, instant form of *wakame* sea vegetable, called *katto wakame*. To make this product, harvested *wakame* is blanched, frozen, cut into small pieces, and completely dried in a machine dryer. Reconstituting *katto wakame* requires only two minutes in cold water. Instant *wakame* is widely available outside Japan, and I always use this type because of the convenience. After reconstitution, the leaves are ready to be used in salad, with sashimi, or in simmered dishes. When used as a soup ingredient, instant *wakame* is added directly to the prepared hot soup.

Note that instant *wakame* swells to about ten times its original volume: 1 tablespoon instant *wakame* makes $1/2$ cup ($1^1/2$ ounces) reconstituted *wakame*. Do not reconstitute more than you need, since reconstituted *wakame* spoils quickly.

No matter which type of *wakame* you use, do not cook it for longer than a few minutes, or it will discolor and become unpleasantly soft.

SOURCES: *Wakame* is sold in the dried-food sections of Japanese, Asian, and health- and natural-food stores. Some large supermarkets also carry this sea vegetable.

WHAT TO LOOK FOR: At Japanese food stores you may find the following three different types of *wakame*: (1) completely dried *hoshi wakame*, (2) moist-looking, salt-covered *yutōshi shiozo wakame*; and (3) instant *katto wakame*. All of these types are sold in clear plastic bags. The easiest to store and use is *katto wakame*, and this type has recently become the most available *wakame* in the large cities of the United States.

STORAGE: Completely dried *wakame* and instant *katto wakame* keep for about a year. Freeze-dried *yutoshi shiozo wakame* can be enjoyed for about two months. Refrigerate an opened package of *yutoshi shiozo wakame*, sealed.

WAKAME AND CUCUMBER IN SANBAIZU DRESSING

Wakame to Kyuri no Sunomono

In this simple and refreshing dish, cucumber and *wakame* are dressed with mellow, sweet *sanbaizu* dressing. The cucumber is treated with a popular Japanese technique: It is cut into paper-thin slices, then soaked in salt water. This removes excess water from the cucumber and makes it more flexible, while retaining its crispiness. Extracting excess water also makes the cucumber absorb the flavor of the dressing more effectively. The same technique can be applied to such vegetables as daikon, radish, carrot, Chinese cabbage, and ordinary cabbage. The addition of cooked crabmeat to this salad provides extra flavor, color, and texture. You might instead use other cooked shellfish or fish, tossed with lemon juice or vinegar.

> 2 teaspoons salt
> 1 Japanese cucumber or ¹/₃ large salad cucumber
> 1¹/₂ tablespoons instant wakame *sea vegetable, soaked in*
>   *water for 2 minutes*
> 1 cup cooked crabmeat, tossed with juice of
>   ¹/₄ lemon (optional)
> ¹/₄ cup sanbaizu *dressing (see page 74)*

Dissolve the salt in 2 cups cold water in a medium bowl. Cut the cucumber into paper-thin slices, discarding both ends, and soak the slices in the salt water for 10 minutes.

Drain the *wakame*. In a colander, rinse it briefly under cold water, and squeeze it firmly to remove excess water. Drain, rinse, and squeeze the cucumber the same way.

Toss the cucumber, the *wakame*, and, if you're using it, the crabmeat with the *sanbaizu* dressing.

• *Yields 4 servings as a side dish*

KOME • Rice

"Let's have a meal" in Japanese is *Gohan ni shiyo* (male speech)/*Gohan ni shimasho* (female speech). *Gohan* literally means "cooked rice" (raw rice is *kome*). So the phrase literally means "Let's eat cooked rice." This illustrates the central role rice plays in Japanese cuisine. My mother always told us at the table that we should not leave a single grain in our rice bowls. Wasting even a grain of cooked rice humiliates the farmers, who went through such difficult yearlong labor to produce it.

Although a piece of toast, Italian bread, or a French baguette now frequently appears at breakfast, lunch, and dinner in Japan, a bowl of plain cooked rice remains the central component of a Japanese meal, a source of carbohydrates and high-quality protein. Indeed, the Japanese have found ways to maintain the central position of rice in the cuisine despite foreign culinary influences.

In the late nineteenth century, the introduction of beef and other foods to Japan gave birth to a number of new dishes. One of these is *gyudon*, beef bowl (page 304). Thinly sliced beef and onions are simmered with *shoyu* (soy sauce) and sugar, and these ingredients together with the simmering broth are placed on top of a bowl of plain cooked rice. *Omu Raisu* (page 316), another rice dish born in this period, was inspired by the French omelette: Rice flavored with tomato ketchup and morsels of chicken is wrapped up in an omelette. Even the name of this dish is borrowed from the West: *Omu* is a contraction of *omelette*, and *raisu* comes from the English *rice*. So while incorporating new ingredients and concepts, *gyudon*, *omuraisu*, and other new dishes kept rice in its central role at the table.

Japanese rice, a short-grain type, is produced in every prefecture of Japan, including the Tokyo Metropolitan district. Major producing prefectures are Niigata, Yamagata, Toyama, Miyagi, Akita, Iwate, Ibaragi, and Hokkaido. Each prefecture has its own distinct regional variety of rice and sells it by discriminating its product from those in other regions. There is a subtle difference in flavor from one variety to another. People continuously debate whether a particular variety of rice tastes better than the others. However, what someone thinks is best may depend on the prefecture from which he or she comes! People in Niigata Prefecture, where my parents come from, always trust their rice, but seldom other types.

In Japan, rice is sold in three different forms: *genmai*, *haigamai*, and *seihakumai*. *Genmai* is unpolished, brown rice: *haigamai* is partially polished; and *seihakumai* is a polished, white variety. Of these three, the most popular is *seihakumai*, even though the polishing process removes much of the nutrients—including thiamine, riboflavin, and niacin—and dietary fiber. Partially polished *haigamai* includes the rice germ and, therefore, the nutrients of that vital part of the grain. *Haigamai* should not be rinsed before cooking, lest the germ be rinsed away.

In addition to ordinary table rice, short-grain *mochigome*, glutinous rice or sweet rice, is also popular in either polished or unpolished form. Glutinous rice is used in rice dishes in which greater stickiness is called for. It is also used to make certain Japanese sweets and *mochi,* glutinous rice cake.

Mochi is made by pounding hot, steamed glutinous rice in a very large wooden mortar. This operation requires two strong, skilled people—one who pounds the rice with a heavy wooden malletlike pestle, and another who helps by turning over the rice after every blow, so that the rice is evenly pounded. It is a rhythmical, high-speed operation. When I was small, watching *mochitsuki*, glutinous rice pounding, was a great thrill. I was always amazed how the man who swung down the heavy wooden mallet from high above his head managed several hundred blows without hitting the hand of his apparently unworried colleague.

Freshly pounded *mochi* is a smooth, soft, silky, snow white dough. When you touch it you will find it very sticky, and when you eat it, although it tastes wonderful, its stickiness may remind you of peanut butter. In a short time the soft dough hardens. Before this happens, the pounded *mochi* is flattened into a thin square and then cut into small cubical cakes, about 1 inch on each side, for storage. Although most *mochi* is made by machine today, *mochitsuki* is still practiced at the end of the year to prepare fresh glutinous rice cake, which is a part of the new year's feast.

To enjoy a bowl of rice at each meal, of course, you have to cook it. Today when you ask Japanese people how to cook rice, their answer is to prepare it in a rice cooker. Now every Japanese household, even a college student living in a tiny one-room apartment, is equipped with a rice cooker, *suihanki*. An example of Japanese electronic ingenuity, the modern rice cooker does more than cook rice. It keeps the cooked rice hot for as long as you wish, allows you to set the start of cooking time in advance, cooks different types of rice—polished or unpolished—and can be used to produce rice dishes with other ingredients, such as vegetables and meat.

To cook rice in a rice cooker, first measure the rice with the cup that came with the machine. Rinse the rice as described on page 152, cover it with water, and let the rice soak for 30 minutes in summer or 60 minutes in winter. Then put the rice into the cooker, and add enough of the soaking water to reach the line on the inside of the cooking pot. Select the button for white or brown, and press Start.

If you do not have a rice cooker, please do not worry. Cooking rice in a regular pot over a gas flame or electric burner is simple and easy to master. Just follow the recipe that begins on page 151.

In Japan, rice is also pulverized into flour. Unlike other Asian countries, however, Japan does not produce noodles made from rice flour. The flour is mainly used in snacks and sweets, such as rice crackers, steamed cakes, and dumplings. There are two kinds of rice flour: *Joshinko* is regular rice flour, made from rinsed, dried, and powdered rice. *Joshinko* is used to make steamed cakes. *Shiratamako* is glutinous rice flour, made from rinsed, soaked, pulverized, and dried glutinous rice. *Shiratamako* is used to make gooey dumplings, which are cooked in boiling water. Both of these flours have a silky, smooth texture and snow white color.

Rice is also made into meal. *Domyojiko*, used in steamed dishes, is made from glutinous rice flour, soaked, steamed, dried, and broken into tiny pieces. *Domyojiko* resembles coarse granulated sugar in texture, and its color is semitranslucent. *Shinbikiko*, toasted *domyojiko*, is composed of uniform, tiny, ball-shaped, snow white granules. *Shinbikiko* is used for coating foods to be deep-fried. When these tiny balls are cooked in oil, they pop up into even larger balls and create a snow white, pearly crust on the cooked food.

SOURCES: Short-grain rice, either polished or unpolished, is available in large supermarkets, Japanese and Asian food stores, and health- and natural-food stores. Medium-grain rice, also sold at these stores, is interchangeable with short-grain rice in all Japanese rice dishes, including sushi. *Mochigome*, glutinous or sweet rice, is found in both whole and flour forms at Japanese and Asian food stores. Rice-meal products are found at large Japanese food stores.

WHAT TO LOOK FOR: Check the year of production, if possible, and purchase rice that is no more than a year old. Newly harvested rice is sold in Japan under the name of *shinmai*, new rice. It contains more water than older rice, and so requires a little less water in cooking. Some rice is sold under the name of sushi rice. This is nothing more than ordinary Japanese short-grain rice.

STORAGE: Brown rice, *genmai*, has a shorter shelf life than white rice, because brown rice contains more fat. At warm temperatures fat quickly oxidizes, causing rancidity. So purchase brown rice in small quantities, refrigerate it in a sealed container, and use it within three months. Partially polished *haigamai* rice and polished, white *seihakumai* rice should be stored in a dark, dry, and cool place, and used within six months after purchase.

BASIC RECIPE

HOW TO COOK RICE ON A STOVE TOP

Gohan no Taki-kata

Water quantity: The ideal water-to-rice ratio can vary slightly, depending on how long the rice has been stored, the type of pot you are using, the weight of the lid, the total volume of rice you are cooking, and the level of heat from the flame or heating element. For example, a small amount of rice cooked on a gas or electric stove needs a little more water, proportionally, than does a larger amount of rice. But here are general rules to remember, for times that you can't check the table that follows:

- Polished, white *seihakumai* rice and partially polished *haigamai* rice require an amount of water equal to about 120 percent of the volume of dry rice. For example, 1 cup polished rice is cooked in $1^1/_5$ cups (or 1 cup plus about 3 tablespoons) water. For sushi rice, less water is used (see page 269).
- Unpolished, brown *genmai* rice requires an amount of water equal to 250 percent of the dry rice volume. For example, 1 cup brown rice is cooked in $2^1/_2$ cups water.
- Newly harvested *shinmai* rice is cooked in a volume of water equal to the volume of dry rice. For example, 1 cup *shinmai* rice is cooked in 1 cup water.
- *Mochigome*, glutinous rice, requires a volume of water equal to 80 percent of dry rice volume. For example, 1 cup glutinous rice requires $^4/_5$ cup (or $^3/_4$ cup plus about 1 tablespoon) water. Further, glutinous rice needs soaking in water overnight before cooking. Soaked, *drained* glutinous rice is usually cooked in a steamer with addi-

tional water sprinkled on the rice several times during cooking (see the recipe on page 153).

Measuring cups: In this cookbook, two different measures are used to specify the quantity of uncooked rice. To cook rice in a pot, follow the measurements given for regular cups. If you own a rice cooker, use the figures for rice-cooker cups, along with the cup that was supplied with the rice cooker when you purchased it. A rice-cooker cup has about four-fifths the volume of a U.S. cup.

RICE AND WATER QUANTITIES FOR STOVE-TOP BOILED RICE

Seihakumai (White Rice) and *Haigamai* (Partially Polished Rice)

RAW RICE	WATER	YIELD (IN POUNDS)
³/₄ cups	1 cup	0.7
1¹/₂ cups	1³/₄ cups + 1 tablespoon	1.4
2¹/₄ cups	2²/₃ cups + 2 teaspoons	2.1
3 cups	3¹/₂ cups	2.8

Genmai (Brown Rice)

RAW RICE	WATER	YIELD (IN POUNDS)
³/₄ cups	2 cups	0.7
1¹/₂ cups	3³/₄ cups	1.4
2¹/₄ cups	5¹/₄ cups + 2 tablespoons	2.1
3 cups	7¹/₄ cups	2.8

Rinsing and soaking rice: Before cooking Japanese white rice or any brown rice, place it in a bowl, cover it with cold water, and rub it in the water for 10 to 20 seconds. Quickly discard the liquid. Add fresh water, and repeat this process three times. After rubbing the rice, do not let it stand in the cloudy water, or the grains will absorb an unpleasant flavor from this liquid. Finally, soak the rice in the measured amount of clean cold water for half an hour in summer and an hour in winter. You will cook the rice in this soaking water.

Neither *haigamai*, partially polished rice, nor American enriched rice needs rinsing.

Rice for sushi should not be soaked, but should be rinsed and drained 1 hour before cooking (see page 267).

Cooking the rice: My method is a bit different from my mother's traditional method and those described in other cookbooks. I have been cooking rice this easy way with the greatest success for years, and I highly recommend it.

Place the rice and measured water in a heavy-bottomed pot. The correct pot size depends on how much rice is to be cooked. Select a pot that is deeper than wide. Because the water and rice will bubble up and down during cooking, and the rice will swell to as much as three times its original volume, the pot should be at least three times deeper than the water level after you have put the rice and water into the pot. Also the pot should have a tight-fitting, heavy lid. At high altitudes, where boiling occurs at lower temperatures, a heavy lid is essential to prevent excessive water evaporation before the rice is completely cooked.

Put the pot over medium heat. Cook the rice uncovered until the water level is decreased almost to the level of the rice. Reduce the heat to very low, cover the pot with a heavy lid, and continue cooking the rice until all the water is absorbed and the rice grains are plump. The exact cooking time depends on the type of pot, the amount of steam that escapes between the pot and the lid, and the quantity and condition of the rice. The standard time for cooking $1^1/_2$ to $2^1/_4$ cups white or partially polished rice is 10 to 15 minutes uncovered and another 10 to 15 minutes covered. The standard time for cooking brown rice is 15 to 20 minutes uncovered and 15 to 20 minutes covered.

Let the cooked rice stand, covered, for 10 minutes. This resting allows the moisture to settle into the rice grains, which makes the rice easier to toss.

Toss the rice gently with a wooden or bamboo rice spatula. It is then ready to serve.

BASIC RECIPE

STEAMED GLUTINOUS RICE

Okowa

Because glutinous rice, *mochigome*, absorbs less water when it is cooked than does ordinary rice, it is prepared in a different way. Glutinous rice requires overnight soaking in cold water. It is then usually cooked in a steamer. Each cooked grain develops a pleasant tender but chewy texture.

To steam glutinous rice in a bamboo or metal steamer, you need a coarsely woven square of cotton cloth. One specifically made for this preparation, 22 inches square, can be purchased at Japanese kitchen equipment stores. A substitute is coarse muslin or triple-layered cheesecloth.

Today there are other ways to cook glutinous rice. One of the latest models of electric rice cookers can be used. So can a microwave oven. These machines make it much easier to prepare *okowa* dishes. Instructions for cooking glutinous rice in a microwave are included here.

Often prepared for special occasions, *okowa* is frequently served with the condiment *gomashio*, a mixture of black sesame seeds and salt. The mixture is available already prepared at Japanese food stores and natural-food stores, but it is easy to make at home.

2 ¹/₄ cups mochigome *(glutinous rice)*
2 tablespoons gomashio *(page 102)*

Rinse the rice as described on page 152. In a bowl of cold water, soak the rice overnight, preferably, or for at least three hours before cooking. A shorter soaking time will require a longer cooking time.

Drain the soaked rice, discarding the water, and transfer the rice to a bowl. Add 1 teaspoon salt to the rice, and toss.

To cook the rice in a steamer, have the steamer ready at high steam production. Lay a steamer cloth on the bottom of the steamer basket. Place the rice in the steamer, and level the top. Make a shallow depression, 2 inches in diameter, in the center of the rice. This will allow the steam to circulate and to cook the rice evenly. Fold the protruding corners of the cloth over the rice to cover it completely. Place the steamer basket on top of the boiling pot of water, cover the steamer basket, and cook the rice over high heat, adding boiling water to the pot as necessary. After 15 minutes of cooking, sprinkle about ¹/₃ cup of tap water evenly over the rice, using a long oven glove for protection from the hot steam. Repeat this process once or twice, about every 15 minutes during the cooking.

After 40 to 50 minutes of cooking, remove the steamer basket from the pot.

To prepare the sweet rice in a microwave oven, drain the soaked rice, reserving the water. Put the rice into a microwave-proof container. Add water in which the rice was soaked until the rice is barely covered. (If you use too much water the cooked rice will be too soft.) Cover the container tightly with plastic wrap. Cook the rice in the microwave oven for 10 minutes, or until the plastic wrap begins to inflate like a balloon. Remove the container from the microwave oven, remove the plastic wrap, and stir the rice. Level the surface of the rice, cover the container with fresh plastic wrap, return the container to the microwave oven, and cook the rice 3 minutes. Remove the rice from the microwave oven, and let it stand, covered, for 5 minutes.

Transfer the cooked rice to a large bowl, and fan it vigorously, using a hand fan or square of cardboard, to cool the rice quickly. Let the cooled rice stand for 5 minutes, and then serve it immediately, garnished with the *gomashio*, or cover it with a dry dish towel. If you will be serving the rice later the same day, refrigeration is not necessary provided the room is cool. If you're making the rice a day ahead, put the rice into a lidded container and refrigerate it. Prepared rice also freezes well. Reheat the rice in the steamer or microwave oven before serving.

MENRUI • Japanese Noodles

Japanese noodles are made from wheat and buckwheat flours, and mung-bean and potato starch. In Japan, rice flour is not used to make noodles.

Soba (Buckwheat Noodles)

Buckwheat, soba, was introduced to Japan from China. Its cultivation is mentioned in the early Japanese history book *Shokunihongi*, written in 797. By the eighth century, the imperial government recommended growing buckwheat along with other grains, including rice and several kinds of millet. In the early days buckwheat seeds were eaten whole, cooked with rice and other grains to make porridge. Later the seeds were ground into flour, and the flour was used in a number of preparations. These included boiled buckwheat-flour dumplings (*sobagaki*), steamed buckwheat-flour dumplings stuffed with sweet azuki bean paste (*soba manju*), and buckwheat cake (*sobamochi*).

Soba noodles, which were first called *sobakiri* and now are simply called soba, did not appear in Japan until the late sixteenth century. But by the beginning of the Edo Era (1600 to 1868), soba noodle dishes had become fashionable; they were the "fast food" sold at numerous food stands in the streets of the busy city of Edo, present-day Tokyo.

Their popularity remains undiminished today. Soba noodles are a preferred lunchtime dish among busy businesspeople, who rush to noodle restaurants to slurp down bowls of hot or cold noodles in 15 minutes or less. Westerners are always amazed by the lightning speed with which a "salary man" can devour a bowl of steaming hot soba noodles.

The quality and price of soba noodles vary greatly from one restaurant to another, depending on whether the noodles are made at the restaurant or in a factory, and on how much other starchy material, such as wheat flour or yam flour, has been added to the buckwheat flour. Buckwheat, which is not a grain, lacks the gluten needed to form a dough that can easily be stretched into noodle form. Besides, noodles made from 100 percent buckwheat flour lack the "bite" of good pasta. So the soba noodles I like best include a small amount of another starch to improve the texture. But since buckwheat flour costs more than other flours, many manufacturers add a large amount of starchy material to lower the cost of noodle production. The resulting noodles are inexpensive, but they lack the rich, nutty flavor and pleasing brown color of good soba. The trick is to find soba noodles that have both the delicious buckwheat flavor and a firm-to-the-bite texture.

Soba noodles are a regional food. Although buckwheat is grown throughout Japan, the cooler the climate, the more fragrant and rich-tasting the buckwheat. Hence, the custom of eating buckwheat noodles has been much more prevalent in cool regions such as northern Japan (Tohoku), the Tokyo region (Kanto), and the central mountainous region (Shinshu). When you walk the streets of the cities and towns in these regions, you will spot soba noodle restaurants on nearly every street corner. Many of these usually modest-quality restaurants have plastic samples encased in glass outside of the building. There you can see soba noodles with tempura (*tempura soba*), soba noodles with duck and *naganegi* long onion (*kamo nanban soba*), soba noodles with mountain vegetables (*sansai soba*), soba noodles with sweet, simmered fried thin tofu (*kitsune soba*), and many other soba dishes. People come into the restaurant all day long to have a quick noodle meal.

Buckwheat flour is nutritious. It contains high-quality protein, and it is rich in B vitamins and minerals such as iron and calcium. For these reasons, soba noodles are favored as a health food in Japan.

Like many Japanese foods, soba noodles also play an important cultural role. They are traditionally eaten on special ceremonial occasions, such as at the end of each year. The end-of-the-year soba noodles, though the same as those eaten year-round, have a special name, *toshikoshi soba*, or "cross-the-year soba noodles." Because of their long, thin form, soba noodles represent longevity and long-lasting happiness. Eating soba noodles at the end of the year assures people that the new year will be a lucky one.

Udon, *Kishimen, Somen,* and *Hiyamugi* (Wheat Noodles)

Japanese wheat noodles are produced in several varieties. First in popularity are **udon**, which are thick, long, white noodles. A primitive form of udon, used to make stuffed dumplings, was introduced from China during the early centuries of the first millennium. By the Muromachi Era (1338 to 1573), udon noodles appeared, but they were mainly consumed at temples. Udon finally reached the commoners during the Edo Era (1600 to 1868). Unlike soba noodles, udon gained more popularity in the Kansai region, which includes Osaka, Kyoto, and the surrounding area.

It was five years ago that I—having spent most of my life in Tokyo—first discovered the great fun and flavor of fresh homemade udon. I attended an udon-making class organized by a leading flour manufacturer. Unlike soba noodles, udon noodles are simple and easy to make from scratch, as you'll see in the recipe on page 326. The ingredients are refined medium-hard wheat flour (or, in the United States, all-purpose flour), salt, and water. The salt is not used to flavor the noodles, but works chemically on the wheat protein to create a pleasant elasticity in the noodles. This prevents the noodles from breaking during storing and cooking.

Udon dishes, which may be served hot or cold, employ toppings similar to those used for soba noodle dishes. As with soba noodles, you will find udon served with tempura, with sweet simmered fried thin tofu (*abura-age*), with duck meat and *naganegi* long onion, with mountain vegetables, and so on. In addition to these, there are specialty udon dishes. *Nabeyaki udon* (page 331) is such a dish, and one that my mother prepared often on freezing winter nights. Udon noodles are cooked in broth in individual earthenware casseroles, *nabe,* with chicken and vegetables over low heat until the noodles have soaked up all the rich flavor of the broth. Finally an egg is broken and dropped on top of the noodles. The mixture is covered with a lid and cooked briefly over a high flame until the egg is half done. Eating steaming *nabeyaki udon* in winter really warmed my entire body.

Miso-nikomi udon (page 329) is another body-warming dish from Aichi Prefecture. Udon noodles are cooked in a rich broth flavored with locally produced soybean miso (*mamemiso*) along with several other ingredients, such as chicken, fried thin tofu (*abura-age*), and vegetables.

Kishimen, flat noodles, are another specialty of Aichi Prefecture. Their flatness reminds Westerners of fettuccini, but *kishimen* noodles have a distinctive chewy bite. They are served either hot or cold.

Somen and **hiyamugi** are thin wheat noodles. *Somen* are as thin as vermicelli, and *hiyamugi* are slightly thicker than *somen*. These summertime noodles are almost always served cold, with a dipping sauce.

Chukasoba (Chinese-Style Noodles)

Another very popular type of wheat noodles is *chukasoba*, which literally means "Chinese-style soba noodles." Despite the name, the noodles contain no buckwheat flour (*soba*), but are made from wheat flour, which is mixed with water and a naturally obtained alkaline agent, *kansui*. The *kansui* provides the noodles with their distinctive elasticity. Today synthesized sodium carbonate or potassium carbonate has replaced natural *kansui*. *Chukasoba* noodles are creamy yellow (although they contain no eggs), curly, and resilient in texture. Unlike other noodles, *chukasoba* are served in a hot, richly flavored broth made from chicken and pork bones.

The most famous dish made from these noodles and broth is called *ramen*. It is served with any of numerous toppings, such as several slices of simmered pork (*chashu*), pickled bamboo shoots (*shinachiku*), and green onion slices. For those who need a stronger kick to their bowl of noodles, grated garlic and spicy chile sauce are served as condiments. Although *ramen* sounds like a Chinese dish and in Japan is served in the local version of Chinese restaurants, it is actually a Japanese dish inspired by authentic Chinese noodle preparations.

Chukasoba are also used to produce another popular snack- and lunchtime dish, *yakisoba*—steamed noodles stir-fried with sliced pork and cabbage and flavored with a special sauce, which tastes like sweetened Worcestershire. If you visit any festival in Japan, you will find a *yakisoba* food stall, where a cook wearing a short-sleeve shirt and a piece of twisted cotton cloth as a hair band will be stir-frying noodles on a large heated griddle with two spatulas. No one can pass by without buying the noodles or, at least, stopping to savor the delicious smell. The aroma of frying *yakisoba* noodles is the nostalgic smell of a Japanese street festival.

When you eat Japanese noodles, forget all of the table manners that your mother patiently taught you. You are allowed, indeed encouraged, to make slurping noises as you suck (not bite) the long noodles into your mouth. You may pick up the bowl in your hand, or lean far over the bowl with the steam clouding your glasses, and you certainly must drink the soup directly from the bowl (except for *ramen*, which for the sake of Chinese tradition is served with a Chinese-style porcelain spoon). I have found that it is easy for Westerners to adopt these rules of etiquette, while Japanese have a hard time not slurping or picking up the bowl while eating soup or spaghetti at high-class Western restaurants.

Ryokuto Harusame (Mung-Bean Noodles)
Harusame (Potato-Starch Noodles)

In the Japanese kitchen, we use two different types of clear, thin starch noodles. One, *ryokuto harusame*, is made from mung-bean starch, and the other, *harusame*, from potato starch. Mung-bean noodles originated in China, but *harusame* were developed in Japan, using potato or sweet-potato starch. The slender, transparent appearance of potato-starch noodles, which are as thin and straight as angel-hair pasta, reminds the Japanese of gentle spring (*haru*) rain (*same*). Dried mung-bean noodles, though also transparent, are as thin as very narrow steel picture wire, and they are wrinkled.

Recent advances in manufacturing have created new types of mung-bean and potato-starch noodles that can be more quickly reconstituted or are better able to withstand longer cooking. So please check the instructions on the package label before following these general directions:

Reconstitute *harusame*, potato-starch noodles, by placing them in a bowl, covering them with boiling water, and letting them stand for 10 minutes. Then drain the noodles, and rinse them in cold water. Cut them into the desired lengths, and use them in salad or soup.

After adding potato-starch noodles to soup, cook them only a few minutes. Overcooking makes the noodles mushy.

Before cooking mung-bean noodles, soak them in lukewarm water for 5 minutes, then cook them in boiling water for 2 to 3 minutes. Drain the noodles, rinse them in cold water, cut them into the desired lengths, and use them in salad, soup, or a simmered dish. Mung-bean noodles have a pleasant bite after cooking.

Generally, mung-bean noodles and potato-starch noodles are interchangeable in cooking. I, however, prefer mung-bean noodles because of their firmer texture and their ability to withstand longer cooking without becoming too soft.

SOURCES: Dried soba (buckwheat noodles), udon and *somen* (wheat-flour noodles), *chukasoba* (Chinese-style noodles), *ryokuto harusame* (mung-bean noodles) and *harusame* (potato-starch noodles) are available at Japanese and Asian food stores and some large supermarkets. Health- and natural-food stores also carry soba and udon. Fresh soba, udon, and *chukasoba*—cooked or not—can be found at Japanese food stores in a refrigerator case. In the freezer case you may also find frozen udon and *chukasoba*. I don't recommend frozen *chukasoba*; the noodles tend to break into small pieces during cooking.

WHAT TO LOOK FOR: Soba noodles are brown in color. From the package label, you may be able to tell the proportion of buckwheat flour and other starch. *Niwari* soba, the best choice, is 80 percent buckwheat flour and 20 percent other starch. Wheat-flour noodles such as udon, *hiyamugi*, and *somen* are white in color, and each comes in a standard thickness. *Chukasoba* is creamy yellow and curly in appearance in both dried and fresh form.

STORAGE: The dried noodles, except thin *somen* noodles, keep for about one year. *Somen* noodles taste best one to two years after production. Store dry noodles in a dry, cool, and dark place. Fresh uncooked noodles should be eaten within two days after the manufacturing date. Refrigerate fresh cooked noodles in a covered container, and consume them within one day.

HOW TO COOK JAPANESE DRIED WHEAT AND BUCKWHEAT NOODLES—SOBA, UDON, AND *SOMEN*

Hoshi Menrui no Yude-kata

Place a large bowl of cold water with some ice cubes in the sink for cooling the cooked noodles.

In a large pot, bring plenty of water to a boil over medium heat. The volume of water required is four to five times that of the dried noodles. Add the dried noodles to the boiling water, and give several stirs with a pair of cooking chopsticks to separate the noodles. After the water returns to a boil, cook the noodles at a brisk simmer for 2 to 8 minutes, depending on the kind of noodles (check the suggested time on the package label). Toward the end of the cooking time, pick up one noodle strand, and bite into it. Stop the cooking when you find a pin-hole-size white uncooked spot in the center.

Drain the noodles immediately, and plunge them into the ice water. Change the water several times as the noodles cool. This prevents further cooking and firms the surface of the noodles. Rinse the cooked noodles in a colander under cold running water, gently rubbing them between your palms to remove excess starch and salt. Drain the noodles, and serve them immediately, if possible. If not, leave them in the colander, covered, for up to an hour. Refresh the noodles under cold running water before serving them.

When serving cooked noodles cold, place them on individual bamboo trays or plates, each with a bowl of the dipping sauce *tsukejiru* (page 67). On the side, provide such condiments as finely grated fresh ginger (for udon), finely grated wasabi (for soba), thinly sliced scallion and freshly toasted white sesame seeds, or julienned nori. Just before eating, each diner adds some of these condiments to the dipping sauce.

To serve noodles hot, warm them in fresh boiling water for no longer than 2 minutes, or they will become unpleasantly soft. Serve the noodles in hot-noodle broth (*kakejiru*, page 66) with condiments. *Shichimi togarashi* (seven-spice powder) is a favorite condiment for hot noodle dishes.

PART TWO

PREPARATIONS
FROM HIROKO'S KITCHEN

TOFU SALAD WITH MISO DRESSING

Tofu Sarada Miso Doresshingu

The texture of fresh tofu, either firm or soft, seems to be unacceptable to some Westerners. This preparation, in which tofu is marinated in miso, pan-fried, and served with assorted salad leaves, may change such an attitude. Try this joyful way to eat healthy tofu.

The miso dressing used in this recipe may become one of your favorites.

> *2 blocks (about 22 ounces) firm tofu*
> *3¹/₂ ounces Saikyo miso (sweet white miso)*
> *¹/₄ cup sake (rice wine)*
> *1 tablespoon sugar*
> *1 clove crushed garlic*
>
> MISO DRESSING
> *1 garlic clove, halved*
> *1 tablespoon tamamiso (miso and egg sauce,*
> *   page 83), or more Saikyo miso*
> *1 teaspoon smooth French-style mustard*
> *1 tablespoon komezu (rice vinegar)*
> *2 tablespoons olive oil or vegetable oil*
> *Tamari*
> *Salt*

> $^1/_4$ kabocha, *seeded but not peeled, preferably,*
>   *or 1 small sweet potato*
> 1 medium lotus root, preferably, *or 1 small potato*
> 1 medium carrot
> Vegetable oil, for deep-frying
> $^1/_4$ cup potato starch or cornstarch
> Mixed salad greens

Cut each tofu block in half horizontally, making four rectangular slices. In a flat-bottomed dish, combine the $3^1/_2$ ounces Saikyo miso, the *sake*, sugar, and crushed garlic. Add the tofu slices, coat them with the miso mixture, and marinate them overnight, covered, in the refrigerator.

Make the dressing: Rub the inside surface of a medium bowl with the halved garlic. Add the 1 tablespoon *tamamiso* or Saikyo miso, the mustard, and *komezu* one at a time, and beat with a whisk. Add the olive oil or vegetable oil little by little, whisking continuously, until the mixture emulsifies. Season the dressing with drops of tamari and salt. Chill the miso dressing in a jar with a tight-fitting lid in the refrigerator.

Cut the piece of *kabocha* in half crosswise, then cut each half into thin lengthwise slices. Cut the root vegetables into thin disks.

In a large pot, heat 3 inches of vegetable oil to 320 degrees F. Add the vegetables to the oil in small batches, and cook them over low heat for about 2 to 3 minutes. Drain the vegetables on a rack. At this point you can set them aside for up to 3 hours.

Increase the temperature of the oil to 360 degrees F. Return the fried vegetables to the oil, and cook them for 30 to 60 seconds, until they are crisp and light golden. Drain the vegetables on a rack, and, while they are hot, sprinkle them generously with salt.

Remove the tofu slices from the miso marinade, and, with a paper towel, wipe off the marinade completely. In a flat-bottomed square container, dredge the tofu slices in the potato starch, patting the slices to remove excess starch from the tofu. Heat a skillet over high heat, and add 5 tablespoons fresh oil. When the oil is hot, add the tofu slices, and cook them over medium heat, turning them once, until they are golden on both sides. Remove the tofu slices from the skillet to a plate, and let them stand for 5 minutes.

In a large bowl, toss the salad greens with the miso dressing. Cut the tofu into $^1/_2$-inch strips and serve them on top of salad greens with crisp vegetables.

• *Yields 4 servings*

SHRIMP AND ASPARAGUS
WITH MUSTARD-VINEGAR-MISO DRESSING

Ebi to Asuparagasu no Karashi Sumiso-zoe

Karashi sumiso, mustard-vinegar-miso dressing, is a loose pastelike dressing made from Saikyo miso (sweet white miso), sugar, *komezu* (rice vinegar), *dashi* (fish stock), and hot mustard. This dressing has a pleasant bitter, sharp taste and is exceptionally good as an accompaniment to parboiled shellfish, sashimi, sea vegetables, and parboiled vegetables. In this dish, bright green asparagus, pink shrimp, and dark green *wakame* sea vegetable are served side by side with the golden yellow dressing over them. I add a little virgin olive oil to the traditional dressing to make it even smoother and glossy.

KARASHI SUMISO DRESSING
1 teaspoon hot mustard paste (see page 55)
3 tablespoons Saikyo miso *(sweet white miso)*
1 tablespoon sugar
3 tablespoons komezu *(rice vinegar)*
1 tablespoon dashi *(fish stock, page 65)*
1 tablespoon virgin olive oil

7 ounces asparagus (16 to 20 spears), tough ends
and tips removed
7 ounces large headless shrimp in their shells,
deveined (see page 22)
2 tablespoons instant wakame *sea vegetable,*
soaked in cold water for 2 minutes, and drained

Make the dressing: In a *suribachi* or other mortar or in a bowl with a whisk, blend the mustard paste and Saikyo miso until smooth. Add the sugar, *komezu*, *dashi*, and olive oil one at a time, blending until smooth. Transfer the mixture to a small saucepan, place it over medium heat, and cook for 2 minutes, stirring all the time. Transfer the dressing to a jar, and let it cool.

Have a bowl of ice water ready for cooling the asparagus and shrimp. In a medium pot of boiling water, boil the asparagus for 1 minute. Drain the asparagus, cool it in the ice water, and wipe it dry with a paper towel.

Insert a wooden skewer through the belly side of each shrimp, from throat to tail, to prevent it from bending during cooking. In a medium pot of salted boiling water, cook the shrimp until they are pink, 2 to 3 minutes. Drain the shrimp, spread them out in a wide colander, and turn the wooden skewers to loosen them, but do not remove them right away. Cool the shrimp in the ice water, and wipe them dry with a paper towel. Then remove the skewers from the shrimp. Peel them, but leave each tail attached. Cut each shrimp open from the belly side without cutting through the back. Gently press the shrimp open with the palm of your hand so that the shrimp maintain a flat shape.

Serve the asparagus, shrimp, and *wakame* sea vegetable side by side, on individual plates or on a communal platter. Pour the dressing over them.

• *Yields 4 servings*

In Japan, dinner is the main meal of the day, served at about seven in the evening. At a Japanese dinner, unless it is a very formal *kaiseki* meal, the prepared dishes are all served at the same time. Each is presented in individual small to medium-size bowls or plates, whose shapes vary: They may be round, triangular, square, rectangular, or shaped like a seasonal flower, leaf, vegetable, or fruit. A typical dinner consists of a bowl of rice, a bowl of soup, a protein dish such as grilled fish, and several vegetable side dishes, including a small plate of pickled vegetables, *tsukemono*. In a Japanese meal, none of these is considered the "main dish." Each dish compliments the others to create a meal ideally balanced in flavor, texture, color, fragrance, and nutritional benefits.

SALMON AND VEGETABLES IN A SWEET VINEGAR MARINADE

Sake to Yasai no Namban-zuke

Several Japanese dishes carry the word *namban* in their names. *Namban* means "southern barbarian." This word was applied to the Portuguese and Spanish, the first Westerners who came to Japan, during the sixteenth century. Until this time, the Japanese had traded predominantly with Koreans and Chinese, with whom they shared similar physical characteristics. The word *namban* reflects the shock the Japanese felt upon encountering Europeans, who had, by comparison, large noses and eyes, hairy bodies, and astonishing height.

Besides introducing a new religion and guns, which contributed to a shift in the political and religious structure of Japan, the Portuguese and Spanish brought new foods and cooking techniques. These included *kabocha*, potatoes, corn, watermelons, chile peppers, figs, sugary sweets, and deep-frying. Dishes prepared in *namban* style typically call for red chile pepper and the combined techniques of deep-frying and marinating.

In this dish, cooked salmon and vegetables are marinated in a sweet vinegar marinade and served chilled or at room temperature. If you like, you can substitute sweet potato, red bell pepper, and asparagus for the *kabocha* and eggplant. This appetizer is always a hit among my guests and students.

MARINADE
1 cup komezu *(rice vinegar)*
¹/₄ cup sugar
2 tablespoons shoyu *(soy sauce)*
1 teaspoon salt
2 akatogarashi *or other small dried red chile*
        peppers, stemmed and seeded

2 Japanese eggplants, preferably, or ¹/₂ large,
        oval eggplant, stemmed
¹/₄ kabocha, seeded but not peeled, and cut into
        12 slices about ¹/₄ inch thick
Vegetable oil, for deep-frying
1¹/₄ pounds skinned and boned salmon fillet
¹/₂ cup all-purpose flour

In a medium pot, combine the *komezu*, sugar, *shoyu*, and salt, and bring the mixture to a boil, stirring. Add the chile peppers, and remove the pot from the heat. Transfer the marinade to a medium flat-bottomed container, and set it aside.

Cut each Japanese eggplant into quarters lengthwise. If you're using half of a large eggplant, cut it into eight pieces lengthwise. Cut the fish into $1^1/_2$-by-3-inch pieces.

In a large, deep pot, heat 2 inches of vegetable oil to 320 degrees F. In small batches, cook the eggplant and pumpkin until slightly golden, about 2 to 3 minutes. Drain the vegetables on a rack.

Put the flour into a bowl, and dredge the salmon with it. Let the salmon stand for 2 minutes.

While the vegetables are still hot, transfer them to the marinade. Remove the eggplant from the marinade to another dish after 5 minutes.

Increase the heat of the vegetable oil to 350 degrees F, add the salmon in small batches, and cook it until it is light golden, about 4 to 5 minutes, maintaining the oil temperature at 350 degrees F. Drain the salmon on a rack.

While the salmon pieces are still hot, add them to the marinade. Marinate them with the vegetables for at least an hour before serving, turning the salmon several times. The salmon and vegetables can be prepared one day in advance and left in the marinade or stored separately, covered, in the refrigerator.

Remove the chile peppers from the marinade, and cut them into thin disks. Serve the salmon and vegetables drizzled with the marinade and garnished with the chile pepper disks and parsley.

• *Yields 6 to 8 servings as an appetizer or 4 servings as a main dish*

DAIKON AND SMOKED SALMON SANDWICHES WITH *KIMIZU* SAUCE

Daikon to Sumoku Sāmon-sando Kimizu-zoe

In this preparation, smoked salmon is cured with *kombu* (kelp) overnight. This technique is traditionally applied to fresh fish to help preserve it. The *kombu* removes water and excess oil from the salmon, tightens its texture, and intensifies its flavor. The smoked salmon is then sliced and layered with daikon pieces to make small, attractive sandwiches. Served with *wakame* sea vegetable, boiled shrimp, and golden yellow *kimizu* sauce, the sandwiches make a dazzling first course.

About 2 ounces kombu *(kelp), enough to cover the
        top and bottom surfaces of the smoked salmon*
7 ounces smoked salmon
*Two 2-inch lengths of thick daikon root, 2¹/₂ to 3
        inches in diameter*
2 tablespoons komezu *(rice vinegar)*
1 tablespoon sugar
Salt
3 tablespoons instant wakame *sea vegetable, soaked in
        cold water for 2 minutes and drained*
*8 medium shrimp in their shells, headed,
        deveined (page 22)*
Kimizu *sauce (page 72)*

Wipe the *kombu* with a moist kitchen cloth, and, with the cloth, cover the *kombu* until it becomes pliable, about 15 minutes. Flatten the *kombu*, and place several pieces on plastic wrap to make a rectangle about 4 inches by 6 inches. Place the smoked salmon on top of the *kombu*, and cover the salmon completely with additional *kombu*. Tightly wrap the *kombu*-sandwiched salmon in the plastic wrap. Place the package between two large flat surfaces such as cutting boards or dinner plates, put a weight of about 2 pounds on top of the upper board or plate, and refrigerate the salmon overnight.

The next day, peel the daikon, and cut it into lengthwise slices about ¹/₄ inch thick, discarding the two round outer slices. You should have at least 24 slices. Transfer the daikon to a bowl, add 1 teaspoon salt, and toss. Let the daikon stand for 15 minutes.

Rinse the daikon thoroughly to remove the salt, and drain the daikon. Wipe it dry with a paper towel.

In a bowl, mix the *komezu*, sugar, and a pinch of salt. Marinate the daikon in the vinegar mixture for 15 minutes.

Drain the daikon, and wipe it dry with a paper towel.

Remove the pressed smoked salmon from the refrigerator and discard the *kombu*. Cut the smoked salmon into pieces the same size as the daikon slices. You will need 16 slices of salmon. Layer the daikon and smoked salmon in eight stacks, starting and finishing each stack with daikon. Each sandwich should have five layers. Wrap the sandwiches tightly in plastic wrap, place them in a container, and weight them with two plates. Refrigerate them for at least 30 minutes and for as long as a day.

Unwrap the sandwiches, and cut off any protruding edges to make neat rectangular shapes. Cut each sandwich in half.

Bring a medium pot of salted water to a boil. Cook the shrimp for 3 minutes.

Drain the shrimp, and quickly cool them in a bowl of cold water. Drain the shrimp, again, and shell them. Cut the shrimp crosswise into halves or thirds.

Place each smoked salmon and daikon sandwich in an individual small bowl, with a portion of the shrimp on top and some of the *wakame* alongside. Pour $1/2$ tablespoon *kimizu* sauce over each sandwich, and serve.

• *Yields 8 servings*

SASHIMI TUNA, RED BELL PEPPER, AND ASPARAGUS IN MISO-VINEGAR DRESSING

Maguro, Akapiman to Asuparagasu no Nuta

Japan has many eateries that serve a variety of small dishes to accompany *sake* (rice wine), beer, and other alcoholic drinks. You might think of these dishes called *ippin-ryori*, as the Japanese version of Spanish *tapas*. *Ippin-ryori* are prepared with all types of cooking techniques and, like their Spanish counterparts, are served in small portions. The function of these little treats is exactly the same in both countries: People drink, eat, talk; talk, drink, eat.

This fish and vegetable salad is a popular *ippin-ryori*. Traditionally it employs *naganegi* long onion and tuna. The long onion is cooked until tender, and then pressed with the back of a knife to remove its somewhat slimy inner juice. The pressed onion is served with sashimi tuna dressed in *karashi sumiso*, mustard-vinegar-miso dressing. In this recipe I use more appealing, non-slimy vegetables, asparagus and red bell pepper. *Sake* is the best drink to accompany this dish.

> *1 red bell pepper*
> *1 teaspoon* tamari
> *1 teaspoon sesame oil*
> *10 asparagus spears, tough ends and tips removed*
> *7 ounces* sashimi-*quality* maguro *(tuna, see page 352)*
> *1 tablespoon* shoyu *(soy sauce)*
> *1 tablespoon* komezu *(rice vinegar)*
> *2 tablespoons instant* wakame *sea vegetable, soaked*
>   *in cold water 2 minutes, and drained*
> Karashi sumiso *(mustard-vinegar-miso dressing,*
>   *page 165)*
>
> GARNISH
> *Julienned* yuzu *citron or lemon rind*

Heat a broiler, and char the red bell pepper on all sides. Remove the bell pepper from the broiler, cover it tightly with plastic wrap, and let it steam in its own heat for 10 minutes. Remove the skin, stem, and white ribs of the pepper, and cut the flesh into 1-inch squares.

In a bowl, combine 1 teaspoon tamari and 1 teaspoon sesame oil with the bell pepper and toss.

In a medium pot, bring plenty of water to a boil. Cook the asparagus for 1 minute, or until it is barely tender. Drain the asparagus, cool it under cold running water, and wipe the asparagus dry with a paper towel. Cut the asparagus into 1½-inch lengths.

Cut the tuna into 1-inch cubes. In a bowl, combine the *shoyu* and 1 tablespoon of the *komezu*, and marinate the tuna for 15 minutes. This process removes excess liquid from the tuna and, at the same time, suppresses strong fishy flavors.

Drain the tuna, discarding the marinade. On individual serving plates, arrange the tuna, *wakame,* asparagus, and red bell pepper, side by side. Pour the dressing over the tuna, and garnish with the *yuzu* or lemon rind.

• *Yields 2 to 4 servings*

STEAMED DUCK BREAST
WITH MUSTARD-VINEGAR-MISO DRESSING

Mushigamo Karashi Sumiso-zoe

Although today duck meat is quite expensive and so is not an everyday food, wild duck has been an important protein source to the Japanese since olden days. My mother prepared this duck dish whenever she could get very fresh duck meat, either from one of my father's patients or from a butcher. She cooked the duck submerged in a flavored broth in the steamer. This indirect heating produced very tender and juicy meat. The duck was then sliced, mounded with strips of long onion, and served with *karashi sumiso*, golden yellow mustard-vinegar-miso dressing. This is still a delicious treat!

> *2 medium duck breast halves (preferably Magret,*
> *a very meaty variety), about 12 ounces each*
> *1 cup* dashi *(fish stock, page 65)*
> *1 cup* sake *(rice wine)*
> *3 tablespoons* mirin *(sweet cooking wine)*
> *2 teaspoons* salt
> *2 teaspoons* usukuchi shoyu *(light-colored*
> *soy sauce)*
> Karashi sumiso *(mustard-vinegar-miso dressing,*
> *page 165)*
>
> GARNISH
> *1* naganegi *long onion, white part only, or a generous*
> *amount of salad greens*

Have ready a bamboo or metal steamer with plenty of water at high steam production. Have a medium pot of simmering water also at hand. Cut the skin from the duck flesh, and scrape away half of the fat attached to the flesh. Make very shallow checkerboard cuts on the remaining fat layer.

Heat a large skillet over moderately high heat. Add the duck halves, fat side down, and cook them until the fat is brown. Turn the pieces over, and cook them until they are lightly browned on the other side. Plunge the browned duck into boiling water to remove excess fat. Quickly remove the duck from the water, and wipe it dry with a paper towel.

In a small saucepan bring the *dashi*, *sake*, *mirin*, salt, and *usukuchi shoyu* to a boil. Transfer the mixture to a heat-proof container that can fit into a steamer. Add the duck to the container, and cover it with plastic wrap. Place the container on the steamer rack, put the lid onto the steamer, and cook the duck over high heat for 10 minutes.

Remove the container from the steamer and the duck from the cooking liquid, reserving the liquid. Push a steel skewer through one end of the duck pieces, and let them hang over a bowl for 10 minutes.

Return the duck to its cooking liquid, and let it cool to room temperature.

Refrigerate the duck in its cooking liquid, covered, for 5 to 12 hours.

If you're using a long onion, cut it crosswise into 3-inch lengths, and then lengthwise into thin strips. In a medium bowl of ice water, soak the onion strips until they are crisp, 15 minutes. Drain them, and gently squeeze them dry in a paper towel.

Remove the duck from the cooking liquid, and cut the meat into thin slices. Serve the duck topped with long onion or on a bed of salad greens, with the mustard-vinegar-miso dressing on the side.

• *Yields 4 servings*

SWEET MISO–VEGETABLE CONDIMENT

Tekkamiso

My mother made sure that *tekkamiso* was always available at our dinner table. This is a condiment in which soybeans, burdock, carrot, and scallions are cooked together and flavored with sweetened *mamemiso*, soybean miso. *Tekkamiso* was our favorite accompaniment to plain cooked white rice. Because of this delicious topping, we frequently ate so much rice that we had no room for anything else.

A
P
P
E
T
I
Z
E
R
S

·

174

> $^1/_2$ *cup dried soybeans, soaked in water overnight and*
>   *drained*
> *2 tablespoons sesame oil*
> $2^1/_2$ *ounces (about* $^1/_2$ *cup) gobo (burdock), scraped,*
>   *julienned, and soaked in 2 cups cold water and*
>   *2 teaspoons vinegar*
> $3^1/_2$ *ounces (*$1^1/_8$ *cup) carrot, julienned*
> *3 scallions, both green and white parts, cut into thin*
>   *disks*
> *5 ounces (*$^1/_2$ *cup) mamemiso (soybean miso)*
> $^1/_3$ *to* $^1/_2$ *cup sugar*
> *2 tablespoons mirin (sweet cooking wine)*
> $^1/_4$ *cup dashi (fish stock, page 65)*
> $^1/_4$ *cup sake (rice wine)*

Heat a skillet over medium heat, add the sesame oil and, when the oil is hot, the soybeans. Cook the soybeans over low to medium heat, stirring occasionally, until the soybeans are light golden, about 8 minutes.

Add the burdock, carrot, and scallions, and cook, stirring, for 4 minutes.

Add the *mamemiso* and sugar ($^1/_2$ cup sugar produces a more traditional taste, but for a less sweet *tekkamiso* use $^1/_3$ cup). Add the *mirin*, *dashi*, and *sake*. Cook the mixture, stirring, until it is no longer watery, about 10 minutes. The soybeans will remain rather crunchy at the end of the cooking.

Serve the *tekkamiso* as a condiment with rice. It keeps for 2 weeks in a covered jar in the refrigerator.

• *Yields* $1^1/_2$ *cups topping*

SOYBEAN HUMMUS

Daizu Hamosu

Since Japanese tofu dressing has some similarity in flavor and texture to Middle Eastern hummus, I experimented with hummus made from firm tofu. The result was a disaster! The tofu, first of all, lacked the sweet taste that chickpeas contribute to hummus. Second, the texture of the tofu after a whirl in the food processor was unpleasantly smooth and rather slimy.

I then tried starting with dried soybeans. The result was a nutritious, delicious, properly textured soybean hummus. Dried beans are soaked in cold water overnight, cooked until soft, and then blended in a food processor. You may cook as many soybeans as you like, and freeze the extra for later use.

Enjoy this creation with crispy rice crackers (page 178).

> ¹/₂ cup dried soybeans, soaked in cold water
>   overnight and drained
> 3 tablespoons Japanese sesame paste, preferably,
>   or tahini
> ¹/₄ cup olive oil
> 1 garlic clove, crushed
> Juice of 1 lemon, fresh-squeezed
> 1¹/₂ teaspoons salt
> 1 teaspoon sugar
> Cayenne and ground cumin to taste

Put the drained soybeans into a large pot, and cover them with fresh water by 4 inches. Cook the beans over medium-low heat until they are tender, 1 to 1¹/₂ hours.

Drain the beans, and discard the cooking water. In a food processor or blender, blend the soybeans and all the rest of the ingredients and ¹/₄ cup warm water into a creamy paste.

Serve the hummus with rice crackers or other crackers, or with vegetable sticks.

• *Yields 1 cup hummus*

BRIGHT GREEN EDAMAME SOYBEAN DIP

Edamame Dippu

In Japan, briefly boiled, lightly salted *edamame*, fresh green soybeans, eaten from the shell with a cold glass of beer, are one of the delights of summer. I was inspired by popular Western dips to find another way of enjoying this excellent summer vegetable. The dip is, of course, best prepared during the summer months, when fresh green soybeans are available. However, frozen *edamame*, found at Japanese and some Asian food stores outside Japan, make it possible for us to enjoy this dip year-round.

> *14 ounces* edamame *(fresh green soybeans)*
> *in their shells*
> *2 ounces feta cheese*
> *6 tablespoons olive oil*
> *3 tablespoons plain yogurt*
> *1¹/₂ teaspoons salt*

In a large pot of salted boiling water, cook the *edamame* until they are tender, 4 to 5 minutes. Drain them in a flat-bottomed colander, and fan them to speed cooling.

Shell the beans, and discard the shells. In a food processor or blender, blend the beans and all the rest of the ingredients to a creamy paste.

Serve the dip with rice crackers (page 178) or other crackers, or with vegetable sticks.

• *Yields 1¹/₂ cups dip*

MISO AND CASHEW (OR WALNUT) SPREAD

Miso to Kashū Batā

I enjoy this spread over toast for my lunch, besides as a dip for crackers or vegetable sticks.

> *1 cup cooked and drained pinto beans*
> *3 tablespoons cashew or walnut butter*
> *2 tablespoons Saikyo miso (sweet white miso)*
> *1 teaspoon akamiso (brown miso)*
> *2 tablespoons lemon juice*
> *1 small garlic clove*

Blend all the ingredients and 3 tablespoons warm water in a food processor or blender until smooth.

Spread the mixture over toast or serve it as a dip with rice crackers (page 178) or other crackers.

• *Yields about 1 1/2 cups spread*

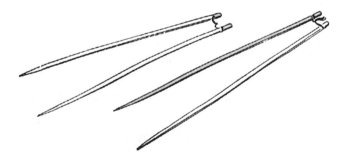

HEAVENLY, CRISPY RICE CRACKERS

Usuyaki Senbei

This simple recipe produces thin, very crisp rice crackers. The sesame seeds added to the dough provide additional texture and sweetness, and a nutty flavor. Poppy seeds are a good substitute for sesame seeds.

> *2 1/2 ounces (about 1/2 cup) cake flour*
> *2 4/5 ounces joshinko (rice flour)*
> *1/2 teaspoon baking powder*
> *3/4 teaspoon salt stirred into 1/2 cup lukewarm water*
> *1 1/2 tablespoons white sesame seeds*
> *1 1/2 tablespoons black sesame seeds*
> *Additional cake flour, for dusting*

In a medium bowl, combine the flours and baking powder. Add the salted lukewarm water to the flour mixture little by little, stirring, until the mixture has a dough-like consistency.

Divide the dough into two portions. Flatten one portion, sprinkle the white sesame seeds on top, and knead them in. Incorporate the black sesame seeds into the other piece of dough in the same way. Shape each piece of dough into a ball. Place the dough balls in a plastic bag, and refrigerate them 1 hour.

Heat the oven to 400 degrees F. On a lightly floured counter, roll each ball into a log about 2/3 inch in diameter. Cut each log into quarters, then each quarter into quarters, to make 32 dough disks. Dredge the cut sides lightly in flour to prevent them from drying out.

With a rolling pin, roll each disk into a circle 2 1/2 inches in diameter. Arrange the thin disks on a baking sheet, and transfer it to the heated oven. Bake the crackers until crisp and light golden, about 15 to 20 minutes, turning the crackers over once halfway through the baking.

Transfer the crackers to a rack to cool, then store them in a jar with a tight-fitting lid. Serve the crackers with *edemame* soybean dip (page 176), soybean hummus (page 175), miso and cashew spread (page 177), or your favorite dip.

• *Yields 32 crackers*

CHILLED SESAME SQUARES

Gomadofu

Gomadofu, "sesame tofu," is a popular summertime dish served at temples and restaurants across Japan. Sesame seeds are ground into paste, mixed with arrowroot starch and *kombu* (kelp) stock, and then cooked until set. Although the dish has the pleasant texture of tofu, tofu is not an ingredient. *Gomadofu* is served chilled, with a little wasabi on top and a little sauce underneath.

To save time and labor, I use prepared white sesame paste in this dish. Please use Japanese sesame paste. Tahini does not have the proper flavor, and Chinese sesame paste, which is often mixed with vegetable oil and sometimes with sugar, has too strong a flavor.

> One 4-inch square piece of kombu (kelp), soaked
>   in 4^1/$_2$ cups water for 1 hour
> 5 ounces arrowroot starch
> 6 ounces Japanese sesame paste
> 1 tablespoon sake (rice wine)
> 1 teaspoon salt
> ^{1}/$_2$ cup dashi (fish stock)
> 2 tablespoons usukuchi shoyu (light-colored
>   soy sauce), preferably, or regular
>   shoyu (soy sauce)
> 2 tablespoons mirin (sweet cooking wine)
>
> GARNISH
> 2 tablespoons wasabi paste

Remove the *kombu* from the stock, and discard the *kombu*. Transfer 1 cup of the *kombu* stock to another bowl. Add the arrowroot starch to the remaining 3^1/$_2$ cups stock, and stir until the liquid is smooth.

Put the sesame paste into a *suribachi* or other mortar, and, little by little, blend in the reserved 1 cup stock. (Or blend the sesame paste and stock in an ordinary bowl with a whisk, but try not to make too much foam.)

In the *suribachi* or in a bowl, stir the stock mixed with arrowroot into the sesame liquid. Strain the mixture through a fine sieve.

Transfer the strained mixture to a medium pot, and add the *sake* and salt. Cook the mixture over medium heat, stirring with a wooden spatula all the time. After 2 to 3 minutes of cooking, you will feel the mixture beginning to thicken. Quickly reduce the heat to low, and cook for 20 minutes more, stirring all the time with the wooden spatula. By the end of the cooking, the mixture will develop a strong elasticity.

Run water all over the inside of a stainless-steel mold or plastic container, about $6^{1}/_{2}$ inches square, then shake the water out. Immediately transfer the arrowroot mixture to the mold; once the mixture is removed from the heat, it instantly sets. With a wet wooden spatula, flatten the surface of the arrowroot mixture. Put 2 to 3 tablespoons cold water in the mold, covering the surface of the mixture to prevent it from drying out. Let it stand until it has cooled to room temperature. Refrigerate it, covered with plastic wrap, for at least 3 hours or for as long as overnight.

In a small saucepan, combine the *dashi*, *shoyu*, and *mirin*, and bring the mixture to a boil. Remove the pan from the heat, and let the sauce cool to room temperature.

Cut the chilled sesame square into 12 or 16 pieces, wetting the knife between cuts. Spoon a little sauce onto individual plates, and serve the sesame squares on top, garnished with a little wasabi.

• *Yields 12 to 16 servings*

BROILED OR GRILLED SUMMER VEGETABLES WITH PONZU DRESSING

Natsuyasai no Yakimono Ponzu-ae

Broiled or grilled vegetables simply seasoned with salt and olive oil or vinegar or both have become a celebrated, international vegetable dish today. Try this popular dish with ponzu, the Japanese dressing of rice vinegar and *yuzu* citron juice. The vegetables are delicious served at room temperature or chilled as well as served hot from the grill or broiler.

> 1 medium zucchini, cut lengthwise into slices
> $^1/_4$ inch thick
> 1 large head radicchio, cut lengthwise into quarters
> 1 large fennel bulb, cut lengthwise into quarters
> 8 ripe cherry tomatoes, stemmed
> 1 garlic clove, crushed
> $^1/2$ teaspoon salt
> 4 tablespoons virgin olive oil, divided
> 2 red bell peppers
> Ponzu dressing (page 73)
>
> GARNISH
> 1 tablespoon minced parsley

In a large bowl, toss all the vegetables except the red bell peppers with the garlic, salt, and 2 tablespoons of the olive oil. Let the vegetables stand at room temperature, covered, for 30 minutes.

Cook the red bell pepper under a broiler or on a grill until the skin is lightly charred. Wrap the pepper in plastic wrap, and let it steam in its own heat for 10 minutes.

Under the broiler or on the grill, cook the oiled vegetables until the outsides are light golden and cooked through.

Stem, seed, and remove the white ribs of the red bell pepper, and cut it into quarters lengthwise.

Serve the hot vegetables drizzled with ponzu dressing and the remaining olive oil. Garnish the dish with parsley.

• *Yields 4 servings*

VEGETABLE SPRING ROLLS

Yasai no Harumaki

Harumaki, spring rolls, are a dish borrowed from the Chinese kitchen. If you search contemporary cookbooks in Japan, you will find spring rolls firmly established as a Japanese dish. Every home cook has his or her own version. Here is my vegetarian spring roll.

FILLING

5 dried shiitake mushrooms, soaked in cold water for
20 minutes
1 ounce ryokuto harusame (mung-bean noodles)
3 tablespoons vegetable oil
1 tablespoon minced garlic
3¹/₂ ounces or ³/₄ cup canned bamboo shoots, julienned
¹/₂ bunch (2 ounces) Chinese chives, preferably, or
scallions, cut into 2-inch lengths
1 egg, beaten
1 teaspoon shoyu (soy sauce)
Pinch of salt

2 tablespoons all-purpose flour, mixed with
3 tablespoons water
8 spring-roll wrappers
Vegetable oil, for deep-frying

CONDIMENTS
Hot mustard paste (see page 55)
Shoyu *(soy sauce)*

Drain the mushrooms, squeeze them to remove excess water, and cut away their stems. Cut the mushrooms into julienne strips.

Bring a medium pot of water to a boil, remove it from the heat, and submerge the mung-bean noodles in the water. Soak them for 2 minutes. Drain them, cool them under cold tap water, and cut them into 2-inch lengths.

In a skillet, heat the vegetable oil, and cook the garlic over low heat for 20 seconds. Increase the heat, and add the mushrooms, mung-bean noodles, bamboo shoots, and Chinese chives. Cook them, stirring, for 2 minutes. Add the egg, and cook for 1 minute. Add the *shoyu* and salt, and cook, stirring, until all the *shoyu* is absorbed. Remove the cooked mixture to a bowl, and let the mixture cool to room temperature.

Have at hand a pastry brush, a moist cotton cloth, and, in a small cup, the flour-water mixture. Cut each spring-roll wrapper in half diagonally to make two triangles. On a clean counter, place two half wrappers, the long edges nearest you. Cover the remaining wrappers with the moist cotton cloth. Place 1 to 2 tablespoons of the mushroom mixture on each triangle, centered on the long edge and closer to that edge than to the others. Brush the edges of the triangles with the flour-water mixture. Fold the long edge over the filling, fold in the sides, and seal them with the flour-water mixture. Then roll the wrapper into a cylinder shape.

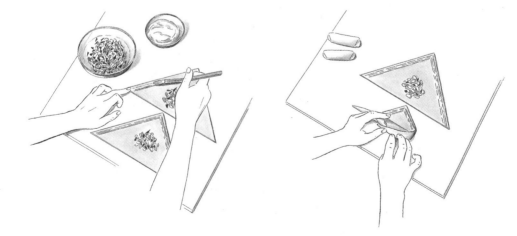

Make the rest of the spring rolls the same way. (You may freeze the rolls at this stage. To cook frozen spring rolls, do not thaw them, but put them directly into oil heated to 340 degrees F. Then raise the heat to 360 degrees F.)

In a skillet, heat 2 inches of vegetable oil to 360 degrees F. Fry the spring rolls in batches until their outsides are golden. Or, if you prefer, bake them in an oven heated to 370 degrees F after brushing them all over with a generous amount of vegetable oil.

Serve the spring rolls hot with mustard paste and *shoyu*.

• *Yields 5 to 8 servings*

ABURA-AGE PIZZA

Yaki Abura-age no Piza

Fried thin tofu can be used in more than traditional preparations. When I want to prepare an easy appetizer, *abura-age*, which is always in my freezer, often plays an important role. I cut each piece in half, make pockets, and stuff them with tomato sauce, assorted cheeses, and basil. This is a quick tofu pizza—good with beer—and everyone loves it.

4 abura-age *(fried thin tofu) sheets*
$^1/_3$ *cup spaghetti-style tomato sauce*
3 *ounces parmesan cheese, cubed*
3 *ounces gorgonzola cheese, cubed*
8 *basil leaves, chopped*

CONDIMENTS
$^1/_3$ *cup grated daikon (optional)*
Shoyu *(soy sauce; optional)*

In a large kettle, bring plenty of water to a boil. Place the *abura-age* sheets in a flat-bottomed, wide colander, and pour the boiling water over them. Turn the *abura-age* over, and pour on more boiling water. This process removes excess oil from the *abura-age*. Cool the *abura-age* under cold running tap water. Drain them, and gently squeeze them to remove excess water.

Cut each *abura-age* in half, and carefully slice open to make a pocket. With a spoon, spread about 2 teaspoons of tomato sauce on the inside bottom surface of each pocket. Stuff the pocket with a portion of the two cheeses and the basil.

Heat the oven to 400 degrees F, or use a broiler. Cook the *abura-age* until the cheese is melted and the top of each "pizza" is golden. Do not overcook *abura-age*; it dries out easily.

Serve the "pizzas" hot, as they are, or cut them in half diagonally to form triangular pieces. For a Japanese-style appetizer, accompany the stuffed *abura-age* with grated daikon and *shoyu*.

• *Yields 4 to 6 servings*

TOFU OMELETTE

Nabeyaki-Dofu

Learning to make an authentic Spanish *tortilla* reminded me of my mother's tofu omelette. It is made of tofu, eggs, and vegetables such as carrot, *gobo* (burdock), and shiitake mushrooms, and flavored with sugar, *sake* (rice wine), and *shoyu* (soy sauce). Although the resulting dish tastes completely different from the Spanish version, the form and method are very similar. This delightful dish could be the centerpiece of a light vegetarian meal.

> *3 dried shiitake mushrooms, soaked in cold water*
> *for 20 minutes*
> *1¹/₂ teaspoons sesame oil*
> *4 tablespoons vegetable oil*
> *1 ounce or ¹/₃ cup gobo (burdock), scraped,*
> *julienned, and soaked in 1 cup cold water*
> *and 1 teaspoon vinegar*
> *1 ounce or ¹/₃ cup lotus root, julienned and soaked in*
> *2 cups cold water and 2 teaspoons vinegar,*
> *preferably, or 1 ounce canned water chestnuts*
> *2 ounces or ²/₃ cup carrot, julienned*
> *1 tablespoon sugar*
> *1 tablespoon sake (rice wine)*
> *1 tablespoon shoyu (soy sauce)*
> *1 block (about 11 ounces) firm tofu*
> *3 large eggs*
> *¹/₂ teaspoon salt*

¹/₄ cup grated daikon
Shoyu *(soy sauce)*

Drain the mushrooms, squeeze them to remove excess water, and cut away their stems. Drain the burdock and lotus root.

Heat a skillet over medium heat. Add the sesame oil and 1 tablespoon of the vegetable oil. When the oil is hot, add all the julienned vegetables. Cook the mixture, stirring, for 2 minutes. Add the sugar and *sake*, and cook, stirring, for 1 minute. Increase the heat to high, add the *shoyu*, and cook until it is absorbed, 30 seconds. Transfer the mixture to a bowl, and let the vegetables cool to room temperature. The vegetables may be prepared to this point in the morning for use later in the day. Refrigerate them, covered, if you won't be making the omelette right away.

Place the tofu in a clean, tightly woven cotton cloth, and squeeze it to remove excess water. Transfer the tofu to a medium bowl, and, with a fork, mash the tofu. In another medium bowl, beat the eggs lightly with a fork. Add the tofu and vegetables to the eggs and mix thoroughly. Season the tofu and egg mixture with the salt.

Heat an 8-inch skillet, and add the remaining 3 tablespoons vegetable oil. When the oil is hot, adjust the heat to medium, and add the tofu mixture. With a rubber spatula, level the surface of the omelette. Cook the omelette, covered, for 1 minute. Decrease the heat to low, and continue to cook the omelette, shaking the skillet gently several times to prevent the omelette from sticking. The omelette is ready to turn when the bottom is golden, after about 4 to 5 minutes of cooking. Check it by lifting the edge of the omelette with a steel spatula.

Place a large platter, preferably one that is completely flat, over the skillet and invert the omelette onto the platter. Return the omelette to the skillet browned side up, and cook, covered, until the other side is golden, about 4 minutes. Remove the skillet from the heat, and let the omelette stand in it for 10 minutes.

Cut the omelette into bite-sized pieces, and serve it with grated daikon and *shoyu* on the side.

• *Yields 4 to 6 servings as an appetizer or 2 to 3 servings as a main dish*

TOFU OMELETTE
WITH COLORFUL SUMMER VEGETABLES

Natsu-yasai Nabeyaki-Dofu

During the hot summer months I often enjoy a Japanese tofu omelette with vegetables that are newer to the Japanese kitchen. In this preparation, small cubes of zucchini, eggplant, and bell pepper replace the traditional shiitake mushrooms, burdock, and carrot. This omelette has an attractive, colorful appearance and a very modern flavor.

> *7 tablespoons olive oil, divided*
> *1 small onion (about 4 ounces), sliced thin*
> *$^1/_2$ zucchini (about 3 ounces), cut into*
>   *$^1/_2$-inch cubes*
> *$^1/_2$ red bell pepper (about 3 ounces), cut into*
>   *$^1/_2$-inch cubes*
> *$^1/_4$ large, oval eggplant (about 2 ounces), cut*
>   *into $^1/_2$-inch cubes*
> *$^1/_4$ cup dashi (fish stock, page 65)*
> *2 teaspoons sugar*
> *$1^1/_2$ teaspoons shoyu (soy sauce)*
> *1 block (about 11 ounces) firm tofu*
> *3 large eggs*
> *$^1/_2$ teaspoon salt*
> *Mixed salad greens tossed with ponzu dressing*
>   *(page 73) or miso dressing (page 163)*

Heat a skillet over medium heat, and add 4 tablespoons of the olive oil. When the oil is hot, reduce the heat to low, add the onion, and cook, stirring, until the onion is soft, about 5 minutes (do not let the onion brown). Adding a pinch of salt during the cooking will help the onion to soften quicker.

Increase the heat to medium, add the cubed vegetables, and cook, stirring, for 2 minutes. Add the *dashi* and sugar, increase the heat to high, and cook the mixture, stirring until the liquid is absorbed. Add the *shoyu* and cook, stirring, for 30 seconds. Transfer the mixture to a bowl, and let the vegetables cool to room temperature. The vegetables can be prepared to this point in the morning for use later in the day. Refrigerate the vegetables, covered, if you won't be making the omelette right away.

Place the tofu in a clean, tightly woven cotton cloth, and squeeze it to remove excess water. Transfer the tofu to a medium bowl, and, with a fork, break and mash the tofu. In another medium bowl, beat the eggs lightly with a fork. Add the tofu and vegetables to the eggs, and fold with a spatula. Season the mixture with the salt.

Heat an 8-inch skillet, and add the remaining 3 tablespoons of olive oil. When the oil is hot, adjust the heat to medium, and add the tofu mixture. Cook the omelette and egg covered, for 1 minute, then reduce the heat to low. Continue cooking, gently shaking the skillet several times to prevent the omelette from sticking. The omelette is ready to turn when the bottom of the omelette is golden, after about 4 to 5 minutes of cooking. Check the bottom by lifting the edge of the omelette with a steel spatula.

Place a large platter, preferably one that is completely flat, over the skillet, and invert the omelette onto the platter. Return the omelette to the skillet, browned side up, and cook, covered, until the other side is golden, about 4 minutes. Remove the skillet from the heat, and let the omelette stand in it for 10 minutes.

Cut the omelette into bite-sized pieces, and serve it on the bed of dressed salad greens.

• *Yields 4 to 6 servings as an appetizer or 2 to 3 as a main dish*

TOFU DAISIES

Mushi Dofu

My students gave the name "tofu daisies" to these dumplings, which consist of tofu and chicken steamed in jackets of julienned wonton wrappers. Each dumpling is garnished with a drop of mustard paste in the center. The resulting appetizer has an attractive flower-like appearance.

Steamed dumplings should be eaten while piping hot, since the surface of the wonton wrappers dries quickly and becomes tough to bite. But sometimes the dumplings may be ready a few minutes before your guests are. Here is a little solution to this problem: Before adding the dumplings to the steamer, make a bed of several lettuce leaves on the bottom of the steamer. This will, first, prevent the dumplings from sticking to the bottom of the steamer during cooking. Further, after you take the dumplings out of the steamer, you can cover them with the hot, softened leaves to keep the dumplings moist and warm for a while.

Wonton wrappers are sheets of dough about 3½ inches square. They are thinner and a little smaller than gyoza wrappers, which are round. Both wonton and gyoza wrappers can be found in the refrigerator or freezer case at Japanese and Asian food stores.

1 small skinned and boned chicken breast half
    (about 5 ounces)
½ teaspoon salt
1 block (about 11 ounces) firm tofu
1½ teaspoons usukuchi shoyu (light-colored
    soy sauce), preferably, or regular shoyu
    (soy sauce)
2 tablespoons thin scallion disks, white parts only
1½ teaspoons peeled, finely grated ginger
½ beaten egg white
½ tablespoon potato starch or cornstarch
2 teaspoons sesame oil, divided
20 to 25 wonton wrappers, preferably, or gyoza
    wrappers, cut into long, thin strips
6 lettuce leaves
12 shungiku (chrysanthemum) leaves, preferably,
    or spinach leaves
2 tablespoons hot mustard paste (see page 55)

CONDIMENT
Nihaizu dressing (rice vinegar and soy sauce dressing,
    page 73)

Chop the chicken fine, transfer it to a bowl, and add the salt. Mix, stirring with a hand, until the chicken feels sticky. Place the tofu in a clean, tightly woven cotton cloth, and squeeze it to remove excess water. Add the tofu to the chicken, and mix thoroughly. One at a time, add the *usukuchi shoyu*, scallion, ginger, egg white, potato starch or cornstarch, and 1 teaspoon of the sesame oil to the tofu and chicken mixture, and blend the mixture by squeezing it in your palms. Refrigerate the mixture, covered, for 30 minutes.

Have at hand a large lightly greased pan, on which twelve 2-inch-diameter dumplings can fit without overlapping. On another large pan, spread the wonton wrapper strips, allowing them to overlap.

Lightly grease your palms with vegetable oil, and form the tofu mixture into 12 balls, each about 1½ inches in diameter. Place the balls on top of the wonton wrapper strips, and gently scatter more strips over the balls until they are completely covered.

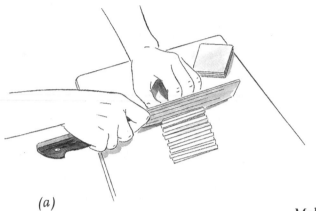

(a)

(b)

Making "tofu daisies": (a) Cut the wonton wrappers into thin strips, (b) place the balls on top of the strips, and (c) cover each ball with the strips.

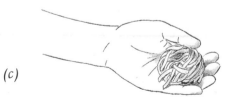

(c)

Place the dumplings on the greased pan, and gently press the center of each dumpling with your thumb to make a shallow depression. This helps the dumplings to cook evenly. The dumplings may be made to this point in the morning for cooking later in the day. Refrigerate them, covered.

Have ready a bamboo or metal steamer with plenty of water at high steam production. Spread the lettuce leaves on the bottom of the heated steamer basket, and arrange the dumplings on top of them, leaving 1/2 inch space between dumplings. Cover the steamer with a lid; if you are using a metal steamer, cover the underside of the lid with a cotton cloth to prevent condensed steam from dripping on the dumplings. Steam the dumplings over high heat for 15 minutes.

Place the cooked dumplings on a bed of chrysanthemum or spinach leaves, and garnish with a drop of mustard paste in the center of each dumpling. If the dumplings are not to be eaten immediately, keep them warm and moist by covering them with some of the steamed lettuce leaves. Serve the dumplings accompanied by *nihaizu* dressing mixed with the remaining 1 teaspoon sesame oil.

- *Yields 4 servings as an appetizer or 2 servings as a main dish*

ROLLED OMELETTE

Tamagoyaki

In my early years at elementary school, my mother prepared a lunchbox for me every morning. Among the many delicious foods in my lunchbox, the one I remember best is the bright yellow, sweet and juicy *tamagoyaki*, rolled omelette. Rolled omelettes are indispensable at sushi restaurants as well as in lunchboxes.

In a *tamagoyaki*, the eggs are cooked in a thin layer in a rectangular skillet, and then rolled to one edge of the skillet. Another thin egg layer is cooked in the same skillet, and this layer is then rolled up with the first. The rolled omelette is then cut into 1-inch cylinders for serving. My mother also made a special-occasion omelette by stuffing it with such ingredients as cooked spinach, *uni* (sea urchin), *unagi no kabayaki* (grilled, flavored eel), crabmeat, or processed cheese.

Rectangular omelette pans, *tamagoyaki-ki,* are available at Japanese cookware shops. A good substitute is a 6-inch round skillet.

4 eggs
1/4 cup dashi *(fish stock, page 65)*
1 tablespoon sake *(rice wine)*
1 tablespoon sugar
Pinch of salt
About 1/4 cup vegetable oil

CONDIMENTS
Grated daikon (optional)
Shoyu (soy sauce; optional)

In a medium bowl, beat the eggs lightly with a pair of chopsticks or a fork. Add the *dashi*, *sake*, sugar, and salt, and combine well.

Heat a Japanese omelette pan or a 6-inch skillet over moderately high heat until the pan smokes. Add 2 tablespoons vegetable oil, and evenly coat the inside of the skillet. Remove the skillet from the heat, pour off the excess oil, and lightly wipe the skillet with a paper towel. Place the skillet over medium heat, and, when the skillet is hot, add about $1/3$ cup of the egg mixture. Swirl the skillet quickly to coat the bottom evenly with the egg mixture. Cook the omelette until the egg mixture is firm on the bottom but still looks wet on top. Do not let the egg brown on the bottom. Adjust the heat as necessary by lifting the skillet.

When the egg mixture has set, use cooking chopsticks or a spatula to quickly roll it from the far end of the skillet toward you. Push the rolled omelette to the far end of the skillet.

Coat the entire skillet again, including the bottom of the rolled omelette, with 1 teaspoon oil. Wipe off any excess oil in the skillet with a paper towel, and add a scant $1/4$ cup of the egg mixture to the skillet. Spread the egg mixture over the bottom of the skillet, lifting the center of the rolled omelette with chopsticks so the egg mixture flows underneath. Cook the egg mixture until the bottom is firm. Roll the new egg layer around the original roll to double its thickness.

Repeat this process until all of the egg mixture is used; you will probably make seven or eight layers in total. When adding oil to the skillet, use only a little, and wipe away any excess. Excessive oil produces a greasy omelette.

Slide the finished omelette out of the skillet, and let the omelette stand at room temperature until it is cool, 15 minutes. At this point you can refrigerate the omelette in a covered container for up to a day.

Cut the omelette into 1-inch cylinders. Serve it as is or with grated daikon and a little *shoyu* on the side.

• *Yields 3 to 4 servings*

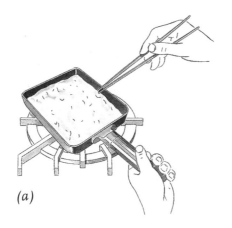

(a)

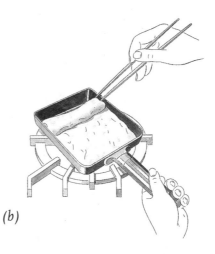

(b)

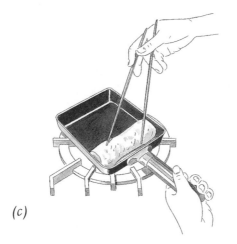

(c)

Making a rolled omelette:
(a) Check that the bottom
of the omelette is firm, and
(b and c) roll the omelette
toward you. Push the
omelette to the far side of
the pan, and (d) begin
again with more egg
mixture. When you have
used up all the mixture,
(e) roll the finished omelette
toward you.

•

193

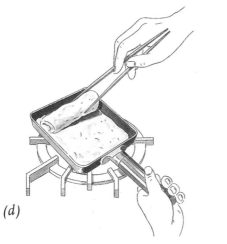

(d)

(e)

ASARI CLAMS STEAMED IN *SAKE*

Asari no Sakamushi

A key to success with this dish is to purchase very fresh clams and to use fairly good *sake*, though not necessarily of *ginjo* (superior) or *daiginjo* (premium) class. The *asari* clam is small, 1½ inches across, and nearly triangular, with fine, shallow striations on the shell. It lives in the inlets where fresh water meets saltwater. The flesh, white with a slight camel tinge, has a rich clam flavor. The clam's season is spring and summer in Japan. When you can't find *asari* clams, use littleneck clams or New Zealand cockles.

The condiments called for in this recipe are *naganegi* long onion and *akatogarashi* chile pepper. Other good condiments are garlic, ginger, lemongrass, parsley, and coriander leaves. Serve a French baguette for soaking up the remaining cooking liquid.

> ½ cup sake *(rice wine)*
> ½ white part of naganegi *long onion,*
>   *preferably, or 2 scallions, minced*
> 1 akatogarashi *or other small dried red chile pepper,*
>   *stemmed, seeded, and cut into thin rings*
> 11 ounces asari *clams, desanded (see page 22)*
>
> GARNISH
> 1 scallion, green part only, *cut into thin rings*
> 1 lemon, *cut into wedges*
> 1 French baguette

In a medium pot, combine the *sake*, minced *naganegi* long onion or scallion, and red chile. Bring the mixture to a boil over medium heat. Reduce the heat to low, and cook, covered, for 3 minutes. Increase the heat to medium, add the clams all at once, and bring the mixture to a boil, covered. Cook the clams, shaking or stirring the pot several times with a wooden spatula, until they are open, 3 to 5 minutes.

Discard any unopened clams. Strain the cooking broth through a fine sieve, reserving the liquid. Serve the clams immediately, in individual soup bowls with the reserved liquid. Garnish each bowl with scallion rings and a lemon wedge. Serve the baguette on the side.

• *Yields 2 servings*

SHRIMP QUENELLES

Ebi no Age-shinjo

The Japanese equivalent of French fish and shellfish quenelles, *shinjo* is made from fish or shellfish, salt, egg white, *dashi* (fish stock), and potato starch. No cream is added to the mixture.

In this recipe, the quenelles are very briefly cooked in oil for extra flavor and color. They are then served hot with tempura dipping sauce. They also taste delicious with just *shoyu* (soy sauce) and mustard paste. Fried or not, they are good in soup, too.

> *2 ounces fresh* shimeji *or* shiitake mushrooms
> *1 cup* dashi *(fish stock, page 65)*
> *¹/₄ teaspoon* shoyu *(soy sauce)*
> *2 teaspoons potato starch or cornstarch*
> *5 ounces headed, peeled, and deveined*
>   *small shrimp*
> *4 ounces skinned and boned sea bass or cod*
> *³/₄ teaspoon salt*
> *1 egg white, lightly beaten*
> *Vegetable oil, for deep-frying*
> *12 shiso leaves, 6 leaves minced and 6 left whole*
> *1¹/₂ cup* tentsuyu *(tempura dipping sauce,*
>   *page 67)*
>
> GARNISH
> *2 tablespoons peeled and grated ginger*

Cut the stems from the mushrooms. Cut *shimeji* mushrooms into ¹/₂-inch lengths, or shiitake mushrooms into ¹/₂-inch cubes. In a saucepan of boiling water, cook the mushrooms for 10 seconds. Drain them in a colander, and spread them to cool. In a small bowl, toss the mushrooms with ¹/₄ cup *dashi* and the *shoyu*.

In another small bowl, combine the potato starch or cornstarch and the remaining ³/₄ cup *dashi*, and stir until smooth. Put the shrimp, fish, and salt into a food processor, and turn the machine on and off until the mixture forms a coarse paste. Transfer the mixture to a *suribachi* or other mortar. Little by little, add first the egg white and then the potato starch or cornstarch liquid, and grind until the mixture is smooth. (If a Japanese mortar is not available, blend the ingredients in a medium bowl with a whisk.) With a spatula, fold in the mushrooms and minced shiso. The mixture should be quite loose.

Have at hand six 8-by-8-inch parchment paper squares, one teacup, and six 6-inch lengths of kitchen string. Place a piece of parchment paper over a teacup, and press the center of the paper to the bottom. Place a sixth of the shrimp mixture into the depression. Squeeze the top of the paper closed to make a round packet. Tie the top with a piece of the kitchen string. Make five more packets the same way.

Bring a large pot of water to a boil over high heat. Reduce the heat to medium, add the packets, and cook them for 6 to 8 minutes. Drain the packets, and cool them at room temperature for 10 minutes. Unwrap the packets, set the quenelles on a plate, and cover them with plastic wrap until you are ready to use them. At this stage, they can be added to a hot soup or refrigerated, covered, for use the next day. Remove them from the refrigerator 20 minutes before further cooking.

In a large, deep skillet heat 2 inches of vegetable oil to 300 degrees F. Cook the six whole shiso leaves one at a time over low heat until they become bright green and translucent, 5 seconds. Transfer the shiso leaves to a rack, and sprinkle them lightly with salt.

Increase the oil temperature to 360 degrees F. Wipe the quenelles with a paper towel, add them to the oil, and cook them in two batches until they are golden. Transfer the quenelles to a rack.

In a medium pot, heat the tempura dipping sauce over medium heat until hot. Serve the quenelles immediately, covered with hot tempura dipping sauce and garnished with grated ginger and fried shiso leaves.

• *Yields 6 servings*

ELEGANT TEMPURA PANCAKES

Kakiage Zensai

I always enjoy devising new, attractive versions of traditional Japanese dishes. Surprisingly small changes can produce big differences in both flavor and appearance.

Kakiage literally means "fried collected ingredients." Unlike most tempura preparations, in which individual ingredients are coated with batter and fried, this preparation uses two to three different foods, cut into cubes, mixed together in batter, and then fried. The resulting appetizer has a pancakelike shape and thickness.

Traditionally, *kakiage* tempura is made in 3-inch disks and served with a lemon wedge, or with tempura dipping sauce and grated daikon. *Kakiage* tempura is also sometimes made into a larger disk, which tops a bowl of rice in the popular lunchtime dish *kakiage donburi*, a favorite among hurried businesspeople. In this recipe, I have transformed this hearty, ordinary rice-bowl dish into an elegant appetizer.

SAUCE
¹/₄ cup shoyu (soy sauce)
¹/₄ cup mirin (sweet cooking wine)
2 tablespoons sugar
1 tablespoon honey

7 ounces headed, peeled, and deveined very fresh
    large shrimp
2 bunches (4 ounces) mitsuba leaves, preferably, or
    watercress
Vegetable oil, for deep-frying
³/₄ cup cake flour
1 egg, beaten in a 2-cup measuring cup
1¹/₂ cups (2 rice-cooker cups) hot cooked short grain
    or medium-grain white rice (see page 151)

GARNISH
¹/₄ cup grated daikon
1 tablespoon minced chives or thin scallion rings
    (green part only)

In a small saucepan, combine the *shoyu*, *mirin*, sugar, and honey with $^1/_2$ cup water, and bring the mixture to a boil over medium heat. Reduce the heat to low, and cook the mixture until it is slightly thickened, 8 minutes. Be careful not to burn the sauce.

Cut the shrimp into $^1/_2$-inch lengths crosswise. Cut the *mitsuba* greens or watercress into 1-inch pieces. In a medium bowl, combine the shrimp and greens, and toss with 1 tablespoon of the flour.

In a large, deep skillet, begin heating 3 inches of vegetable oil over medium heat to 360 degrees F.

Add enough ice water to the egg to make a combined volume of $^3/_4$ cup. In a medium bowl, combine half the egg liquid with half the remaining flour. Stir the mixture with chopsticks or a whisk. Add half the shrimp mixture to the batter, and toss several times.

Pour one-third of the shrimp-batter mixture into a shallow ladle, and pour the mixture gently into the heated oil. Do not submerge the ladle in the oil, or the batter will stick to the ladle. Cook the pancake at 360 degrees F for about 1 minute. Reduce the heat to 340 degrees F, and cook the pancake until it is crisp and light golden, about 3 to 4 minutes. While cooking, skim the oil frequently to remove pieces of batter floating on the surface of the oil.

Transfer the pancake to a rack. Make two more pancakes with the remaining shrimp-batter mixture.

Mix the remaining egg liquid, flour, and shrimp mixture, and make this mixture into three more pancakes.

Using a 3-inch steel ring mold, shape the hot rice into six $1^1/_2$- to 2-inch-tall disks. Place one disk in the center of each of six plates. Spoon 1 to 2 teaspoons of the hot sauce over each rice disk. Place a pancake on the top, and spoon 1 to 2 teaspoons more sauce over each pancake. Decorate the plates with grated daikon, additional sauce, and minced chives.

This appetizer should be eaten hot, so you may wish to serve three dishes at a time, as soon as they are ready. Tell the diners that in Japanese etiquette it is not customary to wait for everyone to be served before starting to eat. It is polite to begin as soon as you are served.

• *Yields 6 servings as an appetizer or 3 servings as a main dish*

GOLDEN BROWN FISH CAKES

Satsuma-age

Satsuma-age, Japanese fish cakes, were invented in Satsuma, the provincial name of present-day Kagoshima Prefecture, on the southern island of Kyushu. Japanese fish cakes remind me of their Thai counterparts, which are served as an appetizer in nearly every Thai restaurant. The concept seems to have been introduced to both countries by the Portuguese and Spanish.

Unlike Thai fish cakes, which contain a substantial quantity of herbs and red chile, the Japanese cakes employ only fish and julienned vegetables, so they have a subtle and delicate flavor. Choosing the freshest fish is the key to success in making Japanese fish cakes.

Japanese fish cakes are served with *shoyu* (soy sauce) and mustard paste.

> 2 ounces or ²/₃ cup gobo *(burdock), scraped,*
> *julienned in 1-inch lengths, and soaked in*
> *1 cup cold water and 1 teaspoon vinegar*
> 2 ounces or ²/₃ cup carrot, *julienned in 1-inch lengths*
> 2 tablespoons vegetable oil
> ¹/₄ cup dashi *(fish stock, page 65)*
> 1 teaspoon sugar
> 2 teaspoons shoyu *(soy sauce)*
> 11 ounces boned and skinned sea bass or cod fillet
> 1 teaspoon sake *(rice wine)*
> 1 large egg white
> 5 tablespoons potato starch or cornstarch
> 2 teaspoons all-purpose flour
> 10 shiso leaves, *preferably, or basil, kaffir lime,*
> *or coriander leaves, cut into thin strips*
> Vegetable oil, *for deep-frying*
>
> CONDIMENTS
> 1 tablespoon hot mustard paste *(see page 55)*
> Shoyu *(soy sauce)*

Drain the burdock and carrot. Heat a skillet over medium heat, and add 2 tablespoons vegetable oil. When the oil is hot, add the burdock and carrot, and cook, stirring, for 2 minutes. Add the *dashi* and sugar, and cook, stirring, until all the liquid is absorbed. Add the *shoyu*, and cook, stirring, for 30 seconds. Transfer the vegetables to a bowl, and let them cool to room temperature.

With a food processor or a knife, chop the fish to a coarse paste. Transfer the fish paste to a *suribachi* or other mortar, and blend in first the *sake* then the egg white. If a Japanese mortar is not available, do the blending in a medium bowl with your hands, squeezing and kneading the mixture. Add the potato starch and flour, one at a time, and grind or squeeze thoroughly. With a spatula, fold in the cooked vegetables and the shiso or other herb. The mixture should be quite soft, but not runny. Refrigerate it for at least 1 hour, covered.

With a spatula, divide the fish mixture into eighths. Grease a large pan on which sixteen 2-inch-diameter fish cakes can fit without overlapping. Grease your hands with additional oil. Pick up half of a one-eighth portion of the fish paste, and make it into a small, flat disk, 2 inches in diameter. Press the center of the fish cake gently to make a shallow depression; this facilitates quicker and even cooking. Place the fish cake on the greased pan, and make the remaining fish paste into cakes. At this point the fish cakes can be refrigerated, covered, for use later in the day. Remove them from the refrigerator 20 minutes before cooking them.

In a large, deep skillet heat 3 inches of vegetable oil to 330 degrees F. In small batches, fry the fish cakes until golden, about 4 to 5 minutes, maintaining the oil temperature at 330 degrees F. Transfer the fish cakes to a rack.

Serve the fish cakes hot, with mustard paste and *shoyu* on the side.

Fish cakes are also delicious served with tempura dipping sauce (page 67), ponzu dressing (page 73), or *sanbaizu* dressing (page 74) with red chile pepper added.

• *Yields 6 to 8 servings*

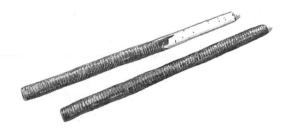

TERIYAKI CHICKEN-AND-ASPARAGUS ROLLS

Asupara-maki Tori no Teriyaki

The cut surfaces of these rolls display white chicken meat with bright green asparagus in the center. You can create other attractive color combinations using strong-colored vegetables, such as red bell pepper.

The rolled chicken is basted with the popular teriyaki sauce. Once the basting sauce is applied, the surface of the chicken burns easily, so please watch carefully as you cook the chicken.

I serve this traditional appetizer on top of salad greens.

> *2 large boned chicken thighs, with skin attached*
> *2 tablespoons* shoyu *(soy sauce)*
> *2 tablespoons* mirin *(sweet cooking wine)*
> *2 tablespoons* sake *(rice wine)*
> *1 tablespoon peeled and finely grated ginger*
> *6 thin asparagus spears, tough ends and tips removed*
> *¹/₂ cup teriyaki sauce (page 77)*
> *Mixed salad greens*
> *Sansho pepper*

Make several very shallow lengthwise cuts on the inner side of each chicken thigh, so that later the chicken will be easy to roll. In a medium bowl, combine the *shoyu, mirin, sake,* and grated ginger. Add the chicken thighs, and marinate them for 20 minutes, turning them over several times. Remove the chicken thighs from the marinade, and wipe them dry with a paper towel.

Bring a medium pot of water to a boil, and blanch the asparagus spears for 20 seconds. Drain them, and wipe them dry with a paper towel.

Tightly roll three asparagus spears in each chicken thigh. Secure each roll with five steel skewers, threaded through the overlapped part of the roll in a fan shape, so that you can hold all five skewers together at one end. They will form a convenient handle by which to turn over the chicken during cooking.

Heat a broiler or grill. Place the chicken rolls in a broiler pan or on the grill rack, 5 to 6 inches from the heat source, and cook the chicken rolls for 10 minutes. Turn them over, and cook them for 6 minutes on the other side. Remove the chicken rolls from the heat source. With a pastry brush, apply the teriyaki sauce on both sides of the chicken rolls. Return them to the heat source, and dry them on both sides for 1 to 2 minutes. Repeat the basting and drying process several times, until the chicken rolls are coated with a glossy layer of sauce.

After the chicken is cooked, turn the skewers to loosen them, but leave them in for 5 minutes.

In a small saucepan, warm the remaining sauce over moderate heat. Unskewer the chicken rolls, and cut each roll into 1-inch slices crosswise. Lay the chicken disks on a bed of salad greens, and drizzle the disks with a little teriyaki sauce. Sprinkle a little *sansho* pepper over the chicken and serve.

• *Yields 4 servings as an appetizer or 2 servings as a main dish*

CHICKEN BREAST FILLETS
IN A CRUST OF MUNG-BEAN NOODLES

Tori Sasami Harusame-age

After learning how to bone chicken many years ago, I frequently accumulated numerous chicken breast fillets, *sasami*, in the freezer. *Sasami* are the slender muscles you find on either side of the breast bone, beneath the large breast muscles, when you bone a chicken. They are the leanest parts of the chicken. In Japan, breast fillets are sold separately from the rest of the chicken breast. They are also sometimes sold separately in U.S. super-markets, where they are usually labeled "tenders."

Now I have a good reason to collect chicken breast fillets: I use them in this elegant preparation. Each fillet is cut and spread into a broad sheet, rolled around a filling, coated with cut mung-bean noodles, and deep-fried. In the hot oil, the mung-bean noodles pop like popcorn, turn snow white, and become an appealing crust. If you don't want to go to the trouble of cutting mung-bean noodles, substitute plain cornflakes, broken into small rough pieces.

8 large chicken breast fillets
Salt
2 tablespoons mamemiso *(soybean miso)*
1 tablespoon sugar

1 teaspoon sesame oil
1/₂ cup all-purpose flour
16 shiso *leaves, or 1/₂ sheet* nori *cut into 8*
     squares and 8 shiso *leaves*
4 green beans, cut in half crosswise
One 2-inch-long piece of carrot, cut lengthwise
     into 8 sticks
3 1/₂ ounces artificial crab sticks
2 egg whites, lightly beaten
5 ounces ryokuto harusame *(mung-bean noodles),*
     cut into 1/₂-inch lengths with scissors
Vegetable oil, for deep-frying

GARNISH
8 shiso *leaves*

Remove the white, string-like tendon from each chicken breast fillet. Make a lengthwise shallow cut in the center of each fillet, and cut each fillet open to make a broader, thin sheet. If this is too difficult, place the fillets between sheets of parchment paper or plastic wrap, and gently beat the fillets with a rolling pin until they are broad and thin. Trim each fillet at both ends to make a clean edge. Lightly salt both sides of the chicken fillets, and let them stand for 10 minutes.

Wipe the salt and exuded juice from the fillets with a paper towel.

In a small bowl, combine the *mamemiso*, 1 tablespoon water, the sugar, and sesame oil, and mix until smooth.

Place the chicken fillets on a clean counter. Using a pastry brush, dust each fillet lightly with flour. Place one shiso leaf or nori (cut into similar size as chicken fillet) over the fillet, and brush the top of the shiso or nori with the miso mixture. Place a bean half, a carrot stick, and a crab stick on the broad end of the fillet. Roll the fillet tightly around the other ingredients, and secure the roll with a toothpick. Make seven more rolls in the same way.

In a large, deep skillet heat 3 inches of oil to 320 degrees F. Dust the chicken rolls with flour. One at a time, dip the chicken rolls in egg white, shake off the excess egg white, and coat the rolls evenly with the mung-bean noodles. Fry the chicken rolls in two batches, turning the rolls once, until they are slightly golden, about 4 minutes.

Transfer the chicken rolls to a rack, and sprinkle them with a little salt. Turn the toothpicks to loosen them, but let the rolls stand for 3 minutes before removing the toothpicks.

Serve the chicken rolls cut into halves or quarters crosswise, on a bed of the remaining shiso leaves.

• *Yields 4 servings*

(a)

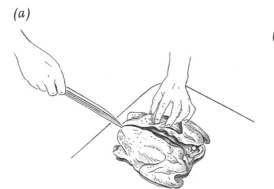

(b)

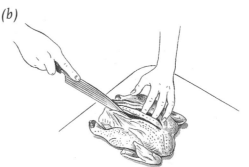

(c)

(d)

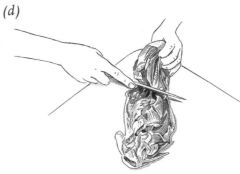

(e)

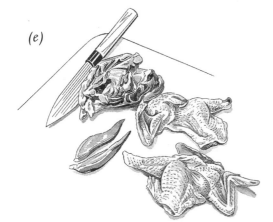

Boning a chicken and extracting the breast fillets:

a. Make one shallow center cut on the back side of the chicken.

b. Make two shallow center cuts next to the breast bone on the belly side.

c. Make a shallow cut on the shoulder in the depression.

d. Pull and separate the wing part from the body. Pull further and separate the breast part, but leaving the breast fillets intact to the center bone, and thigh.

e. Two breast and thigh parts and two breast fillets removed from the center bone.

f. Cut each breast fillet in the center and open to make it into a broad sheet.

(f)

CLASSIC ROLLED BEEF WITH VEGETABLES

Gyuniku no Yasaimaki

Until import restrictions were relaxed in 1991, beef was a very expensive food in Japan. Since then, imports from the United States, Australia, and New Zealand have brought great reductions in the price of beef, and great changes in the way in which beef is consumed in Japan. Now a Japanese family can afford to purchase a thick steak to prepare at home. However, most of the beef sold by Japanese butchers today is still in its traditional thin-sliced form.

You may not be able to buy beef in broad, thin slices, but you can cut it yourself, and then pound the slices into thin sheets. In this preparation, thin sheets of beef are rolled with vegetables and cooked in a strongly flavored sauce. Try this dish with other vegetables, such as scallions, carrots, green beans, or asparagus.

> $^1/_2$ red bell pepper, stem, seeds, and white ribs
> removed
> 14 ounces beef sirloin
> 1 package enokitake mushrooms, stem ends removed
> Salt
> Fresh-ground black pepper
> 12 shishitogarashi peppers, preferably, or 1 medium
> size green bell pepper
> 2 tablespoons vegetable oil
> 2 tablespoons sake (rice wine)
> 2 tablespoons mirin (sweet cooking wine)
> 2 tablespoons sugar
> 2 teaspoons shoyu (soy sauce)
> $^1/_2$ teaspoon tamari

In a medium pot of boiling water, blanch the red bell pepper for 30 seconds. Drain it, and wipe it dry with a paper towel. Cut the bell pepper into thin 2-inch-long strips.

Have parchment paper and kitchen string at hand. Cut the beef into six slices. Place the slices between two pieces of parchment paper, and beat with a meat mallet to make thin, broad sheets about $^1/_{10}$- to $^1/_{12}$-inch thick. Salt and pepper both sides of each beef sheet. Place a sixth of the red bell pepper and mushrooms along a short side of each sheet.

Tightly roll the vegetables into the beef. With kitchen string, bind the rolls tightly in three places.

Prick the *shishitogarashi* peppers all over with a toothpick. If you are using green bell peppers, cut them into 1-inch-wide strips. Heat a large skillet over medium heat, and add 1 tablespoon of vegetable oil. When the oil is hot, add the peppers. Cook them, shaking the skillet, until their skins blister, about 1 minute. Season the peppers with tamari, transfer them to a plate, and set the plate aside, covered.

Clean the skillet with hot water, and wipe it dry with a paper towel. Heat the skillet again over medium heat, and add the remaining 1 tablespoon vegetable oil. Add half the beef rolls to the skillet, and cook them until all sides are brown. Add additional oil, if needed, and then brown the remaining beef rolls. Transfer the beef rolls to a platter, and set it aside, covered.

Clean the skillet with hot water. Add the *sake*, *mirin*, sugar, and ⅔ cup water. Bring the mixture to a boil over medium heat. Return all the beef rolls to the skillet, and cook for 2 minutes, turning the rolls several times in the cooking liquid. Add the *shoyu*, and continue cooking for 1 to 2 minutes. Do not overcook the beef; it can be faintly pink when it is cut. Transfer the beef rolls to the platter, and set it aside, covered.

Increase the heat to high, and boil the remaining cooking liquid until it thickens, about 5 minutes. Return the beef rolls to the skillet, add the tamari, and turn the rolls to coat them with the sauce.

Remove the beef rolls from the skillet, remove the cotton strings, and cut them into quarters. Serve the rolls drizzled with the remaining sauce and accompanied by the fried *shishitogarashi* or green peppers.

• *Yields 4 servings*

STEAMED LAYERED EGG SQUARES

Nishiki-tamago

Nishiki-tamago, brocade egg, is one of the dishes that is part of *osechi-ryori,* the traditional feast eaten during the first three days of the new year. In this dish, hard-boiled eggs are separated into yolks and whites, which are separately pressed through a fine sieve and mixed with salt and sugar. The two mixtures are then layered in a square steel mold and steamed. The finished dish, which displays alternate layers of egg yolk and egg white, reminds the

Japanese of finely woven brocade, *nishiki*. Because of its bright bands of color, *nishiki-tamago* is suitable for any festive occasion.

> *15 eggs*
> *10 tablespoons sugar*
> *1 teaspoon salt*

Remove the eggs from the refrigerator at least 20 minutes before cooking them.

Put the eggs into a pot, and cover them with cold water. Bring the water to a boil, and cook the eggs over medium heat for 15 minutes.

Place the eggs in ice water just until their shells are cool. Drain and shell the eggs, and separate the whites from the yolks. While the egg whites are still warm, set a fine sieve over a plate, and press them through the sieve (as the eggs cool, this process becomes more difficult).

Rinse the sieve, and wipe it dry with a paper towel. Set the sieve over another plate, and press the egg yolks through it.

Add 7 tablespoons of the sugar and $1/4$ teaspoon of the salt to the egg yolks, and toss gently with a wooden spatula. Do not mash the mixture.

Add the remaining sugar and salt to the egg whites, and toss gently.

With a piece of parchment paper cut to fit, cover the bottom of a square steel mold or other heat-proof container about $6^1/_2$ inches square. Line the sides of the mold with additional parchment paper. Spread half the egg white in the mold, cover it with half the egg yolk, then add the remaining egg white, and end with the remaining egg yolk. When spreading the top layer of egg yolk, do not press the surface. The egg yolk should sit on the egg white like freshly fallen snow gently settling on the ground.

Have a bamboo or metal steamer at high steam production. Steam the egg in the mold over medium heat for 8 minutes. Remove the mold from the steamer, and let the egg stand at room temperature until it has cooled completely. Run a small, sharp knife around the edge of the mold to loosen the egg. Lift one side of the egg, and remove it in one piece. Cut it into 16 squares.

• *Yields 16 servings*

STEAMED EGG CUSTARD "SOUP"

Chawanmushi

Chawanmushi, "(food) steamed in a cup," is so popular throughout Japan that special china cups are made for preparing and serving this egg custard soup. The cups come with lids, not for use during cooking but to keep the custard warm for a while after it is served.

Egg custard soup is made from *dashi* (fish stock) and eggs. The subtle, delicate flavor of this non-sweet custard relies on good-quality *dashi,* fresh eggs, and fresh ingredients. These ingredients are usually chicken, shrimp, and mushroom, but seasonal ingredients— gingko nuts, *mitsuba, yuzu* citron, *kinome* (young *sansho* pepper tree leaves), and lily bulb—are sometimes added to express a sense of season.

For a richer, more familiar taste for non-Japanese diners, you can replace the *dashi* with chicken stock.

Use four to six 3-inch-diameter ramekins if Japanese custard cups are not available.

1 chicken breast fillet (see page 205) or 2 scallops
Salt
4 medium shrimp, headed, peeled, deveined, and cut
    into halves
2 fresh shiitake mushrooms, stems removed, quartered
1¹/₂ teaspoons usukuchi shoyu (light-colored soy sauce),
    preferably, or regular shoyu (soy sauce)
2 large eggs
1¹/₂ cups dashi (fish stock, page 65)
¹/₂ teaspoon salt
¹/₂ teaspoon mirin (sweet cooking wine)
8 mitsuba leaves, preferably, or watercress leaves,
    stems removed

GARNISH
¹/₂ yuzu citron or lemon rind, julienned
    (see page 52)

Place a bamboo or metal steamer basket over plenty of water in a deep pot over high heat. Remove the white string from the chicken breast fillet, lightly salt the meat, and let it stand for 15 minutes.

Wipe the chicken with a paper towel to remove the salt and exuded juice. Cut the fillet in half diagonally, then halve the two pieces crosswise.

In a small saucepan of salted boiling water, blanch the chicken and shrimp for 10 seconds. Drain them, and wipe them dry with a paper towel. In a medium bowl, toss the shrimp, chicken, and mushroom with 1 teaspoon *shoyu*, and let the mixture stand for 15 minutes.

Wipe the shrimp, chicken, and mushrooms dry with a paper towel, and divide them among four custard soup cups or ramekins.

In a medium bowl, beat the eggs lightly with a pair of cooking chopsticks or a fork. Add the remaining 1/2 teaspoon *shoyu*, the *dashi*, 1/2 teaspoon salt, and *mirin*, and mix with chopsticks or a fork. Strain the mixture through a fine sieve. Divide the strained egg liquid among the soup cups or ramekins. Transfer the cups or ramekins to the hot steamer. If you are using a metal steamer, cover the underside of the lid with a thick cotton cloth to prevent condensed steam from dripping on the custard. Steam the custard for 2 minutes over high heat, and then reduce the heat to medium to low. (The temperature in the steamer basket should be about 195 degrees F for the rest of the steaming period. Egg custard soup should have a silky, smooth texture similar to that of soft tofu. If the temperature is too high, egg protein coagulates, leaving many tiny air pockets, and the texture of the custard becomes tough.) Steam the custard for 13 minutes more, or until clear liquid runs out when you insert a wooden skewer in the center. Place a *mitsuba* or watercress leaf on top of each cup or ramekin, and steam for another 30 seconds.

Remove the cups or ramekins from the steamer. Serve the custard garnished with *yuzu* citron or lemon rind and covered with a lid if possible. Accompany each serving with a spoon.

- *Yields 4 servings*

ALL-MUSHROOM EGG CUSTARD "SOUP"

Kinokozukushi Chawanmushi

This is my own variation on *chawanmushi*, egg custard soup. A mixture of mushrooms, each of which has a sweet, robust, or otherwise distinct flavor, is steamed in a custard made with chicken broth. The mushrooms give a pleasant chewy texture to the silky-smooth egg custard. This dish can be served hot or chilled.

$\frac{1}{3}$ ounce or $\frac{1}{4}$ cup tightly packed dried porcini
mushrooms, covered with boiling water
and soaked for 15 minutes
2 ounces or about 4 medium fresh shiitake
mushrooms, stems removed
3 ounces or 5 or 6 button mushrooms, stems removed
4 ounces or about 1 cup enokitake mushrooms, stem
ends removed
1 tablespoon vegetable oil
2 teaspoons mirin (sweet cooking wine)
$\frac{1}{4}$ to $\frac{1}{2}$ teaspoon shoyu (soy sauce), depending on
the saltiness of the chicken broth
Fresh-ground black pepper
2 tablespoons minced parsley
1 cup concentrated chicken broth
3 large eggs
Salt to taste

Place a bamboo or metal steamer basket over plenty of water in a deep pot over high heat. Drain the porcini mushrooms in a fine sieve, reserving the soaking liquid. Cut all the mushrooms into $\frac{1}{3}$-inch cubes.

In a medium skillet over high heat, heat the vegetable oil. When the oil is hot, add all the mushrooms. Cook the mushrooms for 1 minute, stirring. Add the *mirin* and *shoyu*, and cook for 1 minute, stirring. Add the ground black pepper and minced parsley, and give several big stirs. Remove the skillet from the heat.

Dilute the chicken broth with the water in which the porcini were soaked, and add water to make 2 cups. In a medium bowl, beat the eggs lightly with a pair of cooking chopsticks or a fork, and add the eggs to the chicken broth. Strain the egg-broth mixture through a fine sieve. Add the mushrooms to the egg-broth mixture, and season the mixture with salt. Fill the custard soup cups or ramekins 80 percent full with the egg-broth mixture, distributing the mushrooms evenly among the cups or ramekins. Transfer the cups or ramekins to the hot steamer. If you are using a metal steamer, cover the underside of the lid with a thick cotton cloth to prevent condensed steam from dripping on the custard. Steam the custard 2 minutes over high heat, and then reduce the heat to medium-low. (The temperature in the steamer basket should be about 195 degrees F for the rest of the steaming period.) Steam the custard for 13 minutes more, or until clear liquid runs out when you insert a wooden skewer.

Remove the cups or ramekins from the steamer. Serve the custard covered with a lid, if possible. Accompany each serving with a small spoon.

• *Yields 4 to 5 servings*

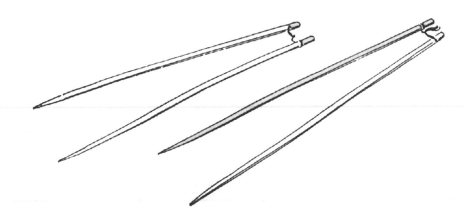

CLEAR SOUP WITH SOFT EGG CAKE

Tamago-jiru

Preparing soft egg cake, the main attraction of this clear soup, is simple and fun. Diners will be impressed with the shape of the sliced cake, but you will have spent nearly no time to prepare it.

The key to successful soft egg cake is to cook the beaten eggs in briskly boiling water very briefly, 3 to 4 seconds. If overcooked, the eggs completely coagulate and cannot be shaped into a smooth cake.

For color and additional flavor, you may add minced parsley or crabmeat to the cake; stir the parsley or crab into the eggs just after draining them.

> *2 eggs*
> *2 teaspoons salt*
> *2¹/₂ cups dashi (fish stock, page 65)*
> *2 teaspoons usukuchi shoyu (light-colored soy sauce),*
>   *preferably, or shoyu (soy sauce)*
> *4 carrot slices, ¹/₃-inch thick, cut into a floral shape*
>   *(see page 27), parboiled 1 minute and*
>   *cooled in ice water*
> *4 small broccoli flowerets, parboiled 30 seconds to 1*
>   *minute and cooled in ice water*

In a medium bowl, lightly beat the eggs and 1 teaspoon salt with a pair of cooking chopsticks or a fork. In a medium pot, bring 1 quart of water to a very brisk boil over high heat. In a sink, place a sieve lined with a cotton cloth.

Add the egg to the boiling water, running the egg over the ends of a pair of chopsticks or a fork so the egg spreads out into a soft cake. The egg will first sink to the bottom of the pot, then quickly swell and float to the surface. As soon as all the egg comes to the surface, which takes only a few seconds, quickly drain the egg in the cloth-lined sieve. Collect the hot cooked egg gently and quickly in the center of the cotton cloth, and squeeze both ends of the cloth tightly closed to make a cake about 4 inches long and 2 inches in diameter. (The egg must be very hot to form into a smooth cake. You may need to wear thin kitchen gloves to protect your hands from the hot water.) Let the egg cake set in the cotton cloth for 20 minutes, until it has cooled to room temperature. You can refrigerate the cooled egg cake, covered, for use later in the day.

Remove the egg cake from the cotton cloth, slice off the misshapen ends of the cake, and cut the cake into four pieces crosswise.

In a medium pot, bring the *dashi* to a boil over medium heat. Season the *dashi* with the remaining salt and the *shoyu*. Warm the egg cake disks, the carrot, and the broccoli in the hot broth for 1 minute. Serve the soup in individual bowls with a slice of egg cake, a broccoli floweret, and a slice of carrot in each.

• *Yields 4 servings*

You can make an egg cake set in various shapes by using two or more chopsticks. For example, if you place two chopsticks opposite each other against the cloth-wrapped cake, and hold them tightly in place with a pair of rubber bands until the cake cools, they will create twin depressions, giving the cut slices the shape of a bottleneck gourd.

CONSOMMÉ WITH SARDINE DUMPLINGS

Iwashi no Tsumire-jiru

Among all fish, sardines (*iwashi*) are ranked one of the highest in eicosapentaenoic acid (EPA) and decosahexaenoic acid (DHA), which are found in unsaturated fish oils. EPA and DHA are known to lower blood cholesterol levels, while raising the level of good cholesterol, HDL. They also work as mild anti-inflammatory agents and, when ingested often, reduce the risk of heart attack.

But for me these nutritional merits are second in importance when I cook sardines. I love their strong but sweet, rich flavor. This sardine dumpling soup has over the years been successfully entertaining many students, who would otherwise never think of trying this oily, "fishy" fish. Sardines are very perishable, so ask at your fish store for the freshest ones for this preparation. As soon as you get them home, scale, gut, and rinse them in a very cool environment, since guts and blood contain enzymes that decompose fish very quickly. Refrigerate the cleaned and wiped sardines, covered, and use them the same day.

The base of this soup is clear *dashi*. It could instead be miso soup or chicken stock.

9 ounces fresh 8-inch-long whole sardines, gutted
1 tablespoon akamiso (brown miso)
1 tablespoon all-purpose flour
1 small egg yolk
1 thumb-size piece of ginger, peeled and grated
1 tablespoon minced scallions
2¹/₂ cups dashi (fish stock, page 65)
1 teaspoon salt
2 teaspoons usukuchi shoyu (light-colored soy sauce),
    preferably, or regular shoyu (soy sauce)
Fresh-ground black pepper

GARNISH
1 tablespoon thin scallion rings, green part only

Rinse the sardines under cold running water, and wipe them dry with paper towels. Cut off the heads. Holding a sardine in one hand, run the thumb of your other hand over one side of the spine, from the top to the tail, to separate the flesh from the bone. Do the same on the other side of the spine, then pull out the spine from the fish. Pull off the skin, too. Bone and skin the remaining sardines the same way.

Chop the sardines coarsely. Do not worry about leaving hairlike rib bones inside. Transfer them to a large *suribachi* or other mortar, and grind them to a paste. Add the miso, flour, egg yolk, and grated ginger, one at a time, grinding until smooth. If a *suribachi* is not available, do this in a food processor, turning the machine on and off just until the mixture is smooth. Do not overprocess the fish.

With a wooden spatula, fold the minced scallions into the dumpling mixture.

In a medium pot, bring plenty of water to a boil over moderate heat. Have a small bowl of water and two soup spoons at hand. Wet the soup spoons in the water, and scoop a heaping spoonful of the sardine mixture with one spoon. Shape the mixture into a ball with the aid of the other spoon. Drop the dumpling into the boiling water, shape the remaining mixture into dumplings, and add them to the boiling water. Cook the dumplings until they are 80 percent done, about 5 to 6 minutes. With a slotted spoon, transfer the dumplings to a clean pan, and cover them to keep them warm. Or refrigerate the dumplings, covered, for use later in the day.

In a medium pot, bring the *dashi* to a boil, and season it with the salt, *shoyu*, and black pepper. Warm the dumplings in the broth until they are heated through. Serve soup with the dumplings, garnished with the remaining scallion slices.

• *Yields 4 servings*

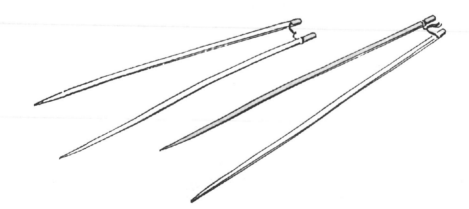

CONSOMMÉ WITH DUCK DUMPLINGS

Kamo no Sumashi-jiru

Compared with sardines, duck is much higher on the culinary ladder, and more expensive. For this reason, duck appears at special-occasion dinners in Japan.

To prepare duck dumplings, ground duck is mixed with sweet white miso and *dashi* (fish stock), and then cooked until tender and juicy. In this recipe the dumplings are served with vegetables in a clear *dashi* broth. You may also enjoy duck dumplings in miso soup or in duck or chicken broth.

3¹/₂ ounces spinach, preferably with root attached
1¹/₂ ounces carrot, julienned in 2¹/₂-inch lengths
   (¹/₂ cup)
1 ounce gobo (burdock) or celery, julienned in 2¹/₂
   inch lengths (¹/₃ cup; if you use gobo, soak it
   in 1 cup cold water and 1 teaspoon vinegar)
5 ounces skinned duck breast
2 ounces skinned and boned sea bass or cod fillet
1 tablespoon Saikyo miso *(sweet white miso)*
1¹/₄ teaspoons salt
1 teaspoon sugar
4 teaspoons usukuchi shoyu *(light-colored soy sauce),*
   preferably, or regular shoyu *(soy sauce)*
2 tablespoons potato starch or cornstarch, mixed with
   3 tablespoons water
1 egg white, lightly beaten
2³/₄ cups dashi *(fish stock, page 65)*
1 teaspoon sesame oil

GARNISH
1 tablespoon thin scallion rings, green part only

In a large pot of salted boiling water, cook the spinach for 2 minutes. Drain the spinach, cool it in ice water, and drain it again. Squeeze it to remove excess water. Cut the spinach into 2¹/₂-inch lengths, discarding the root.

Cook the carrot in the boiling water for 1 minute. Drain it in a colander, cool it in ice water, and then drain it again and squeeze it dry.

In a pot of boiling water with vinegar added (1 teaspoon vinegar to 1 cup water), cook the burdock for 2 minutes. Cool the burdock in ice water, and drain it.

Coarsely chop the duck breast and fish. Transfer them to a *suribachi* or other mortar, and grind them until smooth. One at a time, add the miso, $^1/_4$ teaspoon salt, the sugar, 2 teaspoons *shoyu*, the potato starch or cornstarch water, and the egg white, grinding until smooth. Add $^1/_4$ cup of the *dashi* little by little, grinding continuously. With a spatula, fold in the sesame oil. The mixture should be quite loose. If a *suribachi* is not available, blend the duck and fish with the miso, salt, and sugar in a food processor, turning the machine on and off several times, just until the mixture is smooth. Then transfer the mixture to a large bowl, and add the potato starch or cornstarch water, the egg white, $^1/_4$ cup *dashi*, and the sesame oil one at a time, mixing with a sturdy spatula.

In a large pot, bring plenty of water to a boil over high heat. Have at hand a small bowl of cold water, a $^1/_4$-cup ladle, and a soup spoon. Wet the ladle in the water, and scoop one quarter of the duck-fish mixture into the ladle. Wet the soup spoon in water, and push the mixture out into the boiling water, forming the mixture into an egg shape. Cook the dumplings over medium heat just until they are firm on the outside, about 5 minutes. Transfer them to a pan, and keep them warm, covered. The dumplings can be made in the morning and refrigerated, covered, for use later in the day.

In a medium pot, bring the remaining $2^1/_2$ cups *dashi* to a boil over medium heat. Add the duck-fish dumplings, and warm them through, about 2 minutes. Season the *dashi* with the remaining 1 teaspoon salt and the remaining *shoyu*. Serve the soup hot, allowing one dumpling per person. Fill each soup bowl until about four-fifths of the dumpling is submerged. Decorate each bowl with the three vegetables, arranging them side by side on top of the dumpling, and garnish with scallion disks.

- *Yields 4 servings*

ASARI CLAM SOUP

Asari no Ushio-jiru

Since *asari* clams have a naturally rich, sweet flavor, cooking them in water with a piece of *kombu* (kelp) makes this soup delicious. If *asari* clams are not available, use littleneck clams or New Zealand cockles. This soup is also delicious when made with miso.

12 ounces asari *clams*
1 3-inch square kombu *(kelp)*
1 tablespoon sake *(rice wine)*
Usukuchi shoyu *(light-colored soy sauce), preferably,*
  or regular shoyu *(soy sauce) to taste*
Salt to taste

GARNISH
¹/₂ cup daikon sprouts, roots removed, or watercress
  leaves
¹/₄ yuzu citron or lemon rind, julienned
  (see page 52)

Put the clams into a colander, and place the colander in a large bowl of salted cold water (1 tablespoon salt to 1 quart water). Let the clams stand in a cool place for 2 to 3 hours to expel any sand. Then rub and rinse the clams under cold running water.

In a medium pot, combine 4 cups water, the clams, and the *kombu*, and bring the mixture almost to a boil over medium heat, skimming any foam. Remove and discard the *kombu*. Reserve the clams. Reduce the heat, add the *sake*, and cook the clams, covered, until all are open, 3 to 4 minutes.

Discard any unopened clams. Strain the soup through a sieve lined with a finely woven cotton cloth. Reserve the clams. Return the broth to a pot, and season it to taste with *shoyu* and salt.

When the broth is heated through, serve it in individual bowls, each with a portion of clams and a topping of daikon sprouts and *yuzu* citron or lemon rind.

• *Yields 4 servings*

MISO SOUP WITH FRIED THIN TOFU

Oage no Miso-shiru

This is one of the most popular, nourishing, and quick-to-prepare versions of miso soup. *Abura-age* (fried thin tofu) provides a rich flavor and soft texture contrast with its accompaniment, crisp soybean sprouts. You may decide to keep fried thin tofu frozen in your freezer all the time just so you can enjoy this soup frequently.

Be careful not to overcook the bean sprouts; they should remain crisp and white. When bean sprouts are not available, use tender daikon leaves, broccoli raab, Chinese chives, turnip leaves, or mustard leaves.

1 abura-age *(fried thin tofu)* sheet
1 teaspoon sesame oil
1 cup soybean or mung-bean sprouts
1¹/₂ cups dashi *(fish stock, page 65)*
2 tablespoons thin scallion disks, both green
　　　　and white parts
2 tablespoons akamiso *(brown miso)*
1 teaspoon Saikyo miso *(sweet white miso)*

GARNISH
Shichimi togarashi *(seven-spice powder)*

Rinse the fried thin tofu with boiling water to remove excess oil. Cool the tofu under cold running water, and squeeze it to remove excess water. Cut the tofu sheet lengthwise, and then into thin strips crosswise.

Immediately before serving time, heat the sesame oil in a medium pot, and add the bean sprouts. Cook for 30 seconds, stirring. Add the *dashi*, and bring the mixture to a boil. Add the fried thin tofu and scallion, and cook for 1 to 2 minutes. Add the miso, and stir until it dissolves.

Serve the soup immediately in individual bowls, sprinkled with seven-spice powder.

• *Yields 3 to 4 servings*

MISO SOUP WITH MIXED MUSHROOMS

Kinokozukushi Miso-shiru

When I find various types of mountain mushrooms at markets in autumn or early spring, I make mushroom-studded miso soup. The types of mushrooms available today in Japan are diverse, from traditional shiitake, *maitake, shimeji,* and *enokitake* mushrooms to newly introduced oyster mushrooms, chanterelles, and Portobello mushrooms. Choose and mix those that are in season and available in your neighborhood. This preparation is super-simple!

7 ounces assorted fresh mushrooms
2 teaspoons sesame oil
2 tablespoons diced onion
3 tablespoons thin scallion disks, both green
*   and white parts*
2¹/₂ cups dashi (fish stock, page 65)
2 tablespoons akamiso (brown miso)

GARNISH
Shichimi togarashi *(seven-spice powder)*

Clean the mushrooms quickly under cold running water, and wipe them dry with a paper towel. Cut the mushrooms into thick strips.

Immediately before serving time, heat the sesame oil in a medium pot over medium heat. Reduce the heat to low, add the onion, and cook until the onion is soft, 2 to 3 minutes. Increase the heat to medium-high, add the mushrooms and scallions, and cook, stirring, for 10 to 20 seconds. Add the *dashi*, and bring the mixture to a boil. Add the miso, and stir until it dissolves.

Serve the soup immediately, sprinkled with seven-spice powder.

• *Yields 3 to 4 servings*

CUBED VEGETABLE MISO SOUP

Yasai no Miso-shiru

For miso soup, vegetables are usually sliced into thin rectangular, half-moon, or full-moon shapes, or into julienne strips. This enables the diners to pick up the vegetables with chopsticks. But one day I cut the vegetables into small cubes, and served miso soup in Western soup bowls with spoons as part of a Western-style dinner. It worked very well.

> 2 teaspoons sesame oil
> One 1/2-inch piece ginger, peeled and minced
> 1 medium potato, peeled and diced
> 1 medium carrot, diced
> 1/2 medium onion, diced
> 2 1/2 cups dashi (fish stock, page 65)
> 1 tablespoon akamiso (brown miso)
> 2 tablespoons Saikyo miso (sweet white miso)
>
> GARNISH
> 1 tablespoon minced chives

Immediately before serving time, heat the sesame oil in a medium pot over medium heat. Add the ginger, and cook, stirring, 10 seconds. Add all the vegetable cubes, and cook for 1 minute, stirring. Add the *dashi*, and bring the mixture to a boil.

Reduce the heat to low, cover the pot, and cook the vegetables until they are soft, 15 minutes.

Add the miso, and stir until it dissolves. Serve the soup immediately, garnished with the chives.

• *Yields 3 to 4 servings*

CHICKEN AND VEGETABLE MISO SOUP

Satsuma-jiru

From Satsuma, in Kagoshima Prefecture on the southern island of Kyushu, *Satsuma-jiru* is a rich, full-meal miso soup that is exceptionally good in cold weather. I buy a whole chicken and hack it with a cleaver into bite-sized pieces, bone included. Chicken soup tastes better when the chicken is cooked on the bone.

2 large chicken thighs, with bone and skin

2 ounces gobo (burdock; about 3 inches from the top of the root) or additional carrot

3¹/₂ ounces (1 medium) satoimo (taro root), preferably, or 2 small potatoes, peeled

One ¹/₂-inch piece ginger, peeled and sliced

1 tablespoon sake (rice wine)

3¹/₂ ounces daikon, quartered lengthwise, then cut crosswise ¹/₄ inch thick

1 small carrot, halved lengthwise, then cut crosswise ¹/₄ inch thick

1 naganegi long onion, white part only, or 3 scallions, cut crosswise into 1-inch lengths

3 tablespoons akamiso (brown miso)

GARNISH
1 tablespoon peeled and julienned ginger

Hack the chicken thighs into 1¹/₂-inch pieces, with bone attached. You may remove the skin, if you prefer.

Scrape off the skin of the burdock, and cut the burdock diagonally into ¹/₄-inch slices. In a small bowl, combine 1 cup cold water and 1 teaspoon vinegar. Immerse the burdock until you are ready to use it.

Halve the taro or potatoes lengthwise, then cut them crosswise ¹/₄ inch thick.

Immediately before serving time, combine 1 quart water, the chicken, the sliced ginger, and the *sake* in a medium pot. Bring the mixture to a boil over medium heat, and cook until the foam disappears, skimming constantly. Add the burdock, daikon, and carrot, cover the pot, and cook for 10 minutes.

Add the taro, long onion, and half the miso, and cook the mixture for 5 minutes.

Add the remaining miso, and stir until it is dissolved. Serve the soup immediately in individual bowls, garnished with the julienned ginger.

- *Yields 4 servings*

SEAFOOD MISO SOUP

Kaisen Miso-shiru

Adding fish and shellfish to miso soup produces a full-meal dish. I especially adore the flavor combination of sweet salmon and lobster in miso soup. I must admit that this is quite an expensive soup, and that it goes against the conception of miso soup as an everyday food for every person. But the soup is delicious! So try it for a special occasion. Although the taste is superb, the preparation is very simple and quick.

1 medium fresh lobster, preferably live
5 ounces boned and skinned salmon
4 cups dashi (fish stock, page 65)
1 sprig fresh dill
1 tablespoon olive oil
¹/₂ cup diced carrot
¹/₂ cup diced daikon
¹/₂ cup peeled and diced potato
¹/₂ cup diced celery
¹/₂ cup diced onion
¹/₄ cup Saikyo miso (sweet white miso)
1 tablespoon akamiso (brown miso)

GARNISH
4 watercress leaves

If the lobster is live, bring plenty of salted water to a boil in a large pot. Cook the lobster for 2 minutes.

Put the lobster on a chopping board, back side up. Insert a knife into the space between the body and the meat-filled tail, and cut around in both directions to the belly side. Pull the body apart from the tail, reserving the body and claws.

Place the lobster tail underside up on the chopping board, and make a shallow cut along one side. Remove the thin shell from the underside. With the aid of a knife, gently pull the flesh from the hard shell. Cut the tail flesh into quarters.

Cut the lobster body in half lengthwise, and remove the grey stomach sack. Remove the claws, and crack them with a hammer.

Cut the salmon into $1\frac{1}{2}$-inch squares.

Put the lobster body and claws, the *dashi*, and dill into a medium pot. Bring the mixture to a boil over medium heat, and cook for 5 minutes, skimming any emerging foam.

Strain the broth through a sieve lined with a finely woven cotton cloth. Discard the lobster body and dill, but reserve the claws.

Heat the olive oil in a large pot over medium heat. Add all the diced vegetables, and cook for 2 minutes, stirring. Add the lobster broth, and bring the mixture to a boil. Reduce the heat to low, cover the pot, and cook until the vegetables are soft, about 15 minutes.

Add the salmon, and cook for 3 minutes. Add the miso, lobster tail, and claws, and cook for 2 minutes. Serve the soup immediately in individual bowls, with the lobster and salmon prominently displayed and a watercress leaf in the center of each bowl.

• *Yields 4 servings*

HIROKO'S CLAM AND MISO CHOWDER

Kuramu Chauda Hiroko-fu

Let me call this soup miso chowder even though it employs some ingredients unknown in classical chowder. In this recipe, sweet white miso and soy milk combine with clams and vegetables to create a smooth, flavorful clam soup.

For a richer flavor, replace the soy milk with real cream. When fresh clams are not available, use 6 ounces clams canned in brine.

14 to 16 ounces asari *clams, preferably, or littleneck clams*
One 4-inch square kombu *(kelp)*
1 tablespoon olive oil
1 ounce (about 1 strip) bacon, diced
1 cup diced onion
1 tablespoon all-purpose flour
1 cup diced celery
1 cup peeled and diced potato
1 bay leaf
1 teaspoon fresh thyme leaves, or $^1/_4$ *teaspoon*
    dried thyme
3 tablespoons Saikyo miso (sweet white miso)
Salt to taste
1 cup unflavored soy milk

GARNISH
1 tablespoon minced chives

Put the clams into a colander, and place the colander in a large bowl of salted cold water (1 tablespoon salt to 1 quart water). Let the clams stand in a cool place for 2 to 3 hours to expel any sand. Then rub and rinse them under cold running water.

In a large pot, combine 3 cups water, the *kombu*, and clams, and bring the mixture almost to a boil over medium heat. Remove the *kombu*, and discard it. Bring the mixture to a full boil, and boil it, skimming the foam, until the foam ceases to emerge. Reduce the heat to low, cover the pot, and cook the clams until they open, about 3 to 4 minutes.

Discard any unopened clams. Strain the broth through a sieve lined with a tightly woven cotton cloth. Reserve the clams and broth in separate bowls, covered.

In a medium pot, heat the olive oil. Add the bacon, and cook it over low heat until it is crisp, 2 to 3 minutes.

Pour off the excess oil from the pot, leaving about 1 tablespoon. Add the onion, and cook it until it is soft, 3 to 5 minutes. Add the flour, and toss it with the bacon and onion. Add the reserved broth, the diced vegetables, and the bay leaf and thyme. Increase the heat to medium, and bring the mixture to a boil. Cook, skimming the foam, until the foam ceases to emerge.

Reduce the heat to low, add 2 tablespoons of the miso, and stir until it dissolves. Cover the pot, and cook the mixture until the vegetables are soft, about 15 to 20 minutes.

Add the reserved clams, the remaining miso, and salt to the pot. Increase the heat to medium, and bring the mixture to a boil. Add the soy milk, and cook over medium heat for about 1 minute, until the soup almost comes to a boil. (Soy milk curdles if it boils.) Remove the pot from the heat.

Remove the bay leaf, and discard it. Serve the soup immediately in individual bowls, sprinkled with chives.

• *Yields 4 servings*

SMOOTH SPINACH AND MISO SOUP

Horenso Miso-shiru

In traditional miso soups, the vegetables are never puréed. But I began using this technique to produce a creamy miso soup that does not separate. It works perfectly, and the bright green color and smooth texture please all diners.

CROUTONS
Virgin olive oil
1 slice white bread, crust removed
1 garlic clove, halved

9 ounces spinach leaves
2 cups dashi *(fish stock, page 65)*
3 ounces (about ¹/₂ medium) onion, diced
3 ounces (about ¹/₂ medium) potato, peeled and diced
3 to 4 tablespoons Saikyo miso (sweet white miso)
¹/₂ cup unflavored soy milk or cow's milk

Make the croutons: Heat the oven to 375 degrees F. With a pastry brush, spread the olive oil over the bread. Toast the bread in the oven until it is crisp and light golden.

Remove the bread from the oven, rub the surface with the cut sides of the garlic clove, and cut the bread into twenty-four ¹/₂-inch cubes. Set them aside.

Bring a large pot of salted water to a boil. Cook the spinach for 2 minutes. Drain the spinach, cool it in ice water, and squeeze it to remove excess water.

In a medium pot, combine the *dashi*, onion, and potato, and bring the mixture to a boil over medium heat. Reduce the heat to low, and cook the vegetables, covered, for 20 minutes.

In a food processor or blender, blend the spinach and the other vegetables with the stock to create a smooth purée. At this point the soup base can be refrigerated, covered, for use later in the day.

Immediately before serving time, heat the soup base in a medium pot over medium heat. Add the miso, and stir until it dissolves. Add the soy milk or cow's milk, and cook the soup over medium heat until it almost comes to a boil. Remove the pot from the heat.

Serve the soup immediately in individual bowls, garnished with the croutons.

• *Yields 4 servings*

BRIGHT ORANGE *KABOCHA*-MISO SOUP

Kabocha no Miso-shiru

How squash traveled all the way from South and Central America to Japan is a fascinating story of exploration, exploitation, culture, and linguistics. After discovering the New World, the Spanish brought back pumpkin to Europe, where it was soon introduced to their Portuguese neighbors. The Portuguese brought squash to Japan by way of what is today Cambodia. The Japanese asked the Portuguese the name of this new vegetable. Misunderstanding the question, the Portuguese replied that it came by way of Kampuchea, the Khmer name for Cambodia. What the Japanese heard was *kabocha*. And so this misnamed vegetable found its way into the language and cuisine of Japan.

When cooked, the bright orange flesh of *kabocha* squash becomes very sweet and creamy. I use *kabocha* squash to make pumpkin pie and pumpkin risotto. If *kabocha* is not available, substitute buttercup squash, which is very similar.

> *11 ounces* kabocha *squash or buttercup squash,*
> *seeded but not peeled*
> *One 4-inch square* kombu *(kelp), soaked in 3 cups*
> *water for 1 hour*
> *2 ounces (about ¹/₂)* naganegi *long onion or leek,*
> *white part only, sliced*
> *Ground cinnamon*
> *Fresh-ground nutmeg*
> *2 to 3 tablespoons Saikyo miso (sweet white miso)*
> *¹/₂ cup unflavored soy milk or cow's milk*
>
> GARNISH
> *1 tablespoon minced chives*

Have a bamboo or metal steamer with plenty of water at high steam production. Steam the *kabocha* or buttercup squash with its skin attached until the flesh is soft, 20 minutes. (If you don't have a steamer, you can boil the *kabocha* instead of steaming it, although this will mean throwing away valuable vitamins along with the cooking water.)

With a soup spoon, remove and discard the stringy, soft inner flesh and any remaining seeds from the *kabocha* or squash. Scrape out the flesh, and reserve it.

In a medium pot, combine the *kombu* stock and long onion or leek. Bring the mixture to a boil over medium heat. Reduce the heat to low, and cook until the long onion or leek is soft.

In a food processor or blender, blend the pumpkin or squash with the stock and leek to a smooth purée. At this point the soup base can be refrigerated, covered, for use later in the day.

Immediately before serving time, warm the pumpkin or squash soup base in a medium pot over medium heat. Add a little ground cinnamon and nutmeg. When the soup is heated through, add the miso, and stir until it dissolves. Add the soy milk or cow's milk, and heat the soup through. Avoid boiling the soup after adding the soy milk, which can curdle when overheated.

Serve the soup hot in individual bowls, garnished with the chives.

• *Yields 4 servings*

SMOOTH CARROT-MISO SOUP

Ninjin Miso-shiru

This is another version of creamy puréed vegetable miso soup. The bright orange color of this soup enlivens any meal.

18 ounces (about 3 large) carrots, diced
5 ounces diced onion (about ¼ cup)
3 ounces diced celery (about ¾ cup)
3 garlic cloves
1 bay leaf
¼ cup raw short-grain or medium-grain white rice
One 4-inch square kombu (kelp), soaked in 4 cups
        water for 1 hour
3 to 4 tablespoons Saikyo miso (sweet white miso)
1 cup unflavored soy milk or cow's milk
Cayenne pepper to taste

GARNISH
Eighteen ½-inch square croutons (see page 228)

In a medium pot, combine all the diced vegetables, the garlic, bay leaf, rice, and *kombu* stock, and bring the mixture to a boil over medium heat. Reduce the heat to low, and cook, covered, until the vegetables and rice are soft, 30 to 35 minutes.

Remove the bay leaf, and discard it. In a food processor or blender, blend the mixture until smooth. At this point the soup base can be refrigerated, covered, for use later in the day.

Shortly before serving time, combine the carrot soup base and enough water to make 5^1/$_2$ cups. Bring the mixture to a boil over medium heat. Add the miso, and stir until it dissolves. Add the soy milk or cow's milk, and cook for 1 minute. Avoid boiling the soup after adding the soy milk, which curdles when overheated.

Sprinkle in the cayenne pepper, and give several stirs. Serve the soup hot, garnished with the croutons.

• *Yields 6 servings*

EAT-A-LOT *WAKAME* SEA VEGETABLE SOUP

Wakame Takusan Sūpu

I sometimes crave minerals and vitamin-rich *wakame* sea vegetable and want to eat a lot of it. Upon such a request from my body, this soup provides complete satisfaction.

Using chicken broth rather than *dashi* as a base provides a richer, international flavor to this simple, nourishing soup.

> 1 tablespoon sesame oil
> 2 garlic cloves, minced
> 1 tablespoon peeled and julienned ginger
> 3 scallions, both green and white parts, cut into
>   thin disks
> 4^1/$_4$ cups chicken broth
> ^{1}/$_4$ cup sake (rice wine)
> 1 tablespoon instant wakame sea vegetable, soaked in
>   cold water for 2 minutes, and drained
> 1 tablespoon white sesame seeds, toasted (page 100)
> Tamari to taste
> Ground white pepper to taste

In a medium pot, heat the sesame oil over medium heat until it is hot but not smoking. Add the garlic and ginger, and cook, stirring, 30 seconds.

Add the white part of the scallions, reserving the green part, and cook, stirring, for 1 minute.

Add the chicken broth and *sake*, and bring the mixture to a boil. Add the *wakame* and the sesame seeds. Season the soup with a few drops of tamari and some ground white pepper, and add the green part of the scallions.

Give a few large stirs, and serve the soup piping hot in individual bowls.

• *Yields 4 servings*

DRIED SHIITAKE MUSHROOM SOUP

Hoshi Shiitake Sūpu

Chinese mushroom soup inspired me to create this delicious soup. The base for this soup is chicken stock, which is best prepared from a fresh chicken carcass. Plump shiitake mushrooms of the *donko* variety (see page 107) produce the best result. The reconstituted mushrooms are steamed in chicken stock for almost an hour. The mushrooms acquire a juicy, chewy texture and, in return, give a sweet, fragrant flavor to the chicken stock. Only a little salt and sliced scallions, added immediately before serving, are needed to complete the preparation. To make a full-meal soup, add chicken on the bone, hacked into bite-size pieces along with the mushrooms.

8 dried shiitake mushrooms, soaked in cold water
        for 20 minutes
2 cups chicken stock, preferably homemade
¹/₄ cup sake (rice wine)
2 large chicken thighs with bone and, preferably, skin,
        hacked into 2-inch pieces (optional)
Salt to taste
Ground white pepper to taste

GARNISH
2 scallions, green part only, cut into thin rings

Drain the mushrooms, and reserve the soaking liquid. Cut away and discard the mushroom stems. Strain the mushroom soaking liquid through a sieve lined with tightly woven cotton cloth.

Have a bamboo or metal steamer with plenty of water at high steam production.

In a wide, moderately deep heat-proof bowl that can fit into the steamer, combine the 2 cups of chicken broth and 1 cup of the reserved mushroom soaking liquid. Add the *sake*, mushroom caps, and, if you are using it, the hacked chicken meat. Cover the bowl with plastic wrap. Transfer the bowl to the steamer, and steam the mixture over medium-high heat for 1 hour, occasionally checking the water level in the pot and adding more boiling water as necessary.

Season the soup with salt and white pepper. Serve the soup hot in individual bowls, sprinkled with scallions.

* *Yields 2 servings*

PERSIMMON AND DAIKON IN SWEET VINEGAR DRESSING

Kakinamasu

When bright orange persimmons, *kaki*, dominate fruit markets, it is full autumn in Japan. At the same time, daikon becomes sweeter in the cold weather. The two are perfect mates in this classic Japanese dish. Served as a side dish in individual small bowls, *Kakinamasu* is particularly refreshing as an accompaniment to an oily main dish.

When persimmons are unavailable, you can substitute dried apricots.

DRESSING
$^1/_4$ *cup* komezu *(rice vinegar)*
$^1/_4$ *cup* dashi *(fish stock, page 65)*
2 tablespoons sugar
1 tablespoon plus $^1/_4$ *teaspoon salt*

1 pound upper part of daikon, julienned in
    2-inch lengths
1 medium persimmon, ripe but not too soft, or 4 to 6
    dried apricots, julienned in 2-inch lengths

GARNISH
$^1/_2$ *yuzu citron or lemon rind, julienned (see page 52)*
Peppermint leaves
Tamari

In a medium bowl, combine the rice vinegar, *dashi*, sugar, and ¼ teaspoon salt. Let the mixture stand for 30 minutes.

In a medium bowl, combine the daikon and the remaining 1 tablespoon salt, and toss well. Let the mixture stand for 10 minutes.

Transfer the daikon to a colander, and briefly rinse the daikon under cold running water. Drain the daikon and squeeze it tightly to remove excess water. Taste a strip of daikon. It should taste faintly salty. If it is too salty, rinse it, drain it, and squeeze it again.

In another bowl, toss the daikon and persimmon with the dressing, and let the mixture rest in the refrigerator, covered, for as long as 6 hours. The longer the daikon and persimmon are left in the dressing, the stronger the flavor they will take on.

Serve the salad chilled, with each serving garnished with *yuzu* citron or lemon rind and peppermint leaves and seasoned with a tiny drop of tamari.

• *Yields 4 servings as a side dish*

CHILLED EGGPLANT AND TOMATO SALAD

Hiyashi Nasu to Tomato no Sarada

On sweltering summer days when I was young, my mother frequently prepared a chilled salad of steamed eggplants. I still remember the texture and flavor of those eggplants. Japanese eggplants are less seedy and less watery than their larger, oval counterparts that are so common in U.S. markets. Cooking transforms the flesh of Japanese eggplants into a creamy, sweet treat that is especially good with my mother's spiced sweet and sour dressing. Since steaming dulls the pretty purple color of eggplant skins, I broil the eggplants and peel off the skin when I reproduce my mother's dish.

> 1 tablespoon peeled and minced ginger
> 2 tablespoons minced scallion, white part only
> 4 tablespoons komezu (rice vinegar)
> 2 tablespoons shoyu (soy sauce)
> 1 tablespoon sugar
> 2 teaspoons sesame oil
> 6 Japanese or Italian eggplants, stemmed
> 1 medium tomato, parboiled in water for 30 seconds,
>   peeled, cored, and seeded

In a small saucepan, combine the ginger, scallion, *komezu*, *shoyu*, sugar, and sesame oil. Bring the mixture to a boil over medium heat. Transfer the dressing to a small bowl, and let it cool to room temperature. Then chill the dressing, covered, in the refrigerator.

Heat a broiler or a grill. Cook the eggplants until their skins are lightly charred. Peel the skins, and cut each eggplant in half crosswise. Cut each piece lengthwise into quarters. Cut the tomato into 1/2-inch cubes. Arrange the eggplant on a serving platter, and top with the tomato. Chill the vegetables, covered, in the refrigerator.

Before serving, pour the dressing over the vegetables. At the table, toss the vegetables with the dressing.

• *Yields 3 to 4 servings as a side dish*

GREEN BEANS IN WALNUT-MISO DRESSING

Ingen no Kurumi-miso-ae

Of all nuts, walnuts contain the greatest amount of oil. Because of this, they have long been a favorite food in Japanese kitchens. When the distinctive flavor of walnuts meets that of sweet white miso, they create a delicious harmony.

For this dish, you can use broccoli, asparagus, burdock, or spinach when green beans are not available.

> 7 *ounces green beans, stemmed*
> 2¹/₂ *ounces (¹/₂ cup) walnut meats*
> 1 *tablespoon* Saikyo miso *(sweet white miso)*
> 1 *tablespoon* mirin *(sweet cooking wine)*
> 2 *teaspoons* shoyu *(soy sauce)*
> 1 *teaspoon sugar*
> 2 *to 3 tablespoons* dashi *(fish stock, page 65)*
> *Salt to taste*

In a large pot of salted boiling water, parboil the beans for 2 minutes. Drain them, and spread them to cool in a flat-bottomed colander.

Heat a medium skillet over low to medium heat, add the walnuts, and toast them until they are heated through. Reserve one-fifth of the walnuts, and transfer the rest to a *suri-*

bachi or other mortar or a food processor. Grind the walnuts, until they are smooth and oily-looking.

One at a time, add the miso, *mirin*, *shoyu*, sugar, and 2 tablespoons *dashi* to the mortar or processor, and grind the mixture until it is smooth. The texture should be like that of hummus. If the mixture is too thick, loosen it with another 1 tablespoon *dashi*.

Season the dressing with a little salt. The dressing can be made one day ahead of time and stored in the refrigerator, covered.

Cut the reserved walnuts into small pieces. Immediately before serving, toss the beans with the dressing. Serve the salad garnished with the walnut pieces.

• *Yields 4 servings as a side dish*

SPINACH IN *OHITASHI* DRESSING

Horenso no Ohitashi

Ohitashi literally means "dipped item," although the dressing is actually poured over the leaf vegetables—spinach, mizuna, chrysanthemum, and watercress—that are used to prepare *ohitashi* dishes.

In this preparation, briefly boiled spinach is neatly collected and shaped in a thick cylinder, which is cut into short lengths. The spinach rolls are then garnished with white sesame seeds and served in a mildly flavored dressing.

> OHITASHI DRESSING
> ¹/₂ *cup* dashi *(fish stock, page 65)*
> 1 *tablespoon plus 1 teaspoon* shoyu *(soy sauce)*
> 1 *tablespoon* mirin *(sweet cooking wine)*
>
> 8 *ounces bunch spinach, with root attached*
>
> GARNISH
> ¹/₄ *cup white sesame seeds, toasted (page 100)*

In a small saucepan, combine the *dashi*, 1 tablespoon of the *shoyu*, and the *mirin*. Bring the mixture to a boil over medium heat, and boil it for 30 seconds. Transfer the dressing to a small bowl, and let it cool to room temperature. The dressing may be prepared one day ahead of time and stored in the refrigerator, covered.

In a large pot of salted boiling water, cook the spinach for 1 to 2 minutes. Drain the spinach, and cool it in ice water.

Collect the root ends of the spinach together, and roll the spinach in a bamboo mat. Squeeze firmly to remove excess water. Unroll the spinach, cut off the roots, and divide the spinach bunch in half. Return the spinach to the rolling mat with the stems of the two portions at opposite ends Roll the spinach into a cylindrical form.

Unroll the spinach, remove it from the mat, and sprinkle it with the remaining 1 teaspoon *shoyu*. Roll the spinach in the mat again, and gently squeeze it to distribute the *shoyu* evenly.

Unroll the mat, and remove the spinach. Cut the spinach crosswise into 2-inch lengths. Serve the spinach in bowls, drizzled with the dressing and topped with sesame seeds.

• *Yields 2 servings as a side dish*

PAN-FRIED SWEET ONION WITH TAMARI

Yaki-tamanegi

This onion dish is so simple that it hardly needs a recipe. Juicy, sweet onions and good-quality tamari are the keys to success here.

> 2 large sweet onions
> Tamari
>
> GARNISH
> Minced parsley

Peel the onion, and cut it into 1/2-inch-thick rounds. Do not separate the rings; the slices should maintain their shape throughout the cooking. Heat a large, heavy-bottomed skillet over medium heat. Reduce the heat to low, and lay the onion slices in the skillet. No oil is required. Cook the onion slices until the bottoms are browned and the onions are cooked 40 percent through.

Carefully turn over the onion slices, and cook them until they are golden on the other side. At the end of the cooking, increase the heat to high, and sprinkle about 1 teaspoon tamari over each onion round. Cook until the tamari emits a slightly burnt fragrance, about 5 seconds.

Serve the onion garnished with the parsley, and eat while the onion is piping hot.

• *Yields 2 servings as a side dish*

GRILLED SHIITAKE MUSHROOMS WITH PONZU DRESSING

Yaki Shiitake Ponzu-zoe

When I find fresh large, plump *donko* shiitake mushrooms in the market (see page 58), I simply broil them with a little *sake* (rice wine) and serve them with grated daikon and ponzu dressing. This is the simplest and the most appealing way to enjoy the true flavor of fresh shiitake mushrooms.

> *16 large fresh shiitake mushrooms, preferably* donko
> *(see page 107)*
> *About 3 tablespoons* sake *(rice wine)*
> *¹/₃ to ¹/₂ cup grated daikon*
> *¹/₂ cup ponzu dressing (page 73)*
>
> GARNISH
> *1* yuzu *citron or lemon rind, julienned (see page 52)*

Clean the mushrooms with a moist cotton cloth. Cut away and discard the stems.

Heat a broiler or grill. Place the mushroom caps on a broiler pan or grill rack, gill side down if you're using a broiler or gill side up if you're using a grill. Place the pan or rack close to the heat.

Cook the mushrooms until the tops of the caps are dry. Turn over the mushrooms, and cook them until the insides become wet with the mushrooms' own juice.

If you're using a grill, turn over the mushrooms again. Spoon ¹/₂ teaspoon *sake* into each cap. Cook the mushrooms until the *sake* is bubbling.

Serve the mushrooms garnished with grated daikon and *yuzu* citron or lemon rind strips, and accompanied with ponzu dressing on the side.

- *Yields 4 servings as a side dish*

RED BELL PEPPER AND OKRA
WITH NIHAIZU DRESSING

Yaki Akapiman to Okura Nihaizu-ae

Simply broiled sweet red bell pepper and okra taste delicious with *nihaizu* dressing.

> *2 red bell peppers*
> *5 ounces okra*
> Nihaizu *dressing (page 73)*

Heat a broiler or grill, and cook the red bell peppers until their skins are lightly charred. Place the peppers in a plastic bag, and let them steam for 10 minutes.

Skin, stem, and seed the peppers, and remove their white ribs. Cut the peppers into 2-inch-long strips.

Cook the okra in a broiler or on a grill until the skins turn light golden. Cut the okra into 1-inch slices crosswise.

Serve the vegetables drizzled or tossed with a generous amount of *nihaizu* dressing.

- *Yields 4 servings as a side dish*

STIR-FRIED BURDOCK AND CARROT

Kinpira-gobo

Gobo, burdock, is a long, thin, brown root vegetable. It has a pleasant crispiness and an earthy taste. In this, the most popular burdock dish in Japan, you can enjoy this vegetable's distinguishing characteristics.

Can other vegetables substitute perfectly for burdock in this recipe? Unfortunately, the answer is no. For a similar flavor, you may prepare this dish with only carrot, but the crispiness of burdock will be lacking.

Recently I have spotted fresh burdock at several farmers' markets and supermarkets in Manhattan. You can also find it at Japanese food stores, whole or cut into strips and frozen. Frozen burdock is a good substitute for the fresh root.

Shichimi togarashi (seven-spice powder) is an indispensable condiment in this dish.

> 2 to 3 tablespoons vegetable oil
> 5$\frac{1}{2}$ ounces gobo (burdock), scraped, julienned in
>   2$\frac{1}{2}$-inch lengths (to make about 2 cups), and
>   soaked in 1 cup water and 1 teaspoon vinegar
> 2 ounces carrot, julienned in 2$\frac{1}{2}$-inch lengths
>   (about $\frac{2}{3}$ cup)
> 2 tablespoons sake (rice wine)
> 1 tablespoon mirin (sweet cooking wine)
> 1 tablespoon sugar
> 1 tablespoon shoyu (soy sauce)
> 1 teaspoon tamari
> 2 tablespoons white sesame seeds, toasted (page 100)
> $\frac{1}{3}$ teaspoon shichimi togarashi (seven-spice powder)

In a wok or large skillet, heat the vegetable oil over high heat. Drain the burdock, and cook it, stirring, until it is well coated with oil. Add the carrot and cook, stirring, for 2 minutes.

Add 3 tablespoons water, the *sake*, *mirin*, and sugar. Cook the mixture until almost all the liquid is absorbed, stirring all the time. Add the *shoyu*, and cook for 30 seconds. Season the mixture to taste with tamari. Add 1 tablespoon of the sesame seeds, add the seven-spice powder, and give several large stirs.

Transfer the vegetables to a platter, and let them cool to room temperature. The dish tastes better after a few hours, and can be kept in the refrigerator, covered, for a day. Serve the vegetables at room temperature or chilled, with the remaining 1 tablespoon white sesame seeds.

• *Yields 4 to 6 servings as a side dish*

STIR-FRIED TARO GELATIN IN A FOREIGNER'S WAY

Konnyaku Achara-ni

Achara-ni means "a simmered dish prepared in a foreigner's way." In the nineteenth century, Dutch and Chinese living in Nagasaki were called *achara-san*. *Achara* means "the other side," and *achara-san* implies the people who live on the other side of the street, river, or town. In the Edo Era (1600 to 1868) foreigners lived in a segregated area of town.

In this preparation, *konnyaku* (taro gelatin) is stir-fried in sesame oil, and then flavored with *shoyu* (soy sauce), sugar, and dried red chile pepper. In the Edo Era, a dish that employed chile pepper and the technique of stir-frying was considered foreign.

1 konnyaku *(taro gelatin) cake*
3 tablespoons *sesame oil*
2 tablespoons *sake (rice wine)*
1¹/₂ teaspoons *sugar*
2 tablespoons shoyu *(soy sauce)*
¹/₄ teaspoon shichimi togarashi *(seven-spice powder)*
     or *chile pepper flakes*
1 teaspoon *white sesame seeds, toasted (page 100)*

In a medium pot of boiling water, parboil the taro gelatin for 2 minutes. Drain it, wipe it dry with a paper towel, and cut it into thin 3-inch-long strips.

Heat a wok or large skillet over medium heat, and add the sesame oil. When the oil is hot, reduce the heat to medium-low. Add the taro gelatin, and cook it, stirring, until the surfaces blister and turn partially golden, about 5 minutes.

Pour off any remaining oil from the wok or skillet. Add the *sake* and sugar to the wok or skillet, and cook the mixture, stirring, until almost all the liquid is absorbed. Add the *shoyu*, and continue stirring until it is absorbed, about 30 seconds. Sprinkle in the seven-spice powder or chile flakes and the white sesame seeds, and give several more stirs. Transfer the taro gelatin to a serving dish.

Serve the taro gelatin at room temperature. The flavor matures after half an hour.

• *Yields 3 servings as a side dish*

EGGPLANT AND MISO IN A WOK

Nasu no Abura-miso Itame

Stir-fried eggplant and green bell pepper in a sweetened miso sauce is a popular home-style summer dish. I add red bell pepper to this traditional preparation to give it a striking look. Try this dish with different vegetables, such as zucchini, cabbage, kale, leaf mustard, lettuce, radicchio, asparagus, mushrooms, or tomato. For a hearty lunch or light dinner, serve the vegetables surrounding plain white or brown rice in the center of a dinner plate, sprinkled with minced parsley.

To cut the vegetables, use the *rangiri* technique (see page 28).

2 Japanese or other small green bell peppers, cut
    into 1¹/₂-inch pieces
1 red bell pepper, cut into 1¹/₂-inch pieces
1 tablespoon akamiso *(brown miso)*
1 tablespoon mamemiso *(soybean miso)*
2 tablespoons sake *(rice wine)*
1 to 2 tablespoons sugar
2 tablespoons sesame oil
One 1-inch piece of ginger, peeled and julienned
5 tablespoons vegetable oil
9 ounces (4 to 5) Japanese or Italian eggplants, preferably,
    or 1 large round eggplant, cut into 1¹/₂-inch pieces
A few drops of tamari
Shichimi togarashi *(seven-spice powder)*
    or chile pepper flakes

In a medium pot of boiling water, parboil the green and red peppers for 1 minute. Drain them, cool them in ice water, and wipe them dry with a paper towel.

In a small cup, combine both kinds of miso, the *sake*, and sugar, stirring.

Heat a wok or large skillet over medium-high heat, and add the sesame oil. When the oil is hot, add the ginger, and cook it for 20 seconds. Remove the ginger from the wok or skillet, and reserve it.

Add the vegetable oil. When the oil is hot, add the eggplant, and cook it until all sides are golden. Return the ginger strips to the wok or skillet, add the red and green peppers, and cook, stirring, for 2 minutes.

Add the miso mixture to the vegetables, and toss to distribute the sauce evenly. Add the tamari and seven-spice powder or red chile flakes. Toss again, and serve.

* *Yields 4 servings as a side dish or 2 as a light main dish*

SUMMER VEGETABLES AND SOYBEAN MISO IN A WOK

Natsuyasai no Mamemiso Itame

This is a variation on the preceding recipe. The colorful vegetables create an astonishing look.

SAUCE

1 *tablespoon* mamemiso *(soybean miso)*

2 *tablespoons* sake *(rice wine)*

1 *teaspoon* shoyu *(soy sauce)*

1 *teaspoon* toban jiang *(chile-bean sauce)*

1 *teaspoon* komezu *(rice vinegar)*

1 *tablespoon* honey

$3^1/_2$ *ounces (1 medium-small) green zucchini, cut*
rangiri-style (see page 28) into
$1^1/_4$-inch pieces

$3^1/_2$ *ounces (1 medium-small) yellow summer squash,*
cut rangiri-style (see page 28) into
$1^1/_4$-inch pieces

3¹/₂ ounces broccoli flowerets (about 1¹/₂ cups)
3¹/₂ ounces red bell pepper, cut into lengthwise strips
3 ounces (1 medium) carrot, cut into ¹/₅-inch slices
3 tablespoons vegetable oil
2 garlic cloves, minced
5 ounces cabbage leaves (about 2 large outer leaves),
     cut into 1-inch-wide strips
1 teaspoon tamari
2 teaspoons potato starch or cornstarch, mixed with
     1 tablespoon water

In a small cup, combine the miso, *sake*, *shoyu*, chile-bean sauce, *komezu*, and honey, and blend them into a smooth sauce.

In a medium pot of salted boiling water, parboil the zucchini, yellow squash, broccoli, red bell pepper, and carrot for 30 seconds. Drain the vegetables, and spread them in a wide, flat-bottomed colander to cool quickly. Wipe the vegetables dry with a paper towel.

In a wok or large skillet, heat the vegetable oil. Add the garlic, and cook it over low heat, stirring, for 20 seconds. Increase the heat to high, add the cabbage, and cook for 30 seconds, stirring. Add the parboiled vegetables, and cook for 1 to 2 minutes, stirring.

Add the miso sauce to the wok or skillet, and toss the vegetables with the sauce. Add the tamari, and give several large stirs. Reduce the heat to low, add the potato starch or cornstarch water, and cook until the sauce thickens.

Serve the vegetables hot, with plain white or brown rice.

• *Yields 2 servings as a light main dish*

JAPANESE-STYLE SIMMERED VEGETABLES

Nihon-fu Ratatouille

In this recipe I simmer Western vegetables in the style of ratatouille, but in a broth flavored with miso and other Japanese seasonings. When cutting the vegetables, use the *rangiri* technique (see page 28).

> *²/₃ cup dashi (fish stock, page 65)*
> *2 tablespoons mirin (sweet cooking wine)*
> *2 tablespoons akamiso (brown miso)*
> *2 to 3 tablespoons Saikyo miso (sweet white miso)*
> *3 tablespoons vegetable oil*
> *1 tablespoon sesame oil*
> *2 tablespoons peeled and julienned ginger*
> *4 Japanese or Italian eggplants, preferably, or 1 small*
> *American eggplant, stemmed*
> *1 green zucchini, cut into 1¹/₂-inch pieces*
> *1 yellow summer squash, cut into 1¹/₂-inch pieces*
> *1 red bell pepper, cut into 1¹/₂-inch pieces*
> *1 celery stalk, cut into 1¹/₂-inch pieces*
> *1 large ripe tomato, cut into 1-inch pieces*
> *3¹/₂ ounces Chinese chives or scallions, green part*
> *only, cut into 2-inch lengths*

In a small bowl, combine the *dashi*, *mirin*, and two kinds of miso.

In a large pot, combine the oils, and heat them over medium heat. Add the ginger, and cook it for 20 seconds, stirring. Increase the heat to high, and add all the vegetables except the tomato and Chinese chives or scallions. Cook, stirring, until the vegetables are well coated with oil, 2 to 3 minutes.

Reduce the heat to medium, add the miso mixture, and bring it to a boil. Reduce the heat to medium-low. Cover the vegetables with a drop lid, and cook them for 10 minutes.

Remove the drop lid, add the tomato, and cook for 8 minutes.

Add the Chinese chives or scallions, give a few large stirs, and cook for 1 to 2 minutes.

Transfer the vegetables to another container to cool, then refrigerate them. Serve the vegetables chilled.

• *Yields 6 servings*

SWEET SIMMERED *KABOCHA*

Kabocha no Umani

Because of its natural sweetness and creamy texture, *kabocha* squash is a popular ingredient in Japanese simmered dishes.

Before it is added to simmering broth, *kabocha* is briefly parboiled in water, or, as in this recipe, cooked in a little sesame oil. The latter technique adds a richer flavor to the dish.

> 2 tablespoons sesame oil
> 1^1/$_3$ pounds kabocha or buttercup squash,
>   seeded but not skinned, and cut into
>   1-by-1^1/$_2$-by-2-inch pieces
> 2 cups dashi (fish stock, page 65)
> 1 tablespoon sugar
> 2 tablespoons mirin (sweet cooking wine)
> ^{1}/$_2$ teaspoon salt
> 1 tablespoon shoyu (soy sauce)
>
> GARNISH
> 1 yuzu citron or lemon rind, julienned (see page 52)

In a medium pot, heat the sesame oil over medium heat. Add the *kabocha*, and cook, turning each piece occasionally, until all sides are evenly browned, 2 to 3 minutes. Add the *dashi* to the pot, and bring the mixture to a boil.

Reduce the heat to low, cover the squash with a drop lid (see page 26), and simmer it gently for 5 to 10 minutes, until you can insert a bamboo skewer or toothpick with only a little resistance. The cooking time will vary slightly depending on the time of year. Add the sugar and *mirin*, and cook, covered, for 5 minutes more. Add the salt and *shoyu*, and cook, covered, for a final 5 minutes. During the simmering, do not stir the squash.

Serve the squash hot, with the broth poured over it and the *yuzu* citron or lemon rind sprinkled on top.

• *Yields 4 to 6 servings as a side dish*

GOLDEN BROWN NEW POTATOES
IN SWEET *SHOYU* SAUCE

Shinjaga no Age-ni

Tiny golden brown new potatoes are a perfect accompaniment to a grilled fish or meat dish. Serve the potatoes piping hot.

> *9 ounces small new potatoes of uniform size,*
> *washed but not peeled*
> *Vegetable oil, for deep-frying*
> *¹/₂ cup dashi (fish stock, page 65)*
> *2 tablespoons sake (rice wine)*
> *3 tablespoons mirin (sweet cooking wine)*
> *1 tablespoon sugar*
> *1¹/₂ tablespoons shoyu (soy sauce)*
> *1 tablespoon minced shiso, preferably, or parsley*

Put the potatoes into a medium pot, cover them with cold water, and bring the water to a boil over medium heat. Cook the potatoes uncovered for 15 minutes. Drain the potatoes, and wipe them dry with a paper towel.

In a wok or deep skillet, heat 2 inches of vegetable oil over medium heat to 340 degrees F. Add the potatoes to the oil, and cook them, rolling them occasionally, until their skins are golden, 5 minutes. Transfer the potatoes to paper towels to drain.

In a medium pot, combine the *dashi*, *sake*, *mirin*, sugar, and *shoyu*, and bring the mixture to a boil over medium heat. Reduce the heat to low, and cook until the volume is reduced by half, 5 to 8 minutes.

Add the potatoes to the sauce, and roll them to coat them with the sauce. Sprinkle in the minced shiso or parsley, and serve.

• *Yields 2 servings as a side dish*

CRISP TOFU CUBES
IN PIPING-HOT TEMPURA SAUCE

Agedashi Dofu

Golden brown tofu cubes served in hot tempura dipping sauce is a popular dish at homes, pubs, and restaurants throughout Japan.

Before the tofu is fried, it is lightly dredged in potato starch, which creates an attractive golden, crisp coating during the frying process. Cornstarch, arrowroot starch, or all-purpose flour can be used as a substitute.

Grated daikon or grated ginger is an essential accompaniment to this dish.

1 block (about 11 ounces) firm tofu
6 tablespoons potato starch
Vegetable oil, for deep-frying
1 cup tentsuyu *(tempura dipping sauce, page 67)*
1 akatogarashi or other small dried red chile pepper,
    seeded and cut into thin rings

GARNISH
1 tablespoon thin scallion rings, green part only

CONDIMENT
1/2 cup grated daikon or ginger

Wrap the tofu in a clean cotton cloth, place it between heavy dinner plates, and let it stand 30 minutes.

Put the potato starch on a plate. Cut the tofu block in half along each axis, making eight pieces. Wipe the tofu squares dry with a paper towel, dredge them with potato starch, and let them stand for 2 minutes.

Heat 3 inches of vegetable oil in a large, deep skillet to 340 degrees F. Cook the tofu in the oil, two or three squares at one time, until the outsides are crisp and golden, 3 to 4 minutes. Drain the fried tofu on a rack. In a medium pot, bring the tempura dipping sauce and the red chile pepper to a boil over medium heat.

Place two to four tofu squares in each individual bowl, cover them with a portion of the dipping sauce, and garnish them with sliced scallion. Serve small mounds of grated daikon or ginger on the side.

• *Yields 2 to 4 servings as a side dish*

TEMPURA WITH WESTERN VEGETABLES

Seiyo Yasai no Tempura

Japanese vegetable tempura can employ any fresh vegetables, including sweet potato, carrot, burdock, lotus root, onion, green beans, shiitake mushrooms, okra, *kabocha* pumpkin, chrysanthemum leaves, eggplant, bamboo shoots, and shiso. Today asparagus, button mushrooms, and several other newcomers have joined this traditional group. Use any locally available, seasonal vegetables to enjoy this now very popular preparation.

The oil for tempura is a blend of vegetable oil and sesame oil, usually about 80 percent vegetable oil and 20 percent sesame oil. Increasing the proportion of sesame oil provides a deeper golden color and nuttier flavor to the fried items.

1 egg

1¹/₂ cups cake flour

1 zucchini, cut diagonally into ¹/₃-inch-thick slices

1 fennel bulb, cut into ¹/₃-inch-wide sticks

8 button mushrooms, stems removed

8 large dandelion leaves, stems removed

A blend of sesame oil and vegetable oil, for deep-frying

CONDIMENTS

2 cups tentsuyu (tempura dipping sauce, page 67)

¹/₂ cup grated daikon

In a 2-cup measuring cup, beat the egg lightly, and add enough ice water to make ³/₄ cup liquid, about ¹/₂ cup. Transfer half of the egg liquid to a medium bowl, reserving the rest. Add ¹/₂ cup flour to the egg liquid in the bowl, and immediately give several big stirs with a pair of cooking chopsticks, a fork, or a whisk. Do not stir the batter thoroughly. Overmixing develops the gluten in the flour and produces a lumpy, bready, heavy crust when the batter is fried.

Put ¹/₂ cup flour into a medium bowl for dredging the vegetables. In a large, deep skillet, heat 3 inches of oil to 340 degrees F. Pick up one vegetable slice, and dredge it with flour. Shake off the excess flour, and dip the vegetable slice in the batter. Pull out the vegetable slice, and lightly shake off the excess batter. Carefully add the vegetable slice to the heated oil. This process—dredging and shaking the vegetable slice, dipping it in batter, then placing it in the hot oil—should take only a few seconds.

Cook all the vegetables in the same way, in small batches, three to five pieces at one time (depending on the size of the skillet), until the outsides are light golden and crisp and the vegetables are cooked through. Transfer the fried vegetables to a rack. When you've used half the vegetables, add the remaining egg liquid and $^1/_2$ cup flour to the bowl, and stir. Use this batter to finish cooking the vegetables.

Serve the tempura immediately, with the dipping sauce and grated daikon in separate bowls on the side. Diners should add a little grated daikon to the sauce before dipping the fried items in it.

* *Yields 4 servings as a side dish*

It is always best to eat tempura when it has just been removed from the oil. This makes it necessary for the cook to work without stopping and feed the diners continuously, until they say, "We have had enough!" At the risk of losing some crispiness, however, you can serve all the tempura on a large platter after you finish the frying. In this case, replacing a little of the flour in the batter with cornstarch will prevent the fried items from becoming soggy too soon.

SPINACH IN BLACK SESAME DRESSING

Horenso Goma-ae

Goma-ae, vegetables in black sesame seed dressing, is a popular Japanese salad. Unlike the mild white variety, black sesame seeds have a distinctive, rich flavor. Any seasonal vegetables, such as asparagus, mustard greens, kale, mizuna, broccoli, and eggplant, go very well with this dressing.

5 tablespoons black sesame seeds, toasted (page 100)
1 tablespoon sugar
2 to 3 tablespoons dashi (fish stock, page 65)
1/2 teaspoon tamari

7 ounces spinach

GARNISH
1 yuzu citron or lime rind, julienned (see page 52)

Put the toasted sesame seeds into a *suribachi* or other mortar, and grind them to an oily paste. Add the sugar, blending thoroughly. Add the *dashi* 1 tablespoon at a time, mixing until smooth. Blend in the tamari. If a *suribachi* is not available, blend the seeds, sugar, *dashi,* and tamari in a food processor or blender. The dressing can be stored in the refrigerator for 2 days, covered.

In a large pot of salted boiling water, cook the spinach for about 1 minute.

Drain the spinach, and cool it under cold running water. Squeeze the spinach tightly to remove excess water. Cut the spinach into 1$\frac{1}{2}$-inch lengths.

Just before serving, toss the spinach with the sesame dressing. Serve the salad garnished with *yuzu* citron or lime rind.

• *Yields 2 to 4 servings*

TENDER DAIKON
SIMMERED WITH *YUZU*-MISO SAUCE

Furofuki Daikon Yuzu-miso-zoe

When cold weather arrives, daikon becomes sweeter and sweeter. When daikon is at its sweetest, this dish is at its best.

The daikon is cooked in gently boiling water for hours, until it can easily be broken with chopsticks. The word *furofuki* means "to take a hot bath to get clean and warm." When you observe the daikon cooking, comfortably submerged in hot water in the pot, you can imagine that you are taking a hot bath. The tender daikon is served with a sweetened miso sauce.

My mother cooks the daikon for this dish in water in which rice has been rinsed. This water, she told me, contains some of the fat and enzymes found on the surface of raw polished rice. These constituents help to cook the vegetable softer and quicker. They also seem to remove harsh and bitter flavors.

Substitutes for daikon can be turnips, celery root, and rutabaga. Adjust the cooking time to suit the vegetable used.

> *5 thick daikon disks, 3 inches in diameter by*
> *2 inches in length*
> *One 2-inch square* kombu *(kelp)*
> *5 medium shrimp in their shells, headed*
> *About 1 quart* dashi *(fish stock, page 65)*
> *1 tablespoon* sake *(rice wine)*
> *3 tablespoons* mirin *(sweet cooking wine)*
> *1 teaspoon salt*
> *5 tablespoons black sesame seeds, toasted*
> *1 tablespoon Saikyo miso (sweet white miso)*
> *Juice and julienned rind (see page 52)*
> *of 1 yuzu citron or lime*

With a knife, bevel the edge of each daikon disk, and cut a shallow cross on one of the faces. In a large, shallow pot, combine the *kombu,* daikon, and enough water to cover the daikon by 1 inch (if you have reserved rice-rinsing water, use it instead of fresh water). Cook the daikon uncovered over medium-slow heat for 2 hours or until it is soft, adding water to the pot as necessary. Drain the daikon, discarding the water.

Devein the shrimp (see page 22), and cook them in their shells in salted boiling water for 2 to 3 minutes or until they are done. Cool the shrimp in cold water, drain and peel them, and set them aside.

Return the daikon disks to the pot in which they were cooked, and add *dashi* to cover them. Add the *sake*, 1 tablespoon of the *mirin*, and the salt. Cook for 30 minutes.

While the daikon cooks, grind the sesame seeds to an oily paste in a *suribachi*, preferably, or another mortar. Add the miso, the remaining 2 tablespoons *mirin*, 1 tablespoon *dashi*, and the *yuzu* or lime juice one at a time, grinding continuously. Transfer the mixture to a cup.

When the daikon has cooked 30 minutes, add the cooled shrimp. Cook 1 minute longer.

In each individual serving bowl, place a portion of the hot daikon, and pour over it 2 tablespoons of the cooking liquid from the pot. Top with a shrimp and some of the sauce, garnish with the *yuzu* citron or lime rind, and serve.

• *Yields 5 servings*

EGGPLANT DISKS WITH MISO SAUCE

Nasu no Dengaku

Nasu, Japanese eggplant, is generally short and slim. However, there are several varieties. One of them is *kamonasu,* a specialty in the Kyoto region. *Kamonasu* is larger than an ordinary Japanese eggplant, and its shape is round. Imagine having a soft clay model of a medium American eggplant, and rolling it in your hands to shape it into a ball. This is how *kamonasu* appears. This dense-fleshed variety is suitable for deep-frying, the technique used in this recipe, or for simmering.

In this preparation, the cooked eggplant is topped with a delightful sweet miso sauce. This sauce keeps for two weeks, covered, in the refrigerator. It is a nice condiment to serve with plain cooked white or brown rice.

3 tablespoons mamemiso *(soybean miso)*
2 tablespoons mirin *(sweet cooking wine)*
$^1/_4$ cup sake *(rice wine)*
$1^1/_2$ tablespoons sugar
2 tablespoons minced scallion, green part only
1 teaspoon sesame oil
2 kamonasu *or* 1 medium American eggplant, stemmed
1 tablespoon white sesame seeds *or* white poppy seeds,
        toasted *(see page 100)*
Vegetable oil, for deep-frying

GARNISH
5 shiso leaves, preferably, or mint leaves, julienned

In a saucepan, combine the miso, *mirin*, and *sake*, and mix with a spatula until smooth. Add the sugar, and place the pan over medium-low heat. Cook the mixture until it is no longer watery, about 5 minutes, stirring all the time. Add the scallion and sesame oil, and mix. Remove the saucepan from the heat, and set it aside.

Cut each eggplant into four 2-inch thick disks. Make several shallow cuts in a checkerboard pattern on one cut surface of each disk. With a toothpick, prick the entire surface of the other cut surface.

In a skillet, heat 2 inches of vegetable oil to 340 degrees F. Fry the eggplant over medium heat for 3 to 5 minutes, or until the cut surfaces are golden and the eggplant is cooked through. Drain the eggplant on a paper towel. (As an alternative to deep-frying the eggplant, you can rub it with $^1/_3$ cup oil and bake it at 375 degrees F until it is soft and golden.)

Serve the eggplant hot, topped with the miso sauce and garnished with the sesame seeds and shiso.

• *Yields 4 servings*

SPICY STIR-FRIED FENNEL AND CARROT

Fenneru to Ninjin no Itame-mono

This dish illustrates how to enjoy a vegetable not traditionally found in Japan, fennel bulb, in a Japanese way.

> 2 to 3 tablespoons vegetable oil
> 1 large (6-ounce) fennel bulb, julienned in
>   2¹/₂-inch lengths
> 5 ounces (about 1 medium) carrot, julienned in
>   2¹/₂-inch lengths
> 2 tablespoons dashi (fish stock, page 65) or water
> 1¹/₂ to 3 teaspoons sugar
> 1 tablespoon shoyu (soy sauce)
> Shichimi togarashi (seven-spice powder)
> 1 tablespoon white sesame seeds, toasted (page 100)
> A few drops tamari

Heat a wok or skillet, and add the oil. When the oil is hot, add the fennel and carrot. Cook them over high heat for 1 to 2 minutes, stirring continuously, until the vegetables are well coated with oil.

Add the *dashi* or water and 1¹/₂ teaspoons sugar, and cook until almost all the liquid is absorbed, stirring continuously. Add the *shoyu*, and cook until it is absorbed. Add the seven-spice powder and sesame seeds. Give several large stirs, and check the flavor. Add the remaining sugar, if you like. Drop the tamari onto the hot inner surface of the wok or skillet to burn it instantly, and toss it with the mixture.

Serve the vegetables hot in individual small bowls.

• *Yields 4 servings*

FIVE-COLOR MUNG-BEAN NOODLE SALAD

Ryokuto Harusame Sarada

My mother made this salad during the hot and steaming Tokyo summers. This recipe came from her favorite Chinese cookbook, which actually presented "Japanized" versions of Chinese dishes. The preparation is very simple and quick, taking only 15 minutes. Cucumber, carrot, thin omelette, ham, soybean sprouts, and *ryokuto harusame* (mung-bean noodles) are served with a refreshing dressing. Parboiled broccoli flowerets, asparagus, bok choy, green beans, spinach, bell peppers, and fennel bulb are all good substitutes for the vegetables here. Try steamed and shredded chicken, shrimp, or crabmeat instead of ham.

2 tablespoons sesame oil
¹/₄ cup shoyu (soy sauce)
2 tablespoons komezu (rice vinegar)
1¹/₂ tablespoons sugar
Pinch of chile pepper powder or
*   shichimi togarashi (seven-spice powder)*
1 Japanese cucumber or ¹/₄ salad cucumber
*   (cut crosswise)*
1 medium carrot
2 to 3 cups shredded cabbage, in 2-inch lengths,
*   soaked in ice water 15 minutes*
3¹/₂ ounces cooked ham
1¹/₂ to 2 cups soybean sprouts
2 ounces ryokuto harusame (mung-bean noodles)
2 eggs
Pinch of salt
Vegetable oil

GARNISH
2 tablespoons white sesame seeds, toasted (page 100)

In a saucepan, heat the sesame oil over medium heat. When it is fragrant, add the *shoyu*, *komezu*, and sugar. Bring the mixture to a boil. Remove the pan from the heat, and stir to dissolve the sugar. Add the chile pepper powder or seven-spice powder, and let the mixture cool. Refrigerate the sauce, covered, for several hours.

Cut off both ends of the cucumber, and cut it into three pieces crosswise. Cut each piece into thin sticks. Peel the carrot, and cut it into similar sticks.

Drain the cabbage, discarding the water.

Cut the ham into sticks the size of the cucumber and carrot sticks.

Bring a medium pot of water to a boil. Blanch the soybean sprouts for 30 seconds, drain them, and cool them under cold running water. Drain them again.

Put the mung-bean noodles into a bowl, and cover them by 2 inches with boiling water. Let the noodles stand for 6 minutes.

Drain the noodles, and rinse them under cold running water. Cut the noodles into shorter lengths, about 6 inches.

In a bowl, beat the eggs with the pinch of salt. Heat a small skillet over medium heat. Add 2 tablespoons oil, and tip the skillet to coat the entire surface. Pour out the excess oil. Pour one-fourth of the beaten eggs into the skillet. Cook the thin omelette over low heat until the bottom appears slightly golden when the omelette is lifted with a chopstick but the top is barely cooked.

Flip the omelette over, and cook it 10 seconds more. Slide the omelette onto a cutting board.

Cook three more thin omelettes in the same way, adding $1/2$ teaspoon oil to the skillet, as needed, before cooking each omelette.

Cut the omelettes in half through the center, and then into thin strips the same length of the vegetable strips.

On individual salad plates, arrange a portion of each kind of vegetable, the noodles, and the ham in a radial pattern. Decorate the center of the dish (the "hub" of the "spokes") with a portion of the omelette strips. Pour a generous amount of sauce over each salad, garnish it with white sesame seeds, and serve.

• *Yields 2 to 3 servings*

QUICK SIMMERED SPINACH AND FRIED TOFU

Horenso to Atsuage no Nibitashi

This is very much a home-style dish, such as your mother would make if you were raised in Japan. Each household is proud of the unique flavor of its version. You may replace the *atsuage*, fried tofu, with shelled clams or crisp cooked bacon, and the spinach with mustard greens.

> 1 atsuage *(fried tofu),* or 2 abura-age
>   *(fried thin tofu)* sheets
> 2 tablespoons vegetable oil
> 14 ounces (1 large bunch) spinach or mustard greens
> 1¹/₂ cups dashi *(fish stock, page 65)*
> 2 tablespoons mirin *(sweet cooking wine)*
> 1 tablespoon shoyu *(soy sauce)*
> ¹/₂ teaspoon salt
>
> CONDIMENT
> Shichimi togarashi *(seven-spice powder)*

If you are using *atsuage,* cut it in half horizontally, making two thin rectangular slices. In a skillet, heat the vegetable oil, and cook the fried tofu, turning it once, until both sides are golden.

If you are using *abura-age,* do not half it or fry it. Instead rinse it with boiling water.

Cut the *atsuage* or *abura-age* into ¹/₄-inch-wide crosswise strips.

In a large pot of salted boiling water, cook the spinach for 1 to 2 minutes. Drain the spinach, and cool it under cold running water. Drain the cooled spinach, cut it into 2-inch lengths, and set it aside.

Shortly before serving time, put the *dashi, mirin, shoyu,* and salt into a medium pot, and place the pot over high heat. Bring the mixture to a boil, and add the fried tofu. Bring the mixture to a boil again, and cook it for 2 minutes, or until the tofu is heated through. Add the spinach, and bring the mixture to another boil. Remove the pot from the heat.

Serve the dish hot, sprinkled with seven-spice powder.

• *Yields 2 servings*

HOW TO COOK FRESH BAMBOO SHOOTS

Takenoko no Yude-kata

Somewhat to my surprise, I recently spotted fresh young bamboo shoots at a supermarket near my home in Manhattan. In Japan, baby shoots that haven't yet broken the surface of the soil are dug out, cleaned, and served raw in sashimi style, with wasabi and *shoyu* (soy sauce). Since the sweetness disappears soon after cutting, this juicy, tender treat can be enjoyed only on rare occasions. In cities, this early-spring delicacy is usually found only at first-class restaurants.

Most bamboo shoots available at retail markets in Japan are harvested when they are 5 to 7 inches above ground, and usually a day passes after cutting before they are in the stores. During this time, the shoots develop a harsh astringency, dry out, and toughen. Bamboo shoots at this stage are cooked in water in their brown husks. In Japan, we usually use water to which rice bran and a few dried red chile peppers have been added. Some people, instead of adding rice bran, use water in which rice has been rinsed. These ingredients are said to help to remove harshness from the shoots. The cooked bamboo shoots are then ready to use in various preparations, such as simmered, stir-fried, and deep-fried dishes and soups.

Freshly cooked bamboo shoots have a true bamboo flavor that you can never experience with the canned product. Ask your vegetable seller how to obtain this spring treat, and try the recipe. A bit of detective work is well worth the effort to find these delicious harbingers of spring.

*2 freshly harvested bamboo shoots, preferably no
more than 2 days old (choose shoots that look
moist, not dried out, on the bottom)
2 akatogarashi or other small dried red chile peppers
Rice bran, or water in which rice has been rinsed*

Remove three or four outer brown husks from each shoot. Remove the tiny round, protruding balls from the bottom of the shoot. Make a shallow cut from the top to the bottom through the husk leaves, to make peeling easier later. Remove about 1¹/₂ to 2 inches from the top part of the shoot by making a diagonal cut.

In a large pot, combine the bamboo shoots, chile peppers, and, if you're using plain water, ¹/₄ cup rice bran. Add enough plain water or water in which rice was rinsed to cover the shoots by 1 inch. Bring the mixture to a boil, reduce the heat, and gently simmer the shoots, covered with a drop lid (see page 26), for 3 hours. Add more water as necessary.

Remove the pot from the heat, and let the shoots stand in the cooking liquid to cool.

When the shoots are cool enough to handle, peel off the brown husks, and soak the shoots in cold water for 30 minutes. The shoots will keep for 1 week, covered in cold water, in the refrigerator. Change the water every day.

BAMBOO SHOOTS
TOSSED WITH AROMATIC *SANSHO* LEAVES

Takenoko no Kinome-ae

Takenoko, bamboo shoots, signal the arrival of early spring, and at the same time the *sansho* pepper tree bears its first young, tiny leaves, which are known as *kinome.* Young *sansho* leaf has a very distinctive, refreshing aroma and flavor. As far as I know, there is no other herb that can rival its fragrance.

As basil is used to make pesto, *kinome* is used to produce a bright green, aromatic sauce that is served with tender simmered bamboo shoots. Unfortunately *kinome* is rarely available outside Japan, so I am forced to substitute basil. Yes, basil produces quite a different result, but a tasty one.

By all means, keep on the lookout for *kinome*. Perhaps the popularity of Japanese foods around the world will induce suppliers to import this unique and distinctive ingredient.

7 ounces cooked bamboo shoots (see page 260),
preferably, or white asparagus
1 cup plus 2 tablespoons dashi (fish stock, page 65)
2¹/₂ tablespoons shoyu (soy sauce)
¹/₃ cup loosely packed kinome (young sansho leaves),
preferably, or ¹/₂ cup tightly packed basil leaves
3¹/₂ ounces spinach leaves
¹/₄ cup Saikyo miso (sweet white miso)
2 tablespoons sugar

Quarter the bamboo shoots lengthwise, then cut each quarter crosswise into 1½-inch pieces. In a medium pot, combine the bamboo shoots and 1 cup of the *dashi*, and bring the mixture to a boil over high heat. Reduce the heat to medium, add the sugar, and cook for 3 minutes. Add the *shoyu*, and cook for 5 minutes. Let the bamboo shoots stand in the cooking liquid.

If you are using asparagus, peel the tough skin of the lower part of each spear, and cut off the very bottom of the stalk. Cook the whole spears in boiling water until they are cooked through but still firm.

Drain the asparagus, return it to the pan, and add 1 cup *dashi* and the sugar. Cook over medium heat, covered, for 5 minutes. Add the *shoyu*, and cook, covered, for 3 minutes more. Let the asparagus stand in the cooking liquid.

In a medium pot of boiling water, blanch the *kinome* or basil for 10 seconds. Drain the leaves, and cool them under cold running water.

Fill the pot with water again, bring it to a boil, and cook the spinach until soft, 1 to 2 minutes. Drain it, and cool it under cold running water.

In a *suribachi* or other mortar or food processor, purée the *kinome* or basil and the spinach. One at a time, add the miso, the sugar, and the remaining 2 tablespoons *dashi* to the *suribachi*, grinding between the additions. If you are using a food processor, transfer the *kinome* (or basil) and spinach purée to a bowl, and mix in the other ingredients with a spatula.

Just before serving, drain the bamboo shoots or asparagus, and toss them with the green sauce.

• *Yields 2 to 3 servings*

QUICK SALT-PICKLED CABBAGE

Kyabetsu no Sokuseki Zuke

This is a very quick pickled cabbage preparation. You may be able to find a Japanese pickling pot at a Japanese food or equipment store. The pot has an inner lid that is screwed down to apply the proper pressure to vegetables. If you can't find a Japanese pickling pot, a large stone placed on a plate over the pickles will do the job nicely.

1 pound cabbage, cut into 1¹/₂-inch pieces
1 medium carrot (about 3¹/₂ ounces), julienned
1 umeboshi (pickled plum), pitted and crushed
2 tablespoons mirin (sweet cooking wine)
10 shiso leaves, julienned
1 tablespoon salt

GARNISH
White sesame seeds, toasted (page 100)

CONDIMENT
Shoyu (soy sauce)

Bring 2 quarts of water to a boil. Place the cabbage and carrot in a colander, and pour the boiling water over them. Cool the vegetables under cold running water, and drain them. Mix the pickled plum with the *mirin*. In a bowl, combine this mixture with the vegetables and shiso. Add the salt, and toss.

Transfer the vegetables to a Japanese pickling pot, if you have one, and completely screw down the lid. Or put the vegetables into another container, lay a plate on top to cover them, and weight the plate with a clean stone or unopened food cans weighing about 2 pounds. Refrigerate the pickling pot or other container for about 5 hours.

Remove the pickled vegetables from the pot, and squeeze out the excess water. Serve the vegetables garnished with sesame seeds and flavored with a little *shoyu*.

• *Yields 6 to 8 servings*

SIMMERED CHINESE CABBAGE, FRIED THIN TOFU, AND MUNG-BEAN NOODLES

Hakusai to Abura-age no Nimono

Chinese cabbage, *hakusai,* has the ability to absorb all the good flavors from the other ingredients or the broth with which it is cooked. In this vegetarian preparation, Chinese cabbage is cooked with *abura-age* (fried thin tofu) and mung-bean noodles in a richly flavored *dashi* (fish stock). I add red bell pepper for extra color.

1 red bell pepper

1 pound Chinese cabbage, green and white parts separated

3 *abura-age (fried thin tofu) sheets*

2¹/₂ *ounces* ryokuto harusame *(mung-bean noodles)*

2 *cups* dashi *(fish stock, page 65)*

2 *tablespoons* sake *(rice wine)*

2 *tablespoons* mirin *(sweet cooking wine)*

1 tablespoon sugar

2 *tablespoons* shoyu *(soy sauce)*

¹/₂ *teaspoon sesame oil*

Fresh-ground black pepper

Grill or broil the red bell pepper until the skin is charred. Wrap the pepper in plastic wrap, and let it steam in its own heat for 10 minutes.

Cut the pepper in half lengthwise. Remove the skin, stem, seeds, and white ribs. Cut each pepper half in half crosswise, and then into ²/₃-inch-wide strips.

Cut the Chinese cabbage into ²/₃-inch-wide slices crosswise. Put the thick white parts in one bowl, and the green leafy parts in another.

In a medium pot, bring plenty of water to a boil. Add the fried thin tofu, and cook it for 20 seconds. Rinse the fried thin tofu under cold running water, and squeeze out the excess water. Cut the fried thin tofu crosswise into ²/₃-inch-wide strips.

Fill the medium pot with water again, and bring it to a boil. Remove the pot from the heat, add the mung-bean noodles, and soak them for 6 minutes. Drain the noodles, and cut them in half.

In a medium pot, combine the white part of the Chinese cabbage, the fried thin tofu, mung-bean noodles, *dashi*, and *sake*. Bring the mixture to a boil, and cook it over medium heat, covered with a drop lid (see page 26), for 10 minutes.

Add the *mirin*, sugar, the leafy part of the Chinese cabbage, and the red bell pepper and cook, covered with a drop lid, for 3 minutes. Add the *shoyu*, and cook, uncovered, for 5 minutes, turning the vegetables once or twice. Add the sesame oil and black pepper and stir briefly.

Serve the mixture hot, with plain white or brown rice.

• *Yields 4 servings*

EGGPLANT WITH JAPANESE-STYLE SCRAMBLED EGGS

Nasu to Iritamago no Sarada

This is my mother's favorite summertime salad. The steamed eggplants and scrambled eggs are excellent companions.

> 6 Japanese or Italian eggplants, stemmed
> 1 teaspoon sesame oil
> 3 large eggs, beaten
> 2 scallions, both green and white parts, minced
> 1¹/₂ tablespoons shoyu (soy sauce)
> 1 tablespoon sugar
> 4 tablespoons vegetable oil or melted butter

Have ready a bamboo or metal steamer with plenty of water at high steam production. In a bowl, toss the eggplants with the sesame oil. Steam the eggplants until soft, 15 minutes.

Remove the eggplants from the steamer, and let them cool to room temperature. Cut the eggplants into long strips, and chill them in the refrigerator.

Arrange the chilled eggplants on a serving platter. Into the bowl of beaten eggs, add the scallions, *shoyu*, sugar, and 3 tablespoons of the vegetable oil or melted butter.

In a wok or skillet, heat the remaining 1 tablespoon vegetable oil or butter. When the oil is hot but not smoking, add the egg mixture, and cook it over high heat until it is 80 percent done, stirring with a wooden spatula all the time. Immediately transfer the egg to a bowl.

Serve the eggplant topped with the hot eggs.

• *Yields 2 to 3 servings*

SUSHI RICE

Sushi Gohan

Sushi rice is the base of different kinds of sushi dishes. The key points for preparations are

- Use polished—that is, white—short-grain Japanese rice or medium-grain California rice. Rice sold as "sushi rice" is nothing more than regular polished short-grain Japanese rice.
- Rinse the rice by covering it with cold water in a bowl and rubbing it in the water for 10 to 20 seconds. Discard the liquid. Add fresh water, and repeat the process three times.
- Instead of soaking the rice after its fourth rinsing, drain it, and let it rest in a colander for an hour before cooking. This produces firmly cooked rice, which is perfect for tossing later with vinegar dressing.
- Use good-quality rice vinegar (see page 68).
- For mixing the cooked rice with the vinegar dressing, the best container is a *hangiri* tub. A *hangiri* is made of unfinished *sawara* cypress wood. Because the wood absorbs moisture and retains heat, the rice doesn't become watery after it is tossed with vinegar dressing; nor does it cool too quickly.
- An unfinished wooden salad bowl is a good substitute for a *hangiri*. If you have no hangiri or unfinished salad bowl, substitute a glass or glazed ceramic bowl. A *hangiri* tub, and a large wooden spatula for tossing the rice, require soaking in cold water for 30 minutes before use. If the wood is dry, the rice sticks to it, and the wood absorbs too much of the dressing.
- Prepared sushi rice should be stored at cool room temperature, covered with a moist cotton cloth. Never refrigerate sushi rice, or it will become unpleasantly firm in texture.

> *3 cups (4 rice-cooker cups) short-grain or*
> *medium-grain white rice*
> One 2-inch square kombu *(kelp)*
> *2 tablespoons sake (rice wine)*
>
> V I N E G A R   D R E S S I N G
> *6 tablespoons* komezu *(rice vinegar), plus*
> *2 tablespoons for the utensils*
> *2 tablespoons sugar, to taste*
> *2²/₃ teaspoons salt*

At least one hour before you plan to begin cooking the rice, rinse the rice as described on page 152, and drain it in a colander. At least 20 minutes before beginning to cook the rice, place a *hangiri* tub or an unfinished wooden salad bowl and a wooden spatula in cold water to soak.

Cook the rice with 3 cups (4 rice-cooker cups) water, the *kombu*, and the *sake* as described on page 153.

Make the dressing: As soon as you begin cooking the rice, combine 6 tablespoons of the *komezu*, the sugar, and salt in a small bowl, and stir well. By the time the rice is cooked, the sugar and salt will be almost dissolved. (If you forget to do this step ahead of time, you can heat the mixture in a small saucepan over low heat to facilitate the dissolving, but never boil the mixture.)

When the rice is done, let it stand in the rice cooker or pot, covered, for 5 minutes. While waiting, drain the *hangiri* tub or salad bowl and the spatula, wipe off excess water with a paper towel, and rub the inside surface of the tub and the surface of the spatula with the remaining 2 tablespoons *komezu*. Transfer the cooked rice all at one time into the wooden tub, and, with a large circular motion, quickly pour the vinegar dressing evenly over the rice. Toss the rice thoroughly by cutting into it vertically with the spatula, and then lifting the rice and turning it over. Be careful not to mash the rice. The tossing should take less than 2 minutes.

Toward the end of the tossing, fan the rice briefly with a hand fan or square of cardboard. This facilitates quick cooling, which gelatinizes the surface of the rice, giving it an attractive, glossy appearance.

If no *hangiri* tub or large unfinished wooden salad bowl is available, use the following technique: Put the cooked rice all at one time into a colander placed above a glass or glazed ceramic bowl. Break the rice roughly with a wooden spatula, and pour the vinegar dressing evenly over the rice in a large circular motion. Cutting vertically, lifting, and turning, toss the rice thoroughly. Pour any drops of dressing collected in the bowl back over the rice, and toss it again. Fan the rice briefly.

Collect the tossed rice in the center of the tub, shape it into a mound, and cover it with a moist cotton cloth until you are ready to use it. Sushi rice may be made in the morning for use later in the day. Store the rice in a container with a tight-fitting lid at cool room temperature.

• *Yields 2.8 pounds sushi rice*

By following the table, below, you can vary this recipe to make just as much sushi rice as you need. The quantities of *kombu* (one 2-inch square), *sake* (2 tablespoons), and vinegar for the utensils (2 tablespoons) remain the same for $1\frac{1}{2}$ to 3 cups rice.

PROPORTIONS FOR BASIC SUSHI RICE

RAW RICE AND WATER		VINEGAR	SUGAR (IN	SALT (IN	YIELD
(IN U.S. CUPS)	(IN RICE-COOKER CUPS)	(IN TABLESPOONS)	TABLESPOONS)	TEASPOONS)	(IN POUNDS)
$1\frac{1}{2}$	2	3	1	1	1.4
$2\frac{1}{4}$	3	$4\frac{1}{2}$	$1\frac{1}{2}$	$1\frac{1}{2}$	2.1
3	4	6	2	$2\frac{2}{3}$	2.8

TUNA THIN ROLL

Tekka-maki

Tekka-maki is a thin rolled sushi with a block of *maguro*, tuna, in the center. *Tekka* literally means "iron fire." The roll is so named because the bright red fresh tuna in the center of the white rice reminds people of a red-hot iron bar.

Traditional tuna roll employs lean tuna fish and a little wasabi in the center. Other popular thin rolls have different ingredients in the center. A roll with cucumber is called *kappa-maki*, one with bright yellow pickled daikon is *oshinko-maki,* and one with simmered dried gourd is *kanpyo-maki.*

> *7 ounces sashimi-quality* maguro akami *(lean tuna)*
> *1 tablespoon* komezu *(rice vinegar)*
> *3 sheets nori, toasted and halved crosswise*
> *1.4 pounds sushi rice (page 267)*
> *1 tablespoon wasabi paste*
>
> CONDIMENTS
> *Sweet pickled ginger (page 292)*
> Shoyu *(soy sauce)*

Cut the tuna into 8-by-¹/₃-by-¹/₃-inch strips. Refrigerate the tuna, covered, until you are ready to use it.

Have at hand 2 cups water with the 1 tablespoon *komezu* in a bowl for moistening your hands. Place a half sheet of nori on a bamboo rolling mat, and, with your fingers, sprinkle a little of the vinegar water over the nori. Do not apply too much water, or the nori will become soggy and deform. Moisten your hands with the vinegar water. Spread a sixth of the sushi rice over the nori, about ¹/₄ inch thick, leaving ¹/₂-inch margins along the long edges. Make a shallow lengthwise depression along the center of the sushi rice. Spread ¹/₄ teaspoon wasabi along the center depression. Place one strip of tuna in the depression, and, with the aid of the bamboo rolling mat, make a cylindrical roll. It should be about 1 inch thick. Make five more rolls the same way.

Cut each roll into six pieces crosswise. Serve the sushi with sweet pickled ginger and *shoyu* (soy sauce) in individual small plates on the side.

• Yields 2 servings as a light snack or 4 to 6 servings as an appetizer

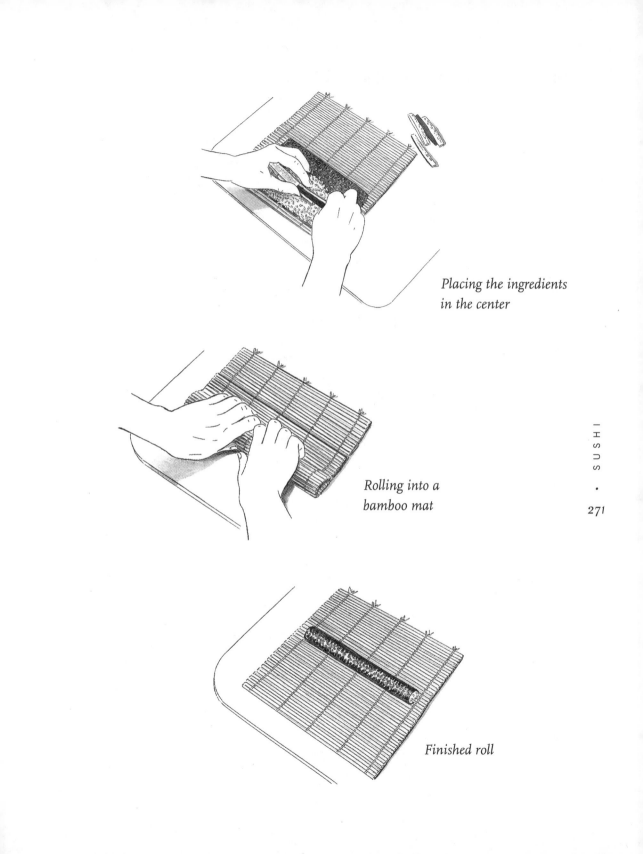

Placing the ingredients in the center

Rolling into a bamboo mat

Finished roll

TRADITIONAL THICK ROLL

Futo-maki

Futo-maki is one of the most popular sushi dishes in Japan. The center ingredients for traditional thick rolls are shiitake mushrooms, *kanpyo* (dried gourd), spinach, sweet fish or shrimp flakes, and rolled omelette. They are all contained in a single sushi roll. These five ingredients produce a delicious harmony of flavors, and at the same time provide a colorful presentation on the cut side.

After trying this authentic thick roll, you may want to explore new ideas by replacing traditional ingredients with others of your choice, such as avocado, pickled vegetables, crabmeat, ham, and smoked fish.

Twelve 8-inch kanpyo *(dried gourd) strips*
Salt
²/₃ ounce (3 large or 4 medium)
        dried shiitake mushrooms
1 cup dashi *(fish stock, page 65)*
5 tablespoons sugar
1 tablespoon shoyu *(soy sauce)*
7 ounces medium shrimp, shelled and deveined
5 ounces spinach, preferably with root attached
1 tamagoyaki *(rolled omelette, page 191)*
1 tablespoon komezu *(rice vinegar)*
3 to 4 sheets nori, *toasted (see page 128)*
2.8 pounds sushi rice (page 267)

C O N D I M E N T S
Shoyu *(soy sauce)*
Sweet pickled ginger (page 292)

Rub the dried gourd with a little salt. Rinse off the salt with water.

In separate medium bowls, soak the dried gourd and shiitake mushrooms, until they are softened, about 20 minutes.

Drain the dried gourd and shiitake mushrooms, reserving ½ cup of the mushroom soaking water. Cut out and discard the mushroom stems.

In a small saucepan, combine the dried gourd, mushroom caps, mushroom soaking water, and *dashi*. The liquid should cover the vegetables by $\frac{1}{2}$ inch; add additional water, if necessary. Bring the mixture to a boil over medium heat. Reduce the heat to low, and simmer the mixture gently, covered with a drop lid (see page 26), for 10 minutes. Add 1 tablespoon sugar, and cook, covered, 3 minutes. Remove the lid, add the *shoyu,* and cook for 5 minutes, turning the vegetables several times so they cook and color evenly.

Remove the dried gourd from the pot, and put it into a colander to cool. Continue to cook the mushrooms, covered with the drop lid, until almost all the cooking liquid is absorbed. Transfer the mushroom caps to a colander to cool.

Cut the dried gourd strips in half, making 4-inch lengths. Cut the mushrooms into thin strips. If you won't be using the vegetables right away, refrigerate them, covered, for up to one day, or freeze them.

In a pot of boiling water, blanch the shrimp 10 to 20 seconds. Immediately drain it, and chop it in a food processor to a rough paste. Blend in the remaining 4 tablespoons sugar and $\frac{1}{2}$ teaspoon salt. Transfer the shrimp to a small ungreased skillet, and cook the shrimp over medium heat, stirring with a wooden spatula, until the shrimp is flaky and almost dry, about 10 minutes. During the cooking, try to break the bigger lumps of shrimp into small flakes, being careful not to burn the shrimp. Transfer the shrimp to a small bowl, and let it cool to room temperature.

In a large pot of salted boiling water, parboil the spinach until it is just done, 1 to 2 minutes. Drain it, and cool it in cold water. Collect all the roots together at one end, place the spinach on a bamboo rolling mat, roll the spinach tightly, and squeeze it to remove excess water. Cut off the root, and discard it.

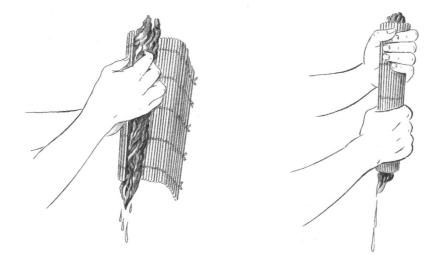

Cut the rolled omelette into quarters lengthwise, and then cut each quarter lengthwise into three long strips.

Have at hand all the five filling ingredients, side by side in a large pan; the sushi rice in the *hangiri* tub, covered with a moist cotton cloth; and a small bowl of 2 cups water with the 1 tablespoon rice vinegar added. Place a bamboo rolling mat in front of you on a counter that isn't slippery, and lay a sheet of nori on the mat, shiny side down. Closest to your body, align a short edge of the nori sheet with a short edge of the mat. Lightly wet your hands in the vinegar water, and sprinkle a few drops of the vinegar water over the nori. Do not wet the nori too much, or it will deform.

Spread a quarter of the sushi rice evenly over the nori, about $1/4$ inch thick, leaving a $1/2$-inch margin in front and a 1-inch margin at the far edge. With the side of your hand, make a shallow lengthwise depression in the center of the rice.

Evenly spread a quarter of each of the five filling ingredients in the center depression. With the aid of the mat, roll the nori, rice, and filling together into a cylinder. It should be about 2 inches thick.

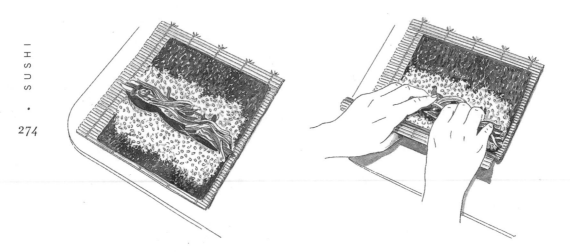

Unroll the mat, and remove the sushi roll. Make three more rolls the same way. Thick rolls can be prepared in the morning for use later in the day. Store them at cool room temperature, covered tightly with plastic wrap.

Before serving, cut each roll into eight or nine disks of equal size. Serve the sushi with *shoyu* and sweet pickled ginger.

• *Yields 8 servings as an appetizer or 4 servings as a main dish*

INSIDE-OUT ROLL

Inside-Out Maki

An inside-out roll is also called a California roll. As the name implies, this type of sushi was invented in California by a young, curious chef, who at a customer's request rolled the nori inside instead of outside the rice. This preparation has become very popular all around the world, including in Japan. However, the majority of sushi chefs at authentic sushi restaurants in Japan still refuse to accept this new invention as true sushi.

This recipe calls for some special Japanese products. You'll find pickled *yamagobo* (mountain burdock) and *takuan* (pickled daikon) at any Japanese food store. *Tobiko* (flying fish) roe, dyed bright orange, is available from Japanese fishmongers and large Japanese supermarkets. If you can't find *tobiko* roe, use sesame seeds instead.

1 teaspoon salt
1 Japanese or salad cucumber
6 roots yamagobo no tsukemono *(pickled mountain*
        burdock) or takuan *(pickled daikon),*
        halved crosswise
1 avocado, cut into thin strips and sprinkled with
        the juice of ¹/₂ lemon
7 ounces smoked salmon, cut into thin strips
1 package daikon sprouts, roots removed
About ¹/₂ cup white sesame seeds, toasted (page 100)
About ¹/₂ cup tobiko *(flying fish) roe, preferably, or*
        more toasted white sesame seeds
1.4 pounds sushi rice
1 tablespoon komezu *(rice vinegar)*
3 sheets nori, toasted (see page 128)

CONDIMENTS
Shoyu *(soy sauce)*
Sweet pickled ginger (page 292)

Spread the salt on a cutting board, and roll the cucumber over the salt. Rinse the cucumber under cold running water, and wipe it dry in a paper towel. Cut the cucumber in half crosswise. If you're using a salad cucumber, seed it. Then cut the cucumber into thin sticks.

Cut the pickled burdock roots in half crosswise.

In a large pan, place the cucumber, burdock or other pickled vegetable, avocado, salmon, and daikon sprouts side by side. Put the sesame seeds and the *tobiko* roe in separate small bowls. Have at hand the sushi rice and a small bowl of 2 cups cold water and 1 tablespoon rice vinegar. Wet a bamboo rolling mat, and wrap it tightly with plastic wrap. Cut the nori sheets in half crosswise.

Place a half-sheet of nori, shiny side down, on the plastic wrap–lined mat, with a shorter side of the nori facing you. Wet your hands with the vinegar water, and sprinkle a few drops over the nori. Cover the nori with one-fifth to one-sixth of the sushi rice, leaving a 1-inch margin at the back uncovered. Sprinkle about $1^1/_2$ tablespoons sesame seeds and $1^1/_2$ tablespoons of the *tobiko* roe, or $1^1/_2$ tablespoons of sesame seeds if you aren't using the *tobiko* roe, evenly over the sushi rice. Flip the sushi rice over, so the nori is on top. Spread a generous amount of each of the five filling ingredients across the nori, a little closer to you than the center of the sheet. With the aid of the mat, gently roll the sushi into a cylinder. Unroll the mat, and remove the sushi.

Make 4 or 5 more rolls the same way, using the rest of the rice and filling ingredients.

Cut each sushi roll into four pieces. Serve the sushi in individual small plates with *shoyu* and sweet pickled ginger on the side.

• *Yields 3 servings as a main dish or 6 servings as an appetizer*

ELEGANT PRESSED SMOKED SALMON SUSHI

Sumoku Sāmon Okizushi

Oshizushi, pressed sushi, is made by pressing sushi rice and a topping in a wooden mold. The toppings vary from vinegar-cured fish to grilled fish, parboiled shrimp, omelette, and vegetables.

I began to use smoked fish as an *oshizushi* topping when sushi-quality fresh fish was unavailable outside Japan. I like the convenience of using smoked fish—there is no filleting, no salting, no curing in vinegar. And sushi rice tastes delicious with this new partner. I serve bite-sized squares of smoked-salmon sushi topped with golden orange salmon roe—an elegant and mouth-watering presentation.

This recipe uses two 3.2-by-6-inch wooden molds. You can substitute four similarly sized plastic containers, two for holding the sushi and two for pressing it.

1 Japanese cucumber or ¹/₄ large
     salad cucumber, diced fine
1 teaspoon salt
1.4 pounds sushi rice (page 267)
2 to 3 tablespoons minced dill
1 tablespoon komezu (rice vinegar)
7 to 9 ounces smoked salmon, sliced into
    the same length as the mold
6 shiso leaves
¹/₄ cup salmon roe

CONDIMENTS
Tamari or shoyu (soy sauce)
Sweet pickled ginger (page 292)

In a bowl, toss the cucumber with the salt. After 5 minutes, transfer the cucumber to a colander, rinse off the salt under cold running water, and pat the cucumber dry in a paper towel. Combine the sushi rice with the cucumber and dill, and mix thoroughly.

Cut four sheets of parchment paper the same size as the bottoms of the wooden molds or plastic containers. Place one sheet on the bottom of each of the two molds. Have at hand 2 cups water and 1 tablespoon rice vinegar combined in a small bowl.

Spread one-quarter of the sushi rice over the bottom of each mold. Place three shiso leaves in each mold, covering the rice. Lay the remaining sheet of parchment paper on top, and press with the lid, if you're using wooden molds, or with another pair of plastic containers to flatten the surface of the rice.

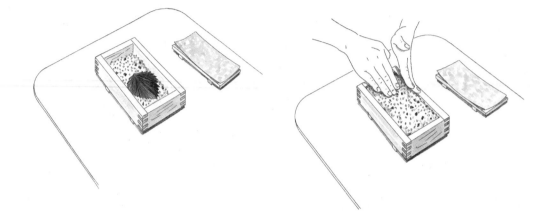

Remove the lids or empty containers and the top sheets of parchment paper, and set them aside. Divide the remaining rice between the two molds, and flatten each surface with your hands. Divide the smoked salmon between the two molds, covering the rice completely. Place the top sheets of parchment paper on top again, and cover with the wooden lids or the empty plastic containers. Press with all of your strength. Cover each mold with plastic wrap, and place a weight of about 3 to 4 pounds on top of the lid. A large rock or brick is excellent for this purpose. If you are using plastic containers, place a weight inside each empty container, and wrap the whole with plastic wrap. Let the sushi stand for 2 to 5 hours at cool room temperature.

Unmold the sushi by simply lifting the sides of each mold away from the base, if you're using wooden molds. If you're using plastic containers, lift out the sushi carefully. Cut each rectangle, with the parchment paper still attached, into eight small squares. Use a *very* sharp knife when cutting the sushi. After each cut, wipe the knife with a moist cotton cloth to remove any rice residue. If you won't be serving the sushi right away, wrap the squares tightly with plastic wrap.

Before serving, decorate each square of sushi with salmon roe. Serve the sushi with tamari or *shoyu* and sweet pickled ginger in individual small plates on the side.

• *Yields 4 servings as an appetizer or 2 as a light main dish*

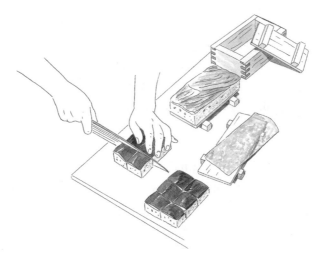

PRESSED SUMMER VEGETABLE SUSHI

Garden *Oshizushi*

My husband affectionately named this colorful new sushi "garden *oshizushi*." What better name could be given to this attractive creation? Sushi rice is pressed together with red and yellow bell pepper, zucchini, and mild feta cheese. The result is a new flavor experience. Enjoy it with a glass of chilled chardonnay or retsina.

This preparation uses two 3.2-by-6-inch wooden molds. You can substitute four similarly sized plastic containers without lids.

1 large red bell pepper

1 large yellow bell pepper

$1^3/_4$ teaspoon usukuchi shoyu *(light-colored soy sauce),*
   preferably, or shoyu (soy sauce)

1 tablespoon plus 1 teaspoon mirin
   (sweet cooking wine)

1 tablespoon dashi (fish stock, page 65)

1 zucchini, cut in half crosswise and then
   in thin slices lengthwise

1.4 pounds sushi rice (page 267)

2 tablespoons virgin olive oil

2 to 3 tablespoons minced parsley

1 tablespoon komezu *(rice vinegar)*

$3^1/_2$ ounces feta cheese, cut into eight thin slices

CONDIMENTS
Tamari or shoyu *(soy sauce)*

Cook the red and yellow bell peppers in a broiler or on a grill until they are slightly charred. Transfer them to a plastic bag, and let them steam for 10 minutes. Remove the skins, seeds, and ribs of the peppers. Cut each pepper into quarters. In a medium bowl, gently toss the peppers with $1/_4$ teaspoon *shoyu*, 1 teaspoon *mirin*, and the *dashi*.

Cook the zucchini slices in a broiler or on a grill, turning them once, until they are slightly golden. Add the zucchini to the bell peppers, and toss.

Remove the vegetables from the *shoyu* mixture, and gently pat them dry with a paper towel. Cut off one end of each pepper slice, if necessary, so that the slices will fit neatly into two 3.2-by-6-inch sushi molds or similarly sized plastic containers.

Toss the sushi rice with the olive oil and parsley.

In a small bowl, combine the rice vinegar with 2 cups water. Cut four sheets of parchment paper the same size as the bottoms of the molds.

In each mold, place one sheet of parchment paper. Evenly spread one-quarter of the sushi rice in the mold. Lay one of the remaining sheets of parchment paper on top, and press with the lid, if you're using wooden molds, or with another plastic container to flatten the surface of the rice.

Remove and set aside the lids or empty plastic containers and the sheets of parchment paper. Add half of the zucchini and feta cheese to each mold, covering the rice completely. Add half of the remaining rice to each mold, and flatten the surface with your hand. Arrange half the bell peppers over the rice in each mold, alternating them from left to right to cover the rice completely. Place a sheet of parchment paper and the lid or empty container on top and press with all of your strength.

Cover each wooden mold with plastic wrap, and place a weight of about 2 pounds on top of the lid. (A large rock or brick is excellent for this purpose.) If you are using plastic containers, place a weight inside each empty container, and cover the whole thing with plastic wrap. Let the sushi stand for 2 to 5 hours at cool room temperature.

Unmold the sushi by simply lifting the sides of each mold away from the base, if you're using wooden molds. If you're using plastic containers, lift out the sushi carefully. With the parchment paper still attached, cut each rectangle into eight small squares. Use a *very* sharp knife for cutting the sushi. After each cut, wipe the knife with a moist cotton cloth to remove any rice residue. If you won't be serving the sushi right away, wrap each square tightly with plastic wrap.

Serve the sushi with a little tamari or *shoyu* in individual small plates on the side.

• *Yields 4 servings as an appetizer or 2 servings as a light main dish*

SUSHI WITH *WAKAME* SEA VEGETABLE

Wakame Sushi

This is a light, refreshing summertime sushi. Sushi rice is tossed with cucumber, *wakame* sea vegetable, shiso, white sesame seeds, and julienned thin omelette. If shiso is not available, use fresh chervil.

> 1 *Japanese or salad cucumber, rolled in* $^1/_4$ *teaspoon*
>   *salt and cut in half lengthwise*
> 2 *teaspoons salt*
> 1 *teaspoon* shoyu *(soy sauce)*
> *Vegetable oil*
> 2 *eggs, lightly beaten*
> 2 *tablespoons white sesame seeds, toasted (page 100)*
> 1 *tablespoon instant* wakame *sea vegetable, soaked*
>   *in cold water for 2 minutes, drained,*
>   *and julienned*
> 10 *shiso leaves, julienned, preferably,*
>   *or 2 to 3 tablespoons minced chervil*
> 1.4 *pounds sushi rice (page 267)*

If the cucumber has a large seed cavity, scrape it clean. Cut the cucumber into paper-thin slices. Soak the slices for 10 minutes in a bowl of 2 cups water with the 2 teaspoons salt.

Drain the cucumber, and squeeze it to remove excess water. Toss the cucumber with the *shoyu*.

Heat a Japanese omelette pan or 6-inch skillet over medium heat until hot. Put 1 tablespoon vegetable oil into the pan, and swirl the pan to coat the bottom evenly. Pour out and reserve the excess oil. Reduce the heat to low.

Add enough egg to thinly coat the bottom of the skillet. Cook the egg until it is done on the bottom but still somewhat moist on top. Turn over the thin omelette, and cook it for 3 seconds more.

Remove the omelette from the skillet, and let it cool. Make more thin omelettes, adding oil to the skillet as necessary, until you have used all the beaten egg. You will have six to eight thin omelettes. The thin omelettes may be made one day ahead of time. Stack them, separated by paper towels, and store them in a covered container in the refrigerator. Or, for later use, freeze them.

Cut the omelettes into 2-inch-long julienne strips. Reserve one-third of the omelette and shiso or chervil to use as garnish. Toss the sushi rice with the cucumber, omelette, white sesame seeds, *wakame* sea vegetable, and shiso or chervil. Serve the sushi garnished with the reserved omelette and shiso or chervil.

- *Yields 4 servings as a light meal*

GOLDEN SWEET SUSHI

Inarizushi

Students always call this small, barrel-shaped, golden-brown sushi "dessert sushi," because of its sweet flavor. The sushi rice itself is not sweetened, but it is packed in fried thin tofu that is simmered in a sweet liquid.

For this preparation, purchase a special type of fried thin tofu called *inari-age.* This type is easy to open into a pocket. If *inari-age* is unavailable, ordinary *abura-age* (fried thin tofu) will do, with care.

When you do not have time to make sushi rice, try packing plain cooked rice in fried thin tofu for another delicious treat.

10 inari-age *sheets (fried thin tofu for sushi; each*
sheet comes cut in half), preferably, or 10
abura-age *sheets (ordinary fried thin tofu)*
$^1/_2$ *cup sugar*
2 tablespoons mirin *(sweet cooking wine)*
6 tablespoons shoyu *(soy sauce)*
2 ounces (1 small) carrot, julienned in 1-inch lengths,
blanched 30 seconds, and drained
$^1/_3$ *cup walnuts, chopped fine and lightly toasted*
2 tablespoons white sesame seeds, toasted (page 100)
10 shiso leaves, julienned
1.4 pounds sushi rice (page 267)

In a large pot of boiling water, blanch the fried thin tofu for 30 seconds, pushing it down into the water, since it will tend to float. Drain the fried thin tofu in a colander, and gently press it with a plastic spatula to remove excess water. If you're using ordinary *abura-age,* cut each sheet in half crosswise. Carefully open each piece to form a pocket.

In a medium pot, combine 3 cups water, the sugar, and the *mirin*. Bring the mixture to a boil over moderate heat. Add the fried thin tofu, and simmer it, covered with a drop lid (see page 26), for 5 minutes. Add the *shoyu*, and cook until the liquid is about 80 percent absorbed, turning the pieces several times to ensure an even color and flavor.

Transfer the fried thin tofu to a colander set over a pot. Let the tofu stand for about 10 minutes.

Gently press the tofu with a plastic spatula to remove more liquid. Reserve the collected cooking liquid. The fried thin tofu can be prepared to this point ahead of time, and stored overnight in a covered container in the refrigerator, or frozen.

Transfer the cooking liquid to a small saucepan, and add the carrot. Cook over low heat, uncovered, until the liquid is absorbed or evaporated.

Add the carrot, walnuts, sesame seeds, and shiso to the sushi rice, and toss.

In a bowl, combine 2 cups water with 1 tablespoon rice vinegar. Pick up one piece of tofu, and, holding it in one hand, open it to make a pocket. Lightly moisten the other hand with vinegar water. Pick up one-twelfth of the sushi rice, gently squeeze it into a small oblong mass, and pack it into the tofu pocket. Fold in the top edges of the pocket to make a small football-shaped container. Fill the remaining pockets the same way.

Serve the sushi with sweet pickled ginger on the side.

• *Yields 4 to 5 servings*

SUSHI RICE TOPPED WITH ASSORTED SASHIMI FISH, SHELLFISH, AND OMELETTE

Edomae Chirashizushi

Chirashizushi is the easiest sushi to prepare at home. For this preparation you do not need a sushi chef's skill in rolling sushi or squeezing sticky rice in the palm. This dish is simply sushi rice in a bowl, decorated with toppings (*chirashi* means "to scatter things"). Toppings can vary from sliced raw fish and shellfish to cooked or vinegar-cured fish and shellfish, cooked vegetables, and rolled omelette.

Employing raw fish produces Tokyo-style *chirashizushi,* because Tokyo is close to the sea, and fish are abundant there. If you have access to very fresh, sashimi-quality fish, as found at Japanese food stores, purchase several varieties. They can include tuna, flounder, salmon, sea bream, squid, and octopus. To make Tokyo-style *chirashizushi,* you just cut the fish into thin slices, and scatter them over sushi rice. Preparing this dish is really an assembly rather than a cooking operation.

7 ounces lotus root (about 5 inches of a 2¹/₂-inch-diameter root), peeled, sliced thin, and soaked in 1 quart cold water and 2 tablespoons komezu (rice vinegar)

²/₃ teaspoon salt

2 tablespoons sugar

3 tablespoons komezu (rice vinegar)

4 to 5 large tiger shrimp (about 6 inches) in their shells, heads attached

3¹/₂ ounces sashimi-quality salmon

3¹/₂ ounces sashimi-quality tuna

3¹/₂ ounces sashimi-quality sea bream or flounder

4 to 5 large sashimi-quality scallops

¹/₂ Japanese cucumber, preferably, or salad cucumber

4 to 5 sweet simmered dried shiitake mushrooms (page 108)

1 rolled omelette (page 191)

2.8 pounds sushi rice (page 267)

Drain the lotus root. In a saucepan, bring $1/4$ cup water, $2/3$ teaspoon salt, and 2 tablespoons sugar to a boil. Add the lotus root, and cook, covered with a drop lid (see page 26), over medium-low heat for 10 minutes. Remove the saucepan from the heat, and let the lotus root stand in the cooking liquid until it is cool. The lotus root can be prepared to this point up to three days in advance, placed in a sterilized jar with a tight-fitting lid, and stored in the refrigerator.

Cook the shrimp on skewers as described on page 166, then cut the shrimp open on the belly side, and press gently to flatten them.

Slice the salmon and tuna $1/4$ inch thick, and the sea bream or flounder a little thinner, about $1/6$ inch thick. Cut the scallops in half crosswise. Refrigerate the fish and shellfish until you are ready to assemble the sushi.

To make a decorative garnish, cut the cucumber diagonally into 2-inch pieces, and then cut each piece in half lengthwise. Make about six evenly spaced diagonal cuts from the skin side, leaving about $1/4$ inch at one side uncut. Soak the cucumber in salted water for 10 minutes. Remove the cucumber from the water, wipe it with a paper towel, and press open the cut ends of each slice to make a fan shape. (If this process seems too complex, just cut the cucumber into thin slices, soak them in salted water, and wipe them dry.)

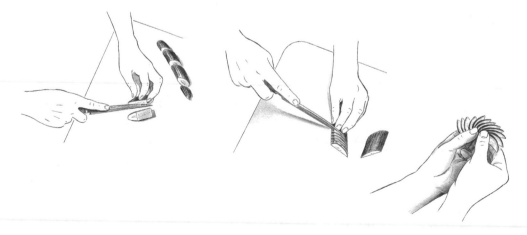

In each individual serving bowl (a deep soup bowl is best), heap one-quarter of the sushi rice, covering the bottom of the bowl but leaving the side exposed. Gently level the top of the rice. Place the cucumber, shiitake mushroom, and lotus root in the center, and arrange the sliced fish, shrimp, and omelette around the vegetables. To make a beautiful arrangement, place items of different colors next to each other and slightly overlapped, so that the presentation does not look flat. Garnish the bowl with wasabi and sweet pickled ginger, and serve *shoyu* or tamari on the side.

To eat *chirashizushi,* apply a little wasabi to a slice of fish, shrimp, or scallop. Pick it up, lightly dip one edge in *shoyu*, place the item back on the rice, and pick it up again together with some rice. Then enjoy! This is a slightly complex, but very rewarding technique. The omelette and shiitake are best eaten without *shoyu*.

• *Yields 4 to 5 servings*

FIVE-COLOR SUSHI

Gomokuzushi

Gomokuzushi is another sushi that's super-easy to prepare, and its elegant, colorful appearance makes it excellent for a party table. The dish does not use raw fish or shellfish. As implied by the name *gomoku,* "five colors and five flavors," the rice is tossed with five ingredients. When you want to make this sushi with more than vegetables and egg, add *unagi no kabayaki* (grilled, flavored eel, which is available refrigerated or frozen at Japanese food stores), cooked shrimp, smoked salmon, or fresh salmon roe. This attractive dish can be the main course of a Western dinner.

> *5 dried shiitake mushrooms, soaked in cold water*
> *for 20 minutes*
> *One 1-ounce package* kanpyo *(dried gourd), rubbed*
> *with salt and soaked in cold water for 20 minutes*
> *1¹/₂ tablespoons* hijiki *sea vegetable, soaked in cold*
> *water for 20 minutes*
> *5 tablespoons plus 1¹/₂ teaspoons sugar*
> *2¹/₂ tablespoons* shoyu *(soy sauce)*

7 ounces lotus root (about 5 inches of a 2¹/₂-inch-
diameter root), peeled, halved lengthwise and
then sliced thin crosswise, and soaked in
1 quart water and 2 tablespoons vinegar
2 tablespoons komezu (rice vinegar)
1¹/₃ teaspoons salt
2 ounces (1 small) carrot, julienned in ¹/₂-inch lengths
4 eggs, beaten
1 tablespoon dashi (fish stock, page 65)
2 tablespoons vegetable oil
15 medium tiger shrimp in their shells; heads,
veins and legs removed (see page 22)
1 unagi no kabayaki (grilled eel), about 9 to 10 ounces
2.8 pounds sushi rice (page 267)
10 shiso leaves, coarsely chopped
1 sheet nori, toasted
¹/₄ to ¹/₃ cup benishoga (pickled red ginger;
see page 58)

Drain the mushrooms, reserving their soaking liquid, and cut off their stems. Drain the dried gourd strips and *hijiki* sea vegetable, discarding the water. In a saucepan, combine the mushrooms, gourd strips, and *hijiki* sea vegetable, and add the reserved mushroom water. Add additional water, if necessary, to cover the vegetables by ¹/₂ inch. Bring the mixture to a boil, and cook, covered with a drop lid (see page 26), over medium-low heat for 10 minutes.

Add 3 tablespoons sugar to the saucepan, turn the vegetables, and cook, covered with the drop lid, for 5 minutes.

Add the *shoyu*, and cook, twice removing the drop lid to turn the vegetables, until almost all the liquid is evaporated or absorbed. Toward the end of the cooking, remove the drop lid to promote quick evaporation.

Drain the vegetables in a colander, discarding the cooking liquid, and let them cool.

Coarsely chop the mushrooms and gourd strips. At this point you can put the mushrooms, gourd strips, and *hijiki* into a covered container and store them in the refrigerator for a day, or, for later use, freeze them.

Drain the lotus root. In a medium pot, combine the *komezu*, 3 tablespoons water, and ²/₃ teaspoon of the salt. Bring the mixture to a boil, add the lotus root, and cook over low heat, covered with a drop lid, for 10 minutes.

Turn off the heat, and add 2 tablespoons sugar, stirring. Let the lotus root cool in its cooking liquid. The lotus root may be prepared to this point a day in advance, then refrigerated in a covered container.

Coarsely chop one-third of the lotus root.

In a small saucepan, bring 1 cup water to a boil. Add the carrot, $^1/_3$ teaspoon salt, and $1^1/_2$ teaspoons sugar, and cook over low heat, uncovered, for 2 minutes. Drain the carrot, discarding the cooking liquid.

To the beaten eggs, add 1 tablespoon sugar, $^1/_3$ teaspoon salt, and the *dashi*. Mix thoroughly.

Heat a 6-inch skillet, add 2 tablespoons vegetable oil, and, when the oil is hot, swirl the skillet to coat the entire inside surface. Pour off the excess oil, and reserve it. Wipe the skillet with a paper towel. Add about $1^1/_2$ to 2 tablespoons of the egg, swirl the skillet to cover the bottom, and cook over low heat until the bottom of the omelette is firm, but not browned. Turn the omelette over, and cook for 3 seconds. Transfer the omelette to a cutting board.

Make more omelettes with the remaining egg mixture, adding some of the reserved oil to the skillet as necessary. You'll have about 8 very thin omelettes. As the omelettes are finished, stack them. If you are making the omelettes a day in advance, stack them with paper towels between them, and then wrap them tightly in plastic wrap. Omelettes also freeze well.

If you have made the omelettes in advance, remove the paper towels from the stack. Cut the omelette stack in half. Then cut each half in half, cutting parallel to the first cut. Julienne each of the four stacks crosswise. Divide the omelette strips into two portions, and set them aside in separate bowls.

In a medium pot of salted boiling water, cook the shrimp for 2 to 3 minutes. Drain them, quickly cool them in ice water, and shell them.

Wrap the eel in plastic wrap and reheat it in a microwave oven, or wrap it in aluminum foil and reheat it in a regular oven preheated to 400 degrees F. Unwrap the eel, and let it cool for 5 minutes. Remove the skin carefully, cut the eel in half lengthwise, and then cut it crosswise into $^2/_3$-inch-wide pieces.

Add to the sushi rice the mushrooms, gourd strips, *hijiki* sea vegetables, chopped lotus root, carrot, half the omelette strips, and the shiso. Toss gently but thoroughly. Transfer the sushi rice to a large serving platter.

Toast the nori (see page 129). With scissors, cut it into quarters crosswise, and then into julienne strips.

Arrange the following items around the platter, in this order: the sliced lotus root, the red ginger, the shrimp, the eel, the omelette, and the nori. Serve without *shoyu* or another condiment, since the dish is fully flavored.

• *Yields 5 to 10 servings*

SUSHI WRAPPED IN THIN OMELETTE

Chakinzushi

A *chakin* is a special square cloth used during a formal Japanese tea ceremony. This sushi acquired its name because the rice is elegantly wrapped in a square thin omelette, which reminds people of a *chakin* cloth. The top third of the omelette is squeezed to make a neck, then tied with blanched *mitsuba* greens. The very top part is left loosely open. This sushi looks like a golden gift pouch.

Diners are always anxious to discover what is inside this striking package. In this recipe I stuff *gomokuzushi* (five-color sushi) and shrimp into the omelette wrapper. But use your own imagination. Try sushi rice with avocado, smoked salmon, or whatever else strikes your fancy.

Chakinzushi can also be made as an oblong block, with the rice wrapped in the omelette as you'd wrap an oblong box in paper. However you do the wrapping, the secret to preparing a thin omelette that will not break during the process is to add potato starch or cornstarch to the beaten egg.

1¹/₂ *tablespoons white sesame seeds, toasted (page 100)*
Meats of 3 walnuts, toasted and coarsely chopped
Gomokuzushi (page 287), prepared without the
 omelette, eel, or benishoga
12 *eggs, well beaten*
1¹/₂ *tablespoons sugar*
1 *teaspoon salt*
1 *tablespoon potato starch or cornstarch mixed with*
 1¹/₂ *tablespoons* dashi *(fish stock)*
Vegetable oil
15 *stalks* mitsuba, *preferably, or scallion with*
 long stems

CONDIMENT
Sweet pickled ginger (page 292)

Add the sesame seeds and walnuts to the *gomokuzushi*.

To the beaten eggs, add the sugar, the salt, and the potato starch or cornstarch mixed with *dashi*. Mix thoroughly, stirring with a pair of cooking chopsticks.

Heat an 8-inch skillet over medium heat, add 2 tablespoons vegetable oil, and pour off the excess, reserving it. Lightly wipe the skillet with a paper towel, and add about 3 tablespoons of the egg liquid, swirling the skillet to cover the bottom. When the bottom of the omelette is firm but not browned, and the top is almost dry, turn over the omelette. Cook the other side for 3 seconds. Transfer the omelette to a cutting board, and cover it with a paper towel.

Make more omelettes, using the reserved oil and more oil as necessary, until you have used all of the egg mixture. You will have about 15 omelettes. They can be made one day in advance; to store them, stack them with paper towels between them, wrap the stack tightly in plastic wrap, and refrigerate it.

In a medium pot of salted boiling water, blanch the *mitsuba* or scallion until wilted, 30 seconds. Drain the greens, and quickly cool them under cold running water. Set them aside to drain.

Place each omelette on a clean counter. Put a little more than $1/3$ cup of the sushi rice in the center of each omelette. Top the rice with the shrimp, and, with both hands, lift the rim of the omelette upright to make a pouch. Hold the neck of the pouch with one hand, and with the other hand, tie the neck closed with one stem of *mitsuba* or spinach.

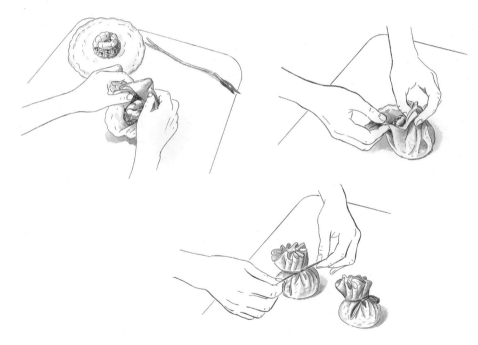

Serve the sushi with sweet pickled ginger. No *shoyu* is necessary, since the dish is fully flavored.

• *Yields about 15 sushi pouches, or 5 to 8 servings*

SWEET PICKLED GINGER

Shoga Amazu-zuke or *Gari*

When you sit down at the counter in a sushi restaurant, a chef may place a small mound of pickled sweet ginger in front of you before asking which sushi you wish to order. Sushi is always served with this slightly pink, sweet, pungent relish. *Gari* is the word for it in sushi restaurants; if you are not Japanese, you can surprise the chef by using this name.

A small bite of ginger eaten after a piece of sushi removes the oiliness of the fish from your mouth and refreshes your palate. Sweet pickled ginger is usually served free of charge.

Sweet pickled ginger is made from young ginger, which appears in the market from early May through August in Japan. You may be able to find young ginger at Asian markets in the United States. Unlike ordinary, more mature ginger, young ginger has a very thin skin, a creamy white color with pinkish knobs, and juicy, tender flesh.

Sweet pickled ginger is easy to find at Japanese and other Asian food stores, but the commercial product often contains preservatives and food coloring. So make your own! If you can't find young ginger you can use a more mature root, but choose one that is thin-skinned and wrinkle-free. Sweet pickled ginger keeps two to three weeks in the refrigerator.

> *14 ounces ginger, preferably young*
> *9 tablespoons* komezu *(rice vinegar)*
> *2³/₄ teaspoons salt*
> *5 to 6 tablespoons sugar, to taste*

Peel the ginger, and cut it lengthwise into paper-thin slices 1 to 1¹/₂ inches long.

In a small saucepan, combine 3 tablespoons water, the rice vinegar, 2¹/₂ teaspoons salt, and the sugar, and bring the mixture to a boil over medium heat. Cook the mixture, stirring, until the sugar and salt are dissolved. Turn off the heat, and transfer the liquid to a clean quart container with a tight-fitting lid.

In a medium pot, bring about 2 quarts water to a boil over high heat. Add the ginger slices all at once, and blanch them for 20 seconds if you're using young ginger, or 30 to 40 seconds if the ginger is mature. Drain the ginger in a large, flat-bottomed colander, spreading the slices so that they dry quickly. Sprinkle the remaining ¹/₄ teaspoon salt over the ginger slices, and toss gently. While they are still hot, transfer the ginger slices to the container of pickling liquid. When the ginger slices contact the vinegar, they will turn a pretty, faint pink color. Refrigerate the ginger for two days, covered, before using it.

• *Yields about 2 cups*

RICE WITH GREEN PEAS

Endomame Gohan

Tiny, sweet green peas turn plain cooked rice into a delicious treat. For this recipe, fresh peas are a must. Frozen peas lack sweetness and texture.

> 2^1/$_4$ *cups (3 rice-cooker cups) short-grain*
> *or medium-grain white rice*
> ^{1}/$_2$ *teaspoon salt*
> *1 tablespoon* mirin *(sweet cooking wine)*
> *1 cup (1^1/$_2$ rice-cooker cups) fresh*
> *shelled green peas*

Put the rice into a bowl, cover it with cold water, and rub it in the water for 10 to 20 seconds. Discard the liquid. Add fresh water, and repeat the process three times. Cover the rice with fresh cold water, and soak it for 30 minutes.

Drain the rice, and let it stand in a colander for 20 minutes before cooking.

Into a rice cooker or heavy-bottomed pot, put the rice, 2^2/$_3$ cup (3^2/$_3$ rice-cooker cups) water, the salt, and *mirin*. If you're cooking the rice on a stove, use the method described on page 151.

While the rice cooks, parboil the green peas for 2 minutes in a small saucepan of salted boiling water. Drain the peas, and soak them in a small bowl of lukewarm water.

If you are cooking the rice on a stove, put the drained peas on top of the rice at the point that you reduce the heat to very low. Cook, covered, until the rice is done. Let the cooked rice rest for 15 minutes before tossing it with the peas.

If you are using a rice cooker, add the peas after the rice is cooked. Let the cooked rice stand for 20 minutes.

- *Yields 5 servings as a side dish*

RICE WITH *SHIMEJI* MUSHROOMS

Shimeji Gohan

When autumn comes I like to cook rice with *shimeji* mushrooms, to bring a delicious sense of season to my family. The mild flavor of *shimeji* makes this rice dish an excellent accompaniment for other dishes, especially those with strong flavors. The plump *shimeji* stems, when cooked, resemble chicken breast in texture, and the round brown caps create an appealing presentation.

$2^1/_4$ cups (3 rice-cooker cups) short-grain or
    medium-grain white rice
5 ounces shimeji *mushrooms*
1 abura-age *(fried thin tofu) sheet*
1 tablespoon mirin *(sweet cooking wine)*
3 tablespoons usukuchi shoyu *(light-colored
    soy sauce), preferably, or regular* shoyu
    (soy sauce)
12 fresh or canned gingko nuts *(see page 36)*
One 2-inch square kombu *(kelp)*
$^1/_2$ teaspoon salt
10 shiso leaves, minced
1 yuzu *citron or lemon rind, grated fine*

Rinse and soak the rice as described on page 152. Drain the rice, and let it stand in a colander for 20 minutes before cooking.

Quickly rinse the *shimeji* mushrooms in a bowl of lightly salted cold water. Drain them, and pat them dry with a paper towel. Cut off the stem ends, and, with your hands, tear the mushrooms into small pieces.

Rinse the fried thin tofu with boiling water. Squeeze the tofu to remove excess water. Cut the fried tofu in half lengthwise and then into thin strips crosswise.

In a medium bowl, combine the mushrooms, fried thin tofu, *mirin,* and *shoyu.* Toss the mixture, and let it stand for 15 minutes.

If you're using fresh gingko nuts, crack and discard their shells. In a medium pot of boiling water, parboil the fresh gingko nuts for 3 minutes. Drain the nuts, and gently press each nut with the back of a spoon to remove the thin skin. Cool the nuts in ice water.

Into a rice cooker or a heavy-bottomed pot, put the rice, $2^2/_3$ cups (or $3^2/_3$ rice-cooker cups) water, the *kombu*, salt, mushrooms, and fried thin tofu. If you're using a rice cooker, add the fresh or canned gingko nuts at this time, too. If you are cooking the rice on a stove, use the method described on page 151, and at the point when you reduce the heat to very low, remove and discard the *kombu* and put the gingko nuts on top of the rice. When the rice is done, let it stand, covered, for 15 minutes.

If you're using a rice cooker, remove the *kombu*.

Add the shiso to the rice, and toss. Serve the rice garnished with grated *yuzu* citron or lemon rind.

- *Yields 5 servings as a side dish*

CLASSIC RICE WITH CHESTNUTS

Kuri Gohan

Chestnuts, *kuri,* are available in Japan from the beginning of October through early winter. Their first appearance in local stores heralds entry into deep autumn. Japanese chestnuts are fairly large, about 1½ inches across, and their flesh is creamy and sweet when it is cooked.

Removing the tough brown shells and thin inner skins of chestnuts is a time-consuming process. When I was a child, my family enjoyed my mother's chestnut rice, *kuri gohan*, so many times, without considering how much time and effort she put in to please us. Today, to make a cook's life easier, peeled chestnuts are available in Japanese stores. Unfortunately, these lack true chestnut flavor.

> 1½ *cups (2 rice-cooker cups) short-grain or*
> *medium-grain white rice*
> 20 to 25 *chestnuts, preferably in their shells*
> ½ *teaspoon salt*
> 1 *tablespoon* mirin *(sweet cooking wine)*
> 2 *tablespoons* sake *(rice wine)*
> 2 *tablespoons black sesame seeds, toasted (page 100)*
> *and mixed with* ½ *teaspoon salt*

Rinse and soak the rice as described on page 152. Drain the rice, and let it stand in a colander for 20 minutes before cooking.

If you're using chestnuts in their shells, put them into a large bowl, and cover them with boiling water by 1 inch. Let the chestnuts stand for 20 minutes.

Drain the soaking chestnuts, and peel off their brown shells and thin skins. Cut each chestnut into four to six cubes.

Into a rice cooker or a heavy-bottomed pot, put the rice, 1¾ cups (2⅓ rice-cooker cups) water, the salt, *mirin*, and *sake*. Put the chestnuts on top of the rice. If you're cooking the rice on the stove, use the method described on page 151. Let the cooked rice stand, covered, for 15 minutes.

Toss the rice gently to distribute the chestnuts. Serve the rice garnished with the mixture of black sesame seeds and salt, making sure a few chestnut pieces are visible in the bowl.

• *Yields 4 servings as a side dish*

FESTIVE RICE WITH BAMBOO SHOOTS AND CRABMEAT

Takenoko to Kani Gohan

Starting in early April, short, plump bamboo shoots, *takenoko*, begin to crowd vegetable markets in Japan. Despite their fragile appearance, the growing shoots have enormous energy. After breaking through hard ground, they can grow ten or more inches in a single day.

Because they are tender, sweet, and juicy, young bamboo shoots are valued as a spring delicacy. Bamboo-shoot dishes are a specialty of the Kyoto region, where several restaurants are famous for serving as many as 15 different bamboo dishes in one meal. A single dinner, which includes raw bamboo shoots served sashimi-style, costs from $300 to $400 per person. Without such a spending spree, though, you can enjoy fresh bamboo shoots at home.

My mother made rice with bamboo shoots frequently during the season. I thank her for teaching me to appreciate the yearly cycle of nature, with its seasonal delicacies and natural flavors. In this recipe I use crabmeat, whose faint pink color reminds diners of cherry blossoms, which appear at the same time as bamboo shoots. It is a beautiful time of year in Japan.

> 2¹/₄ cups (3 rice-cooker cups) short-grain or
>   medium-grain white rice
> 5 ounces cooked fresh bamboo shoots (page 260),
>   preferably, or canned bamboo shoots
> ¹/₄ pound cooked crabmeat
> 2 tablespoons sake (rice wine)
> 2 teaspoons sesame oil
> 1 tablespoon shoyu (soy sauce)
> 2²/₃ cups (3²/₃ rice-cooker cups) dashi
>   (fish stock, page 65)
> ¹/₂ teaspoon salt
> 2 tablespoons minced shiso or chervil leaves

Rinse and soak the rice as described on page 152. Drain the rice, and let it stand in a colander for 20 minutes before cooking.

Cut the bamboo shoots into 1-by-¹/₂-inch thin strips.

In a small bowl, toss the crabmeat with 1 tablespoon of the *sake*.

In a medium skillet, heat the sesame oil over medium heat. Add the bamboo shoots, and cook for 1 minute, stirring. Add the remaining 1 tablespoon *sake* and the *shoyu*. Cook the mixture until almost all the liquid is absorbed or evaporated, stirring occasionally.

Into a rice cooker or a heavy-bottomed pot, put the drained rice, *dashi*, and salt. Place the bamboo shoots on top. If you are cooking the rice on a stove, use the method described on page 151, and add the crabmeat at the point when you reduce the heat to very low. If you are using a rice cooker, add the crabmeat after the cooking is complete.

Let the cooked rice stand, covered, for 15 minutes.

Add the shiso or chervil to the rice, toss gently, and serve.

• *Yields 5 servings as a side dish*

CLASSIC RICE WITH *HIJIKI* SEA VEGETABLE

Hijiki Gohan

In this colorful dish, the striking combination of black *hijiki*, orange carrot, brown shiitake mushrooms, light brown burdock, green peas, and white chicken pieces is appealing to the eyes as well as to the stomach. Brown rice, instead of the usual white rice, enhances the richness of the dish.

When burdock is not available, increase the amount of carrot in the recipe.

1¹/₂ cups (2 rice-cooker cups) short-grain brown rice

3 large dried shiitake mushrooms, soaked in cold
water for 20 minutes

2 tablespoons dried hijiki sea vegetable, soaked in cold
water for 20 minutes

¹/₂ cup fresh or frozen green peas

1 tablespoon sesame oil (see page 100)

2 ounces gobo (burdock), julienned in 1¹/₂-inch
lengths (about ²/₃ cup), and soaked in 1 cup
cold water and 1 teaspoon vinegar

1 small carrot, julienned in 1¹/₂-inch lengths
(about ²/₃ cup)

> $^1/_4$ *pound skinned and boned chicken thigh, cut into*
> $^1/_2$ *-inch cubes*
> $^1/_2$ *cup* dashi *(fish stock)*
> *1 tablespoon sugar*
> *1 tablespoon* usukuchi shoyu *(light-colored soy sauce),*
> *preferably, or regular* shoyu *(soy sauce)*
> *2 tablespoons minced shiso or chervil leaves*

Rinse the rice as described on page 152, and soak it in cold water for 1 hour.

Drain the mushrooms, and cut away and discard the stems. Cut the caps into thin strips.

Drain the *hijiki*, and cut it into $^1/_2$-inch lengths.

In a small saucepan of salted boiling water, parboil the peas for 3 minutes if they are fresh, 1 minute if they are frozen. Drain the peas, and let them stand in lukewarm water until you are ready to use them.

Heat a medium skillet over high heat. Add the sesame oil and, when it is hot, the drained burdock and carrot. Cook the mixture for 1 to 2 minutes, stirring all the time.

Add the mushrooms and *hijiki*, and cook for 1 minute, stirring.

Add the chicken, and cook until the outside surface is white.

Add the *dashi*, and bring the mixture to a boil. Reduce the heat to medium, add the sugar, and cook, stirring occasionally, for 3 minutes.

Add the *shoyu*, and cook for 3 minutes more. Add the drained green peas, and give several stirs.

Drain the cooked vegetables and chicken in a colander set over a bowl, reserving the liquid. Cover the vegetables and chicken, and set them aside.

Pour the reserved cooking liquid into a measuring cup, and add enough water to make $3^3/_4$ cups (or $2^1/_2$ rice-cooker cups or the amount suggested by the rice cooker). Place the rice into a rice cooker or heavy-bottomed pot, and add the measured liquid. If you are using a rice cooker, put the cooked vegetables and chicken on top of the rice. If you are cooking the rice on a stove, use the method described on page 151, and add the cooked vegetables and chicken at the point that you reduce the heat to very low.

After the rice is cooked, let it stand for 15 minutes.

Add the shiso or chervil to the rice, and toss.

• *Yields 4 servings as a side dish or 2 servings as a main dish*

STIR-FRIED *HIJIKI* RICE

Hijiki Gohan Hiroko-fuu

One day I found a bowl of cooked brown rice left from the previous day. I decided to make a quick stir-fried rice with my favorite ingredients in the pantry and refrigerator: *hijiki* sea vegetable, anchovy paste, and parmesan cheese. The resulting dish was so good that I now purposely refrigerate cooked rice to make this *hijiki* rice for the next day's quick lunch or dinner.

Try the dish with an additional ingredient, sun-dried tomatoes. They are a surprisingly good match for the *hijiki*.

> 3 tablespoons hijiki *sea vegetable, soaked in a bowl of*
> *cold water for 20 minutes*
> 4⁴/₅ *cups day-old cooked short-grain brown rice*
> *(from 2 cups raw rice)*
> 2 to 3 tablespoons olive oil
> 1 tablespoon minced garlic
> 2 teaspoons anchovy paste
> ¹/₂ cup freshly grated parmesan cheese
> 1 teaspoon tamari
> ¹/₄ cup minced parsley

Bring a medium pot of water to a boil. Drain the *hijiki*, and boil it for 1 minute. Drain the *hijiki* again, and pat it dry with a paper towel.

Put the cold rice into a medium bowl. With your hands, break the lumps into separate grains.

Heat a wok or large skillet over low heat, and add the olive oil. When the oil is hot, add the garlic, and cook it for 20 seconds. Add the *hijiki* and anchovy paste, and cook for 2 minutes, stirring. Increase the heat to medium-high, add the rice, and cook, stirring, until the rice is heated through.

Add ¹/₃ cup of the parmesan cheese, and toss thoroughly. Season the rice with the tamari, and fold in the minced parsley.

Serve the rice hot, garnished with the remaining parmesan cheese.

• *Yields 2 servings as a main dish*

RICE WITH *ASARI* CLAMS

Asari Gohan

For this preparation, fresh clams are much better than canned ones. If you must substitute canned clams, check their saltiness. You may need to omit the salt or *shoyu* in this recipe.

> 2¹/₄ *tablespoons salt*
> 1¹/₂ *pounds* asari *or* littleneck *clams, or 7 ounces*
>   *shelled, brine-packed canned clams*
> 2¹/₄ *cups (3 rice-cooker cups) short-grain or medium-*
>   *grain white rice*
> 6 *tablespoons* sake *(rice wine)*
> 2 *tablespoons* mirin *(sweet cooking wine)*
> 1 *tablespoon* shoyu *(soy sauce)*
> ¹/₄ *cup thin scallion rings, green part only*

Combine 2 tablespoons salt with 2 quarts water. Put the clams into a colander, and hang it over a bowl. Add salt water until the clams are barely submerged. Let them stand for 2 to 3 hours in a dark, cool place to desand (see page 22).

Rub and rinse the clams under cold running water. Rinse and soak the rice as described on page 152. Drain the rice, and let it stand in a colander for 20 minutes before cooking.

In a medium pot, bring the clams and ¹/₄ cup *sake* to a boil over low heat, covered. Cook the clams until they are open, about 5 minutes. Remove any unopened clams, and strain the cooking liquid through a sieve lined with a cotton cloth. Reserve the cooking liquid. Shell the clams.

In a small saucepan, combine 1 tablespoon *sake*, *mirin*, *shoyu*, and ¹/₄ teaspoon salt. Bring the mixture to a boil over medium heat. Add the clams, and cook for 1 minute.

Drain the clams, reserving their cooking liquid. In a 1-quart measuring cup, combine the first and second clam cooking liquids and enough water to make 2²/₃ cups (or 3²/₃ rice-cooker cups).

In a rice cooker or heavy-bottomed pot, combine the rice, the clam broth and water, the salt, and the remaining 1 tablespoon *sake*. If you're cooking the rice on the stove, use the method described on page 151, and put the cooked clams on top of the rice at the point when you reduce the heat to very low. If you are using a rice cooker, add the clams as soon as the rice is cooked.

Let the cooked rice stand, covered, for 20 minutes.

Add the scallion rings, toss the rice gently, and serve.

• *Yields 5 servings as a side dish or 2 to 3 servings as a main dish*

RICE WITH OYSTERS

Kaki Gohan

Oysters cooked with rice shrink, so they are no longer plump and juicy when the rice is done. But since the rice absorbs all the good flavor from the oysters, this is a simply delicious autumn treat.

> $2^1/_4$ *cups (3 rice-cooker cups) short-grain or*
> *medium-grain white rice*
> *7 ounces small shelled oysters*
> *2 tablespoons* sake *(rice wine)*
> *2 tablespoons* usukuchi shoyu *(light-colored*
> *soy sauce), preferably, or regular* shoyu
> *(soy sauce)*
> *One 2-inch square* kombu *(kelp)*
> *2 scallions, green parts only, cut into thin rings*

Rinse and soak the rice as described on page 152. Drain the rice, and let it stand in a colander for 20 minutes before cooking.

Rinse the oysters in lightly salted cold water. Drain them, and wipe them dry with paper towels.

In a rice cooker or a heavy-bottomed pot, combine the rice, $2^2/_3$ cups ($3^2/_3$ rice-cooker cups) water, the *sake*, *shoyu*, *kombu*, and oysters. If you are cooking the rice on a stove, use the method described on page 151, and remove the *kombu* when you reduce the heat to very low. If you are using a rice cooker, remove the *kombu* after the cooking is complete.

Let the cooked rice stand for 15 minutes, covered.

Add the scallions, toss the rice gently, and serve.

• *Yields 5 servings as a side dish or 3 servings as a main dish*

RICE WITH BEEF, BURDOCK, AND PORCINI MUSHROOMS

Gyuniku, Gobo, Poruchini Gohan

In autumn, the robust, rich flavors of combined beef, *gobo* (burdock), and dried porcini mushrooms satisfies every diner. If burdock is unavailable, substitute carrot.

> *1¹/₂ cups (2 rice-cooker cups) short-grain or*
> *medium-grain brown rice*
> *¹/₃ ounce (about ¹/₄ cup fully packed) dried*
> *porcini mushrooms, soaked in 1 cup*
> *boiled water 15 minutes*
> *1¹/₂ tablespoons* shoyu *(soy sauce)*
> *2 tablespoons sake (rice wine)*
> *1 tablespoon mirin (sweet rice wine)*
> *1 tablespoon sesame oil*
> *3 ounces gobo (burdock), julienned in 2-inch lengths*
> *(about 1 cup), soaked in 1 cup cold water and 1*
> *teaspoon vinegar; or 1 cup julienned carrot*
> *6 ounces beef sirloin, cut into thin*
> *2-by-2¹/₂-inch strips*
> *A scant ¹/₄ teaspoon salt*
> *3 tablespoons minced shiso or parsley*
> *Fresh-ground black pepper*

Rinse and soak the rice as described on page 152. Drain the rice, and let it stand in a colander for 20 minutes before cooking.

Drain the mushrooms, reserving their soaking liquid, and cut them into thin strips. Transfer the liquid to a 1-quart measuring cup, and add enough water to make 3³/₄ cups (2 rice-cooker cups or amount suggested by the rice cooker).

In a small bowl, combine the mushrooms, ¹/₂ tablespoon *shoyu*, 1 tablespoon *sake*, and the *mirin*. Let the mixture stand for 10 minutes.

In a large skillet, heat the sesame oil over medium heat. Add the burdock or carrot and beef, and cook for 1 minute, stirring all the time. Add the remaining 1 tablespoon *sake*, the remaining 1 tablespoon *shoyu*, and the salt, and cook for 1 minute, stirring. Remove the skillet from the heat.

Into a rice cooker or a heavy-bottomed pot, put the rice and the measured mushroom soaking liquid and water. Put the beef, burdock or carrot, and mushrooms on top of the rice. If you are cooking the rice on the stove, use the method described on page 151.

After the rice is cooked, let it stand, covered, for 15 minutes.

Add the minced shiso or parsley and black pepper to the rice, and toss. Serve immediately.

• *Yields 4 servings as a side dish or 2 servings as a main dish*

SWEET SIMMERED BEEF AND ONION OVER RICE

Gyu Donburi

A *donburi* is a dish of plain boiled rice in a large individual bowl topped with cooked foods such as vegetables, fish and shellfish, and meat and chicken. The savory sauce in which the toppings are simmered permeates the rice, creating a wonderful flavor harmony.

Beef was first used in *donburi* around the end of the nineteenth century, when eating beef was no longer forbidden to common people in Japan. The new dish was called *gyu donburi,* beef rice bowl. In this preparation, thin-sliced beef is cooked with onion and egg in a sweet *shoyu* (soy sauce) broth.

Today several informal restaurant chains that specialize in beef rice bowl have been aggressively expanding their business, selling beef rice bowl as a low-priced fast food. A major chain has even established its business in the United States, where the dish is usually called a "beef bowl." I doubt that this popular fast food can become as ubiquitous as McDonald's hamburgers, but you are sure to enjoy trying the dish at home to expand your flavor experience.

> $1^{1}/_{2}$ *cups (2 rice-cooker cups) short-grain or*
> *medium-grain white rice*
> $1^{1}/_{4}$ *cups dashi (fish stock)*
> *2 tablespoons sake (rice wine)*
> *3 tablespoons mirin (sweet cooking wine)*
> $1^{1}/_{2}$ *tablespoons sugar*
> *1 medium onion, cut into thin wedges*
> *7 ounces sirloin beef, sliced thin across the grain*
> *3 tablespoons shoyu (soy sauce)*
> *3 eggs, lightly beaten*

Rinse the rice as described on page 152. Combine the rice in a bowl with 1³/₄ cups (2¹/₃ rice-cooker cups) cold water, and soak the rice for 1 hour.

Cook the rice in its soaking water in a rice cooker or in a heavy-bottomed pot. If you are using the stove, follow the method described on page 151.

When the rice is ready, combine the *dashi*, *sake*, and *mirin* in a medium skillet, and bring the mixture to a boil over medium heat. Add the sugar, and stir until it dissolves. Reduce the heat to low, and cook for 5 minutes.

Add the onion, and cook until it is soft, 3 to 5 minutes. Add the beef, and cook for 2 minutes. Add the *shoyu*, and cook for 2 to 3 minutes more.

Pour the eggs over the beef and onion, and cook, covered, 1 to 2 minutes.

Divide the cooked rice among individual large serving bowls, and top with the beef, onion, and egg mixture. Pour a generous amount of the remaining cooking broth over each serving. Serve the dish with chopsticks and a spoon.

• *Yields 3 servings as a main dish*

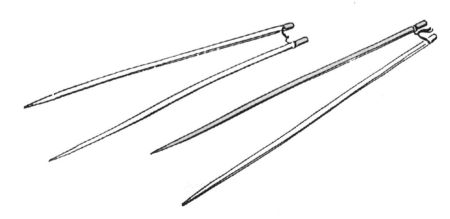

CHICKEN CRUSTED WITH PEANUTS
AND SESAME SEEDS, ON RICE

Tori Donburi

Snow white rice is topped here with chicken in two colors—some pieces are covered with peanuts, and the others with black sesame seeds. This attractive preparation comes with a great-tasting sauce.

To crush the peanuts, wrap them in tightly woven cotton cloth, and squeeze the edges closed. Beat the peanuts with a rolling pin or meat mallet.

Serve the chicken in the traditional way, over rice in a large bowl, or make an elegant appetizer by placing smaller portions of chicken over small molded rice disks.

SAUCE
$^1/_4$ *cup* dashi *(fish stock)*
5 *tablespoons plus* $^1/_2$ *teaspoon* shoyu *(soy sauce)*
3 *tablespoons* sake *(rice wine)*
4 *tablespoons plus* 1 *teaspoon* mirin
 (sweet cooking wine)
2 *to* 3 *tablespoons sugar, to taste*
3 *tablespoons Worcestershire sauce*

$1^1/_2$ *cups* (2 *rice-cooker cups*) *short-grain or*
 medium-grain white rice
2 naganegi *long onions, preferably, or* 1 *slender leek,*
 cut into 2-*inch lengths*
1 *red bell pepper*
13 *ounces skinned and boned chicken breasts, cut*
 into 2-*inch-square pieces*
1 *teaspoon grated ginger*
2 *large or* 3 *medium egg whites*
$^1/_2$ *cup potato starch or cornstarch*
3 *to* 4 *tablespoons black sesame seeds*
$^3/_4$ *cup raw peanuts, broken into small pieces*
Vegetable oil, for deep-frying

In a small pot, combine the *dashi*, 1/4 cup *shoyu*, 2 tablespoons *sake*, 3 tablespoons *mirin*, the sugar, and Worcestershire sauce. Bring the mixture to a boil over medium heat. Reduce the heat to low, and cook the sauce until it is slightly thickened, about 8 minutes. Transfer it to a small bowl, and let the sauce cool to room temperature. The sauce can be stored in the refrigerator, covered, for up to three days.

Rinse the rice as described on page 152. Soak the rice in 1³/₄ cups plus 1 tablespoon (2¹/₃ rice-cooker cups) cold water for 1 hour.

Cook the rice in its soaking water in a heavy-bottomed pot on the stove, as described on page 151, or in a rice cooker.

In a broiler or on a grill, cook the long onion or leek until it is slightly golden on the surface and cooked through. Cook the red bell pepper until its surface is evenly charred. Wrap the pepper in plastic wrap, and let it steam for 10 minutes.

Remove the stem, seeds, and white ribs of the pepper, and peel off the skin. Cut the pepper into eight strips.

In a medium bowl, gently toss the long onion or leek and the red bell pepper with 1/2 teaspoon *shoyu* and 1 teaspoon *mirin*.

In another medium bowl, toss the chicken with the ginger, 1 tablespoon *shoyu*, 1 tablespoon *sake*, and 1 tablespoon *mirin*. Let the chicken marinate for 10 minutes.

In a medium bowl, beat the egg whites with a fork until the thick part of the whites breaks down into a smooth liquid. Put the potato starch, black sesame seeds, and peanuts into separate, medium bowls. Drain the chicken, discarding the marinade, and wipe the chicken dry with paper towels.

In a large, deep skillet, heat 3 inches vegetable oil over medium heat to 340 degrees F. Divide the chicken pieces into two piles of equal size. Dredge half the chicken lightly with potato starch, and shake off the excess. Dip the starch-covered chicken in egg white, pull it out, and shake off the excess. Coat the chicken with black sesame seeds. Add the coated chicken to the oil three to five pieces at one time, depending on the size of the skillet, and cook for 1 minute. Decrease the heat to 320 degrees F, and continue to cook the chicken until it is golden, about 3 minutes. Drain the chicken on a rack.

Coat the rest of the chicken with potato starch, egg white, and the crushed peanuts, and fry it in the same way as the first half.

In a small pot, warm the sauce over medium heat.

For two main-dish servings, place half the cooked rice into each of two large individual serving bowls, and pour 1 to 2 tablespoons hot sauce over the rice in each bowl. Garnish the rice with the two kinds of chicken and the vegetables. Pour an additional 3 to 4 tablespoons sauce over the chicken and vegetables in each bowl.

For six appetizer servings, use a 4- to 5-inch metal ring mold to place a 1½-inch-high disk of hot cooked rice in the center of each dinner plate. Drizzle each rice disk with 1 teaspoon of the hot sauce. Top the rice with the chicken and vegetables. Pour an additional 1 to 2 tablespoons of the hot sauce over each serving of chicken and vegetables.

• *Yields 6 servings as an appetizer or 2 servings as a main dish*

RICE CONSOMMÉ WITH CHICKEN

Tori Zosui

Zosui, rice consommé, is a full-meal dish made from *dashi* (fish stock), a little rice, and vegetables, a protein source, or both. In the olden days, this simple dish was a frugal dinner for country people who could not afford full portions of expensive rice. In this way they could stretch the small portions with *dashi* and vegetables. In today's highly Westernized Japanese diet, which employs much more meat, dairy products, and oil than in the past, rice consommé has ironically made a comeback as a light, refreshing, and nourishing dish.

Although rice consommé is traditionally bland, I flavor it with condiments—fresh-ground black pepper, spicy sesame oil, and dry-roasted peanuts. Another condiment you might try is crisp-fried minced garlic or scallion.

The *mitsuba* greens used in this recipe have a refreshing, faint celery-like flavor. They can be substituted with coriander leaves or watercress.

4 *cups* dashi *(fish stock)*
5 *ounces skinned and boned chicken breast, cut into*
    strips 2 inches long and ¼ *inch wide*
1 *teaspoon* usukuchi shoyu *(light-colored soy sauce),*
    preferably, or regular shoyu *(soy sauce)*
2 *tablespoons* mirin *(sweet cooking wine)*
1 *teaspoon salt*
3 *cups day-old cooked short-grain or medium-grain*
    white rice
3 *eggs, lightly beaten*
Fresh-ground black pepper
Rayu *(chile-flavored sesame oil)*

> *1 bunch* mitsuba, *cut into 1-inch lengths, or leaves of*
> *1 bunch coriander or watercress*
> *2 tablespoons toasted peanuts, chopped fine*

In a medium pot, bring the *dashi* to a boil over medium heat. Add the chicken, bring it to a boil, and skim the foam until no more appears. Reduce the heat to low, and cook for 2 minutes.

Season the stock with *shoyu*, *mirin*, and salt. Increase the heat to medium, add the day-old rice, and bring the mixture to a boil, stirring with a pair of cooking chopsticks or a fork to separate the rice grains. Cook the rice uncovered for 3 minutes.

Little by little, pour the beaten eggs over the ends of the chopsticks or over the fork tines and evenly onto the rice. Cover the rice, and cook it for 1 to 2 minutes over low heat. Add a generous amount of black pepper and chile oil, and give a few large stirs.

Serve the rice consommé garnished with *mitsuba* greens and peanuts.

• *Yields 2 servings as a light main dish*

GLUTINOUS RICE WITH CHESTNUTS

Kuri Okowa

When I was a child and chestnut season arrived, my mother would prepare chestnut rice both with ordinary rice (*kuri gohan*, page 296) and with the glutinous, sweet variety, which makes the dish *kuri okowa*. I preferred *kuri okowa*. The chestnuts add fragrance to the chewy rice. Like other *okowa* (glutinous rice) dishes, this one is served with *gomashio*, a mixture of sesame seeds and salt.

Look for large, heavy, glossy chestnuts for this preparation. You will also need a steamer cloth (see page 25).

> *3 cups* mochigome *(glutinous rice)*
> *1¹/₂ teaspoons salt*
> *1¹/₂ cups shelled, peeled, and quartered*
> *chestnuts (see page 422)*
> Gomashio *(black sesame seeds and salt,*
> *page 102)*

Rinse the rice as described on page 152. In a bowl of cold water, soak the rice for at least three hours, preferably overnight.

Drain the rice, and, in a bowl, mix it with the salt and chestnuts. Steam the rice as described on page 153. Or cook the rice in a microwave oven, as described on page 154. If you use a microwave, precook the shelled and peeled chestnuts in simmering water about 20 minutes before cooking them with the rice.

Transfer the rice to a large bowl, and fan it vigorously with a hand fan or square of cardboard to cool it quickly. Let the rice stand for 5 minutes, and then serve it immediately, garnished with the *gomashio.* Or cover the rice with a dry dish towel and serve later the same day, or refrigerate the rice, covered, and serve it the next day.

Reheat refrigerated *kuri okowa* in a steamer, preferably, or in a microwave.

• *Yields 4 to 6 servings*

FIVE-COLOR GLUTINOUS RICE

Gomoku Okowa

Gomoku means five colors and five flavors. In this popular glutinous rice dish, the rice is cooked with five or more vegetables. For extra flavor, I add Chinese pork sausage, *chozume*, to the traditional ingredients. A delicious and very satisfying dish!

For this preparation you will need a steamer cloth (see page 25).

2¹/₄ cups mochigome *(glutinous rice)*

3¹/₂ ounces cooked fresh bamboo shoots (page 260)
or canned bamboo shoots, cut into small cubes
(about ⁷/₈ cup)

3 tablespoons hijiki sea vegetable, soaked in cold
water for 20 minutes, and cut into small cubes

3 dried shiitake mushrooms, soaked in cold water
for 20 minutes, and cut into small cubes

3¹/₂ ounces gobo (burdock), preferably, or fennel bulb,
cut into small cubes

3¹/₂ ounces carrot, cut into small cubes

1 tablespoon sesame oil

3¹/₂ ounces chozume (Chinese sausage), preferably,
or Spanish chorizo, cut into small cubes

1 tablespoon dried shrimp (available at Japanese and
Asian food stores), soaked in cold water for
10 minutes

¹/₂ cup dashi *(fish stock, page 65)*

1¹/₂ tablespoons sake (rice wine)

1 tablespoon mirin (sweet cooking wine)

1 teaspoon salt

1 tablespoon shoyu (soy sauce)

3 tablespoons minced shiso leaves, preferably, or parsley

Rinse the rice as described on page 152. In a bowl of cold water, soak the glutinous rice for at least 3 hours, preferably overnight.

In boiling water, parboil the bamboo shoots, *hijiki*, shiitake, burdock, and carrot together for 1 minute, and drain them.

In a skillet, heat the sesame oil until it is hot. Add the sausage and dried shrimp, and cook over medium heat, stirring, for 1 to 2 minutes.

Add the vegetables, and cook, stirring, for 1 minute.

Add the *dashi*, *sake*, *mirin*, salt, and *shoyu*, and cook over high heat, stirring, until almost all the liquid is absorbed or evaporated.

Drain the rice. In a bowl, combine the rice with the vegetables, sausage, and shrimp.

Steam the rice as described on page 153.

Transfer the rice to a large bowl, and fan it vigorously with a hand fan or square of cardboard to cool it quickly. Let the rice stand for 5 minutes, and then toss it thoroughly to mix it with the other ingredients. Add the minced shiso or parsley, and toss again. (If you plan to reheat the rice, store it without the shiso or parsley. The reheating process discolors them.)

Since this is a fully flavored dish, no condiment is served with it.

• *Yields 4 to 6 servings as a main dish*

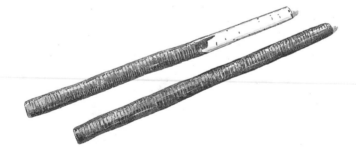

RICE TOPPED WITH CRABMEAT OMELETTE

Kanitama-don

Kanitama-don is a popular menu item at informal Chinese restaurants in Japan. This hearty meal in a bowl is another "Japanized" Chinese dish that has established a firm position in the Japanese kitchen over the past century. In this preparation, piping-hot plain rice is topped with a crabmeat omelette. The omelette is then covered with sauce.

2 dried shiitake mushrooms, soaked in cold water for
*   20 minutes, and drained*
2 ounces cooked fresh bamboo shoots (page 260) or
*   canned bamboo shoots, julienned in 2-inch*
*   lengths (about ¹/₂ cup)*
¹/₂ naganegi long onion, preferably, or 4 scallions,
*   julienned*
2 ounces canned crabmeat, preferably from legs
*   (about ¹/₂ cup)*
1 ounce ham, cubed
6 eggs, lightly beaten
¹/₄ teaspoon salt
4 tablespoons vegetable oil

S A U C E
2 tablespoons sake (rice wine)
³/₄ cup chicken stock
1¹/₂ tablespoons sugar
1¹/₂ tablespoons shoyu (soy sauce)
1¹/₂ tablespoons potato starch, mixed with
*   2 tablespoons water*
1 teaspoon sesame oil
4 to 6 cups hot plain cooked white rice (page 151)

Cut away the stems of the mushrooms, and julienne the caps. In a bowl, combine the mushrooms, bamboo shoots, long onion, crabmeat, and ham. Mix these ingredients with the beaten eggs and salt.

Heat a wok or skillet over medium heat, and add 3 tablespoons of the vegetable oil. When the oil is hot, coat the surface of the wok or skillet with the oil. Turn the heat to high, give several stirs to the egg mixture, and add it all at once to the wok or skillet. Cook until the bottom is golden, giving several large stirs during the cooking. Do not scramble the mixture.

With a broad spatula, turn over the omelette. Add the remaining 1 tablespoon oil to the skillet or wok, and cook until the eggs are set. Slide the omelette out of the wok or skillet.

Into each of two large soup bowls, put half the rice, and, on top, half the omelette.

Wipe the inside of the wok or skillet with a paper towel. Return the wok or skillet to the heat, add the *sake*, and cook away the alcohol. Add the chicken stock, sugar, and *shoyu*, and bring the mixture to a boil over high heat. Reduce the heat to low, add the potato-starch water, and cook the sauce until it thickens. Add the sesame oil, and stir. Pour half the sauce over each omelette.

- *Yields 2 servings as a main dish*

STIR-FRIED RICE AND CHICKEN

Chikin Raisu

Chikin raisu is a Japanese dish that is analogous to macaroni and cheese in the United States. Both are very popular, easy-to-prepare "comfort foods" that anyone can make and enjoy. *Chikin raisu* was created at the turn of the twentieth century as a fusion of two techniques, one a relative newcomer to Japan from France, and the other an old-timer from China. The chicken pieces are cooked with onions softened in butter, and then quickly stir-fried with cooked rice. Ketchup is then added to flavor and color the dish. Children love it.

Once you have mastered this preparation, move on to the rext recipe, *omu-raisu* (omelette and rice). It takes culinary fusion yet one step further.

> *4 cups day-old short-grain white or brown rice*
> *6 tablespoons butter*
> *1 medium onion, minced (about 1 cup)*
> *About $^1/_2$ teaspoon salt, to taste*
> *1 small carrot, minced (about $^1/_2$ cup)*
> *7 ounces boned and skinned chicken breast,*
>   *cut into 1-inch squares*
> *$^1/_2$ cup chicken stock, preferably homemade*
> *$^1/_2$ cup fresh or frozen green peas*
> *$^1/_4$ cup tomato ketchup*
> *Fresh-ground black pepper*

Since day-old rice is lumpy, quickly rinse it under cold tap water. Drain the rice well.

Heat a wok or large skillet over medium heat, add 3 tablespoons of the butter, and, when the butter is melted, add the onion. Reduce the heat to low, and cook the onion until it is soft, about 10 minutes. While the onion cooks, add half of the salt.

Add the carrot, and cook for 1 minute. Add the chicken, and cook until the outside is white. Add the chicken stock and the remaining salt, raise the heat to medium-high, and cook until the liquid is absorbed.

Add the rice and green peas, turn the heat to high, and continuously stir until the rice is heated through and mixed with the chicken. Add the tomato ketchup and black pepper, and stir thoroughly.

Serve the *chikin raisu* with fork and spoon, not chopsticks!

• *Yields 2 servings as a main dish*

OMELETTE WITH STIR-FRIED RICE AND CHICKEN

Omu Raisu

This is another cherished fusion dish that was created at the turn of the twentieth century and has established a permanent position in the Japanese kitchen. *Chikin raisu*, which uses French and Chinese techniques, is enhanced with another French touch: The stir-fried rice is wrapped in an omelette. In this way the rice remains piping hot, and the diners can enjoy more flavor, texture, and color with each bite.

Salt to taste
Fresh-ground black pepper to taste
3 eggs, beaten
2 tablespoons butter
1 1/2 teaspoons vegetable oil
1/2 recipe chikin raisu (page 315)
Ketchup

Stir salt and ground pepper into the beaten eggs. Heat an 8- to 10-inch skillet until very hot, and add the butter. When it sizzles, add the eggs all at once, and quickly swirl the skillet to coat the bottom evenly with the eggs. Cook the eggs over medium-low heat until they are set on the bottom and half-cooked on top.

Spread the *chikin raisu* over half of the omelette, and fold the other half over the rice, covering the rice completely. Eat the omu raisu with ketchup from the bottle.

• *Yields 1 serving as a main dish*

JAPANESE-STYLE SHRIMP CURRY WITH RICE

Ebi no Karei Raisu

Curry preparations reached Japan at the end of the nineteenth century and quickly became popular there. Interestingly, curry was introduced not by Indians but by Westerners, probably the British, who brought curry dishes from their Indian colony. Hence, in those early years curry was regarded in Japan as a sophisticated Western dish and was prepared by chefs who had mastered the arts of French and other Western cuisines. Today's Japanese curry is unrecognizable by lovers of real Indian curry. However, this "new creation," now more than one hundred years old, tastes delicious!

Here shrimp is served in a sweet, spicy, rich curry sauce over white rice. You can replace the shrimp with chicken, pork, or beef; just cut the meat into 1-inch cubes, salt and pepper it, and brown it on all sides in an oiled skillet. When using beef or pork, add potato and carrot pieces to the dish. Cut them into 1-inch cubes, and parboil them for 20 minutes. Add the meat to the curry sauce after cooking the sauce for about 2 hours. Cook for 40 minutes, add the potatoes and carrots, and cook for 20 minutes more.

5 tablespoons butter or vegetable oil

2 medium onions, minced

1 thumb-size piece of ginger, minced

3 garlic cloves, minced

3 tablespoons S&B curry powder (available at Japanese food stores) or any other medium-hot curry powder

1 medium carrot, grated or chopped fine in a food processor

1 apple, grated or chopped fine in a food processor

1 ripe mango, pitted, and grated or chopped fine in a food processor

1/4 cup tomato purée

1 tablespoon mango chutney (available in many supermarkets)

5 cups chicken stock

2 1/2 teaspoons plus a pinch of salt

1 teaspoon sugar

1 teaspoon Worcestershire sauce

1 pound shelled and deveined small shrimp (about 2 inches long), wiped with a paper towel

3 tablespoons brandy

2 tablespoons minced parsley

6 cups hot plain cooked white rice (page 151)

Heat a large skillet over medium heat. Add 3 tablespoons butter or vegetable oil, and, when it is sizzling, add the onions, ginger, and garlic. Cook over low heat until the onion is tender and browned, 20 minutes.

In a small saucepan or skillet, cook the curry powder over medium-low heat until fragrant, 30 seconds. Add the curry powder to the onion mixture, and give several stirs.

Transfer the onion mixture to a pot, and add the carrot, apple, mango, tomato purée and chutney. Add the chicken stock, and bring it to a boil. Reduce the heat to very low. Add the 2$\frac{1}{2}$ teaspoons salt, the sugar, and Worcestershire sauce, and cook, uncovered, for 3 hours. Stir the pot every half-hour so that the mixture does not stick to the bottom and burn. If the mixture reduces too much, add an additional $\frac{1}{2}$ to 1 cup chicken stock.

At the end of the cooking, check the flavor. If you wish to make the curry hotter, add a little ground chile pepper.

In a clean skillet, heat the remaining 2 tablespoons butter or oil. When it is sizzling, add the shrimp and a pinch of salt, and cook the shrimp over medium-high heat, turning it several times, until it is cooked through, about 3 minutes.

Remove the skillet from the heat, and add the brandy. Return the skillet to the heat, and light a flame to burn away the alcohol.

Add the shrimp to the curry. Serve the curry, garnished with parsley, over plain white rice.

• *Yields 4 servings*

STIR-FRIED RICE WITH CURRY

Dorai Karei Raisu

This simple and delicious dish was created upon the introduction of Indian spice powders into the Japanese kitchen. The rice is quickly stir-fried with curry powder. The dish tastes richer if you have a little leftover curry sauce to cook with the rice.

> *6 tablespoons butter or vegetable oil*
> *1 onion, chopped*
> *1 teaspoon salt*
> *1 carrot, chopped*
> *11 ounces beef sirloin, cut into very thin 1-inch squares*
> *6 cups hot plain cooked white rice*
> *$^1/_4$ cup chicken broth*
> *2 tablespoons S&B curry powder (available at Japanese food stores) or any other medium-hot curry powder*
> *3 tablespoons raisins*
>
> CONDIMENT
> *Mango or other chutney (available in many supermarkets)*

Heat a wok or a large skillet over medium heat. Add 2 tablespoons butter or oil, and, when it sizzles, the onion. Add $^1/_2$ teaspoon salt, and cook the onion over low heat for 15 minutes.

Add the carrot, and cook for 5 minutes more. Transfer the onion and carrot to a bowl, and set the bowl aside. Clean the wok or skillet.

In the clean wok or skillet, heat the remaining 4 tablespoons butter or oil. Cook the beef over medium-high heat, turning it several times, until the outside of each piece is pale. Return the onion and carrot mixture to the skillet, add the rice and chicken broth, and cook the mixture over high heat until the cooking liquid is absorbed.

Stir in the curry powder, the remaining $^1/_2$ teaspoon salt, and the raisins. Or, if you have leftover curry sauce from shrimp curry with rice (page 316), use $^1/_4$ to $^1/_2$ cup curry sauce instead of the curry powder, salt, and raisins. This version has a richer curry flavor and wetter texture. Check the flavor, and add curry powder and salt to your taste.

Serve the curry with chutney.

• *Yields 2 to 3 servings*

SOBA WITH SWEET FRIED THIN TOFU IN HOT BROTH

Kitsune Soba

Although *kitsune soba* literally means "fox soba," the dish employs not fox meat but *abura-age*, fried thin tofu, which is said to be the fox's favorite food. Served either hot or cold, *kitsune soba* is one of the most popular and inexpensive dishes at noodle restaurants in Japan. The fried thin tofu absorbs the rich flavor of the broth in which it is cooked, and at the same time adds a delicious, meaty taste. Quickly parboiled spinach provides a beautiful color contrast to the golden brown tofu.

You can substitute udon for the soba, if you prefer.

4 abura-age *(fried thin tofu) sheets*
1 *cup* dashi *(fish stock)*
3 *tablespoons sugar*
2 *tablespoons* shoyu *(soy sauce)*
$^1/_4$ *pound spinach, preferably with root attached*
14 *ounces dried soba*
5 *cups* kakejiru *(broth for hot noodles, page 66)*
4 *scallions, white parts cut into* 1$^1/_2$-*inch lengths,*
    and green parts into thin rings
Shichimi togarashi *(seven-spice powder)*

Rinse the fried thin tofu with boiling water to remove excess oil. Drain the tofu, and halve each sheet crosswise.

In a medium pot, combine the fried thin tofu, *dashi*, and sugar, and bring the mixture to a boil over medium heat. Reduce the heat to low, and cook, covered with a drop lid (see page 26), for 5 minutes. Add the *shoyu*, and cook until the liquid reduces to one-third of the original volume.

In a large pot of boiling water, parboil the spinach for 1 minute. Drain the spinach, and cool it in cold water. Collect the roots together, and squeeze the spinach to remove excess water. Cut the spinach into 2-inch lengths, discarding the roots.

In a large pot of boiling water, cook the noodles al dente, 4 to 6 minutes or as instructed on the package. Drain the noodles in a colander, and rinse them under cold running water, rubbing them between your hands until they are cold and no longer starchy on the outside. Drain them.

In a medium pot, bring the noodle broth to a boil over medium heat. Add the white parts of the scallions, and cook for 1 minute. Add the cooked noodles, heat them through, 1 to 2 minutes.

Divide the hot noodles among three noodle bowls, and pour over the piping-hot broth and large scallion pieces. Serve the noodles topped with the fried thin tofu, and spinach, garnished with the green rings of scallion, and sprinkled with seven-spice powder.

• *Yields 3 servings*

HOT SOBA WITH DUCK AND LONG ONION

Kamonanban Soba

Because it uses duck breast, this is one of the most expensive dishes at noodle restaurants in Japan. Chicken can be used as a cheaper substitute, but the rich flavor of good duck meat in this simple preparation creates a very savory noodle dish.

1 boned duck breast half, excess fat removed
and reserved
14 ounces dried soba
6 cups kakejiru *(broth for hot noodles, page 66)*
1 naganegi *long onion, preferably, or 4 thick scallions*
¹/₄ cup sake (rice wine)
1 bunch mitsuba, *cut into 2-inch lengths, preferably,*
or leaves of ¹/₃ bunch watercress
Shichimi togarashi *(seven-spice powder)*

Slice the duck breast diagonally ¼ inch thick.

In a large pot of boiling water, cook the noodles al dente for 4 to 6 minutes or as instructed on the package. Drain the noodles in a colander, and rinse them under cold running water, rubbing them between your hands until they are cold and no longer starchy on the outside. Drain them again.

In a pot, begin warming the broth over medium heat.

Heat a large skillet over medium heat. Add the reserved duck fat, and cook until oil covers the bottom of the skillet. Remove the solid duck fat, and add the duck breast and long onion or scallions. Cover the skillet, and cook until the surface of the duck turns whitish and the bottom is slightly golden. Turn over the duck and long onion or scallions. Sprinkle the *sake* over the duck, and cook, covered, for 2 minutes.

Transfer the duck and long onion or scallions to the pot of broth. Add the noodles, and reheat them for 1 to 2 minutes.

Divide the noodles among three bowls, and pour over the piping-hot broth. Serve the noodles topped with the duck, long onion or scallions, and *mitsuba* or watercress, and sprinkled with seven-spice powder.

• *Yields 3 servings*

HOT SOBA NOODLES WITH SHRIMP TEMPURA

Ebi Tempura Soba

Soba or udon noodles served with shrimp tempura is nearly everyone's favorite choice at noodle restaurants. Biting into a large, juicy fresh shrimp, coated with a thin, flaky, crisp crust, is a heavenly experience. However, the chances of finding shrimp tempura of such quality is quite small. Most of the time, at least at inexpensive restaurants, small, frozen shrimp are coated with a thick, bready batter, which disguises their low quality and makes them appear much larger than they are. When you bite into such shrimp tempura, you first hit thick dough before reaching the tiny shrimp. It makes sense, therefore, to prepare and enjoy noodles with shrimp tempura at home.

Here are some tips on preparing shrimp tempura:

- Fresh shrimp (the best choice when available) need only a thin batter coating and a brief cooking, 2 to 3 minutes, in oil at a temperature of 360 degrees F. When using shrimp that don't look perfectly fresh or that have been frozen and thawed, use a thicker batter coating, and cook the shrimp thoroughly, about 5 or 6 minutes, at an oil temperature of about 340 degrees F. The thick batter protects the shrimp during the longer cooking period.
- When a shrimp is cooked, its back naturally curves. To prevent this, make shallow diagonal cuts on the belly of the shrimp, and gently straighten the shrimp. Be careful not to cut through the shrimp or bend it too much, lest it break.

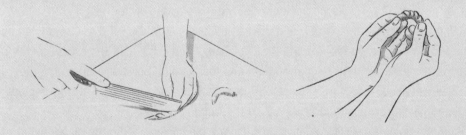

- To remove the vein at the back of the shrimp, use a toothpick.
- Shrimp tempura is always served with the tail attached for an attractive presentation. When peeling the shrimp, remember to leave the tail attached. However, the very end of the tail contains water, which can make the oil splatter during frying. Cut off the very end of the tail, about 1/3 inch.

> 14 ounces dried soba
> 6 large (about 7 inches) fresh shrimp in their shells,
>   heads and tails attached
> A blend of 20 percent sesame oil and 80 percent
>   vegetable oil, for deep-frying
> 2 cups cake flour
> 2 eggs
> 6 cups hot kakejiru (broth for hot noodles)

In a large pot of boiling water, cook the noodles al dente, 4 to 6 minutes or as instructed on the package. Drain the noodles in a colander, and rinse them under cold running water, rubbing them between your hands until they are cold and no longer starchy on the outside. Drain the noodles, and keep them covered with a towel while you make the tempura.

Shell the shrimp and remove their heads, leaving the tails attached. Cut off the tips of the tails, and devein the shrimp with a toothpick. Make two or three shallow diagonal cuts on the belly side of each shrimp to prevent it from curling during cooking.

In a large deep pot, heat 3 inches of the blended oil over medium heat to 360 degrees F if the shrimp is very fresh or 340 degrees F if it is less than perfectly fresh or it has been frozen and thawed. Have a small bowl of $1/2$ cup flour at hand for dusting the shrimp. In a pint measuring cup, beat one egg lightly, and add enough ice water to make $3/4$ cup. Transfer the egg-water mixture to a bowl, add $3/4$ cup flour, and give several big stirs with cooking chopsticks. Do not overstir the batter, or the gluten will develop and make the fried crust lumpy, bready, and heavy. When frying thawed or less fresh shrimp, make a slightly thicker batter, by adding 2 to 3 tablespoons more flour to the egg-and-water mixture.

Pick up one shrimp by the tail, and dredge it with flour. Shake off the excess flour, and dip the shrimp into the batter, keeping the tail clean. Gently shake off the excess batter. Do the same with another shrimp, and drop both into the hot oil. Cook the shrimp until they are slightly golden, about 2 to 3 minutes at 360 degrees F or 5 to 6 minutes at 340 degrees F. Cook the remaining shrimp, two at a time, in the same way.

Drain shrimp on an elevated flat drainer. During the cooking, skim the oil continually to remove bits of burnt batter from the surface. If you run out of batter, make another batch with the remaining egg, ice water, and flour.

Reheat the noodles in boiling water or in the hot broth for 1 to 2 minutes. Divide the noodles among three bowls, and pour the piping-hot broth over. Top each serving with two shrimp tempura, and serve immediately.

• *Yields 3 servings*

SOBA SUSHI

Soba-zushi

Can we make sushi with soba noodles? The answer is yes, and it is a popular preparation in Japan. Cooked noodles with a filling are rolled in nori, in the same fashion as sushi rice, and then cut into bite-sized disks. These are served not with *shoyu* (soy sauce) but with a noodle-dipping sauce. This may be a welcome change if you are having a hard time mastering the art of slurping soba noodles, and constantly splash sauce all over the table and your shirt!

The filling for this sushi can be anything from cucumber or blanched spinach to avocado, simmered *abura-age* (fried thin tofu), *wakame* sea vegetable, boiled shrimp, *unagi no kabayaki* (grilled, flavored eel), smoked salmon, or rolled omelette. Experiment to find your favorite variation.

14 ounces dried soba
7 ounces bunch spinach
2 ounces (about ¹/₄) red bell pepper, julienned
2 abura-age (fried thin tofu) sheets
¹/₄ cup sake (rice wine)
¹/₄ cup mirin (sweet cooking wine)
1 teaspoon sugar
1 tablespoon shoyu (soy sauce)
4 nori sheets, toasted

CONDIMENTS
Tsukejiru (dipping sauce for cold noodles, page 67)
Wasabi
¹/₄ cup scallion rings, green part only

In a large pot, bring plenty of water to a boil. Cook the noodles al dente, 4 to 6 minutes or as instructed on the package. Drain the noodles in a colander, and rinse them under cold running water, rubbing them between your hands until they are cold and no longer starchy on the outside. Drain the noodles well.

In a medium pot, cook the spinach in salted boiling water for 1 minute. Remove the spinach with chopsticks, and cool it under cold running water. Squeeze tightly to remove excess water in a bamboo rolling mat (page 24), and cut off the roots.

Put the red bell pepper into a fine-meshed strainer that will fit into the pot of boiling water. Blanch the red bell pepper for 20 seconds. Remove the pepper, and cool it under cold running water.

In the same pot of boiling water, blanch the *abura-age* for 20 seconds, turning it over once. Drain the *abura-age*, and cool it under cold running water. Cut the *abura-age* in half lengthwise and then into thin strips crosswise.

In a small saucepan, combine the *abura-age*, *sake*, and *mirin*. Add enough water to cover the *abura-age*. Bring the mixture to a boil, add the sugar, cover the pan with a drop lid (see page 26), and cook over medium-low heat for 5 minutes. Add the *shoyu*, and cook until almost all the liquid is absorbed.

Place a bamboo rolling mat on a counter. Lay one nori sheet on it shiny side down, with a short edge of the nori aligned with a short edge of the mat directly in front of your body. Cover the nori with one-quarter of the noodles, leaving 1 inch uncovered at the far end for sealing the roll. Evenly distribute the spinach in a thin strip across the center of the noodles. Place the bell pepper on top of the spinach, and the *abura-age* on top of the pepper. With the aid of the bamboo mat, gently roll up the sushi.

Make three more rolls the same way. Cut each roll into eight disks. Serve the sushi with individual small bowls of noodle-dipping sauce, wasabi, and scallions. The wasabi and scallions are mixed into the dipping sauce in the quantity desired.

• *Yields 3 servings*

326

HOMEMADE UDON WITH GINGER-SESAME DIPPING SAUCE

Teuchi Udon to Gomadare

Preparing udon is easy and fun. At restaurants in Japan where large quantities of udon dough are made every day, the dough is placed in a sturdy plastic bag between large, clean towels. The noodlemaker, wearing crisp, clean Japanese-style socks, kneads the dough by stepping on it.

This recipe makes a small batch of dough, so do the kneading by hand. The freshly made noodles are served here with a creamy, ginger-flavored sesame-seed dipping sauce, but it can be served with other cold noodles such as soba, *somen,* or *hiyamugi.*

Both the noodles and the sauce can be made one day ahead of serving time and stored, covered, in the refrigerator.

DOUGH
1 tablespoon salt
4 cups all-purpose flour, plus additional flour,
           for dusting

SESAME-SEED DIPPING SAUCE
$^{1}/_{4}$ cup shoyu *(soy sauce)*
1/4 cup mirin *(sweet cooking wine)*
1/2 cup katsuobushi *(bonito flakes)*
6 tablespoons white sesame seeds, toasted *(page 100)*
3 tablespoons sesame seed paste, preferably Japanese
1 tablespoon peeled and finely grated ginger

$^{1}/_{2}$ sheet nori, shredded

In a small bowl, mix the salt with $^{1}/_{2}$ cup plus 4 teaspoons lukewarm water. Stir until the salt is completely dissolved.

Sift the flour into a large bowl. Make a well in the center of the flour, and add the salt water. Thoroughly combine the flour and water by rubbing the mixture between your hands.

On a floured counter, knead the dough for 5 minutes. Transfer the dough to a plastic bag, and let the dough stand at room temperature for 30 minutes.

Knead the dough with your hands, as if it were bread dough, for 10 to 15 minutes. Return the dough to the plastic bag, and let the dough stand at room temperature for 3 hours.

In a small saucepan, combine the *shoyu, mirin,* and 1 cup plus 8 teaspoons water. Bring the mixture to a boil over high heat. Reduce the heat to low, add the bonito flakes, and, when the mixture comes to a boil again, turn off the heat. Let the mixture stand for 2 minutes. Strain the mixture through a sieve lined with a tightly woven cotton cloth, and discard the fish flakes.

In a *suribachi* (preferably) or other mortar, grind the sesame seeds until they appear oily. Add the sesame paste, and grind some more. Add 5 tablespoons of the *shoyu-mirin-water* mixture 1 tablespoon at a time, and mix until smooth. Add all of the remaining broth and the ginger, and mix, stirring. Chill the sauce, covered, in the refrigerator.

Dust the counter with flour, and roll out the dough into a sheet just a little thinner than $1/4$ inch. Dust the dough with flour, and fold it into thirds. With a broad, sharp knife, cut the dough into strips between $1/4$ and $1/8$ inch. Hang the noodles on a rack to dry for 1 hour.

In a large pot, bring plenty of water to a boil. Add the noodles, and gently stir several times with a pair of cooking chopsticks to prevent the noodles from sticking to one another. Cook the noodles al dente, 8 to 10 minutes. Check the doneness by removing a noodle and biting it.

Drain the noodles in a colander, and rinse them under cold running water, rubbing them between your hands until they are cold and no longer starchy on the outside. Serve the noodles on individual bamboo trays or platters, garnished with the shredded nori. Serve the sesame dipping sauce in individual small bowls on the side.

• *Yields 3 servings*

HOT UDON NOODLES WITH CHICKEN AND EGG

Oyako Udon

In this dish, udon noodles are topped with chicken and egg. *Oyako* literally means "parents and children." The egg is clearly the child of the chicken! Soba can also be used in this preparation.

> *1 pound dried udon*
> *1 quart* kakejiru *(broth for hot noodles, page 66)*
> *1 boned and skinned chicken breast, cut into*
> *   1-inch cubes*
> *4 whole scallions, the white parts cut into $1^1/_2$-inch*
> *   lengths crosswise, and the green parts into*
> *   thin rings*
> *3 eggs, lightly beaten*
> Shichimi togarashi *(seven-spice mixture)*

In a large pot of boiling water, cook the noodles al dente, about 4 to 6 minutes or as instructed on the package. Drain the noodles in a colander, and rinse them under cold running water, rubbing them between your hands until they are cold and no longer starchy on the outside. Set them aside to drain.

In a medium pot, bring the broth to a boil over medium heat. Add the chicken and the white parts of the scallions, and cook until the chicken is done, about 3 minutes.

Add the cooked noodles to the broth, and bring the broth to a boil. Add the eggs and cook, partially covered, for 1 minute.

Divide the noodles among three bowls, and top the noodles with the chicken and long scallion pieces. Pour in the hot broth, garnish each bowl with scallion rings, and sprinkle with seven-spice powder.

- *Yields 3 servings*

HEARTY HOT UDON
IN A RICH *MAMEMISO* BROTH

Miso Nikomi Udon

Aichi Prefecture is famous for its udon noodles cooked in rich *mamemiso* (soybean miso) broth, in a *donabe* earthenware pot. Unlike in other udon dishes, the noodles are cooked long enough in the hot broth that they absorb its rich flavor.

If you have no earthenware pot, do all the cooking in one pot. An enameled pot is a good substitute.

$5^1/_2$ *cups* dashi *(fish stock)*
$^1/_2$ *cup* katsuobushi *(bonito flakes)*
3 tablespoons mamemiso *(soybean miso)*
$1^1/_2$ *tablespoons* Saikyo miso *(sweet white miso)*
$^1/_4$ *cup* mirin *(sweet cooking wine)*
2 abura-age *(fried thin tofu) sheets*
3 eggs
9 ounces dried udon
5 ounces boned and skinned chicken thighs
1 naganegi *long onion, preferably, or 1 slender leek,*
cut into 1-inch lengths

CONDIMENT
Shichimi togarashi *(seven-spice powder)*

In a medium pot, bring the *dashi* to a boil over medium heat. Reduce the heat to low, add the bonito flakes, and cook for 10 minutes. Strain the *dashi*, discarding the fish flakes.

In a *suribachi* or other mortar or medium bowl, mix the two kinds of miso, and soften the mixture with *mirin*. Mix ¼ cup of the hot *dashi* into the miso mixture to further soften it. Stir the miso mixture into the remaining *dashi*.

Rinse the fried thin tofu sheets with boiling water, and cut them each into eight small triangles. Break the eggs into a small bowl, but do not beat them.

In a large pot, bring plenty of water to a boil over medium heat. Cook the noodles al dente, about 4 to 6 minutes or as instructed on the package. Drain the noodles in a colander, and rinse them under cold running water, rubbing them between your hands, until the noodles are cold and no longer starchy on the outside.

In a pot, bring the broth to a boil over medium heat. Add the chicken and fried thin tofu, and cook for 2 minutes. Add the noodles. When the broth begins to boil again, carefully transfer the contents of the pot to a *donabe*.

Bring the mixture in the *donabe* to a boil over medium-low heat. Add the long onion or leek, and cook for 8 minutes.

Drop the eggs gently on top of the noodles without breaking the yolks. Spread the eggs so that they cover the entire surface. Cover the pot, and cook until the eggs are barely done, about 3 to 4 minutes, lifting the lid and scooping the broth over the eggs several times during the cooking.

Take the *donabe,* covered with the lid, to the dining table. Diners should be supplied with individual small bowls, chopsticks, and soup spoons. Each diner reaches inside the pot with chopsticks, transfers noodles and other ingredients to his or her bowl, and, with a ladle, pours some of the hot broth over. Pass the seven-spice powder to sprinkle on top.

• *Yields 3 servings*

PIPING-HOT UDON IN AN EARTHENWARE POT

Nabeyaki Udon

This is another dish that is traditionally cooked and served in a *donabe*, an earthenware pot. Earthenware retains heat very well, so the udon and broth remain hot for a longer time. If you do not have a *donabe*, use an enameled pot instead.

3¹/₂ ounces bunch spinach
1 pound dried udon
5 cups kakejiru *(broth for hot noodles, page 66)*
¹/₄ pound boned and skinned chicken thighs,
      cut into 1¹/₂-inch pieces
Four ¹/₄-inch thick slices kamaboko *(steamed fish cake)*
1 naganegi *long onion, preferably, or 4 thick scallions,*
      white parts cut into 1¹/₂-inch lengths and
      green parts into thin rings
4 eggs

CONDIMENT
Shichimi togarashi *(seven-spice powder)*

In a medium pot of boiling water, parboil the spinach without separating the leaves, for 1 minute. Drain the spinach, cool it in cold water, and squeeze it to remove excess water. Cut the spinach into 2-inch lengths, discarding the roots.

In a large pot of boiling water, cook the noodles al dente, 4 to 6 minutes or as instructed on the noodle package. Drain the noodles in a colander, and rinse them under cold running water, rubbing them between your hands until the noodles are cold and no longer starchy on the outside.

In individual *donabe* pots, a communal *donabe*, or a large enameled pot, bring the broth to a boil over medium heat. Add the chicken, steamed fish cake, and the white parts of the Japanese long onion or scallions, and cook, continually skimming any foam, for 4 minutes.

Add the cooked noodles, and bring the mixture to a boil. Reduce the heat to low, and cook for 5 minutes.

Add the long onion or scallion rings and the spinach. Break the eggs, and drop them gently on top of the noodles without breaking the yolks. Spread the eggs so that they cover the whole surface. Increase the heat to medium, cover the pot, and cook until the eggs are barely done, about 3 minutes.

Bring the pot, covered with a lid, to a dining table. Since the noodles and broth will be steaming hot, the diners should be supplied with small individual bowls and spoons. Each diner picks up a small portion of noodles and other ingredients from the pot with chopsticks, transfers them to his or her bowl, and, with a ladle, pours a generous amount of the broth over the noodles. Pass the seven-spice powder to sprinkle on top.

• *Yields 4 servings*

STIR-FRIED *CHUKASOBA* NOODLES FOR A PARTY

Gochiso Yakisoba

Wherever outdoor festivals are held in Japan, they are accompanied by traditional and contemporary festival foods sold from outdoor, makeshift food stalls. There are octopus dumplings, apricots covered with millet or rice syrup, shaved ice with colorful syrup, grilled sweet corn, grilled chicken pieces on skewers, and boiled potatoes with butter. And always there is *yakisoba,* stir-fried *chukasoba* noodles.

A *yakisoba* stand, which is similar in size to a New York City hotdog stand, is equipped with a large square iron griddle. A cook behind the stand, wearing a white undershirt and a twisted cotton hair band, holds a large steel spatula in each hand for quickly moving the ingredients around the hot grill. He cooks a mixture of shredded cabbage, pork strips, and *chukasoba* noodles. Then he adds a special sauce—a commercial product similar to Worcestershire sauce, but thicker, more peppery, and sweeter—and gives several final tosses to the fragrant dish. Watching the cook's vigorous stir-frying demonstration, his hands and body in constant motion, is great fun. The performance and aroma combined keep people from leaving without tasting the result.

In this preparation, suitable for your next party, *chukasoba* noodles are stir-fried with more celebrated ingredients, including shrimp, scallops, and bamboo shoots. Each serving must be individually prepared, so share the fun of wokking the noodles with your friends.

The "thin sticks" in the recipe are about $1/8$ by $3/16$ inch by $1\frac{1}{2}$ inches—a little thicker than julienne.

5 medium shrimp, peeled and deveined, but tail left on
2 scallops, cut in half horizontally to make
      thinner disks
$1/2$ small chicken breast fillet (see page 205),
      cut into thin 2-inch-long strips
2 tablespoons sake (rice wine)
$1/4$ teaspoon salt
$1/2$ beaten egg white
2 teaspoons potato starch
1 dried shiitake mushroom, soaked in cold water
      20 minutes
$1/2$ cup vegetable oil
1 large outer leaf of head cabbage (about 2 ounces),
      cut into 1-inch-wide strips
$1/2$ small carrot, cut into thin sticks
1 ounce cooked fresh or canned bamboo shoots,
      cut into thin sticks (about $1/4$ cup)
1 ounce green bell pepper, cut into thin sticks
      (about $1/4$ cup)
1 cup soybean sprouts
3 peeled thin ginger slices, julienned
1 ounce onion, cut into thin strips (about $1/4$ cup)
4 ounces fresh chukasoba noodles for yakisoba
      (available at Japanese food stores, in the
      refrigerator case)
$1/3$ cup chicken stock
$1 1/2$ teaspoons shoyu (soy sauce)
1 teaspoon oyster sauce (a Chinese condiment
      found at regular supermarkets)
1 to 2 teaspoons Worcestershire sauce
$1/2$ teaspoon sugar
Ground white pepper to taste
Tamari to taste

In a bowl, toss the shrimp, scallops, and chicken with 1 tablespoon *sake* and the salt, then with the egg white, and finally with the potato starch. Let the mixture stand in the refrigerator for 20 minutes. Cut away the stem of the shiitake mushroom, and cut the cap into thin strips.

Heat a wok or skillet, and add the $1/2$ cup oil. When the oil is moderately hot, cook the scallops until they are firm on the outside. Turn the scallops out of the wok or skillet into a strainer set over a bowl, reserving the oil. Transfer the scallops to another bowl.

Return the oil to the wok or skillet, and cook the shrimp, and then the chicken, in the same manner. Drain the shrimp and chicken in the strainer, and then transfer the shrimp and chicken to the bowl with the scallops, reserving the oil.

Add 3 tablespoons of the reserved oil to the wok or skillet, and stir-fry the cabbage, carrots, bamboo shoots, green bell peppers, and soybean sprouts over high heat, 1 to 2 minutes. Drain the vegetables, and set them aside in another bowl.

Add 1 tablespoon of the reserved oil to the wok or skillet, and cook the ginger over low heat for 20 seconds. Increase the heat to high, add the onion and the shiitake mushroom, and stir-fry for 30 seconds. Add the noodles, and stir-fry them until they are well coated with oil. Return the shrimp, scallop, chicken, and vegetables to the wok or skillet, and cook the mixture until the noodles are thoroughly mixed with the other ingredients, 1 minute.

Add the remaining 1 tablespoon *sake* to the wok or skillet, and cook away the alcohol. Add the chicken stock, *shoyu*, oyster sauce, Worcestershire sauce, sugar, and white pepper. Cook the mixture, stirring, for 1 to 2 minutes. Check the flavor, and add a few drops of tamari.

Serve the noodles on a large platter.

• *Yields 1 serving*

BASIC STOCK FOR *RAMEN* NOODLES

Ramen Sutokku

Ramen is a "Japanized" Chinese noodle dish that has become, over the years, one of the signature dishes of Japan, served at restaurants across the country. They vary from tiny food stands, resembling a New York hotdog stand, to casual chain restaurants, local restaurants, and fancy eateries. There are regional differences and specialties. There is Sapporo *ramen* from the north island of Hokkaido, and Hakata *ramen* from the south island of Kyushu. Every restaurant boasts that it serves the best *ramen* in Japan, and keeps its recipes for the *ramen* broth and noodles as top secrets.

The classic Japanese comedy film *Tampopo* tells the story of one gutsy woman and her struggling *ramen* shop. She is determined to have the best *ramen* shop in her neighborhood. To do this she visits competitors, noting this ingredient, that technique, this flavor, and that texture all by observing the chefs and tasting their dishes. Her oldest and wisest customer tells her that the secret of successful *ramen* is all in the stock. At one point she is so overwhelmed by her desire to master the preparation of perfect stock that she dreams of fainting upon finding a large pig's head in her stock pot.

And here is the recipe for the best stock! After trying it you may wish to go into the *ramen* business yourself. Good luck!

> *2 pounds pork knuckles and rib bones*
> *2 pounds chicken thighs with bones*
> *1 small onion, cut into quarters*
> *1 leek, green part only*
> *1 ounce ginger (about the size of a table-tennis ball)*
> *with skin, sliced*
> *½ head garlic (cut the head in half crosswise)*
> *One 4-inch square* kombu *(kelp)*
> *1 teaspoon salt*

Ask your butcher to crack the large pork bones. Hack the chicken thighs into three to four pieces each. Put plenty of water into a large pot, and add the pork and chicken. Bring the mixture to a boil, and cook for 1 minute.

Drain the pork and chicken, discarding the water. Rinse the pork and chicken under cold running water. Clean the pot.

Return the pork and chicken to the clean pot. Add the onion, leek, ginger, garlic, and *kombu*. Add water to cover the ingredients by 1 inch, and bring the mixture to a boil. Turn the heat to low, and gently simmer, uncovered, for 7 hours, adding water as necessary to keep the bones covered.

Strain the stock through a sieve lined with cotton cloth, and discard the bones and vegetables. Add 1 teaspoon salt, stirring, and let the stock cool at room temperature. The stock keeps 1 week refrigerated, and can be frozen for later use. Leave the fat on the surface if you're refrigerating the stock, but remove the fat before freezing the stock. Use the stock in any of the *ramen* recipes from page 339 to page 342.

• *Yields about 2 quarts*

SIMMERED PORK FOR *RAMEN*

Chashu

Simmered pork, cut into thin slices, is used as a topping for *ramen* noodles. By itself, with ample coriander leaves and mustard, sliced *chashu* is a tasty appetizer.

> 1¹/₂ *pounds pork flank (the cut in which fat and*
>   *meat are layered, used to make bacon;*
>   *Chinese butchers carry this cut)*
> 3 *to 4 garlic cloves, peeled and halved*
> 1 *ounce ginger (about the size of a table-tennis ball),*
>   *peeled and sliced*
> 1 *teaspoon salt*
> 2 *tablespoons* sake *(rice wine)*
> ²/₃ *cup* shoyu *(soy sauce)*

Trim the skin and the pork across the grain into several 6- to 7-inch blocks.

Put the pork pieces into a large, shallow pot in which they can fit without overlapping and cover them with water. Add the garlic, ginger, salt, *sake*, and *shoyu*. Bring the mixture to a boil, and skim any foam. Reduce the heat to medium-low, cover with a drop lid (see page 26), and gently simmer the pork for 40 minutes.

Remove the pot from the heat, and let the pork stand in its cooking liquid for 15 minutes.

Remove the pork from the pot, and let the broth cool to room temperature. Use the pork in *shoyu ramen* (page 338), *miso ramen* (page 339), or chilled *ramen* (*hiyashi chukasoba*, page 346). Reserve the broth for making sweet simmered bamboo shoots (*menma*, page 337), another *ramen* topping. The broth is also an important ingredient in *shoyu ramen*.

The pork and its broth keep for 1 week in the refrigerator, and can be frozen for later use.

SWEET SIMMERED BAMBOO SHOOTS

Menma

The pleasant, crisp texture and rich, earthy flavor of sweet simmered bamboo shoots is indispensable for all types of *ramen* dishes. Japanese and other Asian food stores often sell *menma* packed in jars or plastic bags. These products are convenient, but they may contain chemical additives and preservatives. Besides, homemade *menma* tastes the best.

To make *menma,* use unsalted dried bamboo shoots, not the canned variety. Dried bamboo shoots are sold at Chinese food stores in long strips the color of yellow mustard. They must be soaked for three hours in cold water.

> 1 package (6 ounces) dried bamboo shoots
> ¹/₂ cup chashu broth (page 336)
> ¹/₂ cup mirin (sweet cooking wine)

In a large bowl of cold water, soak the bamboo shoots for 3 hours.

Drain the bamboo shoots, discarding the soaking water. In a medium pot, combine the bamboo shoots, *chashu* broth, 1 cup water, and the *mirin*. Bring the mixture to a boil, reduce the heat to low, and cook, covered with a drop lid (see page 26), for 30 minutes.

Let the bamboo shoots cool in their cooking liquid. *Menma* keeps for 1 week in the refrigerator, or can be frozen for later use.

Use *menma* in *shoyu ramen* (page 338) or *miso ramen* (page 339).

GARLIC PASTE

Ninniku-dare

Casual *ramen* eateries frequently have a long eating counter that separates the kitchen from the dining area. At your order, the chef prepares your dish in front of you with skill and speed. A steaming hot bowl of noodles, with just the ingredients you've ordered, will land in front of you in 5 minutes or less.

While watching the chef and studying the restaurant, you will notice that there are small containers with condiments placed every few feet along the counter. One condiment is white, and the other is red. The red one is *toban jiang* (chile-bean sauce), and the white one is garlic paste. After receiving your bowl of noodles, you are in charge of using the condiments to add flavors to your bowl.

Here is the recipe for *ninniku-dare*, garlic paste. It is a wonderful flavoring ingredient!

> *2 ounces pork fat*
> *4 to 5 garlic cloves, peeled*
> *3 tablespoons lard or vegetable oil*

In a food processor, chop the pork fat and garlic to a smooth paste.

In a small skillet, heat the lard or vegetable oil until it is hot but not smoking. Add the garlic-fat paste, and cook over low heat until the mixture is barely golden. Remove the skillet from the heat, and let the mixture cool to room temperature.

Garlic paste keeps for 1 month in the refrigerator, in a jar with a tight-fitting lid. Enjoy garlic paste with any *ramen* dish.

RAMEN BROTH FLAVORED WITH SOY SAUCE

Shoyu Ramen

This recipe uses the rich *shoyu*-flavored broth of *chashu* (simmered pork), the pork itself, and garlic paste to produce a delicious, hearty bowl of soup and noodles.

> *12 to 20* chashu *(simmered pork) slices (page 336)*
> *1 cup homemade or commercial* menma
> *(sweet simmered bamboo shoots, page 337)*
> *2 scallions, green parts only, cut into thin rings*
> *1 nori sheet, cut into 8 rectangles*
> *4 cups* ramen *stock (page 334)*
> *13 ounces dried* chukasoba *noodles*
> *4 teaspoons garlic paste (page 337)*
> *³/₄ cup* chashu *(simmered pork) broth (page 336)*
>
> CONDIMENTS
> *Ground white pepper*
> *Additional garlic paste*

Place four noodle bowls in a hot oven or in hot water to warm. Place the topping ingredients—pork, simmered bamboo shoots, scallions, and nori—on a platter at hand. In a large pot, heat the *ramen* broth to a gentle simmer.

In another large pot, bring plenty of water to a boil. Cook the noodles al dente, about 3 to 5 minutes or as instructed on the package. Check for doneness by removing a noodle and biting it. When the noodles are ready, drain them, discarding the water.

Into each hot noodle bowl, put 1 teaspoon garlic paste and 3 tablespoons of the *chashu* broth. Divide the noodles among the bowls, and add 1 cup piping-hot *ramen* stock to each bowl. With a pair of cooking chopsticks or tongs, lift and stir the noodles several times to mix them with the garlic paste, *chashu* broth, and *ramen* stock.

Serve the noodles piping hot, topped with the pork, simmered bamboo shoots, scallions, and nori. Serve the ground white pepper and additional garlic paste on the side.

• *Yields 4 servings*

RAMEN IN MISO-FLAVORED BROTH

Miso Ramen

Next to *shoyu ramen* in popularity is *miso ramen*. In this dish, *chukasoba* noodles are served in a hearty, miso-flavored broth. The dish is rich in both flavor and texture.

1¹/₂ *teaspoons* mamemiso *(soybean miso)*
¹/₂ *cup Saikyo miso (sweet white miso)*
About 1 teaspoon toban jiang *(chile-bean sauce),*
        to taste
Pinch of sansho *pepper*
1 garlic clove, crushed
4 cups ramen stock *(page 334)*
1¹/₂ *tablespoons lard or vegetable oil*
4 scallions, white parts only, julienned in 2-inch
        lengths and soaked in cold water until needed
12 to 20 slices chashu *(simmered pork, page 336),*
        preferably, or cooked ham
¹/₂ *cup homemade or commercial* menma
        (sweet simmered bamboo shoots, page 337)
4 nori sheets, shredded in 2-inch lengths
13 ounces dried chukasoba *noodles*
4 teaspoons garlic paste (page 337)

In a bowl, combine the *mamemiso* and Saikyo miso. Stir in the *toban jiang, sansho* pepper, and crushed garlic.

In a pot, bring the *ramen* stock to a simmer over low heat.

In a small skillet, heat the lard or vegetable oil. Add the miso mixture, and cook it over low heat, stirring, for 5 minutes. Transfer the mixture to a small container, and set it aside.

Place the noodle bowls in a hot oven or in hot water to warm.

Drain the scallions, and pat them dry in a paper towel. Place them on a platter with the pork or ham, simmered bamboo shoots, and nori.

In a large pot, bring plenty of water to a boil. Cook the noodles al dente, about 3 to 5 minutes or as instructed on the package. Test for doneness by removing a noodle and biting it.

In each individual noodle bowl, place 1 tablespoon of the miso mixture and 1 teaspoon garlic paste. Drain the cooked noodles, and divide them among the bowls. Add 1 cup piping-hot *ramen* stock to each bowl. With a pair of chopsticks or tongs, lift and stir the noodles several times so that the miso and garlic paste dissolve. Serve the noodles topped with the pork or ham, simmered bamboo shoots, nori, and scallions.

- *Yields 4 servings*

RAMEN WITH PORK-AND-MISO SAUCE

Buta-miso Ramen

Almost any topping you can think of is good with hot *ramen* noodles. In this dish, noodles in hot broth are served with a sauce of miso and chopped pork. Instead of using ground pork from the butcher, I buy a piece of pork shoulder and chop it with a knife into small pieces. In this way I get a nice, crumbled texture in the sauce.

The dark brown color of this sauce may not look very appetizing, but the wonderful flavor will sweep your doubts aside. Brighten up the presentation with a companion such as shiso or coriander. Cold noodles served with this sauce are another treat, especially on a hot summer day.

5 1/2 ounces pork shoulder or ground pork
3 tablespoons sake (rice wine)
3 tablespoons mamemiso (soybean miso)
1 1/2 tablespoons akamiso (brown miso)
2 tablespoons sugar

1¹/₂ naganegi *long onions, preferably, or*
    5 *scallions, white parts only*
2 *tablespoons vegetable oil*
2 *garlic cloves, minced*
¹/₂ *teaspoon* toban jiang *(chile-bean sauce; optional)*
A few drops of tamari
1 *teaspoon grated ginger*
10 *shiso or large coriander leaves, minced*
13 *ounces dried* chukasoba *noodles*
4 *cups* ramen *stock (page 334)*

If you're starting with pork shoulder, chop the meat fine with a heavy-duty knife, or chop it in a food processor by turning the machine on and off several times.

Put the chopped or ground pork into a bowl. Add 1 tablespoon *sake* and stir to loosen the texture.

In another bowl, combine the two kinds of miso, the remaining 2 tablespoons *sake*, and the sugar, stirring until smooth.

Mince half a long onion or 2 scallions. Cut the remaining long onion or 3 scallions into julienne strips, about two inches long, and soak them in ice water until you are ready to use them. Before using them, drain them and pat them dry with a paper towel. This process removes the slippery liquid from the long onions or scallions, and makes them crisp.

Heat a skillet, and add the oil. When the oil is hot, add the minced long onion or scallion and the garlic, and cook over low heat, stirring, for 20 seconds.

Add the chile-bean sauce, and cook for 10 seconds (if you prefer a less spicy dish, omit the chile-bean sauce). Add the pork, and cook until it is pale and crumbled. Add the miso mixture, and cook over medium-low heat for 3 minutes, stirring. At the end of the cooking, add the tamari, ginger, and half of the shiso or coriander.

Remove the skillet from the heat. Let the sauce cool to room temperature, and then refrigerate it in a jar with a tight-fitting lid. The sauce will keep for one week in the refrigerator and may be frozen for later use.

Place the noodle bowls in a hot oven or in hot water to warm. Drain the long onion or scallion strips, and pat them dry with a paper towel.

In a large pot, bring plenty of water to a boil. Cook the noodles al dente, about 3 to 5 minutes or as instructed on the package. Test for doneness by removing a noodle and biting it.

While the noodles cook, bring the *ramen* stock to a simmer in another pot.

When the noodles are ready, drain them, and divide them among four individual noodle bowls. Pour 1 cup of piping-hot *ramen* stock over the noodles in each bowl, and top each serving with 3 tablespoons of the pork-and-miso sauce. Serve the noodles garnished with the long onion or scallion strips and the remaining shiso or coriander.

• *Yields 4 servings*

RAMEN WITH STIR-FRIED VEGETABLES

Yasai-itame Nose Ramen

In this preparation, *ramen* noodles in hot broth are topped with a quickly stir-fried vegetable mixture. The vegetables used here can be replaced with seasonal varieties of your choice. When selecting vegetables, be aware of how the colors and textures will mix. This is my favorite combination.

Kikurage, described on page 115, is available at Japanese and other Asian food stores.

4 dried shiitake mushrooms, soaked in cold water
         for 20 minutes
1/3 ounce dried black kikurage (1/2-inch-square piece)
         soaked in cold water for 30 minutes
3 ounces cooked fresh or canned bamboo shoots
1/2 small carrot, sliced thin crosswise
3 scallions, cut into 1-inch lengths diagonally
8 asparagus spears, tough ends and scales removed,
         cut into 1-inch lengths
2 Chinese cabbage leaves, cut into 1-inch slices
         crosswise
1/2 red bell pepper, cut into 2 1/2-inch-long strips
1/2 cup snow peas
1/2 cup vegetable oil
13 ounces dried chukasoba noodles
4 1/2 cups ramen stock (page 334) or chicken broth
1 tablespoon sake (rice wine)
1 teaspoon salt
1 teaspoon sugar

> *¹/₂ teaspoon tamari*
> *2 teaspoons potato starch or cornstarch, mixed with*
> *1 tablespoon water*
> *¹/₄ teaspoon ground white pepper*
> *1 teaspoon sesame oil*

Cut away the stems of the shiitake mushrooms, and cut the caps into halves or thirds. Cut the *kikurage* into ¹/₂-inch strips.

Cut the bamboo shoots into 1-by-¹/₂-inch strips. Combine the mushrooms, *kikurage*, and bamboo shoots in a bowl.

In another bowl, combine the carrot, scallions, asparagus, Chinese cabbage, and red bell pepper. Put the snow peas into a third small bowl.

Heat a wok or large skillet over high heat. Add the oil. When the oil is very hot, cook the mixed vegetables 40 seconds, stirring, in several batches.

Remove the vegetables to a large colander to drain.

Add the mushrooms, *kikurage*, and bamboo shoots to the oil, and cook for 30 seconds, stirring. Remove the mushrooms, *kikurage*, and bamboo shoots to the colander.

Add the snow peas to the oil, and cook them for 10 seconds. Remove the snow peas to the colander.

Clean the wok or skillet. Place individual noodle bowls in a hot oven or in hot water to warm.

In a large pot bring plenty of water to a boil, Cook the noodles al dente, 3 to 5 minutes or as instructed on the package. Test the noodles for doneness by removing one and biting it. While the noodles cook, bring 4 cups of the *ramen* stock or chicken broth to a gentle simmer in another pot. Place the cleaned wok or skillet over high heat. Add the *sake* and the remaining ¹/₂ cup *ramen* stock or chicken broth to the wok or skillet, and bring the mixture to a boil. Add all the vegetables, and cook for 1 to 2 minutes, stirring. Add the salt and sugar, stirring. Add the tamari, white pepper, and sesame oil, give several large stirs, and reduce the heat to low. Add the potato-starch or cornstarch water, and cook until the sauce is thickened, stirring all the time. Remove the wok or skillet from the heat.

When the noodles are ready, drain them. Divide them among four individual noodle bowls. Pour 1 cup of piping-hot *ramen* stock over each bowl of noodles, and top with the vegetables.

• *Yields 4 servings*

PAN-FRIED CRISP *CHUKASOBA* WITH VEGETABLES AND SEAFOOD

Age-chukasoba Itame-yasai to Shi-fu-do

Chukasoba noodles can be served hot in a broth, cold with dressing, or stir-fried. This recipe provides yet another method for preparing and enjoying these versatile noodles.

My mother used to cook *chukasoba* completely submerged in heated oil. Cooked that way the noodles were completely crisp, golden, and delicious. However, I remember that the dish, which closely resembled the famous Chinese-American dish chow mein, was a bit heavy on my stomach. My version of fried *chukasoba* is lighter. I pan-fry the cooked noodles in the shape of large, flat disks, so that both surfaces acquire a golden color and crisp texture. The noodles are then topped with quickly stir-fried vegetables and seafood. The dish is delicious!

To butterfly the shrimp, cut most of the way through from the belly side, and spread the shrimp open.

13 ounces dried chukasoba *noodles*

1 teaspoon sesame oil

3 1/2 ounces snow peas

2 cups soybean or mung-bean sprouts

2 ounces canned bamboo shoots, cut into
    1-by-1 1/2-inch strips (about 2/3 cup)

1 small broccoli head, separated into flowerets

1 1/4 cups vegetable oil

8 medium shrimp, shelled, deveined, and butterflied

8 scallops, cut in half

1 cup chicken stock

2 tablespoons sake (rice wine)

1/2 teaspoon sugar

1 tablespoon shoyu (soy sauce)

1/4 to 1/2 teaspoon salt, to taste

1 tablespoon potato starch, mixed with
    1 1/2 tablespoons water

Ground white pepper

In a large pot, bring plenty of water to a boil. Add the noodles, and cook them al dente, about 3 to 5 minutes or as instructed on the package. Test for doneness by removing and biting a noodle. Drain the noodles, toss them in a bowl with sesame oil, and set the bowl aside.

In another bowl, combine the snow peas, soybean or mung-bean sprouts, and bamboo shoots. Put the broccoli into a third bowl.

In a wok or skillet, heat $1/2$ cup vegetable oil. Cook the shrimp and scallops separately over medium-high heat until they are firm on the outside. Drain them, and set them aside, reserving the oil.

In a medium pot of boiling water, parboil the broccoli for 30 seconds, and then the snow peas, soybean sprouts, and bamboo shoots for 10 seconds. Drain the vegetables, and set them aside.

Return the wok or skillet to the heat, and add 3 tablespoons fresh oil. When the oil is hot, add one-quarter of the noodles, and press them with a spatula to make a flat disk about 7 inches in diameter. Cook the noodle disk over medium-low heat, turning it once, until both surfaces are golden and crisp.

Remove the noodle disk from the wok or skillet and cook three more noodle disks the same way. Place each noodle disk on a large individual plate.

Return the wok to the heat, and add 2 tablespoons of the reserved oil. When the oil is hot, add the shrimp and scallops, and give several large stirs. Add the vegetables, and stir-fry them for 1 to 2 minutes. Add the chicken stock, *sake*, sugar, *shoyu*, and salt, and bring the mixture to a boil. Reduce the heat to low, add the potato-starch water, and cook until the sauce is thickened. Add a generous amount of ground white pepper.

Serve the noodle disks topped with the vegetables and seafood.

• *Yields 4 servings*

SUMMERTIME CHILLED *CHUKASOBA*

Hiyashi Chukasoba

When the hot and sticky summer approaches, Chinese-style restaurants across Japan begin to carry on their menus a special summer *chukasoba* noodle dish called *hiyashi chukasoba*. The noodles are served cold with various toppings, and bathed in a refreshing sauce flavored with rice vinegar and sesame oil. This dish was one of my husband's favorite during his thirteen-year stay in Japan. He often said that these cold *chukasoba* noodles were absolutely necessary for surviving the heat and humidity of a Tokyo summer.

Toppings for this noodle dish can be just about anything—seafood such as shrimp, crabmeat, or squid; meat such as *chashu* (simmered pork), ham, or cooked chicken; and vegetables varying from lettuce to carrot, fennel bulb, bell peppers, cucumber, asparagus, broccoli, and *wakame* sea vegetable. Important tips for selecting the toppings are (1) combine materials of different color and texture, and (2) shred the topping materials fine. Thin strips of omelette are always included.

SAUCE
$^1/_4$ *cup* mirin *(sweet cooking wine)*
1 *tablespoon sugar*
$1^1/_3$ *cups* ramen *stock (page 334) or chicken stock*
$^1/_3$ *cup* shoyu *(soy sauce)*
$2^1/_2$ *tablespoons* komezu *(rice vinegar)*
1 *tablespoon sesame oil*
1 *to 2 teaspoons ginger juice (page 58), to taste*

3 *cups soybean or mung-bean sprouts*
2 *ounces mung-bean noodles, soaked*
    in boiled water for 6 minutes
1 *Japanese or salad cucumber, julienned in*
    $2^1/_2$*-inch lengths*
8 *cherry tomatoes, each cut in half*
10 *slices* chashu *(simmered pork, page 336)*
    or cooked ham or chicken breast,
    julienned in 2-inch lengths

THIN OMELETTES
Pinch of salt
1 teaspoon sugar
4 eggs, lightly beaten
1¹/₂ tablespoons vegetable oil

13 ounces dried chukasoba *noodles*
2 teaspoons sesame oil

GARNISHES
2 tablespoons white sesame seeds, toasted (page 100)
Hot mustard paste or smooth French-style mustard

In a saucepan, bring the *mirin* to a gentle boil to evaporate the alcohol. Add 1 tablespoon sugar and the *ramen* stock or chicken stock, and bring the mixture to a boil. Add the *shoyu*, and, when the mixture boils again, transfer it to a clean jar. Add the *komezu*, 1 tablespoon sesame oil, and the ginger juice. Let the mixture cool, and then refrigerate it for 2 to 3 hours.

In a medium pot of boiling water with a little vegetable oil added, blanch the soybean or mung-bean sprouts for 30 seconds. Drain them, and set them aside.

Drain the mung-bean noodles, cool them under cold running water, and cut them into 6-inch lengths.

Stir 1 teaspoon sugar and the pinch of salt into the beaten eggs.

Heat an 8-inch skillet over medium heat until hot. Put the 1¹/₂ tablespoons vegetable oil into the pan, and swirl the pan to coat the bottom evenly. Pour out and reserve the excess oil. Reduce the heat to low.

Add enough beaten egg to thinly coat the bottom of the skillet. Cook the egg until it is firm on the bottom but still somewhat moist on top. Turn the omelette over, and cook it for 3 seconds more.

Remove the omelette from the skillet, and let it cool. Make more thin omelettes, adding the reserved oil to the skillet as necessary, until you have used all the beaten egg. You should have eight thin omelettes.

Cut the omelettes into 2-inch-long julienne strips.

In a large pot of boiling water, cook the *chukasoba* noodles al dente, 3 to 5 minutes or as instructed on the package. Test them for doneness by removing a noodle and biting it. Drain the noodles, and rinse them under cold running water. Drain the noodles again. Toss them with 2 teaspoons sesame oil.

Divide the noodles among four individual shallow bowls. Decorate the noodles with the cucumber; tomatoes; simmered pork, ham, or chicken; soybean or mung-bean sprouts; mung-bean noodles; and omelette strips. In the traditional presentation, the items are placed in separate mounds like the colorful spokes of a wheel. Pour some of the sauce over each dish, and garnish with some sesame seeds on top and a dab of hot mustard on the rim of the bowl.

- *Yields 4 servings*

CHILLED *CHUKASOBA* WITH SPICY SESAME SAUCE

Hiyashi Chukasoba Mushidori to Gomadare

This preparation draws large crowds who seek a spicier, richer chilled *chukasoba* noodle dish than regular *hiyashi chukasoba* (page 346). The noodles are topped with steamed chicken, cucumber, and tomato, and then bathed in a spicy, creamy sauce of sesame and scallions. Experiment with different toppings of your choice.

2 boned and skinned chicken breasts
2 teaspoons salt

S A U C E
2 tablespoons sesame oil
1 teaspoon toban jiang *(chile-bean sauce)*
¹/₄ cup sesame paste, preferably Japanese
¹/₄ cup hot brewed unscented black tea
2 tablespoons shoyu *(soy sauce)*
1 tablespoon sugar
1 tablespoon komezu *(rice vinegar)*
3 tablespoons chopped scallion, white part only

13 ounces dried chukasoba *noodles*
2 Japanese or salad cucumbers, cut into
    ¹/₈-by-³/₁₆-by-3-inch sticks
1 large tomato, seeded and cut into thin
    3-inch-long sticks

In a medium pot, bring 1 quart water to a boil. Add the chicken breast, reduce the heat to medium, and simmer for 12 minutes. Remove the pot from the heat, add the salt, and let the chicken steep in its cooking liquid for 30 minutes. Prepared in this way, the chicken stays juicy.

Remove the chicken from its cooking liquid, plunge it into ice water, and let it stand for 10 minutes. Drain the chicken, wipe it with a paper towel, and shred it into 3-inch lengths.

In a skillet, heat 1 tablespoon sesame oil. Add the *toban jiang,* and cook it until it is fragrant, 10 to 20 seconds. Transfer the mixture to a bowl, and add the sesame paste. Stir with a whisk until the mixture is smooth. Add the hot tea 1 tablespoon at a time, stirring between additions until the mixture is smooth. Add the *shoyu*, sugar, *komezu,* and scallion, and mix until smooth. Set the sauce aside.

In a large pot of boiling water, cook the noodles al dente, 3 to 5 minutes or according to the package instructions. Test the noodles for doneness by removing one and biting it.

Drain the noodles in a colander, and rinse them under cold running water. Drain them again, and toss them with the remaining 1 tablespoon sesame oil. Divide the noodles among four individual bowls. Decorate each serving with the chicken, cucumber, and tomato. Top with the sauce, and serve.

- *Yields 4 servings*

JAPANESE STUFFED PANCAKE

Okonomiyaki

Okonomiyaki is a stuffed pancake similar to a crêpe, filled with vegetables and meat, shellfish or both. Various Japanese cities—Tokyo, Osaka, and Hiroshima—are proud of their versions of this popular fast food, which is often prepared and sold at food stands on the streets and at festival grounds. There are also informal restaurants, *okonomiyaki-ya,* that serve only this dish.

An *okonomiyaki* restaurant is equipped with a large steel griddle along a long communal table, or individual tables with built-in griddles in the middle. You sit in front of the heated griddle to place your order. The waiter brings a bowl of batter, your choice of filling ingredients, and a pair of steel spatulas.

At these eateries, you are the chef. First you mix the batter and filling ingredients in the bowl, and then you pour the mixture all at once onto the hot cooking surface, making a disk about 7 inches in diameter. Don't be discouraged if your pancake is not perfectly round. When the bottom is golden and the top looks dry, you flip over the pancake with the aid of the two spatulas. With every passing minute, the aroma becomes more enticing. Then you baste the *okonomiyaki* with a special thick sauce, similar to *tonkatsu* sauce (page 93). Now the pancake is ready to eat, and you are happy to learn that, despite your lack of training and experience, you can cook!

Let us introduce this very enjoyable dish to your own kitchen. You, your family, and your friends will love it.

SAUCE
$^1/_4$ *cup tomato ketchup*
$1^1/_2$ *tablespoons Worcestershire sauce*
$^1/_4$ *teaspoon smooth French-style mustard*
2 *tablespoons* mirin *(sweet cooking wine)*
1 *tablespoon sugar*
1 *teaspoon* shoyu *(soy sauce)*

BATTER
1 *cup cake flour*
1 *cup water or* dashi *(fish stock)*
$^1/_2$ *teaspoon salt*

3 *tablespoons grated* yama-imo *(Japanese mountain taro, available at Japanese food stores), preferably, or 2 tablespoons potato starch*

2 *ounces beef sirloin, cut into thin strips*
One 2-ounce slices pork sirloin, cut into thin strips
4 *headed, peeled, and deveined raw medium shrimp, cut in half lengthwise*
$3^1/_2$ *ounces cabbage (about $^1/_8$ small head), shredded*
$^1/_4$ *cup thin green scallion rings*
2 *tablespoons minced* benishoga *(pickled red ginger, see page 58; available at Japanese food stores)*
2 *eggs*
2 *to 3 tablespoons vegetable oil*
2 *tablespoons toasted and crumbled* nori
$^1/_4$ *cup* katsuobushi *(bonito flakes; optional)*

In a small saucepan, combine the ketchup, Worcestershire sauce, mustard, *mirin*, sugar, and *shoyu*. Bring the mixture to a boil, and cook it over low heat for 3 minutes. Remove the saucepan from the heat, and set it aside.

Sift the flour into a bowl. Add the water or *dashi*, salt, and grated mountain taro or potato starch, and mix, stirring. Divide the batter between two bowls.

Put half the beef, pork, shrimp, cabbage, scallion, and pickled ginger into each bowl, and press the center of each bowl to make a small depression. Break the eggs, and drop one into the center depression of each bowl.

Heat a large skillet, add 2 to 3 tablespoons vegetable oil and swirl the skillet to coat the entire bottom. When the oil is hot, pour out the excess, and reserve it. Reduce the heat to low. With a soup spoon, mix the batter and other ingredients in one of the bowls. Raise the heat under the skillet to medium, and pour all of the batter in that bowl into the skillet. Spread the batter into a disk about 6 to 7 inches in diameter. Cook the pancake over medium heat until the bottom is golden.

Turn the pancake over with the aid of two spatulas, press it to flatten the bottom, and cook until the other side is golden.

With a pastry brush, spread some of the sauce over the surface of the pancake. Sprinkle half of the nori and bonito flakes if you're using them, on top, and transfer the pancake to a plate.

Add the reserved oil to the pan, and prepare the second pancake in the same way as the first. Cut each pancake into six pieces, like a pizza, and serve them hot.

• *Yields 2 servings*

SELECTING, CLEANING, AND CUTTING FISH FOR SASHIMI OR SUSHI

Sakana no Erabikata to Sanmai Oroshi

Sashimi is thin-sliced, very fresh raw fish. Fish is also often used raw in sushi. Any fish that is to be eaten raw should be very fresh.

Freshness depends only partially on when the fish was caught. Suppose you go to the fishmonger around ten in the morning, and the fishmonger tells you that a fish was caught early on the same morning, so it is very fresh. Does this mean the fish is fresh enough to use in sashimi? The answer is maybe, depending on how the fish was handled after being caught and while it was being transported to the store. The most important thing is whether the fish was kept in an insulated case with plenty of ice from the time it left the ocean until the time you purchase it.

Here are tips on determining whether a fish is fresh enough for use in sashimi, or any fish preparation.

- Check the eyes. They should be clear, watery-looking, and plump, not depressed. No trace of blood should be seen in the eyes.
- Check the skin. A fresh fish has a slight sliminess, which protects the skin in water.
- Check the scales. They should be firmly attached to the body.
- Open and check the gills. Blood concentrates in the gills, so they should be blood-red.
- Check the belly of the fish by looking at it or gently touching it. A fresh fish has a very elastic, firm belly. The intestines, like the blood, contain many enzymes that decompose fish proteins very quickly. A soft belly is a bad sign. Cutting the belly open and looking at the intestines really tells you the condition of a fish. A fresh

fish has very firm, undamaged intestines, and the blood is very red and not clotted. In contrast, old fish have soft, mashed, broken intestines with brown blood sticking to the center bone.

To master the skill of checking fish for freshness, make frequent visits to fish stores that sell whole fish. If all of the conditions just described are met, purchase the fish whole, not filleted.

To clean and fillet your fish, you'll need several tools. Japanese cooks use a very sharp, heavy-duty, pointed, slightly broad and thick knife called a *deba bocho* for filleting fish, but you can use any very sharp, heavy-duty pointed knife. To completely remove the blood that is clotted to the center bone, there is a special utensil. Called a *sasara*, it is a bundle of thin, flat bamboo sticks. When this tool is not available, use a new, firm toothbrush. You will need tweezers, too, to remove the thin bones from the fish.

Finally, one of the most important rules in preparing fish for sushi and sashimi is that, to avoid transferring your body heat to the fish, you should always work quickly when you handle the fish—keeping in mind that you are using a very sharp knife. Speed is key in the astounding show you see at sushi bars or any high-quality Japanese restaurant. You may not achieve the proficiency of a master chef, but you can make the same cuts and do it quickly. Try it, practice a bit, and you will be very proud of your accomplishment.

> One 3-pound whole sashimi-quality sea bass
> or sea bream
> Salt

Cleaning fish. Have at hand two large bowls of salted ice water (about 3 percent salt, by weight, or $1^1/_2$ tablespoons fine salt per quart). Rinse the fish under cold running water. This simple process removes a great deal of the bacteria on the skin. Scale the fish and cut off the head; discard the head, or preserve it for a fish soup. Cut open the belly, remove the intestines, and discard them. Transfer the fish to one of the bowls of salted water, and, with a *sasara* (see above) or toothbrush, completely remove any blood that is clotted on the center bone. Rinse the fish in the other bowl of salted water. Wipe the fish dry with a paper towel. If you won't be using the fish right away, stuff its belly with clean paper towels, wrap the fish in a moist paper towel, and refrigerate the fish, covered. Use the fish the same day.

Filleting fish. Clean the cutting board, and wipe it dry with paper towels. If you are right-handed, place the fish on the cutting board with its head on the right and its belly facing you. Cut open the belly side from the head to the tail, by running the tip of a knife over the lower part of the bones. Turn the fish around so its head is on the left and its back is facing you. Cut open the back side, by running a knife over the upper part of the bones from the tail toward the head end. Finally, run the knife over the backbone to separate the fillet from the bones. If you are left-handed, start with the fish's head on the right, then turn the fish so its head is on the left and its back facing you.

Turn the fish upside down, and remove the second fillet in the same manner. The Japanese call this basic filleting *sanmai oroshi,* "three-piece cutting," because it produces two fillets and a flesh-webbed carcass. Discard the carcass, or reserve it along with the head for fish soup. With a knife, remove the thin bones attached to the upper belly side of each fillet. The fillets are now ready to be broiled, grilled, steamed, or simmered.

If you are going to use the fish for sashimi or sushi, you need to go through more cutting and skinning processes. You will separate each large fillet into two narrower ones, the back side and the belly side. In the center of each large fillet, where the backbone was located, is a row of small bones perpendicular to the surface. Remove them by making two long cuts on either side of the center line. Discard this narrow strip containing a row of fine bones.

The fillet has now been divided into two parts. Repeat the process with the other fillet. If you won't be using the fish immediately, wrap it in cotton cloth and refrigerate it for up to half a day.

Filleting a fish: (a) Cut off the head, (b) cut open the belly side, (c) cut off the back side, and (d) remove the fillet. (e) Turn the fish over, and fillet the other side.

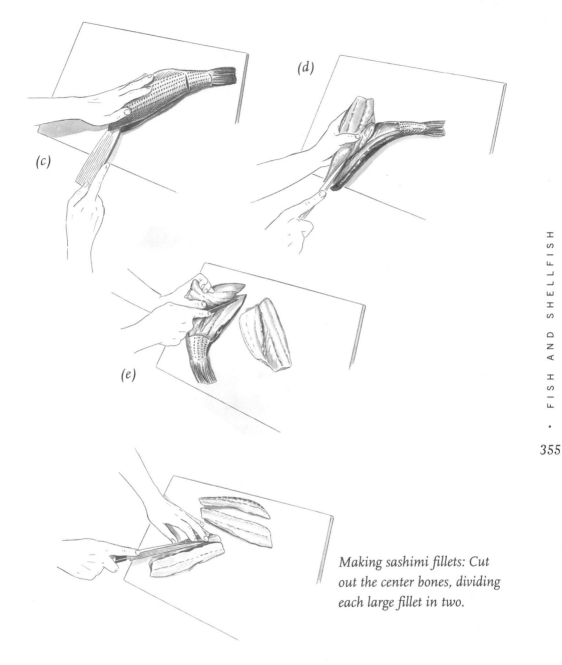

(c)

(d)

(e)

Making sashimi fillets: Cut out the center bones, dividing each large fillet in two.

Skinning fish. The next step is to skin each narrow fillet. Start with a back fillet, which has thicker flesh and is much easier to skin than the belly fillets. Place the fish skin side down on a cutting board. Hold the tail end with one hand, and make a shallow vertical cut ½ inch from the end. Cut through the fish to the skin, but no deeper. Then angle the knife, pull the tail, and carefully cut along between the skin and the meat, pulling the skin with a back and forth motion.

Remove the skins of the other fillets. The fish is now ready to slice for sashimi or sushi.

Skinning a fillet: Pull the skin back and forth while cutting just above it.

Shimofuri. Instead of skinning the fish, you may leave the skin on and give it an instant boiling water bath. This technique is called *shimofuri*. To do it, have at hand a kettle of boiling water and a large bowl of ice water. Place the fillet sections skin side up on a cutting board. Cover the fish with a thin cotton cloth or triple layers of cheesecloth. Bring the cutting board to a sink. Tilt the board, and pour about $1/2$ cup of boiling water per sashimi fillet evenly over the skin. This cooks the skin and makes it tender to bite. Then immediately plunge the fish into the ice water so that the flesh does not cook. Drain the fish, and wipe it dry in paper towels. The fish is now ready to be sliced for sashimi or sushi.

To eat sashimi, mix some of the spicy condiment—wasabi or ginger—into the *shoyu* or tamari. Use only a little wasabi; too much would overwhelm the delicate flavor of the fish. Then dip each fish slice into the sauce just before putting the slice in your mouth. Be careful not to drown the fish in the sauce; merely touch the edge of each fish slice to it.

SEA BREAM SASHIMI

Tai Sashimi

Sashimi is always presented with three partners: *ken, tsuma,* and *karami. Ken* is the primary garnish, on which the fish slices rest when they are served. Popular materials for *ken* include julienne strips of daikon, carrot, and cucumber. The primary garnish does two things. First, it absorbs any fishy flavor from the fish slices, so the fish stays fresh longer. Second, a little of the primary garnish eaten after a slice of fish refreshes the palate.

Tsuma, the secondary garnish, is generally seasonal. Secondary garnishes include shiso leaves, young shiso buds, small cucumber or pumpkin flowers, and young buds of *myoga* ginger. A secondary garnish adds a seasonal touch and aroma to the dish.

Karami are spicy condiments. They include wasabi and ginger.

In this recipe the primary garnish is marinated carrot slices, which must be prepared a day ahead, and julienned daikon. The condiment is wasabi. Use the seasonal garnish of your choice. After learning how to prepare and serve authentic sashimi, you may want to explore your own ways to complement the delicate flavor of raw fish.

To cut fish fillets into fine sashimi slices, Japanese cooks use a thin knife, *sashimi bocho,* whose blade is about 11 inches long. If you have no sashimi knife, use a long-bladed knife or a meat slicer.

> One 2-inch length of carrot
> $^1/_4$ cup komezu (rice vinegar)
> 2 tablespoons sugar
> $^1/_4$ teaspoon salt
> One 3-inch length of daikon, peeled
> 2 back and 1 belly sea bream sashimi fillets,
>   skinned or treated with shimofuri
>   (see page 356)
>
> CONDIMENTS
> Wasabi
> Shoyu (soy sauce), tamari, or a mixture of the two

Cut the carrot in half crosswise. Square each half, and then cut it lengthwise into $^1/_5$-inch-thick rectangular slices.

In a small saucepan, bring some water to a boil over medium heat. Add the carrot, and cook it for 30 seconds. Drain it, and wipe it dry in a paper towel.

In the saucepan, combine the *komezu,* 2 tablespoons water, the sugar, and the salt, and bring the mixture to a boil over medium heat, stirring to dissolve the sugar and salt. Transfer the mixture to a bowl. Add the carrot, let the mixture cool to room temperature, and refrigerate it overnight, covered.

Cut the daikon into thin julienne strips. In a medium bowl of cold water, soak the daikon until it is crispy, 20 minutes. Gently pat the daikon dry with a paper towel. Refrigerate the daikon, covered, until you are ready to use it.

If the fillets are skinned, cut them into sashimi slices. Start with a back fillet. Lay it on a cutting board in front of you, skin side up, with the thinner edge facing you. Hold the sashimi knife inclined to the right and make a diagonal cut through the fish in one movement, starting with the end of the blade near the handle and finishing with the very tip of the knife. Do not saw. To do this the way a chef does, take a deep breath, cut through the fish in one stroke, then take another breath, and make another cut. Each slice should be about $1/4$-inch thick and broad. While cutting, don't press on the fish or handle it more than necessary.

Slice the remaining fillets in the same way.

If the fillets still have their skin attached, first make two lengthwise, shallow cuts on the skin side. Hold the knife vertically, and cut crosswise slices $1/4$ inch thick.

Mound the daikon on individual serving plates, slightly off center, toward the back. Neatly lean five fish slices against the front of the daikon. Rest three more fish slices against the first five. Garnish the area to the right front of the fish with the pickled carrot and a baby cucumber with the flower still attached, or some other seasonal touch. Place a small mound of wasabi next to it.

Serve the dish with *shoyu,* tamari, or a mixture of the two in a small plate on the side.

• *Yields 4 servings*

SEA BREAM IN MODERN STYLE

Seiyo-fu Tai Sashimi

For this dish, cut fresh sea bream into very thin, broad slices, by tilting the knife deeply toward the cutting board. Serve the slices with a little lemon juice mixed with olive oil and soy sauce. This type of presentation is finding its way into more and more Western restaurants.

> *2 skinned back-side sea bream or sea bass*
>   *sashimi fillets (page 354)*
> *3 tablespoons virgin olive oil*
> *¹/₂ teaspoon sesame oil*
> *Wasabi*
> *Salt*
> *1 tablespoon fresh-squeezed lemon juice*
> *1 teaspoon tamari*
> *1 cup mixed baby spinach leaves and mesclun*
>   *or baby spinach leaves*
> *1 tablespoon seeded and finely diced tomato*
>
> **GARNISH**
> *1 teaspoon minced chives*

Cut the sashimi fillets into paper-thin, broad slices. Refrigerate them, covered.

Mix 4 teaspoons olive oil with the sesame oil and a little wasabi to taste. With a pastry brush, spread half the mixture over a large platter on which the fish slices can fit without overlapping.

Place the fish slices on the platter. Brush the remaining oil mixture over the top of the fish. Sprinkle it with a little salt. Cover the fish with plastic wrap, and refrigerate it for 15 minutes.

To make the dressing, in a bowl, whisk the lemon juice with the remaining olive oil and the tamari. Arrange the spinach and mesclun in the center of a serving plate, and top with the tomato. Arrange the fish slices around the greens, overlapping them slightly. Serve the fish and greens drizzled with a generous amount of the dressing and sprinkled with chives.

• *Yields 2 servings*

VINEGARED MACKEREL
FOR SUSHI AND SASHIMI

Shimesaba

Have you tried *shimesaba,* mackerel cured with salt and vinegar, either on its own as a sushi dish or as a sushi topping? Did you enjoy the refreshing taste of this rich, sweet fish? If the answer is yes, you are a real fish lover.

Because mackerel migrate over a long distance, they develop a large amount of red muscle meat on the back side, just as tuna and yellowtail do. The most important key to preparing *shimesaba* is getting very fresh mackerel, *saba.* Unfortunately, outside Japan I find it difficult to purchase mackerel that is of the very best quality. An oily fish, mackerel deteriorates very quickly. During the process of aging, one of the amino acids is converted to a chemical that may cause allergic symptoms in some people. This is another reason that the fish should be very fresh. Mackerel season in Japan is during the cool autumn, and that is when Japanese most often prepare and enjoy this special treat.

1 whole sashimi-quality mackerel, about 1¹/₂ pounds
    (see page 352)
1 cup sea salt
1 cup plus 1 tablespoon komezu (rice vinegar)
3 tablespoons sugar
1¹/₂ teaspoons shoyu (soy sauce)

FOR SASHIMI
One 2-inch length of daikon, julienned and soaked
    in ice water for 20 minutes
4 shiso leaves
1 tablespoon instant wakame sea vegetable, soaked in
    cold water for 2 minutes, and drained

CONDIMENTS
2 teaspoons wasabi
Shoyu (soy sauce)

Remove and discard the head and intestines of the mackerel. Rinse the fish thoroughly under cold running water, and then ice water. Wipe the mackerel dry with paper towels.

Fillet the mackerel by the *sanmai oroshi* method, to produce only two fillets (see page 353). Do not divide each fillet into back and belly sections, and do not skin the fish.

Place the mackerel fillets on a bamboo rolling mat set in a rectangular pan. Spread one-third of the salt over the fillets, turn them over, and cover them with the rest of the salt. Cover the pan with plastic wrap, and refrigerate the fish for 3 hours.

In a small saucepan, combine 1 cup of the *komezu*, the sugar, and *shoyu*. Bring the mixture almost to a boil over medium heat, stirring to dissolve the sugar. Transfer the marinade to a pan large enough to hold the fish in one layer, and let the marinade cool to room temperature.

In a large bowl, combine 2 quarts cold water and the remaining 1 tablespoon *komezu*. Remove the mackerel from the refrigerator, and rinse off the salt under cold running water. Plunge the mackerel into the water with the vinegar added, and rinse the fish again. Wipe the mackerel with a paper towel. With tweezers, pull out the small bones from the center of each fillet. Place the mackerel skin side down in the pan with the *komezu* and sugar marinade and lay a piece of plastic wrap directly on the fish and the marinade. Let the fish stand until its outer flesh becomes white with a faint pinkish tint, about 20 to 30 minutes.

Remove the mackerel from the marinade, and wipe off the excess liquid with a paper towel. Remove the skin by gently pulling it with your hand, from the head end to the tail end.

For sashimi, slice each fillet crosswise $^3/_8$ inch thick, alternating between partial cuts, halfway through the fillets, and complete cuts.

Drain the daikon, and pat it dry with a paper towel. Mound the daikon on four individual serving plates. Place one shiso leaf on the front side of each daikon mound. Place one-quarter of the *wakame* sea vegetable at the foot of each daikon mound. Lean three mackerel slices together against the shiso leaf. Lean two more fish slices together against the others. Mound $^1/_2$ teaspoon wasabi on the right front part of the plate. Accompany each serving with a little *shoyu* in a small plate on the side.

For a sushi topping, cut the fish diagonally into broad $^1/_4$-inch-thick slices. Place each fish slice on top of sushi rice squeezed by hand into an oval shape.

- *Yields 4 to 6 servings*

CLASSIC SALT-GRILLED FISH

Sakana no Shioyaki

Simply salting and then grilling very fresh fish is the best way to enjoy its true flavor. Neither marination nor sauce, either of which may mask the natural, delicate flavor of the fish, is necessary. Salting fish does two major things: It removes the fishy-tasting juice from the flesh, and it firms the fish protein.

In Japan, salt-grilling is called *shioyaki*. Favorite fish to prepare in this style include *aji* (horse mackerel), *iwashi* (sardine), *ayu* (a sweet-tasting freshwater fish), *sanma* (pike), *nishin* (herring), *saba* (mackerel), *hirame* (sole), and *tai* (sea bream). These small fish are cooked whole with the head attached. Large fish such as *buri* (yellowtail), *suzuki* (sea bass), *kajikimaguro* (swordfish), and *sawara* (Spanish mackerel) are filleted, cut into smaller pieces, and then salt-grilled.

From the preceding list you may notice that the Japanese enjoy many oily fishes, which are juicier and sweeter than white-fleshed fish. For many Westerners, excluding the sardine-loving Portuguese and Spanish, *fish* generally means a white fish fillet. If you have never tried grilled—or, at least, broiled—oil-rich fish, I hope you will. Before long you will acquire a taste for these rich fish. The salt-grilling method is the best way to embark on this new taste journey.

> *Four 8-inch* iwashi *(sardines), or 6-ounce*
> *swordfish steaks*
> *Salt*
> *1 cup grated daikon*
> *4 teaspoons* shoyu *(soy sauce)*
> *1 lemon, cut into wedges*

To clean the sardines, have at hand a large bowl of cold salted water. Rinse the whole fish under cold running water. This simple process removes a great amount of bacteria on the shin. Scale the fish. Cut open the belly, and remove the gills and intestine without damaging them. Rinse the inside of the belly thoroughly but gently. Don't use a toothbrush, because sardines are very tender. Rinse the fish again in the salted water. Drain the fish, and wipe it dry with paper towels.

If you are using swordfish steaks, rinse them in cold salted water ($1^{1}/_{2}$ tablespoons fine salt per quart of water) very briefly. Once fish is filleted and cut into pieces it loses its flavor quickly in water. Drain the steaks, and wipe them dry with paper towels.

For a more attractive presentation of cooked whole fish, you can remove the gills and intestine together without cutting the belly. To do this, insert a pair of disposable wooden chopsticks through the mouth of the fish and deep into the belly. Rotate the chopsticks several times, and then gently pull them out, with the intestine and gills sandwiched between them.

If you won't be cooking the fish for several hours, wrap it in plastic, and refrigerate it.

Salt the fish using the proper amount of salt (see page 364), and let it stand for 20 minutes.

During the salting period, fire up a grill or broiler. Heat the grill rack or broiler pan to a very high temperature before placing the fish on it. This will prevent the fish from sticking to the rack or pan.

Rinse the fish in a bowl of salted cold water ($1^{1}/_{2}$ tablespoons fine salt per quart of water). Wipe the fish dry with a paper towel.

Place the fish on the hot grill rack or broiler pan, about 4 inches from the heat source, with the side that will face the diner toward the heat. Cook the fish over high heat until its surface has attained a nice golden color. Turn over the fish just once. A 1-inch-thick fish takes about 8 to 10 minutes of total cooking time.

Mix the daikon with the *shoyu*. Accompany each serving with a little tinted daikon and two lemon wedges.

• *Yields 4 servings*

Tips on Salt-Grilling

No matter which type of fish you salt-grill, the kind and quantity of salt and the length of salting time together determine whether the grilled fish will taste fishy or sweet and flavorful.

Sea salt is best for salt-grilling. With its extra minerals, such as magnesium chloride, it extracts more water than ordinary table salt, and thus removes more of the fishy-tasting liquid from the fish protein.

The quantity of salt to use depends on whether the fish is oily or lean, and on how fresh it is. A good rule is to use 2 percent of the weight of the fish. Therefore, for a 7-ounce fish, a little less than 1 teaspoon fine salt is necessary. Oily fish and slightly old fish need a little more salt than this, to draw out more of the fish juice.

When salting fish do not place them directly in the bottom of a pan. Arrange them instead on a bamboo rolling mat or steel rack set inside the pan, so that the fish won't be bathed in its own juice.

About one-half hour before serving, lay the fish on a bamboo rolling mat or steel rack set inside a pan. Sprinkle the fish with half of the salt, turn the fish over, and sprinkle with the remaining salt.

Let the fish stand for 20 minutes, or if it is not absolutely fresh, 25 minutes. The time required for salting is generally 20 minutes. However, this varies depending on the type, thickness, and freshness of the fish. The oilier, thicker, or older the fish, the longer the required salting time—as long as 50 minutes.

After salting oily fish, rinse it in water with 2- to 3-percent brine (about 1½ tablespoons fine salt per quart of water). Wipe the fish with a paper towel before cooking it. After salting a lean type of fish, you may skip the rinsing, and simply wipe off the exuded liquid with a paper towel.

A charcoal fire is the ideal heat source for grilling fish. When I was small, my mother cooked fish on a small portable charcoal brazier that she set in our garden. The grilled fish had a truly delicious flavor. But you can instead use a wood- or gas-fired grill, or even broil the fish.

Serve the grilled or broiled fish with a small mound of condiment. If you are serving an oily fish, the condiment might be grated daikon tinted with a little *shoyu*. Lemon wedges and vinegar-pickled vegetables such as daikon, turnip, carrot, cucumber, and ginger are good with any kind of grilled or broiled fish. But you can instead use a wood- or gas-fired grill, or even broil the fish.

YELLOWTAIL TERIYAKI

Buri no Teriyaki

Buri, yellowtail, is a full-flavored, oily fish that tastes best during the cold months. In Japan, the fish undergoes several name changes according to its size and age. *Buri* is three-year-old, fully grown yellowtail, weighing around 13 pounds. Smaller one- or two-year-old fish are called *hamachi,* a name you may have heard at a sushi restaurant.

> $^1/_4$ *cup* shoyu *(soy sauce)*
> $^1/_4$ *cup* mirin *(sweet cooking wine)* ·
> *1 teaspoon peeled, finely grated ginger*
> *Two 1-inch-thick skinned and boned yellowtail fillets*
> *(about 1$^1/_4$ pounds)*
> *6 tablespoons teriyaki sauce (page 77)*
>
> CONDIMENT
> *Sweet pickled ginger (page 292)*

In a pan large enough to hold the fish in a single layer, combine the *shoyu, mirin,* and grated ginger. Add the fish to the pan, and marinate the fish for 15 minutes.

Remove the fish from the pan, and wipe it dry with paper towels. Discard the marinade.

Heat a broiler or grill. Place the fillets on the broiler rack or grill, 4 inches from the heat source. Cook the fish until the surface is light golden, about 3 minutes.

Turn over the fish, and cook it for 2 minutes.

Remove the fish from the heat, and place it on a plate. With a pastry brush, spread 2 tablespoons of the teriyaki sauce on both sides of the fish. Return the fish to the heat, and cook it for 2 minutes to dry the surface of the fish.

Remove the fish from the heat, and baste both sides with 2 tablespoons of the remaining teriyaki sauce. Return the fish to the heat, and cook it for another 1 to 2 minutes.

Repeat the basting process one more time with the remaining sauce. Use caution, since basted fish burns easily. If the fish starts to burn, cover it with aluminum foil.

Serve the fish with sweet pickled ginger or with baked, mashed, or fried potatoes.

• *Yields 4 servings*

SWORDFISH IN *YUAN* STYLE

Kajikimaguro no Yuan Yaki

Yuan yaki is a traditional and popular Japanese grilling technique. Fish fillets are first marinated in a marinade that includes slices of *yuzu* citron, and then grilled. The dish takes its very distinctive and refreshing flavor from the citron. If *yuzu* citron is not available, use a combination of lime, lemon, and orange slices. The cooked fish is fully flavored, so no sauce is served with it.

In this recipe I pan-fry the fish instead of grilling it. To complement the soft, juicy texture of cooked swordfish, I serve this dish with crisp fried burdock or lotus root chips. Adding salad or parboiled or grilled vegetables—and of course miso soup and rice—makes a complete meal.

> $^1/_4$ *cup* shoyu *(soy sauce)*
> $^1/_4$ *cup* mirin *(sweet cooking wine)*
> $^1/_4$ *cup* sake *(rice wine)*
> *6 slices* yuzu *citron, preferably, or 2 slices each*
>   *lime, lemon, and orange*
> *Four $^1/_2$-pound swordfish steaks*
> *5 ounces* gobo *(burdock), or 7 ounces lotus root*
>   *(about 5 inches of a $2^1/_2$-inch-diameter root)*
> *2 cups plus 2 tablespoons vegetable oil*
> $^1/_3$ *cup all-purpose flour*
> *1 tablespoon minced shiso leaves, preferably, or parsley*

In a pan large enough to hold all the fish in a single layer, combine the *shoyu*, *mirin*, *sake*, and *yuzu* citron. Add the steaks to the pan, and marinate them for 30 minutes, if they are $^1/_2$-inch thick, or a little less time if they are thinner.

If you're using burdock, scrape the skin with a knife, and julienne the burdock in 3-inch lengths. If you are using lotus root, peel it and cut it into thin slices. Soak the burdock or lotus root in a bowl of 2 cups cold water and 2 teaspoons vinegar.

In a large, deep skillet, heat 2 cups oil over medium heat to 320 degrees F. In small batches, cook the burdock or lotus root until it is crisp and lightly golden. Remove each batch all at one time with a large skimmer, and drain the vegetables on a rack.

Remove the fish from the marinade, and reserve the marinade, discarding the citron slices. Wipe the fish dry with paper towels. Coat the fish lightly with flour, and pat it to remove excess flour.

Heat a large skillet over medium heat. Add the remaining 2 tablespoons oil. When the oil is hot, add the fish, and cook until the bottom is golden. Turn the fish over and cook until the other side is golden. Reduce the heat to low, and cook the fish until it is done, about 8 minutes for a 1-inch-thick steak. Transfer the fish to a platter, and cover with aluminum foil.

Rinse the skillet with hot water to remove the oil. Dry the skillet with paper towels, and add the reserved marinade. Bring the marinade to a boil over medium heat. Reduce the heat to low, and cook for 2 to 3 minutes.

Return the fish to the skillet, and cook the fish over medium-high heat for about 1 minute, basting until the fish is well coated with the sauce. Serve the fish garnished with the fried burdock or lotus root and sprinkled with minced shiso or parsley.

• *Yields 4 servings*

SESAME-CRUSTED SEARED TUNA

Maguro no Goma-age

Archaeological remains indicate that *maguro,* tuna, has been eaten in Japan since ancient times. But it was relatively recently, toward the end of the Edo Era (1600 to 1868), that tuna gained its present popularity. Thoroughly cooking tuna firms and dries its flesh. In Japan, therefore, tuna is eaten mainly as sashimi or in sushi, although there are some traditional recipes in which tuna is cooked, such as *negima-nabe* (page 393).

Recently tuna has become a popular fish at restaurants outside Japan, both Japanese and non-Japanese. The most popular new style of preparation is searing. I suppose this method was born out of a Japanese chef's search for a good way to serve sashimi-quality fish to clients who might resist ordering raw fish.

To sear fish is to cook the surface quickly with intense heat while barely cooking the interior. Searing can be done with any heat source, wet or dry. In this preparation I marinate tuna, coat it with sesame seeds, and then sear it in oil.

Cutting the cooked tuna requires a little practice, since the outside of the cooked fish easily falls apart. Let the cooked fish stand for 10 minutes, and then cut it with a very sharp knife, such as a meat slicer.

Serve the sliced tuna on a bed of salad greens.

1 pound sashimi-quality tuna (see page 352)
2 tablespoons black sesame seeds, toasted (page 100)
¹/₂ cup plus 1 teaspoon shoyu (soy sauce)
¹/₂ cup mirin (sweet cooking wine)
1 teaspoon smooth French-style mustard
1 tablespoon komezu (rice vinegar)
¹/₄ teaspoon peeled, grated ginger
¹/₂ teaspoon sugar
1 teaspoon sesame oil
1 to 2 tablespoons virgin olive oil
¹/₂ cup all-purpose flour
Vegetable oil, for frying
A mixture of salad leaves and sliced cherry tomatoes

Cut away any deep red part of the tuna, and cut the rest of the meat into four 1-inch-thick steaks. In a *suribachi* or other mortar, grind the sesame seeds until they are just broken.

In a pan large enough to hold the steaks in one layer, combine ¹/₂ cup of the *shoyu*, the *mirin*, and sesame seeds. Place the tuna in the pan, and marinate it for 15 minutes.

In a large bowl, combine the mustard, the remaining 1 teaspoon *shoyu*, the *komezu*, grated ginger, sugar, sesame oil, and olive oil, and whisk until smooth. This is the dressing for the salad greens.

In a large, deep skillet, heat 1 inch vegetable oil over medium heat to 360 degrees F.

While the oil heats, drain the tuna, discarding the marinade but reserving the sesame seeds. Coat the tuna with the sesame seeds, and then the flour..

Add the tuna to the skillet, and cook the tuna, turning it with tongs and a spatula, until both sides are golden. The center of the fish should be rare and pink, but cook it longer if you prefer.

Remove the fish from the oil, and drain it on a rack for 10 minutes. With a very sharp knife, cut the tuna diagonally to produce broad slices ¹/₄-inch thick.

Toss the salad greens with the dressing, and serve the tuna on a bed of greens, garnished with tomatoes.

• *Yields 4 servings*

CLASSIC MISO-MARINATED SALMON WITH GREEN SAUCE

Sake no Saikyo Misozuke

Saikyo miso, sweet white miso, is made in Kyoto Prefecture. Kyoto was the capital of Japan for a thousand years. The technique of marinating fish in miso was born out of necessity, because, unlike other major cities such as Tokyo, Kobe, and Osaka, Kyoto is situated inland. Marinating fish in miso was a method of preserving fresh-caught fish for the long journey from the fishing port to the capital. Today, we marinate fish not to preserve it, but rather to enjoy the sweet flavor that the fish acquires during marination.

Broiled or grilled miso-marinated fish, one of the most popular fish preparations in Japan, can appear on any dining occasion. You may find it in an ordinary box lunch or at a formal dinner, *kaiseki ryori*, at a first-class Japanese restaurant.

In this traditional preparation, lightly marinated salmon is broiled with a spinach-miso sauce. To keep the miso marinade from adhering to the salmon, you will need two tightly woven, thin cotton cloths, about 12 inches square, or four similarly sized pieces of cheesecloth.

A Chilean sea bass also works well in this recipe.

1¹/₂ pounds salmon fillet, skin attached, cut into 4 pieces
5 teaspoons salt
8 ounces Saikyo miso (sweet white miso)
¹/₄ cup sake *(rice wine)*
¹/₄ cup mirin *(sweet cooking wine)*

SPINACH-MISO SAUCE
3¹/₂ ounces Saikyo miso (sweet white miso)
1 tablespoon sugar
Yolks of 2 small eggs
2 tablespoons sake, mixed with 2 tablespoons water
3¹/₂ ounces spinach leaves, 4 small leaves reserved

CONDIMENT
Sweet pickled ginger (page 292)

Salt the fish on both sides, and place it on a steel rack set over a pan. Put the fish in the refrigerator for 1 hour.

In a medium bowl, soften the 8 ounces miso with the *sake* and *mirin*. In a pan large enough to hold all the fish without overlapping, spread one-third of the miso mixture. Place a tightly woven cotton cloth or two layers of cheesecloth over the miso. Wipe the salt from the fish with a paper towel, and place all the pieces on the cloth in the pan. Cover the fish with another tightly woven cotton cloth or two layers of cheesecloth. Spread the remaining miso mixture over the cloth, covering the surface completely. Wrap the entire pan with plastic wrap, and refrigerate the fish for about 5 hours to overnight.

In a large pot of boiling water, parboil the spinach, excluding the 4 leaves, 1 to 2 minutes. Cool the spinach in ice water, and drain the spinach. In a food processor or blender, purée the spinach, adding 1 to 2 tablespoons water if necessary.

In a skillet, heat 1 inch oil over medium heat to 320 degrees F. One at a time, add the 4 reserved spinach leaves to the oil, and cook them until they are bright green and translucent, 10 to 15 seconds. Transfer the spinach to paper towels to drain.

In a *suribachi* or other mortar, grind the 3¹/₂ ounces miso, the sugar, the egg yolks, and the *sake* mixed with water, adding the ingredients one at a time. Transfer the mixture to the top of a double boiler and cook over simmering water until the mixture thickens.

Remove the top of the double boiler from the heat, and cool the mixture in a bowl of ice water. Stir in the puréed spinach.

Heat a broiler and a broiler pan. With a pastry brush, grease the pan lightly. Transfer the salmon to the broiler pan, and cook, turning once, until both sides are slightly golden, about 8 minutes. Just before the cooking is finished, spread the spinach sauce over the fish. Cook the fish close to the fire until the sauce is lightly charred.

Serve the fish garnished with the fried spinach leaves and accompanied by the sweet pickled ginger on the side.

- *Yields 4 servings*

BROILED OR GRILLED MISO-MARINATED SALMON WITH SPINACH SAUCE

Sake no Saikyomiso-zuke Horenso Sōsu

Because miso-marinated fish is strongly flavored by the marinade, the cooked fish is traditionally served without any sauce. In this preparation, however, I break with convention by serving miso-marinated salmon with a bright green spinach sauce underneath. To adjust the flavor balance, the fish is marinated for a shorter time than is traditional. For a more authentic presentation, try the preceding recipe.

This preparation requires two tightly woven, thin cotton cloths, about 12 inches square, or four similarly sized pieces of cheesecloth. The cloth keeps the salmon from direct contact with the miso, and makes it easy to remove the salmon from the miso marinade without any residue adhering to the fish. The marinated fish should not be rinsed in water, since water would wash away the delicate flavor.

> $1^1/_4$ *pounds fresh salmon or cod fillets, skinned or not,*
> *cut into 4 pieces*
> *5 teaspoons salt*
> *8 ounces Saikyo miso (sweet white miso)*
> $^1/_4$ *cup* sake *(rice wine)*
> $^1/_4$ *cup* mirin *(sweet cooking wine)*
> $^1/_4$ *cup dry white wine*
> $^1/_4$ *cup* komezu *(rice vinegar)*
> *1 tablespoon minced shallot*
> $3^1/_2$ *ounces spinach leaves, 4 medium leaves reserved*
> *Vegetable oil, for frying*
> *2 tablespoons tamamiso (miso-and-egg sauce, page 83)*
> *6 to 8 tablespoons virgin olive oil, to taste*

Salt the fish on both sides, and rest it on a steel rack set over the pan, for 1 hour in the refrigerator.

In a medium bowl, soften the miso by stirring in the *sake* and *mirin*. Spread one-third of the miso mixture in the bottom of a large pan in which the fish can fit without overlapping. Lay a tightly woven cotton cloth or two layers of cheesecloth over the miso in the pan.

Wipe the salted salmon with a paper towel to remove the salt and the liquid exuded from the fish. Place all the salmon pieces on the cloth in the pan, and cover them with another tightly woven cotton cloth or two layers of cheesecloth.

Spread the remaining miso mixture over the cloth, covering the surface completely. Wrap the entire pan with plastic wrap, and refrigerate it for 5 hours.

In a small saucepan, combine the dry white wine, *komezu,* and shallot. Bring the mixture to a boil over medium heat. Reduce the heat to very low, and cook the mixture until it is reduced to 1 tablespoon syrup.

In a large pot of boiling water, parboil the spinach, excluding the 4 leaves, 1 to 2 minutes. Cool the spinach in ice water, and drain the spinach well. In a food processor, purée the spinach.

In a skillet, heat 1 inch oil over medium heat to 320 degrees F. One at a time, add the 4 reserved spinach leaves to the oil, and cook them until they are bright green and translucent, 10 to 15 seconds. Transfer the spinach to paper towels to drain.

Lift the top cloth (or cloths) from the salmon, and remove the salmon from the marinade. Discard the marinade, or reserve it to use as a fish marinade one more time within 2 weeks, after heating it through and adding more miso and *sake*, or for making miso soup. If there is any miso residue on the fish, gently wipe it away with a paper towel. At this point you can refrigerate the fish, in a well-sealed plastic bag, for up to 3 days, or freeze it for a longer period.

Heat a broiler or grill, and the broiler pan or grill rack. With a pastry brush, lightly grease the pan or rack. Transfer the salmon to the pan or rack, and cook the salmon, turning once, until both sides are light golden. A 1-inch-thick salmon steak needs about 8 minutes' total cooking. Marinated fish burns easily, so you may need to cover the fish with aluminum foil as it cooks.

In a small saucepan, combine the miso-and-egg sauce with the reduced vinegar-wine syrup. Place the saucepan over low heat, and cook until the mixture is heated through. Transfer the mixture to a medium bowl, and add the spinach purée. Little by little, whisk in the olive oil. Serve the salmon with the spinach sauce underneath and garnished with the fried spinach leaves.

• *Yields 4 servings*

BROILED SEA BASS WITH SESAME SEEDS

Suzuki no Gomamiso-yaki

This is another variation on broiled miso-marinated fish. The marinade in this preparation uses *tamamiso,* miso-and-egg sauce, as a base. The *tamamiso* is mixed with white sesame seeds to make a rich, nutty marinade.

In this preparation the marinating period is only 10 minutes, much shorter than in *Sake no Saikyo Misozuke* (page 369). Some of the marinade in this recipe, however, is spread on the fish while it is cooking. A little charring of the marinade here and there gives excellent color and flavor to this dish.

> 13 ounces suzuki *(sea bass)*, *Chilean sea bass,*
> *Spanish mackerel, or red snapper fillet*
> 1¹/₂ *teaspoons salt*
> 3 *tablespoons white sesame seeds, toasted (page 100)*
> ¹/₂ *cup* tamamiso *(miso-and-egg sauce, page 83)*
> 2 *tablespoons* mirin *(sweet cooking wine)*
> 2 *tablespoons* sake *(rice wine)*
> *Sweet pickled ginger (page 292)*

Salt the fish on both sides, and rest it on a steel rack set over a pan, for 30 minutes in the refrigerator.

Wipe the fish with a paper towel to remove the salt and the exuded liquid. Remove any remaining bones with tweezers. Cut the fish into four portions.

In a *suribachi* or other mortar, crush or beat 2 tablespoons of the sesame seeds.

In a medium bowl, combine the miso-and-egg sauce, *mirin*, *sake*, and crushed sesame seeds. Transfer the mixture to a pan large enough to hold the fish in one layer, and marinate the fish for 10 minutes.

Remove the fish from the marinade, and gently wipe off the excess. Reserve the marinade.

Heat a broiler and a broiler pan. With a pastry brush, lightly grease the pan. Lay the fish on the pan, and broil the fish, turning once, for 6 to 7 minutes. Toward the end of the cooking, spoon a ¹/₄-inch-thick layer of the reserved marinade on the surface of the fish, and sprinkle the fish with the remaining sesame seeds. Cook the fish close to the heat source until the surface turns golden.

Serve the fish with sweet pickled ginger.

• *Yields 4 servings*

CRISP FRIED SOLE WITH PONZU DRESSING

Karei no Kara-age Ponzu-zoe

Kara-age is a deep-frying technique in which the food is first coated with flour or other starch and then cooked in oil until crisp. The idea of frying a whole fish is borrowed from Chinese cooking (*kara* means "Chinese," and *age* means "deep-frying"), but the types of fish and style of serving in Japan make this dish look and taste very different from its Chinese counterparts. *Karei* (sole), *okoze* (stingfish/stonefish), *ainame* (rock trout), and *iwashi* (sardine) are popular fish in this preparation. The crisp cooked fish is served not with a sweet, starchy sauce as in China, but with refreshing, light ponzu dressing.

MAIN DISHES

374

> 2 karei *(sole), 1 to 1¹/₄ pounds each*
> 12 shishitogarashi *peppers, preferably,*
>   *or 1 small green bell pepper*
> *Vegetable oil, for deep-frying*
> *3 tablespoons* joshinko *(rice flour)*
> *1 teaspoon cornstarch*
> *Four ¹/₄-inch-thick, 2-inch-square pieces of* kabocha,
>   *pumpkin, or buttercup squash, skin attached,*
>   *or sweet potato*
> *12 paper-thin, peeled ginger slices*
>
> CONDIMENTS
> *¹/₃ cup grated daikon*
> *2 shiso leaves*
> *¹/₄ cup ponzu dressing (page 73)*

Scale, gut, and clean each fish. Wipe the fish with paper towels. Place one fish on a cutting board white side (back side) up, and make a large crosscut in the flesh. Turn over the fish so the dark side (front) is up, and make shallow cuts along both edges of the fish, without piercing the bottom surface, to separate the flesh from the fins. Make a long lengthwise cut across the center. Moving the knife away from the center, cut along the bones from the head of the fish, and partially open out the flesh on both sides of the backbone. Do not separate the flesh completely from the bones. Fold the flesh flaps inside-out. Secure the folded back flaps of the cut-open side with toothpicks woven into the exposed surface. Repeat the same process for another fish.

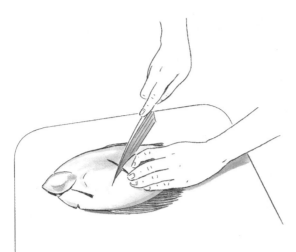

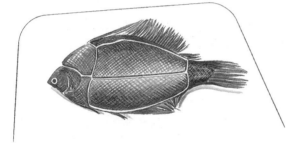

*Preparing the sole:
(a) Cut a large
cross on one side.
(b) On the other
side, make a long
lengthwise cut
across the center;
make shallow cuts,
perpendicular to the
center cut, along
both the head and
tail sides. (c) Fold
out the flaps of fish.*

Prick the *shishitogarashi* peppers with a toothpick all over the skin; this prevents the peppers from exploding while they are cooking. If you are substituting the bell pepper, cut it into eight lengthwise slices.

In a pot large enough to fit one of the fish, heat 4 inches of oil over medium heat to 340 degrees F.

In a small bowl, combine the rice flour and cornstarch. With a pastry brush, sprinkle each fish with the flour mixture. Let the fish rest.

In two batches, fry the *shishitogarashi* peppers or bell pepper slices in the hot oil until the skins blister slightly. Drain the peppers on a rack.

Add the *kabocha* squash to the oil, and cook until the pieces are slightly golden. Drain them on the rack.

Reduce the oil temperature to 320 degrees F. Add one of the fish, and cook it about 20 minutes, turning it once, until it is slightly golden. Before removing the fish from the oil, increase the temperature of the oil to 360 degrees F, and cook the fish for 2 to 3 minutes longer. This makes the outside of the fish crisp and golden brown. Drain the fish on the rack.

Cook the other fish in the same way.

After removing the second fish from the oil, reduce the heat to very low, or even turn off the heat, to return the oil temperature to 320 degrees F. Add the ginger, and cook it until it is golden and crisp. Drain the ginger on the rack.

Put each fish on a plate with half of the peppers, ginger, and *kabocha*. Next to the fish, at the right front, place a shiso leaf, and mound half of the grated daikon on the leaf. Serve the ponzu dressing in a small bowl on the side. At the table each diner takes a portion of the fish with some grated daikon and some of the dressing.

• *Yields 4 servings*

STEAMED GINGER-FLAVORED SEA BASS

Suzuki no Saka-mushi

Although oily or old fish should never be cooked this way, steaming is the best method for cooking very fresh, delicately flavored fish. This method preserves all the natural, sweet flavor of the fish, and maintains a very juicy texture.

Sake (rice wine) and ginger are frequently used in steaming fish. They enhance the sweet flavor of the fish and, at the same time, eliminate any unpleasant flavor characteristics.

To judge when a fish is done steaming, look at the eye. It becomes snow-white and pops up when the fish is ready!

> *Two 4-inch squares* kombu *(kelp)*
> *One 3-pound whole sea bass, sea bream, red snapper,*
>   *or other white fish*
> *2 tablespoons salt*
> *4 fresh shiitake mushrooms*
> *8 small broccoli flowerets*
> *One 2-inch piece ginger, peeled and sliced thin*
>   *crosswise*
> *5 tablespoons* sake *(rice wine)*
> *2 tablespoons peeled julienned ginger*
> *1* naganegi *long onion, preferably, or 5 thick scallions,*
>   *julienned in 3-inch lengths*
> *1 tablespoon sesame oil*
> *1 cup* nihaizu *dressing (page 73)*

Wrap the *kombu* in a moist cotton cloth, and let it stand until softened, 30 minutes.

Gut the fish, clean it, and wipe it dry with a paper towel. Transfer the fish to a steel rack set over a pan, or to a rack on top of a pan, and salt the fish on both sides. Let the fish stand for 30 minutes.

Rinse the shiitake mushrooms, and cut away and discard their stems.

In a medium pot of salted boiling water, parboil the broccoli for 30 seconds. Drain it, and spread it in a colander to cool.

Set a large pot of water over high heat. Set a bamboo or metal steamer basket over plenty of water in another large pot, and set it over high heat, too. Place the softened *kombu* on a platter that can fit into the steamer.

Wipe the fish with a paper towel to remove the salt and exuded liquid. When the water in the first pot comes to a boil, add the fish. If the whole fish will not fit into the steamer, cut the fish in half. Blanch it for 30 seconds.

Carefully remove the fish from the water, using two large spatulas, and transfer the fish to the *kombu*-lined platter. Stuff the belly cavity with half the sliced ginger, and scatter the remaining ginger slices over the fish.

Transfer the platter to the hot steamer. Sprinkle the fish with the *sake*. If you are using a metal steamer, line the underside of the lid with a cotton cloth to prevent condensed steam from dripping over the fish. Cover the steamer, and steam the fish over high heat for 18 to 20 minutes or until the eye turns very white and pops up. About two minutes before the fish is done, add the shiitake mushrooms and broccoli to the steamer and steam the fish and vegetables together.

Using two large spatulas, carefully transfer the cooked fish to a large serving platter. Arrange the vegetables next to the fish. Garnish the top of the fish with the julienned ginger and long onion or scallion.

In a small saucepan, heat the sesame oil until it is sizzling but not smoking. Pour the sesame oil over the fish.

Serve the fish with *nihaizu* dressing in a small bowl on the side. At the table the host may serve the fish to each of the diners, removing the flesh from the bone. Be careful not to swallow bones.

- *Yields 4 servings*

MISO-FLAVORED SIMMERED MACKEREL

Saba no Miso-ni

In Japan, *saba,* mackerel, is often simmered in a rich broth flavored with brown miso, whose strong flavor suppresses the oily flavor of mackerel. Personally, I prefer salt-grilled mackerel, in which I can taste the true natural flavor of this fish. But from time to time I enjoy using this recipe of my mother's for delicious miso-flavored mackerel.

> $1\frac{1}{2}$-*pound whole mackerel*
> *6 scallions, cut into* $2\frac{1}{2}$-*inch lengths*
> *One 2-inch piece ginger, peeled and sliced*
> *thin crosswise, julienned*

> $^1/_2$ cup mirin *(sweet cooking wine)*
> $^1/_2$ cup sake *(rice wine)*
> 4-inch square kombu *(kelp), soaked in*
>   1 quart water for 1 hour
> 2 tablespoons plus 2 teaspoons akamiso *(brown miso)*
> 4 to 8 teaspoons mamemiso *(soybean miso), to taste*
> 1 thumb-size piece ginger, peeled and julienned

Remove and discard the head and intestine of the mackerel. Rinse the mackerel thoroughly under cold running water. Wipe the mackerel dry in paper towels. Fillet the fish in *sanmai oroshi* fashion (see page 354), but do not divide the two fillets into four narrower ones, as you would for sashimi. Instead, cut each fillet into three pieces crosswise.

In a medium pot of boiling water, cook the scallions for 10 seconds. With a skimmer, transfer them to a large bowl of ice water. Drain the scallions, and set them aside.

In the same pot of boiling water, cook one piece of fish on the skimmer until the outside of the fish turns white, about 10 seconds. Immediately plunge the fish into ice water, and rub the fish gently. Transfer the fish to a bowl. Cook the remaining fish pieces in the same way.

In a large shallow pot in which the fish can be placed without overlapping, distribute the ginger slices. Place the fish pieces on top, skin side up, without overlapping them. Add the *mirin*, *sake*, and enough of the *kombu* liquid to cover the fish by $^1/_2$ inch.

Bring the mixture to a boil over medium heat, skimming off any foam. Reduce the heat to low, and cook the fish, covered with a drop lid (see page 26), at a gentle simmer for 10 minutes.

In a small cup, soften the two kinds of miso with a generous amount of cooking liquid from the pot. Add the miso mixture to the simmering broth, and cook for 5 minutes. Turn off the heat, and let the cooked fish stand in the pot for 5 minutes.

Carefully transfer the fish to a large platter, and cover the fish with aluminum foil to keep it warm. Strain the cooking broth through a fine sieve. Return the broth to the pot, and cook it over medium heat until the broth thickens, about 5 minutes.

Return the fish to the pot, add the scallions, and baste them with the cooking broth. Turn off the heat, and let the cooked fish and the scallions stand in the pot for 5 minutes.

Arrange the fish pieces on a large serving platter with the scallions on top and the remaining cooking broth poured over. Garnish the fish with the ginger strips, and serve.

• *Yields 2 to 3 servings*

SARDINES IN SWEET *SHOYU* SAUCE

Iwashi no Kabayaki

Kabayaki is a popular Japanese cooking technique most often applied to eel. An eel, *unagi,* is cut open, cleaned, boned, steamed, grilled over a charcoal fire, and then basted with a thick, sweet soy-based sauce, *tare*. The finished dish is called *unagi no kabayaki*. The eel's oily taste and texture are very well complemented by the sauce, making *unagi no kabayaki* one of the most favored delicacies in Japan.

Eel, however, is expensive and hard to handle at home. Home cooks, therefore, frequently use a substitute. Oily fishes such as sardine, mackerel, and pike are well suited for *kabayaki* cooking. Fish lovers all adore this inexpensive version of *kabayaki*.

Sansho pepper, which has a minty, refreshing aroma, is an indispensable condiment for *kabayaki* preparations.

4 medium sardines
¹/₂ cup all-purpose flour

TARE SAUCE
¹/₄ cup mirin *(sweet cooking wine)*
2 tablespoons sugar
¹/₄ cup shoyu *(soy sauce)*

6 tablespoons vegetable oil

GARNISH
¹/₂ teaspoon sansho *pepper*

Scale and clean the sardines. Remove the tails and heads, and butterfly each fish. You may need only your hands and not a knife to butterfly them, since sardines are very delicate. Leave the skins attached.

Dust the sardines with flour, and let them stand for 5 minutes.

In a saucepan, bring ¹/₄ cup water, the *mirin,* and sugar to a boil. When the sugar is dissolved, add the *shoyu*, and cook the sauce over medium-low heat for 10 minutes.

In a skillet, heat 3 tablespoons vegetable oil until hot, but not smoking. Cook two of the sardines over medium heat, turning them once, until both sides are slightly golden. Remove the sardines from the skillet, and set them aside.

Put the remaining 3 tablespoons oil into the skillet, and cook the remaining sardines in the same way. Remove the sardines from the skillet, and set them aside with the others.

Rinse the skillet with boiling water. Wipe the skillet with a paper towel, and place it over medium-high heat. Add the *tare* sauce, return the sardines to the skillet, and cook until the fish is thoroughly coated with the sauce.

Serve the sardines garnished with $1/8$ teaspoon *sansho* pepper each, and accompanied by plain cooked white or brown rice. Or serve the rice in a soup bowl, topped with the fish, and drizzled with the remaining sauce in the skillet.

- *Yields 2 servings*

PAN-FRIED SQUID PATTIES

Ikayaki

My mother from time to time makes a squid-dumpling hot pot. While watching this preparation one day, I became very hungry. So I stole a little of the dumpling mixture from my mother's bowl, and pan-fried the mixture. On that night, my family found this new inspiration very delicious.

To make this dish, prepared squid is mixed with pork, and flavored with scallions and ginger. The mixture is formed into small patties, about the size of a blini, and pan-fried. A brush of *shoyu* (soy sauce) and *mirin* (sweet cooking wine) over the patties is the only additional step.

This dish makes a very good party appetizer. For such an occasion, make the patties smaller.

> *10 ounces cleaned and peeled squid, including legs*
> *3 1/2 ounces pork shoulder*
> *1/2 teaspoon salt*
> *1/3 cup minced scallions, green part only*
> *1 tablespoon potato starch or cornstarch, mixed with*
>   *1 1/2 tablespoons dashi (fish stock) or water*
> *1 tablespoon ginger juice (page 58)*
> *1 teaspoon sesame oil*
> *1 tablespoon tamari*
> *2 tablespoons mirin (sweet cooking wine)*
> *1/4 teaspoon shichimi togarashi (seven-spice powder)*
> *Vegetable oil*

With a heavy-duty knife, coarsely chop the squid, including the legs, and, separately, the pork. Or cut the squid and pork into small pieces and chop them separately in a food processor by turning the machine on and off. Do not overprocess them, or they will become slimy paste.

Combine the squid and pork in a bowl, and add the salt, scallions, potato-starch or cornstarch liquid, ginger juice, and sesame oil one at a time, stirring.

In a small cup, mix the tamari, *mirin*, and *shichimi togarashi*. Heat the oven to 300 degrees F.

Heat a skillet, and add 1 tablespoon vegetable oil. When the oil is hot, add 2 tablespoons of the squid mixture. Spread it into a flat patty, about 3 inches in diameter. Make one or two more patties, depending on the size of your skillet. Cook the patties over medium-low heat until the bottom is golden. Turn the patties over, and cook them until the other side is golden. The total cooking time should be about 4 to 5 minutes.

Transfer the patties to a baking dish, and brush them with the tamari-and-*mirin* mixture. Keep the cooked patties warm in the oven while you make the rest, adding vegetable oil to the skillet as necessary.

- *Yields 8 to 10 patties or 4 servings*

SEA BREAM STEAMED WITH SWEET RICE

Tai no Sakuramushi

Tai, sea bream, is a favorite fish in Japan because of its delicate and sweet flavor. It becomes most delicious in spring when the pretty pink color of cooked sea bream skin is associated with the beautiful cherry blossoms of spring.

Tai no sakuramushi is a celebrated spring dish. In this preparation, glutinous rice, usually tinted a faint pink, is steamed with sea bream wrapped in salt-pickled young cherry leaves. This elegant presentation gives diners a strong sense of the season, a concept that is very important in Japanese cuisine. The dish is simply served with a sauce of flavored *dashi* (fish stock).

In this preparation I add bacon to provide more depth to this traditional broth. French béchamel and lemon butter are other possibilities for dressing this delicate dish. Sea bass, red snapper, cod, or salmon can be substituted for the sea bream.

1¹/₂ cups mochigome (glutinous rice)

Drop of red food coloring (optional)

8 salt-pickled cherry leaves (available in Japanese food
stores), preferably, or shiso or basil leaves

Four 4-inch-wide pieces boned sea bream fillet,
skin attached (about 1 pound)

Potato starch or cornstarch

10 ounces nanohana (rape blossoms, sometimes
available in Japanese food stores),
or young, thin broccoli raab

2 cups dashi (fish stock)

3 slices bacon

1 tablespoon shoyu (soy sauce)

1 teaspoon sugar

2 tablespoons mirin (sweet cooking wine)

In a bowl of cold water, soak the rice with a drop of food coloring for at least 3 hours or overnight. A shorter soaking will necessitate longer cooking.

Drain the rice, discarding the water.

Soak the pickled cherry leaves in a little salted water (1¹/₂ tablespoons salt per quart) for 30 minutes. If you are using shiso or basil, omit this step.

Mince the cherry or herb leaves. If you are using shiso or basil, toss the minced herb with ¹/₄ teaspoon salt.

On each piece of fillet skin side down, make a very shallow cut along the center line of the fish, and then cut parallel to your work surface toward the outside edges. Carefully open the back of the fish in butterfly fashion. Salt the fish on both sides, and let it stand for 1 hour in a flat-bottomed colander.

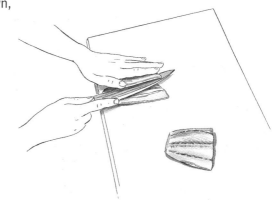

Butterflying a fillet

Wipe the fish with a paper towel to remove the salt and exuded liquid.

Have ready a bamboo or metal steamer with plenty of water at high steam production. Place the drained rice in a square of coarse cotton cloth or triple-layered cheesecloth, transfer the bundle to the heated steamer, and cover the rice completely with the edges of the cloth. Steam the rice over high heat for 30 to 40 minutes. During the steaming, sprinkle $\frac{1}{2}$ cup cold water over the rice every 15 minutes.

Remove the rice from the steamer, and fan it vigorously with a hand fan or square of cardboard to cool the rice quickly. Toss the rice with the minced cherry or herb leaves.

On a counter, place four sheets of plastic wrap, each about 10 inches by 12 inches. Place a piece of fish, skin side down, on each sheet of plastic wrap. With a pastry brush, dust the fish with potato starch or cornstarch.

Place one-quarter of the cooled rice across the center of each fish piece, parallel to the short sides, and roll the fish and rice into a tight cylinder. Wrap the fish rolls tightly in the plastic wrap.

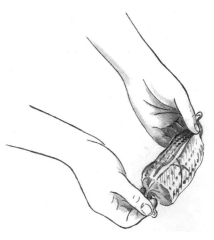

Transfer the wrapped fish rolls to the heated steamer, and cook them over high heat for 12 to 15 minutes.

Remove the fish rolls from the steamer, and let them stand for 10 minutes.

In a pot of boiling water, parboil the rape blossoms or broccoli raab until they are heated through but still crisp, 1 to 2 minutes. Cool the vegetables under cold running water, drain them immediately, and squeeze them to remove excess water. Cut them into 2-inch lengths, and set them aside.

In a saucepan over medium heat, bring to a boil the *dashi*, two slices of bacon, the *shoyu*, the sugar, and the *mirin*. Cook the mixture for 3 minutes. Remove the saucepan from the heat. Remove the bacon from the stock, and discard it.

In a skillet or hot oven, cook the remaining slice of bacon until crisp. Cut the cooked bacon into small pieces.

Return the sauce to a gentle simmer, and reheat the vegetables in it. Drain the vegetables, reserving the sauce, and arrange them on individual plates.

Unwrap the fish rolls, and arrange each over a portion of vegetables. Pour the sauce over the fish. Garnish the fish with the crisp bacon, and serve.

• *Yields 4 servings*

BRAISED FISH IN THE JAPANESE WAY

Nizakana

Braising is a favorite way of cooking fish in Japan; it is second only to grilling in popularity. Seasonal fish, whole or filleted, is cooked in a broth flavored with *sake* (rice wine), *mirin* (sweet cooking wine), and *shoyu* (soy sauce). Miso, vinegar, salt, pickled plums, and herbs and spices are added in the braising of strongly flavored, oily fish, such as sardine, mackerel, and pike.

Popular fish for braising are *karei* (sole), *tai* (sea bream), *iwashi* (sardine), *aji* (horse mackerel), and *saba* (mackerel). I use salmon in this recipe to provide an easy introduction to Japanese-style braising with a fish that is available nearly everywhere throughout the year.

> *Four 1-inch thick salmon steaks*
> *2 slices peeled ginger*
> *1 cup* sake *(rice wine)*
> *3 tablespoons* mirin *(sweet cooking wine)*
> *1 tablespoon sugar*
> *3 tablespoons* shoyu *(soy sauce)*
> *Vegetable oil, for frying*
> *1 thumb-size piece ginger, peeled and julienned*
> *10 ounces spinach*

Place the salmon in a large, flat-bottomed colander. Pour boiling water evenly over the fish. Turn the fish carefully and do the same on the other side of the fish. This process removes any strong fishy flavor or foreign matter from the skin of the fish. Wipe the fish gently with a paper towel.

Into a large, shallow pot that can hold all the salmon without overlapping, put the fish and ginger slices. In a small saucepan, bring the *sake* and *mirin* to a gentle boil. In a kettle, bring about 2 cups water to a boil. Add the *sake* mixture to the salmon in the shallow pot. Add enough boiling water to barely cover the fish. Bring the mixture to a boil over medium heat, and skim off the foam until no more appears.

Reduce the heat to medium-low, add the sugar, and cook, covered with a drop lid (see page 26), for 5 minutes.

Add the *shoyu*, and cook, covered with the drop lid, for 18 to 20 minutes, maintaining a gentle simmer. During the cooking, tilt the pot several times, and scoop the broth over the fish.

While the fish simmers, cook the ginger and spinach. Heat $1/2$ inch oil in a skillet over medium heat until hot, and cook the julienned ginger until crisp and light golden. Remove the ginger from the skillet, and set it aside to drain on a paper towel.

In a medium pot of salted boiling water, parboil the spinach until barely done, 1 to 2 minutes. Drain the spinach, and cool it under cold running water. Squeeze the spinach gently to remove excess water.

When the fish is cooked, add the spinach to the pot, and let the spinach absorb the cooking liquid.

To serve, place the fish and spinach next to each other in shallow bowls, and top with the crisp ginger strips. Pour the remaining broth into each bowl.

- *Yields 4 servings*

FRIED OYSTERS

Kakifurai

Oysters, *kaki,* are eaten in several ways in Japan: raw with a sweet rice-vinegar sauce, cooked with rice, stir-fried, deep-fried, and in hot-pot preparations. Whether they are for eating raw or for cooking, oysters are sold already shucked in Japan. Before using them we rinse them with watery grated daikon radish to remove any foreign matter.

Kakifurai, fried oysters, are a very popular lunch and dinner menu item at all classes of restaurants and in school and office cafeterias across the country. Using very fresh oysters is the key to the success of this dish. Biting into a briefly cooked, juicy oyster trapped in a crisp breadcrumb coating is a real treat. The fried oysters are served with a mayonnaise sauce or Worcestershire-based *tonkatsu* sauce.

For this recipe you will need *panko* breadcrumbs, which are available in Japanese food stores and some supermarkets. Especially made for deep-frying, *panko* breadcrumbs produce a very light, crispy coating.

1 cup grated daikon
$1/4$ teaspoon salt
20 very fresh oysters, in their shells or shucked
1 cup all-purpose flour
2 eggs and 1 egg yolk, thoroughly beaten together
2 cups panko *breadcrumbs*

MAYONNAISE SAUCE (OPTIONAL)

¹/₂ cup mayonnaise
2 hard-boiled eggs, minced
¹/₄ cup sweet or sour pickle relish
¹/₄ cup minced onion, soaked in cold water
for 10 minutes and drained
1 tablespoon minced parsley
¹/₄ teaspoon salt
Vegetable oil, for deep-frying
Assorted salad leaves
Tonkatsu *sauce (page 94; optional)*

Into a bowl, put the grated daikon and ¹/₄ teaspoon salt. Add the oysters, and gently rub them. Add cold water to the bowl, stir several times, and drain the oysters, discarding the water and daikon. Change the water several times until it is clear. Drain the oysters. Do this entire process quickly, using no more water than necessary.

Wipe the oysters gently with a paper towel. Lightly salt and pepper them.

Put the flour, eggs, and breadcrumbs into three separate bowls. Dust each oyster with flour, and then coat it with egg. Return the oyster to the flour, and pass it through the egg again. Dredge the oyster with breadcrumbs, patting gently to assure that it is well coated. Finish coating all the oysters.

Make the mayonnaise sauce: In a bowl, mix the mayonnaise, hard-boiled egg, relish, onion, parsley, and remaining ¹/₄ teaspoon salt. Set the bowl aside.

In a deep skillet, heat 3 inches vegetable oil to 350 degrees F. Cook the oysters in small batches, turning only once, until the coating is golden, 2 to 3 minutes. Skim the oil from time to time with a fine-netted skimmer to remove bits of breadcrumb. Remove the oysters from the oil, and drain them on a rack.

Serve the hot oysters alongside salad leaves with the mayonnaise sauce or *tonkatsu* sauce in a saucer on the side.

• *Yields 4 servings*

FRIED SHRIMP

Ebifurai

When I was a child, *ebifurai* was my favorite dish at restaurants called *yoshoku-ya,* which specialize in "Japanized" Western dishes. The menus at these restaurants include such adopted dishes as croquettes, beef stew, curry, fried shrimp, fried oysters, and steak. *Yoshoku-ya* originated at the end of the nineteenth century, when Japan opened the country to foreign trade after almost three hundred years of isolation. During this period, new ideas, science, technology, and cuisine flooded into Japan from Western countries.

Fried shrimp came along with the tide. It is a dish in which impressively large, fresh shrimp are cooked crisp with a *panko* breadcrumb coating. The dish is served with ample shredded cabbage and a mayonnaise sauce.

> 8 large shrimp, in their shells, with heads attached,
>   each about 5 ounces in weight and 7 inches
>   from head to tail
> Salt and ground black pepper
> ²/₃ cup all-purpose flour
> 2 eggs thoroughly beaten
> 2 cups panko breadcrumbs (see page 386)
> Vegetable oil, for deep-frying
> 4 cups finely shredded head cabbage
> 1 tomato, cut into wedges
> 1 Japanese or salad cucumber, sliced thin crosswise
> Mayonnaise sauce (page 387)

Peel the shrimp, leaving their heads and tails attached. Cut off the very ends of the tails, about ¹/₈ inch, since this part contains water. Briefly rinse the shrimp in cold water. Drain the shrimp, and wipe them dry with a paper towel. Make a very shallow lengthwise cut on the back of each shrimp, and devein it. Make several shallow diagonal transverse cuts on the belly side, and bend the head and tail back to stretch the belly side. This prevents the shrimp from curling during cooking. Lightly salt and pepper the shrimp. Put the flour, eggs, and breadcrumbs into three separate bowls. Dust each shrimp with flour, and coat it with egg. Return the shrimp to the flour, dip it into the egg again, and then coat it with the breadcrumbs.

In a deep skillet, heat 3 inches oil to 330 degrees F. Cook the shrimp one or two at a time for about 3 to 4 minutes. At the end of the cooking, increase the heat to 355 degrees F to achieve a light golden color and crisp texture. Drain the shrimp on a rack.

Serve the shrimp hot, with cabbage, tomato, and cucumber, with mayonnaise sauce in a saucer on the side.

- *Yields 4 servings*

FRIED SHRIMP WITH TWO SAUCES IN A SANDWICH

Ebifurai-sando

Putting crisp, juicy fried shrimp, *ebifurai*, between toasted slices of white bread makes a delicious sandwich. Before being placed on the bread, the shrimp is basted with two sauces—one mayonnaise-based and the other Worcestershire-based *tonkatsu* sauce. These create a sensational harmony of flavor and texture in your mouth.

> *8 slices white bread, toasted*
> *Butter*
> *Smooth French-style mustard*
> *Mayonnaise sauce (page 387)*
> *8 ebifurai (fried shrimp, page 388, but remove the heads and tails and cut the shrimp open in butterfly fashion before cooking them)*
> *Tonkatsu sauce (page 94)*
>
> GARNISH
> *4 sprigs curly parsley*

Spread the butter and mustard on one side of each slice of bread. With a spoon, spread a thin layer of mayonnaise sauce over four of the slices. Place two fried shrimp on each mayonnaise-covered slice. Apply about 1 tablespoon *tonkatsu* sauce over the two fried shrimp.

Close the sandwiches with the remaining four bread slices. Gently press down on the top of each sandwich. Cut each sandwich in half.

Serve the sandwiches with parsley.

- *Yields 4 servings*

FISH STEAMED WITH SOBA, SHINSHU-STYLE

Sakana no Shinshu-mushi

Shinshu is a region between Tokyo and Kyoto, in the middle of the main island of Japan. The area is mountainous, with many small rivers and gorges. The air and water in this region are much cleaner than in many other parts of the country. In summer Shinshu is full of lush greenery, which attracts many hikers. In winter the area is heavily blanketed with snow, and crowded with skiers.

Shinshu is also known for its production of high-quality buckwheat and wasabi. Soba (buckwheat) noodles are the base for many popular dishes in the region. The noodles are served not just in bowls of hot broth or cold with dipping sauce, but in special ways, too.

A good example is *shinshu-mushi*. In this dish soba is wrapped in a fish fillet and steamed. The fish is served garnished with wasabi and bathed in a hot broth similar to that used in the more common soba dishes. In this recipe I serve the fish with a mixture of sesame oil and *shoyu* (soy sauce) to provide a greater depth of flavor.

Cha-soba, buckwheat noodles flavored with green tea, are available in Japanese and other Asian food stores.

*Four 5-ounce red snapper, sea bass, sea bream,
        cod, or salmon fillets*
1/3 cup plus 1 tablespoon vegetable oil
*1/2 naganegi long onion or 1/4 leek, white part only,
        julienned in 3-inch lengths*
1 thumb-size piece ginger, peeled and julienned
*3 1/2 ounces dried cha-soba (buckwheat noodles
        flavored with green tea), preferably,
        or plain soba noodles*
1/4 cup potato starch or cornstarch
1 egg white, lightly beaten
10 ounces spinach or kale
2 tablespoons sesame oil
2 tablespoons shoyu (soy sauce)

GARNISH
Wasabi

Salt the fish, and let it rest on a rack for 1 hour.

In a skillet, heat $\frac{1}{3}$ cup vegetable oil. When the oil is hot, cook the long onion or leek until it is slightly golden and crisp. Drain it on a paper towel, and cook the ginger in the same way. You can prepare the long onions or leeks and the ginger in the morning for use later in the day, if you like.

Wipe the fish with a paper towel to remove the salt and exuded liquid. With each piece of fillet skin side down, make a very shallow cut along the center line of the fish, and then cut parallel to your work surface toward the outside edges. Carefully open the back of the fish in butterfly fashion.

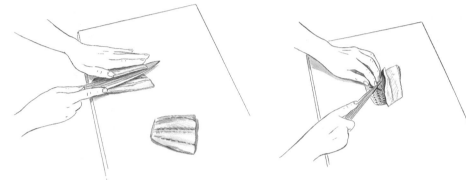

Divide the noodles into two portions, and tightly tie one end of each noodle bundle with cotton kitchen string. This will prevent the noodles from becoming separated during cooking.

Bring a large pot of water to a boil, and cook the noodles al dente, about 3 to 4 minutes.

Drain the noodles, discarding the cooking water, and rinse them in cold water to remove surface starch. Do this carefully, so that the tied ends do not become loose.

Drain the noodles, and place them on a counter. With a pastry brush, apply potato starch or cornstarch all over each noodle bundle. Pass the noodles through the egg-white liquid. Gently squeeze the noodles to remove excess egg white.

Lay the fillets open on the counter, skin side down. With a pastry brush, dust the fish with potato starch or cornstarch. Place a bundle of noodles on one fillet, along the center line of the fish, with the tied end of the noodle bundle protruding to one side. Roll the fillet tightly around the noodles. Cut off and discard the tied end of the noodle bundle. Cut off the ends of the noodles protruding from the opposite side of the roll, but instead of discarding them, reserve them for the second fillet.

With the seam of the roll down, cut a shallow cross, about 2 inches wide, on the upper side of the roll. This will promote even, rapid cooking and prevent the skin of the fish from tearing.

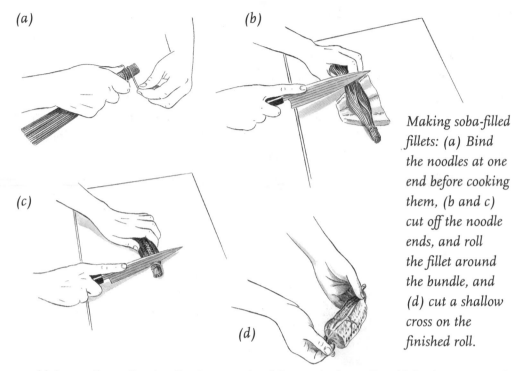

(a)

(b)

(c)

(d)

Making soba-filled fillets: (a) Bind the noodles at one end before cooking them, (b and c) cut off the noodle ends, and roll the fillet around the bundle, and (d) cut a shallow cross on the finished roll.

Make another roll using the loose ends of the cooked noodles. Make two more rolls using the second noodle bundle.

Wrap the fish rolls tightly in plastic wrap. If you won't be cooking them right away, refrigerate them until later in the day.

Have ready a bamboo or metal steamer at high steam production. Place the rolled fish in a heat-proof dish, and cook the fish in the steamer over high heat for 10 minutes. Remove the fish from the steamer, and let it stand for 10 minutes.

In a pot of boiling water, cook the spinach or kale for 1 minute. Drain the greens, squeeze them to remove excess water, and cut them into 3-inch lengths.

In a skillet, heat the remaining 1 tablespoon vegetable oil, and cook the spinach or kale for 2 minutes, stirring. Salt the greens. Arrange them on four individual serving plates.

Carefully remove the plastic wrap from the fish, reserving the trapped juices in a small container, and arrange a rolled piece of fish on top of the spinach on each plate.

In a skillet, heat the 2 tablespoons sesame oil. When it is hot and fragrant, add the 2 tablespoons *shoyu*, and bring the mixture to a boil. Add 1 to 2 tablespoons of the reserved fish juice.

Serve the fish with the greens, drizzled with the sesame-oil-and-*shoyu* sauce. Garnish with the long onion or leek, the ginger, and a dab of wasabi on top of each fish roll.

• *Yields 4 servings*

TUNA AND LEEK HOT POT

Negima-nabe

Tuna has been the favored fish for sashimi and sushi since the eighteenth century. But although today's chefs and diners prefer the oily belly of the fish, *toro*, for sashimi and sushi, in the old days raw tuna belly was regarded as inedible. So cooks developed grilled or stewed dishes just to use the oily belly. Times and tastes do change!

Negima-nabe is a traditional hot-pot dish in which tuna belly, long onion, and several other vegetables are cooked together. Since today the oily belly is one of the most expensive parts of the tuna, I use the more reasonably priced red meat, *akami,* instead of the belly meat.

Like other hot-pot dishes, this one is cooked and eaten at the table.

> 1 pound maguro akami *(red tuna),*
> *cut into 1¹/₃-inch cubes*
> 6 naganegi *long onions or tender leeks, white part*
> *only, cut into 1-inch pieces crosswise*
> 1 bunch chrysanthemum leaves, cut into halves
> 1 thumb-size piece ginger, peeled and julienned
> One 4-inch square kombu *(kelp), soaked in*
> *2 quarts water for 2 hours*
> ¹/₂ cup sake *(rice wine)*
> 2 tablespoons shoyu *(soy sauce)*
> ¹/₂ teaspoon salt
> 1 yuzu *citron or lime, cut into wedges*
> Shichimi togarashi *(seven-spice powder)*
> 2 cups fresh-cooked or day-old plain
> white or brown rice
> 2 to 3 eggs, lightly beaten
> 1 tablespoon green scallion disks
> Fresh-ground black pepper

Arrange the tuna on a platter. On another platter, arrange the long onions or leeks, the chrysanthemum leaves, and the ginger side by side.

Remove the kelp from its soaking liquid, and discard the kelp, reserving the stock. In a *donabe* earthenware pot or an enameled pot, combine the kelp stock and *sake,* and bring the mixture to a gentle simmer. Add the *shoyu* and salt.

If you have a tabletop gas stove, set it on the dining table. Transfer the hot pot to the tabletop stove, and invite the diners to the table. If you do not have a tabletop stove, finish the cooking in the kitchen.

First add about eight pieces each of long onion or leek and ginger to the pot, and cook them over medium heat for 2 to 3 minutes, or until the onion or leek is tender. Add 2 to 3 pieces per person of tuna, and cook for 1 to 2 minutes, depending on your preference. Add a handful of chrysanthemum leaves, and cook for 1 minute. During the cooking, skim off the foam occasionally.

Each diner should now transfer some of the fish and vegetables to an individual serving bowl, ladle over a little of the simmering broth, add a squeeze of *yuzu* or lime juice and a generous sprinkle of seven-spice powder, and eat.

Repeat the simmering process until all the tuna and vegetables are cooked and eaten.

At the end of the cooking, some of the fully flavored broth will be left in the hot pot. Add the cooked rice to the broth. The liquid should barely cover the rice; add water, if needed. Cook the rice over low heat, covered, for 4 to 5 minutes.

Add the beaten eggs, pouring them evenly over the rice. Cook the mixture, covered, 1 to 2 minutes.

Serve the rice topped with scallion rings and a little ground black pepper.

• *Yields 4 servings*

FISHERMEN'S MACKEREL SOUP

Senba-jiru

Senba-jiru was originally assembled quickly by fishermen, right on their boats. In this dish, mackerel is cooked with daikon—a simple combination that produces a delicious soup.

The best season for mackerel is autumn, when this fish becomes richer in flavor and creamier in texture. Fishermen know that the best way to enjoy mackerel, whose flesh quickly deteriorates, is to eat it immediately after it is caught. To be sure your fish is fresh, choose one whose eyes are plump and clear, whose gills are blood red, and whose belly is plump and firm to the touch.

If you are not an oily-fish lover, try this recipe with salmon, substituting broccoli for the carrot for an attractive color contrast.

> *1 large whole mackerel (about 1.3 pounds),*
>   *cleaned and filleted (see pages 352 to 356),*
>   *or 1 pound salmon fillet*
> *2 to 3 teaspoons salt*
> *11 ounces daikon (about 12 inches of a medium root)*
> *1 medium carrot, or 1 small broccoli head*
> *2 tablespoons julienned ginger*
> *$^1/_4$ cup sake (rice wine)*
> *One 2-inch square kombu (kelp)*
> *3 quarter-size slices ginger, peeled*
> *$^1/_4$ teaspoon tamari*
> *$^1/_4$ teaspoon komezu (rice vinegar)*
> *$^1/_3$ cup coriander leaves cut into 1-inch lengths*

Cut the fish into eight to ten pieces, about 2 by 2$^1/_2$ inches each, holding the knife at a shallow angle to the cutting board to make the surface area of the cuts large. Place the fish in a flat-bottomed colander, and sprinkle salt all over it using 1 tablespoon salt for the mackerel or 2 teaspoons for the salmon. Let the fish stand for 30 minutes.

While the salted fish rests, peel the daikon and carrot, and cut them, *rangiri*-style (see page 28), into 1-inch pieces. If you are using broccoli, cut it into small flowerets. Put the daikon and carrot into a medium pot, and add water to cover them by 1 inch. Bring the mixture to a boil, and cook over medium heat for 2 minutes. If you are using broccoli, parboil it for 1 minute. Drain the vegetables, and set them aside.

In a saucepan of boiling water, blanch the julienned ginger. Drain the ginger, cool it under cold running water, and wipe it dry with a paper towel. Set it aside.

Rinse the fish gently under cold running water to remove the salt and exuded liquid. Bring a medium pot of water to a boil. Place two or three fish pieces at a time in a small colander, and blanch the fish by lowering the colander into the boiling water. When the fish turns white, remove the colander from the water, and rinse the fish gently to remove any foreign matter.

In a medium pot combine the fish, *sake*, *kombu*, and raw ginger slices, and add water to cover the fish by 1 inch. Bring the mixture to a gentle boil over medium heat. Turn the heat to low, and cook, uncovered, for 10 minutes.

Carefully remove the fish pieces from the cooking liquid, set them aside on a plate, and cover them with plastic wrap. Remove the *kombu* from the pot, and discard it.

Add the daikon and carrot to the pot, cover the pot with a drop lid (see page 26), and cook, covered, until the vegetables are soft, about 15 to 20 minutes. Add the tamari and *komezu.* If you are using broccoli, add it after the tamari and *komezu,* and heat the broccoli just until it is warm. If you won't be serving the soup until later in the day, let it cool, and refrigerate it and the fish separately.

Immediately before serving time, heat the pot of soup, return the fish to it, and add the coriander. Serve the soup garnished with the blended julienned ginger.

• *Yields 3 to 4 servings*

KURIMU KOROKKE

Creamy Croquettes

The use of béchamel sauce in this preparation clearly signals the French origin of this "Japanized" dish. Besides béchamel sauce, crabmeat and canned corn are the main constituents of these croquettes, although my mother often substituted canned salmon or chopped hard-boiled egg for the corn. The mixture is shaped into small barrel forms and then fried crisp with a coating of *panko* breadcrumbs. Creamy croquettes are usually accompanied by shredded cabbage, potato salad, sliced tomato and cucumber, and, on the side, *tonkatsu* sauce or ketchup. Make smaller croquettes as a delicious salad ingredient or appetizer.

$^{1}/_{4}$ *cup butter*

1 medium onion, minced

$^{3}/_{4}$ *cup all-purpose flour, plus some for dusting hands*

2 cups whole milk

7 ounces crabmeat, or flaked salmon

7 ounces canned sweet corn, drained

Salt and ground black pepper to taste

3 eggs, beaten

2 cups panko *breadcrumbs (see page 386)*

Vegetable oil, for deep-frying

Tonkatsu *sauce (page 94), or tomato ketchup*

Assorted salad greens

In a skillet, heat the butter until it is hot but not smoking. Add the onion, and cook it over medium-low heat, stirring, for 5 minutes.

Add $1/4$ cup of the flour, and cook for 5 minutes, stirring.

Stir in the milk little by little, and cook until the mixture is smooth and thickened. Add the crabmeat or salmon and sweet corn, and mix. Stir in the salt and pepper. Spread the mixture on a baking sheet, and let it cool.

Refrigerate the cooled mixture, covered with plastic wrap, for 1 hour. Chilling makes the mixture firm and easy to shape.

Put some flour into a small bowl. Dust your palms with some of the flour, and pick up $1/3$ cup portion of the mixture in a large spoon. Drop the mixture into a floured hand, and shape the mixture into a small barrel. Use the rest of the mixture to make about fourteen more barrels, dusting your palms with flour between barrels. At this point you can refrigerate the barrels, covered, to cook later in the day.

Put the beaten eggs, remaining $1/2$ cup flour, and the breadcrumbs into three separate bowls. If the breadcrumbs are large, crumble them in your palms. Dust each barrel once more with flour, dip it into the egg, and coat it with breadcrumbs. At this point you can freeze the croquettes for later use.

In a skillet, heat 2 inches vegetable oil to 360 to 370 degrees F. Cook the barrels, several at a time, until they are golden and crisp. (If the oil isn't hot enough, the barrels will burst and absorb excess oil. Properly cooked croquettes are very crisp outside and tender and juicy inside.) Frozen barrels should be cooked straight from the freezer without thawing first.

Serve the croquettes on a bed of salad greens with *tonkatsu* sauce or tomato ketchup in a saucer on the side.

• *Yields about 15 croquettes, or 4 servings as a main dish*

EEL BURGER

Unagi Bagaa

Let's have a change from hamburger! Why not prepare burgers with *unagi no kabayaki,* grilled and flavored eel? The prepared eel is sold at every Japanese store. Look for it in the freezer or refrigerator case. Chop the eel, mix it with onion and *panko* breadcrumbs, shape the mixture into burgers, and cook them in a skillet. Very simple, I guarantee. Serve the burgers in buns with two sauces, *tonkatsu* and mayonnaise sauce.

Children will love these burgers, but it may be best to tell them what they have eaten only after they have devoured it.

> 3 to 4 tablespoons vegetable oil
> 1 cup minced onion
> 1 unagi no kabayaki (grilled, flavored eel,
>   about 10 ounces)
> 1 egg
> 1 cup panko breadcrumbs (see page 386)
> ¹/₄ cup all-purpose flour
> 4 hamburger buns, cut into halves and toasted,
>   cut side up, in the oven
> Butter
> 2 cups shredded lettuce
> 1 Japanese or salad cucumber, cut into 2-inch lengths,
>   then sliced thin lenghwise
> 1 small tomato, cut into thin disks
> Tonkatsu sauce (page 94)
> Mayonnaise sauce (page 387)
> Pickled cucumber slices

In a skillet, heat 2 tablespoons of the vegetable oil. Cook the onion over low heat until it is soft, about 5 minutes.

While the onion cooks, pull off and discard the eel skin. Cut the meat into small pieces. Add the eel to the skillet, and cook for 3 minutes.

Transfer the eel and onion to a bowl, add the egg and breadcrumbs, and mix. Shape the mixture into four flat patties. Dredge the patties in the flour, and pat them to remove excess flour.

Clean the skillet in which you cooked the onion and eel. Heat the skillet, and add 1 to 2 tablespoons oil. Cook the patties over medium-low heat, turning once, until both sides are golden.

Butter the hamburger buns. Place some shredded lettuce, cucumber, and tomato on the bottom part of each bun. Apply 1 to 2 tablespoons mayonnaise sauce over the vegetables, place the eel patty on top of the mayonnaise sauce, and top it with 1 to 2 tablespoons *tonkatsu* sauce. Cover with the top part of the bun.

Serve the eel burgers with cucumber pickles.

• *Yields 2 to 4 servings*

FRIED GINGER-FLAVORED MACKEREL

Saba no Tatsuta-age

In this preparation, mackerel is marinated in a mixture of *shoyu* (soy sauce) and ginger, coated with potato starch, and cooked in oil. The mackerel can be substituted with shrimp, tuna, salmon, or cod. Only a small mouth freshener, such as sweet pickled ginger, need accompany the dish. Or serve the fish with salad greens.

3 tablespoons shoyu *(soy sauce)*
1 tablespoon sake *(rice wine)*
1 tablespoon mirin *(sweet cooking wine)*
2 tablespoons minced shiso, preferably, or parsley
1 tablespoon grated ginger
1 pound mackerel fillets, cut into 2-inch-square pieces,
    skin attached
¹/₃ cup potato starch
Vegetable oil, for frying
Mixed salad greens
Shoga amazu-zuke *(sweet pickled ginger,*
    page 292)

In a bowl, combine the *shoyu*, *sake*, *mirin*, shiso, and ginger. Marinate the fish in this mixture for 20 minutes.

Drain the fish, discarding the marinade. Wipe the fish with a paper towel, and lightly coat each piece with potato starch. Let the fish stand for 2 minutes.

Heat $1\frac{1}{2}$ inches vegetable oil in a deep skillet to 340 degrees F. Fry the fish, several pieces at a time, until they are slightly golden and cooked through. Drain them on a rack.

Serve the fish on top of the salad greens, accompanied by sweet pickled ginger.

• *Yields 2 to 3 servings*

DUCK TERIYAKI

Kamo no Teriyaki

In this preparation, duck is cooked in Japanese broth with a little added orange juice. Serve the duck with plain cooked white or brown rice, which will soak up all the delicious broth left on the plates.

> *2 medium duck breast halves (preferably Magret,*
> *a very meaty variety), about 12 ounces each*
> *1 naganegi long onion, preferably, or 5 scallions, white*
> *part only, julienned in 2¹/₂-inch lengths and*
> *soaked in ice water for 20 minutes*
> *²/₃ cup sake (rice wine)*
> *3 tablespoons mirin (sweet cooking wine)*
> *2 tablespoons sugar*
> *3 tablespoons shoyu (soy sauce)*
> *¹/₂ cup fresh-squeezed orange juice*
> *¹/₂ tablespoon tamari, to taste*
> *Komezu (rice vinegar) or balsamic vinegar, to taste*
> *Plain cooked white or brown rice*

Remove any protruding skin from the duck. Cut off half of the fat attached to the flesh. Make very shallow checkerboard cuts on the fat side.

Drain the long onion or scallion pieces, and wipe them dry with a paper towel. Set them aside.

Have a medium pot of boiling water at hand. Heat a large skillet over moderate heat until hot but not smoking. Put the duck into the skillet fat side down, and cook the duck until the bottom is golden. Turn the duck over, and cook the flesh side until golden.

Remove the duck from the skillet, and plunge it into boiling water. Immediately remove the duck from the water, and wipe it dry with paper towels. This process removes excess oil from the duck skin.

Clean the skillet with hot water, and wipe it dry with a paper towel. Return the duck to the skillet skin side down, and add the *sake*, *mirin* and sugar. The duck should be barely covered with liquid. If necessary, add water to the skillet. Bring the mixture to a boil over medium heat. Reduce the heat to medium-low, and cook, covered with a drop lid (see page 26), for 5 minutes.

Add the *shoyu*, and cook, uncovered, until the simmering broth reduces to three-quarters of its original volume. Check for doneness by pressing the meat with your fingers. When it is resilient but still tender inside, remove the duck from the skillet. Duck meat can be eaten when it is still pink, so do not overcook it.

Transfer the duck to a platter, and cover it with aluminum foil to keep it warm. Increase the heat, add the orange juice to the skillet, and cook the mixture until it is thickened. Check the flavor, and add tamari and *komezu* or balsamic vinegar to taste.

Return the duck to the skillet, and baste the duck with the cooking broth. Remove the skillet from the heat, and let the duck stand in the broth for 10 minutes.

Cut the duck into $3/16$-inch slices. Arrange the slices on individual dinner plates with plain cooked white or brown rice on the side. Pour some of the cooking broth over each serving, and garnish with the long onion or scallion.

• *Yields 2 to 3 servings*

DUCK PREPARED IN KAGA STYLE

Kamo no Jibuni

My mother learned to make this dish while we lived in Kanazawa City, Ishikawa Prefecture, a region known as Kaga during the Tokugawa shogunate (1600 to 1868). The city is often called Little Kyoto, because it is one of the most culturally refined and sophisticated cities in Japan, second only to Kyoto, the acknowledged center of Japanese culture. Over the centuries, Kanazawa's proximity to the Korean Peninsula and China has enriched the city's cuisine and led to the creation of many new dishes.

Kamo no jibuni is traditionally made with wild duck. The duck is sliced thin, coated with a protective layer of flour, and parboiled in a richly flavored stock. This recipe includes another step: I sear the skin, to remove excess fat, add a caramelized color, and give a better flavor to the finished dish. This is a delicious way to enjoy duck.

> *2 cups* dashi *(fish stock)*
> *1 cup* sake *(rice wine)*
> *1 cup* mirin *(sweet cooking wine)*
> *¹/₂ cup* shoyu *(soy sauce)*
> *2 to 3 tablespoons sugar*
> *3 duck breast halves, with skin*
> *¹/₂ cup bread flour*
> *¹/₂ cup buckwheat flour, preferably,*
> *   or all-purpose flour*
> *2* naganegi *long onions, preferably, or young,*
> *   thin leeks*
> *Wasabi*
> *18 carrot slices, cut into floral shapes (see page 26)*
> *   and parboiled for 1 minute*

In a pot, combine the *dashi, sake*, *mirin*, *shoyu*, and sugar. Bring the mixture to a boil, reduce the heat to low, and simmer for 2 minutes. Remove the pot from the heat.

Cut off the excess skin and fat from the duck, and reserve the skin and fat. Heat a skillet until very hot, and cook the duck, skin side down, until golden. Do not turn the pieces over.

Remove the duck from the skillet, and put it in ice cold water to cool. Quickly remove it from the water and wipe it dry with a paper towel. Cut each breast half diagonally into slices a little less than $1/4$ inch thick. Make tiny, shallow cuts along the border between the fat and meat. This will prevent the skin from shrinking in later cooking.

In a bowl, combine the bread flour and buckwheat flour. Coat the duck slices with the flour mixture, pat gently to remove excess flour, and let the slices stand at room temperature for 20 minutes, or in the refrigerator, covered, for several hours. Reserve the remaining flour mixture.

Cut the white parts of the long onions or leeks into $1^1/2$-inch lengths diagonally. Reserve the green parts.

Add the duck skin and the green parts of the long onions or leeks to the prepared broth, and bring the broth to a boil over medium heat. Remove the onions or leeks and the duck skin. Add the white parts of the onions or leeks to the broth.

Coat the duck slices again with the flour mixture, add them to the broth, and cook until the duck is done, about 2 minutes.

Serve the duck in individual shallow soup bowls with the long onions or leeks and carrots alongside, $1/4$ teaspoon wasabi on top, and a little broth poured over the duck.

• *Yields 4 servings*

Yakitori: Chicken on Skewers

Yakitori is a dish of chicken cut into bite-sized pieces, threaded on skewers, and cooked over a charcoal fire. During the cooking, the chicken is simply salted or is basted with a sweet basting sauce, depending on the part of the chicken being cooked and on the preference of each diner. The word *yakitori* is also used to refer to all the skewered and grilled foods served in a *yakitori* restaurant, *yakitori-ya*. These casual, small specialty restaurants are found all across Japan. In them, customers sit at a long counter in front of the chef and order beer or *sake* (rice wine) to accompany the dishes. It is great fun to observe every one of the chef's movements while sipping your drink. He adjusts the fire; salts the chicken; grills it, periodically turning the skewer; and bastes the meat with a glossy sauce. He also grills seasonal vegetables, shrimp, and other foods in a similar fashion to make the dinner complete.

Purchase chemical-free, free-range chicken and use your own grill to enjoy the *yakitori* experience at home.

BASTING SAUCE FOR *YAKITORI*

Yakitori: Tare

Each *yakitori* restaurant in Japan boasts of its own delicious basting sauce, *tare*. The exact ingredients and preparation methods are kept secret by every chef. But *tare* is always a mixture of *sake* (rice wine), *mirin* (sweet cooking wine), and *shoyu* (soy sauce). What makes *tare* so tasty is the way it is treated. During cooking, the grilled chicken on the skewer is dipped into the *tare* pot. The *tare* thereby acquires some chicken flavor every time a skewer is dipped into it. This continuously improves the flavor of the *tare*. Some restaurants claim that they have been using the same *tare* base for ten years. This recipe produces a delicious *tare* without requiring that you be in the *yakitori* business for a decade.

Tasty grilled or broiled chicken wings are a wonderful by-product of *tare* making. Do not throw them away, but serve them as a snack with a glass of beer or *sake*. Delicious!

> *8 chicken wings*
> *³/₄ cup* sake *(rice wine)*
> *1¹/₃ cups* mirin *(sweet cooking wine)*
> *3 tablespoons sugar*
> *1¹/₃ cups* shoyu *(soy sauce)*

In a broiler or on a grill, cook the chicken wings until they are charred over about half their surfaces.

In a medium pot, bring the *sake* and *mirin* to a boil over high heat. Reduce the heat to medium, add the sugar, and cook until the sugar is dissolved, stirring. Add the *shoyu* and chicken wings, and bring the mixture to a boil. Cook over low heat for 30 minutes. At the end of the cooking, the sauce will be thick and glossy.

Strain the sauce through a strainer lined with cotton cloth, reserving the chicken wings. Let the sauce cool to room temperature, then refrigerate it for as long as a month.

Reheat the *tare* before using it, and once every week between uses.

* *Yields about ¹/₂ cup sauce*

CHICKEN THIGH OR BREAST
WITH LONG ONION ON SKEWERS

Yakitori: Negima

Negima is one of the most representative and popular *yakitori* dishes. Pieces of chicken thigh or breast are placed alternately on a skewer with sections of long onion. The meat and onion are simply salted or are dipped in *tare* during the grilling.

If you're using only salt to flavor the chicken, apply it before cooking, not during cooking or afterward.

Chicken cooked with its skin is juicier and tastier, but you can remove the skin if you prefer.

> *1 chicken thigh, boned, with or without skin attached*
> *1 chicken breast, boned, with or without skin attached*
> *4 naganegi long onions, preferably, or young, thin*
> *leeks, white parts only*
> *Tare basting sauce (page 405)*

Soak 12 bamboo skewers in water for at least 1 hour.

Cut the chicken thigh and breast into small pieces, about 1 by $1^1/_4$ inches. Cut the white part of each long onion or leek into $1^1/_4$-inch lengths. Thread two pieces of chicken and three pieces of long onion or leek alternately on each skewer. When using chicken with skin, fold in the edges of the skin, and tuck them between the chicken meat and the long onion or leek to prevent the skin from burning.

Heat a grill or broiler until hot. Cook the skewered chicken and long onion or leek for 4 minutes, turning the skewers several times. Remove the chicken from the heat, and, with a pastry brush, baste it with *tare*.

Return the chicken to the heat, and cook for 2 minutes, turning the skewers several times. Remove the chicken from the heat, and baste again.

Return the chicken to the heat, and cook it for 2 minutes, turning it. Remove the chicken from the heat, baste it once more, and serve it hot.

• *Yields 4 servings*

CHICKEN BREAST FILLETS ON SKEWERS WITH PICKLED PLUM AND SHISO

Yakitori: Sasami no Ume-shiso

Sasami, chicken breast fillets, are the leanest part of a chicken, the fine-grained, delicate meat of the chicken breast. When *sasami* are really fresh they may be eaten raw as sashimi, and they are served in this fashion at restaurants in Japan. Since *sasami* have such a delicate flavor, they are basted with only a small quantity of condiments, such as *umeboshi* (pickled plum) or wasabi. Do not overcook *sasami*; they dry out easily.

> 4 *chicken breast fillets (see page 205)*
> 1 umeboshi *(pickled plum), pitted and chopped*
> 2 tablespoons sake *(rice wine)*
> 1 tablespoon mirin *(sweet cooking wine)*
> 4 shiso leaves, julienned

Soak four bamboo skewers in water for at least 1 hour.

Remove the white, stringlike tendon from each chicken breast fillet. Make a long cut on one side of each fillet. Run a knife deeper into the fillet, from the top to the bottom, to make a long pocket. Do not cut through to the other side of the fillet.

In a small cup, mix the pickled plum, *sake*, and *mirin*. Apply this paste in a thin layer to one side of the inside pocket of each fillet. Scatter shiso on top of the paste. Close the open edge of each breast fillet with a bamboo skewer.

Heat a grill or broiler. Salt the outside of the fillets liberally on both sides, and cook the chicken on the grill or in the broiler, turning the skewers several times, until the chicken is cooked through, about 8 minutes. Serve the chicken hot.

• *Yields 4 servings*

MISO-MARINATED CHICKEN BREAST FILLETS ON SKEWERS

Yakitori: Sasami no Misozuke-yaki

In this variant of *yakitori*, chicken breast fillets are briefly marinated in miso before they are grilled or broiled.

> *3¹/₂ ounces* Saikyo miso *(sweet white miso)*
> *3 to 4 tablespoons* mirin *(sweet cooking wine)*
> *1 teaspoon* shoyu *(soy sauce)*
> *4 chicken breast fillets (see page 205)*
> Sansho *pepper*

Soak four bamboo skewers in water for at least 1 hour.

In a small bowl, combine the miso, *mirin,* and *shoyu*. Add the chicken breast fillets, and marinate them for 3 hours.

Remove the fillets from the marinade, and wipe them with a paper towel to remove excess marinade. Thread each breast fillet onto a bamboo skewer.

Heat a grill or broiler. Cook the breast fillets, turning several times, until done, about 8 minutes. Serve them sprinkled with *sansho* pepper.

• *Yields 4 servings*

CHICKEN LIVERS ON SKEWERS

Yakitori: Rebaa

Juicy, *tare*-marinated chicken livers are a real treat as part of a *yakitori* dinner. Use the freshest livers, and do not overcook them.

> *1 pound chicken livers, cut into 1¹/₂-inch pieces*
> Tare *sauce (page 405)*
> Sansho *pepper*

Soak five bamboo skewers in water for at least 1 hour.

Thread three to five pieces of liver onto each skewer. Liver is soft and fragile, so do not squeeze or push too hard, and make sure that the skewer goes through the center of each piece of liver.

Heat a grill or broiler. Cook the liver for about 2 minutes, and then turn the skewers, and cook the other side until the liver is almost done, about 5 to 6 minutes.

Remove the livers from the heat, and, with a pastry brush, baste them with the *tare*. Return the livers to the heat, and dry their surfaces.

Remove the livers from the heat, baste them again with *tare*, and return them to the heat.

When their surfaces are dry, remove the livers from the heat, baste them once more with *tare*, and sprinkle them with *sansho* pepper. Serve the livers hot.

• *Yields 2 to 3 servings*

CHICKEN WINGS ON SKEWERS

Yakitori: Tebasaki

The part of the wing used in this preparation is the second joint of the chicken wing, called *tebasaki*. Use the first joint and the end joint, in chicken stock preparation.

Tebasaki is delicious simply cooked with salt.

> *Second joints (the parts with 2 bones) of*
> *8 chicken wings*
> *Sea salt*
> *1* yuzu *citron or lime, cut into wedges*

Soak four bamboo skewers in water for at least 1 hour. Heat a grill or broiler.

Lay the wing joints flat on the cutting board, and slit each of them, running a small knife along first the thin bone and then the thick bone. Insert the knife under the thin bone, and remove it. Leave the thick bone in place. Open out the meat on the thick bone butterfly fashion, to make a flat piece. Remove any excess skin or fat from the chicken.

Thread two wings on each skewer, running the skewer between the thick bone and the skin. Salt the chicken liberally on both sides, and cook it on the grill or in the broiler until golden, 8 minutes.

Serve the hot chicken wings with *yuzu* or lime wedges.

• *Yields 4 servings*

GRILLED OR BROILED GOLDEN CHICKEN DUMPLINGS

Yakitori: Tori no Tsukune

Chicken dumplings are a popular grilled item at *yakitori* restaurants. The dumplings are made from ground chicken, shaped into small balls, threaded on bamboo skewers, and then grilled. During the cooking, the meat is basted with sweet *tare* sauce. The preferred spice for the dumplings is *sansho* pepper, which provides a refreshing sharp, mintlike flavor to complement the sweet, juicy chicken.

> *7 ounces skinned and boned chicken thighs*
> *7 ounces skinned and boned chicken breasts*
> *$^1/_2$ teaspoon salt*
> *$^1/_2$ teaspoon fresh-ground black pepper*
> *$^1/_2$ naganegi long onion or 3 scallions, both green
>   and white parts, minced*
> *1 teaspoon peeled, finely grated ginger*
> *1 egg white, lightly beaten*
> *2 teaspoons sesame oil*
> *2 to 3 tablespoons vegetable oil*
> Sansho *pepper*
> Tare *sauce (page 405)*

Soak six bamboo skewers in water for at least 1 hour.

Chop the chicken to a paste with a heavy-duty knife or a food processor. Transfer the chicken to a medium bowl, and add the salt. Squeeze the mixture continuously with your hands until it becomes sticky and pale pink in color. One at a time, add the black pepper, minced long onion or scallions, grated ginger, and egg white, while continuing to squeeze the mixture. Add the sesame oil, and mix.

Lightly grease a large pan. Grease your hands with a little vegetable oil, and form the chicken mixture into 12 balls, each about $1^{1}/_{2}$ inches in diameter. Press the center of each ball with your thumb to make a shallow depression, which will facilitate even and quicker cooking. Place the balls on the greased pan.

Heat a large skillet over medium-high heat until hot. Thinly coat the bottom of the skillet with vegetable oil. In several batches, cook the dumplings over medium-low heat, turning them, until they are white and firm all over, 1 to 2 minutes.

Transfer the dumplings to a paper towel, and let them stand for 10 minutes. The dumplings can be made to this point in the morning for use later in the day. Refrigerate them if you will be finishing the cooking later. Remove the dumplings from the refrigerator 20 minutes before cooking them further.

Heat a broiler or grill. Thread two to three dumplings together on each skewer. Broil or grill the dumplings $2^{1}/_{2}$ inches from the heat source, turning them once, until they are golden on both sides, about 4 minutes.

Remove the dumplings from the broiler or grill, and dip them in the *tare* sauce. Shake off the excess sauce, and return the dumplings to the broiler or grill.

Cook the dumplings until they are dry, about 1 to 2 minutes. Repeat the basting and drying process, and then remove the dumplings from the heat and baste them once more.

Serve the hot dumplings on the skewers, sprinkled with *sansho* pepper.

• *Yields 4 servings as an appetizer or 2 servings as a light main dish*

PAN-FRIED FLAVORED CHICKEN

Tori no Usugiriyaki

This is a very quick, delicious dish of thin-sliced chicken, briefly marinated and then pan-fried. Served here with parboiled spinach and plain cooked rice, the chicken also makes a good salad topping.

> *1 pound boned and skinned chicken thighs or breasts*
> *3 tablespoons white sesame seeds, toasted (page 100)*
> *¼ cup minced* naganegi *long onion, or scallions*
> *2 garlic cloves, minced*
> *3 tablespoons* shoyu *(soy sauce)*
> *1 tablespoon honey*
> *Fresh-ground black pepper*
> *2 tablespoons sesame oil*
> *4 to 6 tablespoons vegetable oil*
> *10 ounces spinach or soybean or mung-bean sprouts,*
> *cooked in boiling water for 1 minute,*
> *and drained*

Cut the chicken thigh or breast diagonally into ½-inch-wide slices. In a *suribachi* or other mortar, roughly crush the sesame seeds.

In a bowl, combine the sesame seeds, long onion or scallion, garlic, *shoyu*, honey, black pepper, and sesame oil. Add the chicken, and marinate it for 20 minutes.

Heat a skillet until hot, and add 2 tablespoons of the vegetable oil. When the oil is hot, reduce the heat to medium-low, add several slices of chicken, and cook them until they are golden on both sides and cooked through, 2 to 3 minutes. Cook the rest of the chicken in the same way, adding oil to the skillet as necessary. Keep the chicken warm while you cook the spinach or lettuce.

Rinse the skillet with hot water, wipe it with a paper towel, and place the skillet over medium heat. Add 1 tablespoon vegetable oil. When the oil is hot, add the spinach or sprouts, and cook for 1 minute, stirring.

Serve the chicken with the spinach or lettuce, accompanied by plain cooked white or brown rice.

• *Yields 3 to 4 servings*

CHICKEN TERIYAKI WITH ORANGE

Tori no Teriyaki

Chicken teriyaki is one of the most popular dishes on the menus of Japanese restaurants outside of Japan. In this preparation, I add orange juice to traditional teriyaki sauce. I serve the chicken in a nontraditional way, with mashed sweet potatoes and braised Chinese cabbage and long onion or leek.

¹/₄ cup fresh-squeezed orange juice
¹/₂ recipe teriyaki no tare (teriyaki sauce, page 77),
     cooked with 2 cloves added
2 boned and skinned chicken breasts
2 skinned chicken thighs, with bones attached
Salt and fresh-ground black pepper
3 tablespoons vegetable oil
2 cups chicken stock
1 naganegi long onion or leek, cut into 2-inch lengths
8 Chinese cabbage leaves, cut into 2-inch strips
1 large orange, peeled and sectioned (remove all
     membranes and white, inner rind)

Add the orange juice to the teriyaki sauce, and simmer the sauce for 10 minutes. Set it aside.

With a toothpick or sharp steel skewer, prick the chicken breasts and thighs all over. Salt and pepper the chicken.

Heat a large skillet over medium heat, and add the vegetable oil. When the oil is hot, add the chicken to the skillet. Cook the chicken until it is golden on the bottom. Reduce the heat to low, turn over the chicken, and cover the skillet with a lid. Cook the chicken until it is cooked through. The total cooking time for the breasts should be about 12 to 15 minutes, for the thighs about 20 minutes. Transfer the chicken to a large platter, and cover it with aluminum foil.

Rinse the skillet with hot water, and wipe it with a paper towel. Place the skillet over medium heat. Add the teriyaki sauce to the skillet, and then add the chicken. Cook the chicken for 1 to 2 minutes, or until it is well coated with the sauce, using a spoon to baste the chicken frequently.

While the chicken cooks, bring the chicken stock to a boil in a medium pot. Add the long onion or leek and the Chinese cabbage, and cook over low heat, covered, for 15 minutes.

Drain the vegetables well, reserving the stock for another use. Serve the chicken, accompanied by the orange sections and simmered vegetables, with the remaining teriyaki sauce from the skillet poured over the chicken.

• *Yields 4 servings*

CHICKEN, CASHEWS, AND MISO IN A WOK

Tori to Kashunattsu no Miso Itame

This recipe is inspired by the popular Thai and Chinese chicken-and-cashew or chicken-and-peanut preparations. Without using bottled oyster sauce, which is usually full of artificial ingredients, I can make a similar dish with healthy ingredients and great taste. Serve the dish with plain cooked white or brown rice.

10¹/₂ ounces boned and skinned chicken breasts,
cut into 1-inch cubes
Pinch of salt
4 tablespoons sake (rice wine)
1 egg white
2 teaspoons potato starch or cornstarch
1 teaspoon sesame oil
2 tablespoons akamiso (brown miso)
3 tablespoons sugar
2 to 3 tablespoons vegetable oil
4 to 5 akatogarashi or other small dried
red chile peppers
1 tablespoon minced garlic
3 ounces (¹/₂ medium) onion, cut into
³/₈-inch-thick wedges
3 scallions, both green and white parts,
cut into 1-inch lengths
1 cup raw cashew nuts
About 2 teaspoons tamari
Plain cooked white or brown rice

In a medium bowl, toss the chicken with the salt and 1 tablespoon of the *sake*. Add the egg white, potato starch or cornstarch, and sesame oil one at a time, vigorously tossing the mixture with your hands between additions. Refrigerate the chicken, covered, for 20 minutes.

In a small cup, combine the miso, sugar, and the remaining 3 tablespoons *sake*.

Bring a medium pot of water to a boil over high heat. Drop the chilled chicken into the boiling water. Stir with cooking chopsticks to separate the pieces. Cook the chicken until the outside of each piece turns white. Drain the chicken, discarding the water, and set the chicken aside.

Heat a wok or large skillet over medium-high heat. Add the vegetable oil and, when it is hot, the chile peppers. Stir-fry until their skins become dark, about 5 seconds.

Add the garlic, lift the wok or skillet away from the heat, and stir-fry for 20 seconds. Add the chicken, and stir-fry over high heat for 1 to 2 minutes.

Add the onion, and cook for 30 seconds, tossing vigorously. Add the scallions, and give a few more tosses.

Add the miso mixture, and stir-fry for 1 minute. Add the cashew nuts, and stir-fry for 1 to 2 minutes more. Season the mixture to taste with tamari.

Serve the chicken and cashew nuts with plain cooked white or brown rice on the side.

• *Yields 3 to 4 servings*

CHICKEN IN SPICY VINEGAR MARINADE

Tori Namban-zuke

Elsewhere in the book you may have found the recipe for salmon *namban-zuke*. Here is another popular *namban-zuke* preparation. In this treat, cooked chicken is marinated overnight in sweet chile-flavored, vinegar-based *namban* sauce. In the traditional way, the marinated and sliced chicken is served cold with long green onion—an ideal summertime platter. You can instead serve the chicken as a salad topping or with mixed grilled vegetables. Reheated, the chicken also tastes delightful. Serve it with fried potatoes and smooth French-style mustard.

> 2 boned chicken thighs, with or without skin
> One 2-inch square kombu (kelp), soaked in 1 cup
>   water 2 hours
> 1 cup komezu (rice vinegar)
> ²/₃ cup sugar
> ¹/₂ cup shoyu (soy sauce)
> 3 akatogarashi or other small dried red chile peppers,
>   seeded and sliced into thin rings, or ¹/₄ to
>   ¹/₂ teaspoon red chile pepper flakes
> 2 tablespoons vegetable oil
> 2 naganegi long onions, or young, thin leeks,
>   white parts only

If you are using chicken with its skin, prick the skin all over with a sharp steel skewer or toothpick.

Remove the *kombu* from its soaking liquid. Discard the *kombu*. In a saucepan, bring the *kombu* stock, *komezu*, sugar, and *shoyu* to a gentle simmer, stirring. When the sugar is dissolved, remove the saucepan from the heat, and add the chile rings or flakes. Set the saucepan aside.

Heat the oven to 350 degrees F.

In a skillet, heat the vegetable oil over medium heat. When the oil is hot, add the long onions or leeks, and cook them over medium heat until they are slightly golden. Drain the vegetables, and transfer them to the vinegar marinade.

Put the chicken into the skillet, and cook it over medium heat, turning it once, until both sides are golden.

Drain the chicken, and transfer it to an oven-proof pan. Bake the chicken for 20 to 25 minutes.

Place the baked chicken in the vinegar marinade. Let the chicken cool to room temperature, and then refrigerate it in the marinade, covered, overnight or for as long as five days.

Cut the marinated chicken into slices, and serve it cold, accompanied by the long onions or leeks and sauced with a generous amount of vinegar marinade. Or reheat the uncut chicken and the long onion or leek in a steamer or microwave, and serve them with fried potatoes or mashed sweet potatoes.

• *Yields 2 servings*

CRISP CHICKEN CUTLET

Chikin-katsu

This popular take-out dish is sold at butcher shops across Japan. The boned, skinned chicken breasts are fried in a coating of *panko* breadcrumbs, which provide a pleasant crispness and at the same time trap moisture, making the meat tender and juicy.

The cutlets are eaten with a sauce called *tonkatsu*. You can buy prepared *tonkatsu* sauce at a Japanese or Asian food store, but it is simple to make from scratch, and your homemade *tonkatsu* sauce will be free of chemical additives.

Serve the cutlets with plenty of shredded cabbage, which is rich in vitamin C. They are also delicious sandwiched between bread slices or in buns. You can substitute thick sliced ham for the chicken.

> *4 boned and skinned chicken breast halves*
> *¹/₂ cup all-purpose flour*
> *3 eggs, lightly beaten with ¹/₃ cup water*
> *2 cups* panko *breadcrumbs (see page 386)*
> *Vegetable oil, for deep-frying*
> *¹/₂ head cabbage, shredded*
> Tonkatsu *sauce (page 94)*

Make large, shallow cuts in a checkerboard pattern on each side of the chicken breasts, and gently beat them flat with a meat mallet or rolling pin. This prevents the chicken from shrinking and promotes even cooking.

Put the flour, egg-and-water mixture, and *panko* breadcrumbs into three separate bowls. Dredge the chicken with flour, and pass it through the egg mixture. Shake off the excess egg, dredge the chicken with flour again, and once more pass it through the egg. Repeating the flour-and-egg dredging process produces a very crisp coating. Cover the chicken with the *panko* breadcrumbs.

In a deep pot, heat 2 inches vegetable oil to 345 to 350 degrees F. Cook the chicken over medium-low heat for 4 minutes, and then turn over the chicken. Cook until both sides are golden, about 4 to 6 minutes more.

Drain the chicken, and serve it with abundant shredded cabbage and *tonkatsu* sauce.

- *Yields 4 servings*

JAPANESE-STYLE FRIED CHICKEN

Tori no Kara-age

Before Kentucky Fried Chicken came to Japan, we Japanese had our own popular version: *tori no kara-age,* chicken coated with potato starch and fried. My mother, who has loved chicken since her childhood, frequently cooked this dish when I was growing up. At the table during dinner, while everyone was busy eating the piping-hot fried chicken with our hands, my mother would repeat the story of how she became so attached to the flavor of chicken. Her father, who operated a rural pediatric clinic, received one or two live chickens almost every other day from patients who could not afford to pay the doctor's fee in cash. Her mother therefore prepared many chicken dishes, including this one. Rather than getting fed up with chicken, my mother grew to love it.

After my sister and I left home and my father passed away, I asked my mother whether she was still cooking her favorite fried chicken for herself at home. She told me in a very small voice that she sometimes cannot pass a Kentucky Fried Chicken store without buying a piece! I should visit her frequently and cook this chicken for her.

> 1¹/₄ *pounds chicken thighs, bones and skin attached*
> ¹/₄ *cup* shoyu *(soy sauce)*
> ¹/₄ *cup* mirin *(sweet cooking wine)*
> 2 *tablespoons* sake *(rice wine)*
> 1 *tablespoon peeled, finely grated ginger*
> 2 *garlic cloves, crushed*
> ¹/₄ *teaspoon ground chile pepper*
> ¹/₈ *teaspoon ground allspice*
> 10 *coriander seeds, toasted and crushed*
> 1 *cup potato starch or cornstarch*
> *Vegetable oil, for deep-frying*
> *Lemon wedges*

With a cleaver, hack the chicken on the bone into 2-inch pieces.

In a large bowl, combine the *shoyu, mirin, sake,* ginger, garlic, cayenne, allspice, and crushed coriander seeds. Add the chicken to the bowl, toss it with the seasonings, and let it stand for 30 minutes in the refrigerator, covered.

Remove the bowl from the refrigerator, and drain the chicken in a colander, discarding the marinade. Wipe each chicken piece with a paper towel.

Put the potato starch or cornstarch into a large pan. Add the chicken pieces to the pan, and lightly coat them with the starch. Pat each chicken piece to remove excess starch. Let the chicken stand for 3 minutes.

In a large, deep pot heat 3 inches of vegetable oil to 320 degrees F. Cook the chicken pieces in small batches, turning them once or twice, until they are slightly golden, 6 to 7 minutes. Drain the chicken on a rack.

Increase the oil temperature to 360 degrees F. Fry the chicken again, in small batches, to make the outsides crisp and golden. Drain the chicken on the rack.

Serve the chicken with lemon wedges.

- *Yields 4 servings*

CRISP ROLLED CHICKEN

Tori no Maki-age

In this preparation chicken breast is rubbed with *mamemiso* (soybean miso), rolled with crisp bacon and shiso, and then cooked to a golden hue. The cut surface of the rolls have an elegant appearance.

The chicken is traditionally served with grated daikon with drops of *shoyu* (soy sauce). Sliced, the chicken is also an ideal topping for fresh salad greens or grilled vegetables. Toss the salad greens with miso dressing (page 163).

4 boned and skinned chicken breasts, halved
Salt
12 slices bacon
2 teaspoons mamemiso (soybean miso)
2 teaspoons mirin (sweet cooking wine)
Potato starch or cornstarch
16 shiso or basil leaves
1 sheet nori, cut with scissors into 12 long strips
Vegetable oil, for deep-frying
¼ cup grated daikon
A few drops of shoyu (soy sauce)
1 lemon, cut into wedges

Beat the breast halves with a meat mallet or rolling pin, and press them into flat sheets. Salt both sides of the breast halves, and let them stand 10 minutes.

Wipe the chicken with a paper towel to remove exuded water.

In a skillet, cook the bacon over medium heat until it is crispy. In a small cup, mix the miso and *mirin*.

Spread the four chicken halves on a counter. With a spoon, spread the miso mixture over each chicken breast. With a pastry brush, sprinkle a thin layer of potato starch or cornstarch over the chicken.

Place four shiso or basil leaves on each chicken breast, and lay three bacon slices lengthwise on top. With the pastry brush, sprinkle another thin coat of potato starch or cornstarch over the chicken. Roll the chicken crosswise tightly around the stuffing. Wrap each roll with three strips of nori, being careful not to pull too tight and tear the nori. Place the rolls with the sealed ends down, so that the nori will naturally stick to itself as the juices exude. With the pastry brush, apply potato starch or cornstarch to the outside of each chicken roll.

In a pot, heat 2 inches vegetable oil to 320 degrees F, and cook the chicken rolls, turning them 90 degrees three times, until the outsides are golden, 8 minutes. At the end of the cooking, increase the oil temperature to 360 degrees F to make the outsides crisp. Remove the chicken rolls from the oil, and let them stand for 5 minutes.

Cut each chicken roll into bite-size pieces. Serve them with grated daikon, *shoyu*, and lemon wedges on the side.

• *Yields 4 to 6 servings*

CHIKUZEN-STYLE SIMMERED CHICKEN AND VEGETABLES

Tori no Chikuzen-ni

Chikuzen was the name given to present Fukuoka Prefecture on the southern island of Kyushu during the Edo Era (1600 to 1868). This is the region where Chinese, Dutch, and other European influence first reached Japan and remained strongest over the years.

In this preparation, chicken is first cooked in oil, and then simmered in a Japanese broth. Although the traditional recipe does not call for this step, I lightly flour the chicken before cooking it in oil. This gives the chicken a nice color and flavor.

The vegetables in this preparation are mostly root vegetables, which can endure long cooking without changing their color or losing their firm texture. *Sato-imo,* taro, is always included. Its primary constituent, starch, gives the cooked broth a pleasant, thick texture. Taro appears in the market from autumn through winter at Japanese and other Asian food stores.

Instead of using mostly root vegetables, you can substitute such vegetables as broccoli, cauliflower, and asparagus. When using these vegetables, cut them up into small pieces, parboil them in water, and add them to the pot at the very end of the cooking. In this way they will preserve their color and texture.

10 ounces skinned chicken thighs, with bones attached

3 tablespoons shoyu *(soy sauce)*

2 tablespoons all-purpose flour

5 ounces gobo *(burdock), cut* rangiri-*style (see page 28)*
     into 1¹/₂-inch pieces, and soaked in 2 cups
     cold water and 2 teaspoons vinegar

5 ounces lotus root, cut rangiri-*style into 1¹/₂-inch*
     pieces, and soaked with the burdock

4 medium sato-imo *(taro), cut* rangiri-*style into*
     1¹/₂-inch pieces, and soaked in cold water

1 tablespoon sesame oil

2 tablespoons vegetable oil

1 medium carrot, cut rangiri-*style into*
     1¹/₂-inch pieces

10 green beans, stemmed and cut into halves

2 tablespoons sugar

2 tablespoons mirin *(sweet cooking wine)*

Tamari *to taste*

Shichimi togarashi *(seven-spice powder) to taste*

2 tablespoons minced parsley

Plain cooked white or brown rice

With a cleaver, hack the chicken on the bone into 1¹/₂-inch pieces. In a large bowl, toss the chicken with 1 teaspoon *shoyu.* Let the chicken stand for 10 minutes.

Drain the chicken, and wipe it dry with a paper towel. In a bowl, toss the chicken with the flour. Pat the chicken to remove excess flour, and let the chicken stand for 3 minutes.

Drain the burdock, lotus root, and taro in a colander.

In a medium pot, heat the sesame and vegetable oils over medium heat. Add the chicken, and cook until all sides are lightly browned, about 3 to 4 minutes.

Remove the chicken from the pot, and add the burdock, lotus root, taro, and carrot. Cook the vegetables, stirring, until all the pieces are well coated with oil, 1 to 2 minutes.

Return the chicken to the pot, and stir the chicken with the vegetables. Add enough water to the pot to barely submerge all the ingredients. Bring the mixture to a boil over medium heat. Gently simmer the mixture, covered with a drop lid (see page 26), for 5 minutes.

Add the beans to the pot, and give several stirs. Add the sugar and *mirin*, and cook, covered with a drop lid, for 5 minutes.

Add the remaining 2 tablespoons plus 2 teaspoons *shoyu*. Cook the mixture, uncovered, for 5 minutes, stirring occasionally so that the vegetables and chicken do not stick to the bottom of the pot.

Season the mixture with tamari and seven-spice powder. Serve the dish sprinkled with parsley and accompanied by plain cooked white or brown rice.

• *Yields 3 to 4 servings*

SIMMERED AUTUMN CHICKEN AND CHESTNUTS

Tori to Kuri no Umani

When chestnuts appear in the market, I think of preparing this chicken and chestnut dish to appreciate the abundance of the season. In Japan, supermarkets sell already shelled and skinned chestnuts, ready to use. For a while after I left my parents' house, I was spoiled by using this type. One day I visited my mother and found her peeling and skinning chestnuts. On that night she prepared for me chestnut rice and a dish of chicken with chestnuts. The freshly peeled chestnuts tasted so sweet and delicious that I stopped buying the more convenient type.

Peeling chestnuts requires extra time and labor. However, once you learn the technique, this process won't overburden you. Soak the chestnuts in freshly boiled water for 20 minutes. Use a sharp, small knife to remove the hard shells. The inner skin is easily removed from soaked chestnuts, but be very careful not to cut yourself. Be sure to place the knife so that, if it slips, it moves away from your hand. I have made two trips to the hospital to repair my hand after chestnut-peeling accidents! Since then, I have learned to respect the tough chestnut skin and my sharp peeling knives.

In this preparation, chestnuts and chicken are cooked in a sweet broth flavored with *shoyu* (soy sauce). The chicken is served with broccoli, which absorbs the rich flavor from the chicken and chestnuts. Serve this dish with plain cooked white or brown rice.

20 large chestnuts, in their shells
10 ounces chicken thighs, with bones and
   skin attached
3 tablespoons sesame oil
3¹/₂ tablespoons sugar
1 cup dashi (fish stock)
2 tablespoons sake (rice wine)
1 tablespoons mirin (sweet cooking wine)
2 tablespoons shoyu (soy sauce)
A few drops of tamari
Fresh-ground black pepper to taste
1 large broccoli head, separated into small flowerets
   (reserving the stem for a later use)
1 tablespoon minced shiso, preferably, or parsley

In a medium pot, bring plenty of water to a boil. Remove the pot from the heat and add the chestnuts, and soak them for 20 minutes.

With a small, sharp knife, shell the chestnuts, and remove their thin skins. Soak the skinned chestnuts in cold water for 15 minutes. Drain the chestnuts, and set them aside.

With a cleaver, hack the chicken thighs on the bone into 2-inch pieces.

In a medium pot, heat the sesame oil. Cook the chicken several pieces at a time over medium heat, turning them, until all sides are golden.

Put all the browned chicken into the pot, and add 1¹/₂ tablespoons sugar. Cook the chicken, stirring, until the sugar caramelizes.

Add the chestnuts to the pot, and cook, stirring, until they are well coated with oil, 1 minute.

Add the *dashi, sake*, and *mirin* to the pot, and bring the mixture to a boil. Add the remaining 2 tablespoons sugar, and cook the mixture over medium-low heat, covered with a drop lid (page 26), 10 minutes, shaking the pot occasionally so that the chicken does not stick to the bottom.

Add the *shoyu*, turn the heat to medium-high, and cook, uncovered, until 80 percent of the liquid is absorbed. At the end of the cooking, add a few drops of tamari and some black pepper.

In a large pot of salted boiling water, cook the broccoli for 1 to 2 minutes. Drain the broccoli, and gently squeeze it to remove excess water.

Serve the hot chicken and broccoli side by side, garnished with shiso or parsley and accompanied by plain cooked white or brown rice or mashed potatoes.

- *Yields 3 to 4 servings*

STEAMED FLAVORED CHICKEN, SHIITAKE, AND LONG ONION

Tori, Shiitake to Negi no Mushimono

This is a very simple and quick dish that my mother used to make when she had very little time to spend in the kitchen. The preparation is adopted from the Chinese kitchen. The chicken is tossed with shiitake mushrooms, long onions, and seasonings, and steamed. The steaming process transforms these simple ingredients into a comforting, delicious chicken dish. You might add asparagus, broccoli, or carrot for additional color and flavor.

1 pound chicken thighs, with skin and bones attached
4 dried shiitake mushrooms, soaked in cold water
    for 20 minutes
1 naganegi long onion, preferably, or 5 scallions,
    cut into 1-inch lengths
2 thumb-size pieces ginger, peeled and sliced thin
1 teaspoon salt
1 1/2 teaspoons sugar
1 tablespoons shoyu (soy sauce)
2 tablespoons sake (rice wine)
2 teaspoons sesame oil
1 tablespoons potato starch or cornstarch mixed with
    1 1/2 tablespoons water
Plain cooked white or brown rice

With a cleaver, hack the chicken on the bone into 1^1/$_2$-inch cubes. If you wish, remove the skin.

Drain the mushrooms, cut away their stems, and cut each cap in half.

In a bowl, toss together all the ingredients but the rice. Refrigerate the mixture, covered with plastic wrap, for 20 minutes.

Have ready a bamboo or metal steamer with plenty of water at high steam production. Transfer the chicken mixture to a heat-proof container that can fit into the steamer. Steam the mixture for 20 minutes.

Serve the dish piping-hot with plain cooked white or brown rice.

• *Yields 2 to 3 servings*

STEAMED CHICKEN BREAST WITH GOLDEN *KIMIZU* SAUCE

Tori no Sakamushi Kimizu-zoe

Here chicken breast is placed on top of *kombu* (kelp), sprinkled with rice wine, and then steamed. This is one of the best ways to enjoy the subtle, sweet flavor of good-quality chicken. If possible, purchase free-range, chemical-free chicken for this dish. The golden yellow *kimizu* (egg-vinegar sauce) and green asparagus served with the chicken make a stunning presentation.

> 2 boned chicken breast halves, with skin attached
> Salt
> Two 5-inch squares kombu *(kelp)*
> ^{1}/$_4$ cup sake *(rice wine)*
> 1 lemon, cut into thin disks
> Kimizu *sauce (page 72)*
> A few drops of tamari
> 12 to 16 asparagus spears, tough ends and
>   scales removed

Have ready a bamboo or metal steamer with plenty of water at high steam production. Prick the chicken skin all over with a toothpick or a sharp steel skewer, and rub the chicken with salt.

In a heat-proof dish that can fit into the steamer, place the *kombu* squares. Arrange the chicken over them. Sprinkle the *sake* over the chicken, and cover the chicken with lemon slices. Steam the chicken over high heat for 12 minutes.

While the chicken cooks, make the *kimizu* sauce. Stir in the tamari, and set the sauce aside. Add the asparagus to the steamer. Steam for 3 minutes more.

Remove the chicken and asparagus from the steamer, and arrange them on individual serving plates. Serve the chicken, garnished with *kimizu* sauce.

• *Yields 2 servings*

HEARTY CHICKEN HOT POT

Tori-nabe

Sharing a large pot of chicken and vegetables cooked in broth at the table is entertaining, fun, and soul-warming. As a child I frequently quarreled with my sisters over trivial things, and we created an icy atmosphere inside the house. My mother, who did not like to see us in such a condition at the dinner table, prepared this chicken hot pot. She was clever, knowing that sharing this hearty dish melted our hostility toward each other.

Chicken hot pot differs from home to home. At my friend's house, the chicken was cooked in water with a piece of kelp and served with ponzu dressing. My mother's recipe uses a lightly flavored broth to cook the chicken. The chicken is then eaten with the broth, with a little squeeze of *yuzu* citron juice. Remaining in the pot at the end of dinner is a delicious broth, in which all the chicken and vegetables were cooked. How not to waste this? My mother added plain cooked rice to the broth and cracked in a few eggs. The rice, of course, absorbed all the good flavors.

To enjoy any hot pot dinner, you will need the following three items: (1) a *donabe* earthenware pot or *tetsunabe* iron pot (see page 9) or a medium-sized shallow enameled pot; (2) a *takujo konro,* tabletop gas stove, or another heat source that can be used at the table; and (3) propane-filled bottles or other fuel. *Donabe* and *tetsunabe* pots, tabletop stoves, and propane gas bottles are found at large Japanese supermarkets and some general Asian stores. If these items are not available, do all the cooking in the kitchen.

2 boned chicken breast halves

2 chicken thighs, with bones attached

7 ounces ground chicken

1¹/₂ teaspoons shoyu *(soy sauce)*

¹/₄ cup plus ¹/₂ teaspoon sugar

3¹/₂ tablespoons minced scallions, both green
and white parts

3 eggs

1 block firm tofu, cut in half lengthwise

2 naganegi *long onions, or young, tender leeks,*
cut into 2-inch lengths

8 fresh shiitake mushrooms, stems removed

1 bunch chrysanthemum leaves, preferably, or spinach
leaves cut into halves

One 4-inch square kombu (kelp)

3 tablespoons usukuchi shoyu *(light-colored*
soy sauce), preferably, or regular shoyu
(soy sauce)

2 tablespoons sake *(rice wine)*

2 yuzu citrons, preferably, or lemons, cut into wedges

Shichimi togarashi *(seven-spice powder)*

4 cups plain cooked white or brown rice, in a
ceramic bowl

With a cleaver, hack the breast halves and thighs into 2-inch pieces. Transfer these pieces to a platter.

In a medium bowl, combine the ground chicken, 1¹/₂ teaspoons *shoyu*, and ¹/₂ teaspoon sugar. Mix with your hands until the mixture is sticky. Add the scallions, and mix well.

Transfer the mixture to a medium serving bowl. Press the center to make a shallow depression, and drop one whole egg into the center without breaking the yolk.

Cut each half of the tofu block into eight crosswise slices. Arrange the tofu and all the vegetables—long onions, shiitake mushrooms, and chrysanthemum leaves or spinach—side by side on a large serving platter.

In a *donabe* or enameled iron pot, combine 1 quart water, the *kombu, usukuchi shoyu,* the remaining ¹/₄ cup sugar, and the *sake.*

Just before serving time, set a tabletop gas stove in the center of the dining table. Carry to the dining table two soup spoons, one soup ladle, the vegetable and chicken platter, the bowl of ground chicken, the bowl of cooked rice, two eggs in a small cup, and a jar of cold water. In the kitchen, place the earthenware pot or substitute pot over medium heat, and bring the mixture to a boil. Light the tabletop stove, and bring the hot pot to the stove flame. Call all diners to the table.

Now the cooking and eating can begin! Remove the *kombu* from the broth. Discard the *kombu*. Add some of the chicken pieces to the pot. With a spoon, break the egg yolk on top of the ground chicken, and blend the egg into the meat. Scoop a little of the ground chicken with a soup spoon, and, with the other soup spoon, shape the ground chicken into a ball and push it into the broth. Add several more balls. Add small portions of the tofu, long onions, and shiitake mushrooms, and heat until the ingredients are almost cooked through. Add a portion of the chrysanthemum leaves.

When all the ingredients are done, each diner picks some up with chopsticks, transfers the foods to his or her bowl, ladles over a little broth, squeezes on a little *yuzu* citron or lemon juice, and adds some seven-spice powder. Now, you can enjoy!

Cook another batch of chicken, chicken balls, and vegetables while you eat, and repeat the process, adding water to the pot, if necessary, until all the ingredients are cooked and eaten.

When only the cooking broth is left in the pot, add the cooked rice. It should be barely covered with broth; add extra water, if needed. Bring the mixture to a boil over medium heat. Reduce the heat to low, and cook the rice for 2 to 3 minutes.

In the small cup, break the remaining two eggs, and beat them lightly with chopsticks or a fork. Add the eggs to the pot, and cook, covered, for 2 minutes. Eat the rice with ceramic spoons or ordinary soup spoons.

• *Yields 4 servings*

PORK CUTLET
FLAVORED WITH SOYBEAN MISO

Miso-katsu

In this recipe, sliced pork is rolled with shiso leaves and sweet, rich *mamemiso* (soybean miso) sauce. The rolls are sliced and threaded on bamboo skewers, creating an elegant appearance. They are then coated with *panko* breadcrumbs and fried crisp. Serve the rolls on the skewers as an appetizer, or off the skewers on top of plain cooked rice, drizzled with *tonkatsu* sauce.

Have your butcher slice the pork for you, if possible. If you will be slicing it yourself, the task will be easier if the meat is partially frozen. Transfer the meat from the freezer to the refrigerator half a day before cutting it.

¹/₂ teaspoon salt
1 tablespoon sake (rice wine)
1 tablespoon ginger juice (see page 58)
1 pound pork shoulder, cut into twelve
        3-by-5-by-¹/₄-inch slices
2 tablespoons mamemiso (soybean miso)
2 tablespoons mirin (sweet cooking wine)
15 to 20 shiso, preferably, or basil leaves
²/₃ cup all-purpose flour
3 eggs, beaten
2 to 3 cups panko breadcrumbs (see page 386)
Vegetable oil, for frying

Lemon wedges (optional)
Plain cooked white or brown rice (optional)
Tonkatsu sauce (page 94; optional)

Soak four bamboo skewers, each about 6 inches long (you can cut longer skewers with a cleaver or kitchen scissors), in water for 30 minutes.

In a medium bowl, combine the salt, *sake*, and ginger juice. Marinate the pork in this mixture for 20 minutes.

In a small bowl, combine the miso and *mirin*, stirring with a spoon until smooth.

Spread a thin layer of the miso paste over one pork slice, and place three to four shiso or basil leaves on the paste. Cover with another pork slice, and spread a thin layer of miso paste over the top slice of pork. Roll the pork tightly into a 3-inch cylinder.

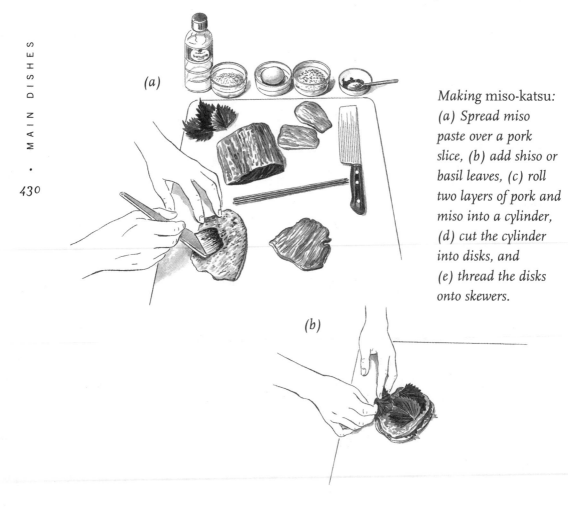

(a)

(b)

Making miso-katsu: *(a) Spread miso paste over a pork slice, (b) add shiso or basil leaves, (c) roll two layers of pork and miso into a cylinder, (d) cut the cylinder into disks, and (e) thread the disks onto skewers.*

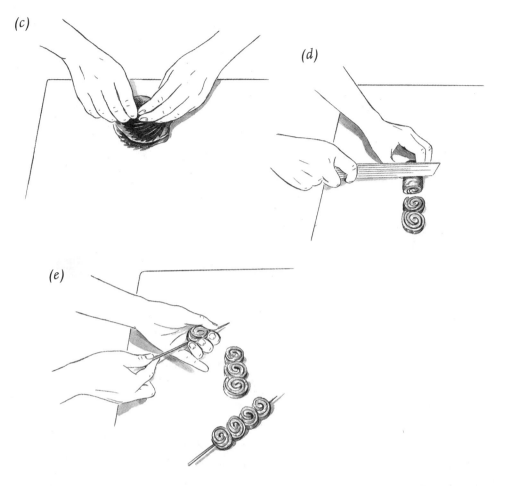

(c)

(d)

(e)

Make four or five more rolls with the remaining pork and miso paste. Cut each pork roll into four disks.

Thread three disks onto each skewer, securing the ends of the rolls with the skewer.

Put the flour, beaten eggs, and *panko* breadcrumbs into three separate pans that are long enough to hold the skewers. Dredge the skewered pork with the flour and then the egg. Dredge the pork again with the flour, then with the egg, and finally with the *panko* bread-crumbs. Gently press the rolls so that the breadcrumbs adhere well.

Heat 1¹/₂ inches oil in a wide, deep skillet to 330 degrees F. Fry the pork on the skewers over low heat, two or three at a time, until the outside is golden and cooked through, about 5 minutes. Drain the pork on a rack.

Serve the pork on the skewers with lemon wedges, or off the skewers on top of plain cooked white or brown rice and drizzled with *tonkatsu* sauce.

• *Yields 4 servings*

FRIED PORK AND LONG ONION ON SKEWERS

Kushikatsu

Kushikatsu is a variation on *tonkatsu*, fried pork cutlet. *Tonkatsu* is a very unusual name. It is a combination of the Japanese word *ton*, "pork," and a corruption of the English *cutlet*. Fried pork cutlet was born along with modern Japan when political power was returned to the Meiji emperor from the Tokugawa shogunate at the end of the nineteenth century. The Meiji government reopened the country to foreign commerce and culture after a hiatus of almost three hundred years. Suddenly the Japanese population was encouraged to adopt scientific and technological advances, medicines, and customs from the West so that Japan could catch up with the rest of the world after a long period of near total isolation. The Japanese quickly abandoned the daily wearing of the kimono for Western clothes, shoes, and hats. The taboo against eating meat was also abolished, and meat consumption was promoted. This led to the creation of many new meat dishes, among them *tonkatsu*, fried pork cutlet.

Tonkatsu is a dish of pork sliced $1/2$ inch thick, dipped in flour and beaten egg, coated with breadcrumbs, and deep-fried. The cooked meat is then cut into bite-sized pieces suitable for eating with chopsticks. *Tonkatsu* is served with a special sauce and, on the side, shredded raw cabbage. When you bite through the golden, rather thick and crispy crust, the meat inside is juicy and tender.

In this preparation I use cubes of pork instead of cutlets. I thread the pork cubes on bamboo skewers, alternating them with pieces of long onion. This is *kushikatsu*, or fried pork on skewers. It is a lighter treat on the stomach than a fried pork cutlet.

Successful preparation of *kushikatsu* depends on creating a thick, crisp, but non-oily crust that protects the meat as it cooks, keeping it tender and juicy. To accomplish this, the skewered pork and onions are dredged in flour and egg twice before being coated with breadcrumbs. The frying temperature is also important. When you first put the pork into the oil, its temperature should be around 360 degrees F. This cooks the outside firm, sealing it quickly. The rest of the frying is done at a lower temperature, around 300 degrees F. If you don't lower the temperature, the outside will be burnt while the center remains undercooked.

> 9 ounces boneless pork loin, excess fat removed,
>   cut into 12 cubes
> Salt and ground black pepper
> 9 ounces naganegi long onions, preferably,
>   or young, slender leeks, white part only
> 1/2 cup all-purpose flour
> 2 eggs, lightly beaten
> 2 cups breadcrumbs
> Vegetable oil, for deep-frying
> Tonkatsu sauce (page 94)
> 1 quart shredded cabbage

Soak six bamboo skewers, each about 6 inches long (you can cut longer skewers with a cleaver or kitchen scissors), in water for 30 minutes.

Lightly salt and pepper the pork on both sides, and let it stand for 15 minutes.

Cut the long green onion or leek into 1½-inch lengths crosswise.

Thread two pork pieces and two long onion or leek pieces on each skewer, alternating the pork and long onion or leek.

Put the flour, beaten eggs, and breadcrumbs into separate pans that are long enough to hold the skewers. One at a time, dredge each skewer of pork and long onion or leek with flour, pat to remove the excess flour, and dip the skewer into the egg. Shake off the excess egg, and return the skewer to the flour. Coat the meat and onion or leek with flour once more, and dip the skewer in the egg again. Shake off the excess egg, and dip the skewer into the breadcrumbs. Gently press the pork and long onion so that the breadcrumbs adhere well. Turn the skewer to coat the other side.

In a wide, deep skillet, heat 3 inches of vegetable oil over medium heat to 360 degrees F. Add the skewered pork and long onion to the heated oil two to three skewers at a time, depending on the size of the skillet. Cook until the crust becomes barely golden. Reduce the temperature of the oil to 300 degrees F, and cook until the crust is quite golden, about 8 minutes. Put the skewers on a rack to drain.

Serve the pork and long onion or leek on the skewers, with *tonkatsu* sauce and ample shredded cabbage.

• *Yields 2 to 3 servings*

BRAISED PORK AND CHINESE CABBAGE

Butaniku to Hakusai no Kasane-ni

When the weather becomes chillier and chillier, my family asks me to make a dish that warms the body and satisfies a winter appetite. This is one such cold-weather dish. In this preparation, leaves of Chinese cabbage are layered in a pot with pork and bacon. The mixture is cooked in chicken broth until the cabbage becomes soft and absorbs flavor from the broth. This dish proves that a very quick and simple preparation can produce a very satisfying, complete dinner. Serve the dish with plain cooked white or brown rice.

Chinese cabbage, *hakusai,* becomes sweetest in winter, especially from the end of November through February. Purchase head that are heavy for their size, unwilted and without black spots. Endive can be a good substitute for the Chinese cabbage.

If your butcher doesn't slice the pork for you, you'll have an easier time slicing it yourself if the meat is partially frozen. Freeze it overnight, and then let it stand in the refrigerator half a day before cutting it.

> *1 tablespoons* shoyu *(soy sauce)*
> *1 tablespoon* sake *(rice wine)*
> *1 teaspoon grated ginger*
> *1 teaspoon grated garlic*
> *10 ounces boneless pork loin, sliced thin*
> *1 pound Chinese cabbage leaves*
> *1 small carrot, julienned in 2-inch lengths*
> *6 slices bacon, cut into halves*
> *2 tablespoons chopped ginger*
> *1 cup chicken broth*
> *A few drops of tamari (optional)*
> *2 teaspoons potato starch or cornstarch mixed*
> *with 1 tablespoon water*
> *Fresh-ground black pepper*

In a bowl, combine the *shoyu, sake,* grated ginger, and garlic. Marinate the pork for 20 minutes.

Make several shallow, lengthwise cuts on the thick base of each cabbage leaf to keep the leaf from curling during cooking.

Divide the cabbage and carrot into four portions. Divide the pork, bacon, and chopped ginger into three portions. Place one portion each of cabbage and carrot on the bottom of a large, shallow pot. Cover with one portion each of pork, bacon, and ginger. Add another portion each of cabbage and carrot, followed by more pork, bacon, and ginger. Repeat this process once more, and then finish the layering with cabbage and carrot.

Pour in the chicken broth, cover the pot with a tight-fitting lid, and bring the mixture to a boil over medium heat. Cook the mixture for 20 to 25 minutes.

Taste, and add a few drops of tamari, if you like. Reduce the heat to low, and stir in the potato-starch or cornstarch liquid. Cook the mixture for 1 to 2 minutes, uncovered, until the broth thickens. Add a generous amount of fresh-ground black pepper.

Serve the pork on individual dinner plates, with the broth poured over and bread or plain cooked white or brown rice alongside.

• *Yields 3 to 4 servings*

BRAISED PORK CHINESE-STYLE

Buta no Kakuni

This dish, which originates in Nagasaki Prefecture on Kyushu Island, is an adaptation of a Chinese pork dish called *tonporo.* Nagasaki was the chief port city where the Japanese received ships from the outside world during the sixteenth, seventeenth, and eighteenth centuries. The city was exposed to strong culinary influence from the Chinese, Portuguese, Spanish, and Dutch. This is one of the most celebrated dishes from that period.

In the Chinese version of this dish, fatty pork belly, or flank, is first cooked in oil and then simmered in a flavored broth. Japanese cooks changed the first step from deep-frying to steaming. To steam the pork, my mother uses a large quantity of grated daikon. Because daikon is rich in digestive enzymes such as protease and diastase, two to three hours of steaming removes a substantial portion of the fat from the pork and turns the meat tender and juicy.

The ginger used in the sweet simmering broth provides a sharp flavor contrast.

3 cups peeled and grated daikon, with juice
1¹/₂ pounds unsalted pork flank
    (available from Chinese butchers)
One 2-inch piece ginger, peeled and sliced
One 4-inch piece kombu (kelp), soaked in
    1 quart water for 1 hour
¹/₂ cup sake (rice wine)
3 tablespoons mirin (sweet cooking wine)
¹/₄ cup shoyu (soy sauce)
¹/₄ cup sugar
7 ounces bunch spinach
1 tablespoon thin hot mustard paste (see page 55)

Set a bamboo or metal steamer over plenty of water in a deep pot over high heat.

Into a deep, heat-proof dish about 8 inches wide (it must fit into the steamer) put one-third of the grated daikon. Put the pork on top of the daikon, and cover the pork with the remaining daikon. Cover the container with plastic wrap, and transfer it to the hot steamer. Cook the pork over high heat for 2 hours. During the cooking, occasionally check the level of water in the pot, and add boiling water as necessary.

Steaming pork: Cover the meat with the daikon, and cover the dish with plastic wrap.

Place a bowl of lukewarm water in the sink. Remove the container of pork from the steamer, put the pork into the lukewarm water, and rinse the pork gently and thoroughly. Drain the pork, and wipe it dry with paper towels. Cut the pork into 2-inch-thick crosswise slices. At this point you can refrigerate the pork, covered, for as long as one day.

Scatter the ginger slices in a pot large enough to hold the pork in one layer. Lay the pork on the ginger slices.

Remove the *kombu* from its soaking liquid, and add the liquid to the pot, discarding the *kombu*. Add the *sake* and *mirin*. Bring the mixture to a boil over medium heat. Reduce the heat to very low, and cook at a gentle simmer, covered with a drop lid (see page 26) for 30 minutes.

Add the *shoyu*, and cook for 20 minutes, turning the pork several times for even flavoring and coloring. At this point you can refrigerate the pork, covered, for use later in the day. If you do, reheat the pork, covered, over very low heat before proceeding with the recipe.

Add the sugar to the pork, and cook, uncovered, over very low heat for 3 to 5 minutes. By this time the sauce should be quite thick. If not, remove the pork and ginger, and cook the sauce a little more to reduce it.

In a medium pot of boiling water, parboil the spinach for 1 minute. Cool the spinach in ice water, and drain it. Cut the spinach into 2-inch lengths.

Arrange the spinach on a large platter. Place the pork on top, and drizzle it with the sauce left in the pot. Garnish the dish with a little mound of mustard paste on the edge of the platter.

• *Yields 4 servings*

JAPANESE-STYLE BRAISED SPARERIBS

Supearibu no Nikomi

Spareribs are not traditionally used in Japanese cooking. However, this recipe proves that the traditional Japanese braising liquid, a combination of *sake* (rice wine), *shoyu* (soy sauce), and *komezu* (rice vinegar), turns spareribs into a mouth-watering treat. For the fullest flavor and a denser sauce, cook the spareribs early in the morning and reheat them at dinnertime.

Chopsticks are not the proper utensils for eating these spareribs. Just pick up the meat and bite into it as you would with the best of American barbecued ribs. You may need a lot of paper napkins.

1¹/₂ pounds pork spareribs

3 tablespoons shoyu *(soy sauce)*

1 teaspoon Worcestershire sauce

¹/₂ teaspoon toban jiang *(chile-bean sauce)*

1¹/₂ tablespoons honey

2 tablespoons vegetable oil

¹/₄ cup sake *(rice wine)*

2 tablespoons sugar

3 tablespoons komezu *(rice vinegar)*

1 teaspoon sesame oil

10 ounces chrysanthemum or spinach leaves

Plain cooked white or brown rice

Cut the meat into individual ribs.

In a bowl, combine 1 tablespoon of the *shoyu*, the Worcestershire sauce, the chile-bean sauce, and the honey. Marinate the spareribs in this mixture for 30 minutes.

Remove the spareribs from the marinade, and discard it.

Heat a medium skillet, and add the vegetable oil. When the oil is hot, add the spareribs. Cook them over medium heat until all sides are brown. Remove the spareribs from the skillet, and set them aside.

Into a medium pot, put the spareribs, *sake*, sugar, and ¹/₂ cup water. Bring the mixture to a boil, and cook it over low heat, covered, for 20 minutes.

Add the remaining 2 tablespoons *shoyu* and the *komezu* to the pot, and cook, uncovered, for 10 minutes, basting the spareribs several times with the cooking liquid.

In a medium pot of salted boiling water with 1 teaspoon sesame oil added, cook the chrysanthemum leaves or spinach for 1 to 2 minutes. Drain the greens, and cool them under cold running water. Roll the greens in a bamboo rolling mat, and squeeze them to remove excess water. Unroll the mat, cut off the root end, and cut the greens into 2-inch lengths. Place the spareribs on a bed of the greens, and pour the remaining cooking liquid over them. Serve the dish with plain rice.

• *Yields 4 servings*

SWEET-AND-SOUR BRAISED PORK WITH PICKLED PLUMS

Buta no Ama-umeni

Sweet-and-sour pork, a popular Chinese preparation, was long ago adopted by the Japanese kitchen. As always, this "Japanization" resulted in a dish that is quite different from the Chinese original. This sweet-and-sour pork dish is neither too sweet nor too starchy. The tartness comes from *umeboshi,* pickled Japanese green plums.

Umeboshi are available at Japanese food stores. For this recipe, choose plums that are large and soft.

> *1 pound boneless pork shoulder,*
> *   cut into 1¹/₂-inch cubes*
> *1 teaspoon salt*
> *¹/₂ teaspoon fresh-ground black pepper*
> *4 tablespoons* sake *(rice wine)*
> *1 egg white, beaten*
> *1 tablespoon potato starch or cornstarch*
> *1 large (about 14-ounce) Japanese sweet potato,*
> *   preferably, or regular sweet potato*
> *1 medium onion, cut into thin wedges*
> *1 cup vegetable oil*
> *¹/₂ cup* dashi *(fish stock)*
> *5 tablespoons sugar*
> *¹/₂ ounce (two large) pitted* umeboshi, *mashed with*
> *   the back of a spoon*
> *1¹/₂ tablespoons* shoyu *(soy sauce)*
> *1 to 2 teaspoons* komezu *(rice vinegar; optional)*
> *6 shiso leaves, minced*
> *Plain cooked white or brown rice*

Rub the pork with the salt and black pepper. Put the pork into a bowl, and toss the meat with 2 tablespoons of the *sake,* then with the egg white, and finally, with the potato starch or cornstarch. Refrigerate the pork, covered, for 30 minutes.

While the pork rests, peel the sweet potato, and cut it into 1¹/₂-inch pieces *rangiri*-style (see page 28). Soak the sweet potato in a bowl of salted water for 20 minutes.

Drain the sweet potatoes, and wipe them with a paper towel. Cut the onion into thin wedges.

In a wok or skillet, heat the vegetable oil to 330 degrees F. Cook the pork in small batches over medium-low heat until all sides are golden. Drain the pork, and set it aside.

Cook the sweet potato in the hot oil over medium-low heat until it is golden, about 5 minutes. Drain the sweet potato, and set it aside.

Into a medium pot, put the *dashi*, the remaining 2 tablespoons *sake*, and 4 tablespoons of the sugar, and bring the mixture to a boil. Add the pork, onion, and sweet potato, and cook over low heat, covered with a drop lid (see page 26), for 5 minutes.

Add the pickled plum and *shoyu*, and cook, covered, for 15 minutes, stirring gently several times. At the end of the cooking, taste the pork, and, if you like, add the remaining 1 tablespoon sugar, a little more *shoyu*, or the *komezu*. You can refrigerate the dish, covered, to reheat later in the day.

Serve the pork garnished with the shiso and accompanied by plain rice.

• *Yields 4 servings*

STEAMED PORK IN SPICY GARLIC SAUCE

Mushibuta no Shoyu Ninniku-zuke

This is another simple steamed pork dish. The steamed pork is marinated overnight in a full-flavored, spicy garlic sauce, cut into thin slices, and served with lettuce, vegetable strips, and herbs. At the table, each diner rolls some of the pork, vegetables, and herbs in a lettuce-leaf wrapper. The spicy garlic marinade is used as a sauce. The marinated pork is also delicious as a sandwich filling or noodle topping.

3 cups grated daikon
1³/₄ pounds boneless pork loin, trimmed of excess fat
³/₄ cup sake (rice wine)
1 naganegi long onion, preferably, or leek, cut in half,
    plus 1 cup julienned naganegi or tender leek
    cut into 3-inch lengths
One 1-inch piece ginger, peeled and quartered
¹/₃ cup shoyu (soy sauce)
¹/₄ cup mirin (sweet cooking wine)
1 tablespoon komezu (rice vinegar)

2 garlic cloves, crushed

¹/₂ to 1 teaspoon toban jiang (chile-bean sauce)

1 tablespoon sugar

2 teaspoons sesame oil

10 coriander seeds, toasted and roughly crushed in a
    suribachi or other mortar

12 large leaves of romaine lettuce

1 cup julienned carrot in 3-inch lengths

1 cup julienned celery in 3-inch lengths

1 cup julienned daikon in 3-inch lengths

10 shiso leaves

1 bunch coriander leaves

Set a bamboo or metal steamer basket over plenty of water in a deep pot over high heat.

In a deep heat-proof dish that can fit into the steamer, put 1 cup of the grated daikon. Spread the daikon to cover the bottom of the dish. Add the pork, and pour over ¹/₂ cup of the *sake*. Place the long onion or leek halves and the ginger on top of the pork, and cover the pork with the remaining grated daikon. Cover the dish with plastic wrap, and put it into the hot steamer.

Steam the pork over high heat for 1 hour. During the cooking, occasionally check the level of water in the pot, and add boiling water as necessary.

In a small pot, combine the remaining ¹/₄ cup *sake*, and the *shoyu*, *mirin*, *komezu*, garlic, chile-bean sauce, sugar, sesame oil, and coriander seeds. Bring the mixture almost to a boil over medium heat. Transfer the mixture to a bowl, and let the mixture cool to room temperature.

Place a medium bowl of lukewarm water in the sink. Remove the dish of pork from the steamer, transfer the pork to the lukewarm water, and rinse the pork, discarding the long onion or leek and the ginger. Wipe the pork with a paper towel, and when the pork has cooled, transfer it to the *shoyu* marinade. Marinate the pork in the refrigerator overnight.

Remove the pork from the marinade, reserving the marinade. Cut the pork into thin slices or strips.

In a small saucepan, bring the marinade to a boil. Strain it through a sieve lined with a cotton cloth.

Serve the pork with the lettuce leaves; the julienned carrot, celery, daikon, and long onion or leek; and the shiso and coriander leaves. Serve the remaining marinade in a saucer on the side.

• *Yields 4 to 6 servings*

GINGER-FLAVORED PAN-FRIED PORK

Buta no Shogayaki

Here thin-sliced pork is marinated in ginger juice and soy sauce for a very short period, and then is pan-fried. The preparation is as simple as its description. By adding condiments or spices such as garlic, black pepper, mustard paste, *mirin*, seven-spice powder, or chile-bean sauce to the marinade, you can create a variety of tasty dishes. This very popular, quick lunch dish is usually served together with a bowl of rice and a bowl of miso soup.

> *2 teaspoons ginger juice (see page 58)*
> *2 tablespoons* shoyu *(soy sauce)*
> *9 ounces pork loin, trimmed of excess fat*
> *and sliced thin*
> *1 tablespoons sesame oil*
> *2 tablespoons vegetable oil*
> *2 cups bean sprouts*
> *7 ounces Chinese chives or scallions, cut into*
> *2-inch lengths*
> *Salt to taste*
> *Plain cooked white or brown rice*

In a medium bowl, combine the ginger juice and *shoyu*. Add the pork, and marinate it for 2 minutes—no longer, or it will become too salty and tough. Drain the pork, discarding the marinade.

In a large skillet, heat the sesame oil and 1 tablespoon of the vegetable oil over medium heat. When the oil is hot, add the pork, two to three slices at a time. Do not let them overlap. Cook the pork, turning it once, until both sides are slightly golden, about 3 minutes.

In another large skillet heat the remaining 1 tablespoon vegetable oil, and add the bean sprouts. Stir-fry them over high heat for 30 seconds. Add the Chinese chives or scallions, and stir-fry for 30 seconds more. Season the mixture with salt.

Serve the pork alongside the vegetables with plain rice on the side.

• *Yields 3 servings*

JAPANESE POT-STICKERS

Gyoza

In this dish adapted from the Chinese kitchen, rounds of wheat dough, about 3 inches in diameter, are stuffed with minced pork and cabbage. In China such dumplings are usually steamed or cooked in boiling water. In Japan we pan-fry them before steaming them in the skillet.

According to legend, the pan-fry method of cooking dumplings was born out of necessity in China. It is said that the servants of a wealthy family had to eat cold cooked, leftover dumplings. Instead of resteaming or reboiling them, the servants heated up the dumplings by pan-frying them, to give them a pleasant, crisp texture and additional flavor. This style of preparation became dominant in Japan, where *gyoza* are served with hot mustard and *shoyu* (soy sauce).

Homemade dough gives *gyoza* a distinctive taste and texture. If you do not have time to make wrappers, however, you may purchase them ready-made. They are available at every Japanese and general Asian food store in the refrigerator or freezer case, at very reasonable prices.

2 cups all-purpose flour,
    plus additional flour, for dusting
$^3/_4$ teaspoon salt
7 ounces Chinese cabbage, upper leafy part only,
    or bibb lettuce
7 ounces ground pork, or $3^1/_2$ ounces ground pork and
    $3^1/_2$ ounces chopped shrimp or flaked crabmeat
2 teaspoons shoyu (soy sauce), plus more
    for drizzling on the dumplings
1 teaspoon grated ginger
1 garlic clove, grated
1 tablespoon minced scallion, green part only
Pinch of sugar
$^1/_2$ teaspoon fresh-ground black pepper
6 tablespoons sesame or vegetable oil
Hot mustard paste (see page 55)

Sift the flour into a large bowl, and stir in $^1/_4$ teaspoon salt. Add about $^1/_2$ cup boiling water to the flour little by little, stirring with chopsticks, until you can shape the mixture into a ball. Let the dough stand, covered with a moist cloth, for 1 hour.

On a floured work surface, knead the dough for 5 minutes or until it is smooth. Form the dough into a long log, and cut the log crosswise into 40 disks. Dust each cut side with additional flour to prevent the surfaces from drying out.

Roll each piece of dough into a 3-inch disk, making the rim thinner than the center. Dust the wrappers liberally with additional flour, and stack them. Wrap the stack tightly in plastic wrap.

Mince the Chinese cabbage, and toss it with the remaining ½ teaspoon salt. Let the cabbage stand for 10 minutes.

Squeeze the cabbage firmly to remove excess water.

In a bowl, toss the ground pork with the *shoyu*, and mix until the pork is sticky. Mix in the cabbage, ginger, garlic, scallion, sugar, and black pepper.

Have a small bowl of water at hand. Place a wrapper in one hand, wet half the rim of the wrapper with water, and place a little of the stuffing in the center of the wrapper. Fold the wrapper in half by placing the dry edge over the wet edge. While sealing the dumpling, make six to eight pleats in the top, dry edge, starting at one side and continuing around the rim.

Bring a kettle of water to a boil, and keep it simmering. Over medium heat, heat a skillet large enough to hold 20 dumplings, and add 2 tablespoons oil. When the oil is hot, add 20 dumplings to the skillet, pleated sides up, and cook until their bottoms are golden and crisp.

Making gyoza: Pleat the top edge of the wrapper as you seal it.

In a bowl, combine 1 cup boiling water and 2 tablespoons oil. When the dumplings are golden, add enough of this mixture to the skillet so the liquid reaches to one-third the height of the dumplings. Immediately cover the skillet, and cook the dumplings over low heat for 8 minutes.

Place a cold, wet, thick towel in the sink. Remove the lid of the skillet, turn the heat to high, and cook away any remaining liquid. Place the skillet on the wet cloth to cool the bottom quickly. With a spatula, carefully remove the dumplings from the skillet.

Cook the remaining 20 dumplings in the same way, using 2 tablespoons more oil. Serve the dumplings hot, with *shoyu* and mustard paste.

• *Yields 4 servings*

STEAMED PORK WITH PONZU DRESSING

Mushibuta Ponzu-zoe

Simply steamed pork with ponzu dressing is a light dinner dish. To keep the pork juicy and tender, it is cooked with grated daikon, whose digestive enzymes give the pork a most desirable texture. Other sauces, such as sesame-flavored *shoyu* (soy sauce) dressing (page 92) or spicy garlic sauce (page 440), can be used instead of the ponzu dressing.

1¹/₂ pounds boneless pork tenderloin,
*   trimmed of excess fat*
Salt and ground black pepper
1 naganegi long onion, preferably,
*   or 3 scallions, green parts only*
2 cups grated daikon
²/₃ cup sake (rice wine)
1 onion, cut into paper-thin rings
¹/₄ cup buckwheat flour
Vegetable oil, for frying
2 cups shredded head cabbage or lettuce
1 carrot, julienned in 2-inch lengths
1 Japanese or salad cucumber,
*   julienned in 2-inch lengths*
¹/₂ green bell pepper, julienned in 2-inch lengths
¹/₂ red bell pepper, julienned in 2-inch lengths
Ponzu dressing (page 73)

Place a bamboo or metal steamer basket over plenty of water in a deep pot over high heat.

Cut the pork into two thick logs. Rub them with salt and pepper. Let the pork stand for 10 minutes.

Into a heat-proof dish that can fit in the steamer, spread half the long onion or scallions and one-third of the grated daikon. Place the pork on top, and pour the *sake* over the meat. Scatter the remaining daikon and long onion or scallion on top of the meat. Cook the pork in the heated steamer over high heat for 45 to 50 minutes.

Remove the dish of pork from the steamer, and let it stand at room temperature for 15 minutes.

In a bowl of lukewarm water, rinse the pork to remove the daikon. Wipe the pork dry with a paper towel, and set the pork aside, covered with aluminum foil.

In a bowl, toss the onion slices with the buckwheat flour. In a wok or skillet, heat 1 inch vegetable oil. Cook the onion slices in batches until they are golden. Drain them on a paper towel.

Cut the pork into thin slices, a little less than 1/4 inch thick. Serve the pork with the raw vegetables alongside, the fried onions on top, and the ponzu dressing, for dipping the meat, in a saucer.

• *Yields 4 servings*

STIR-FRIED LIVER AND CHINESE CHIVES

Nira-reba Itame

In Japan every local shopping district has one or two Chinese restaurants. Chefs at these restaurants, naturalized Chinese or native Japanese, cook up "Japanized" but delicious, reasonably priced Chinese-style dishes for lunch and dinner. *Nira-reba itame*, stir-fried liver and Chinese chives, is one of the most popular lunchtime offerings at these very informal eateries. I sometimes crave a liver dish, so this platter appears from time to time at our dinner table.

To keep it soft and juicy, the liver is precooked in oil before it is quickly stir-fried.

> 7 ounces pork or beef liver, cut into thin slices,
> a little less than $^1/_4$ inch thick
> 2 tablespoons sake (rice wine)
> $^1/_4$ teaspoon salt
> 2$^1/_2$ teaspoons shoyu (soy sauce)
> 2 pinches of ground white pepper

> 1 tablespoon potato starch or cornstarch
> 2 teaspoons sesame oil
> ¹/₂ cup plus 1 tablespoon vegetable oil
> 10 ounces Chinese chives, cut into 2-inch lengths
> One 1-inch piece ginger, sliced thin
> 2 scallions, white parts only, cut into thin disks
> ¹/₄ cup chicken stock
> ¹/₂ teaspoon sugar
> 1 teaspoon potato starch or cornstarch,
>   mixed with 2 teaspoons water
> Plain cooked white or brown rice

Have a large bowl of ice water at hand. In a medium pot of boiling water, blanch the liver until the outside turns pale, about 20 seconds.

Drain the liver, and plunge it into the cold water. Rinse the liver in the cold water, stirring gently. Drain the liver again, and pat it dry with a paper towel.

In a bowl, combine 1 tablespoon of the *sake*, salt, 1¹/₂ teaspoons of the *shoyu*, and a pinch of white pepper. Add the liver to the bowl, and toss. Add 1 tablespoon potato starch or cornstarch, and stir gently. Add 1 teaspoon of the sesame oil, and stir again. Refrigerate the mixture, covered, for 20 minutes.

Heat a wok or skillet, and add ¹/₂ cup vegetable oil. Heat the oil to 360 degrees F. Add half the liver, and cook until the outside is golden, about 1 to 2 minutes. Remove the liver from the oil, and partially cook the remaining liver in the same way. Set the liver aside.

Remove most of the oil from the wok or skillet, leaving about 3 tablespoons. Turn the heat to high. When the oil is hot, add the Chinese chives, and stir-fry them until they begin to wilt, 30 seconds. Remove the chives from the wok or skillet, and set them aside.

Add 1 tablespoon fresh vegetable oil to the wok or skillet, and cook the ginger and scallion over low heat for 20 seconds. Increase the heat to high, and return the liver to the wok or skillet. Add the remaining 1 tablespoon *sake*, the chicken stock, the remaining 1 teaspoon *shoyu*, and the sugar. Cook the mixture for 2 minutes, tossing vigorously.

Return the chives to the wok or skillet, and stir-fry for 30 seconds.

Reduce the heat to low, and add the starch-water mixture. Cook until the sauce thickens.

Add the remaining 1 teaspoon sesame oil and pinch of white pepper, and toss. Serve the dish piping-hot, with plain cooked white or brown rice.

• *Yields 1 to 2 servings*

PORK DUMPLINGS AND MUNG-BEAN-NOODLE HOT POT

Nikudango to Ryokuto Harusame no Sūpu

Mung-bean noodles, *ryokuto harusame*, are ideal for use in soups. Unlike *harusame* (potato-starch noodles), mung-bean noodles can be cooked a long time without losing their shape or texture. In this full-meal soup, they are cooked with pork dumplings and vegetables in chicken broth. The long cooking allows the noodles to absorb all the delicious flavors from the meat and vegetables.

The dumplings can be made from pork alone, a mixture of pork and chicken, or a mixture of pork and shrimp.

10 ounces ground pork
$^1\!/_2$ teaspoon salt
1 teaspoon shoyu *(soy sauce)*
2 tablespoons minced scallion
1 tablespoon minced ginger
1 teaspoon minced garlic
1 small egg
$^1\!/_4$ cup minced coriander leaves
$^1\!/_2$ teaspoon ground white pepper
6 dried shiitake mushrooms, soaked in
      cold water for 20 minutes
$3^1\!/_2$ ounces ryokuto harusame *(mung-bean noodles)*
1 quart chicken broth, preferably homemade
1 medium carrot, cut diagonally into thin pieces
1 naganegi long onion, preferably, or 4 to 5 scallions,
      cut diagonally into 1-inch pieces
7 ounces Chinese cabbage, cut crosswise into
      1-inch pieces
$^1\!/_3$ cup whole coriander leaves

In a bowl, mix the pork with 1 tablespoon water to loosen the texture. Add the salt and *shoyu*, and mix until the pork is sticky. Add the minced scallion, ginger, and garlic. Add the egg, and mix, stirring with your hand. Add the minced coriander and $^1\!/_4$ teaspoon of the white pepper, and mix again.

Bring a large pot of water to a boil. Shape the pork mixture into 18 balls, each about 1 inch in diameter. Boil the dumplings, in three batches, 2 to 3 minutes, until the dumplings feel firm on the outside but tender on the inside when pressed with a finger. Drain the dumplings.

Drain the mushrooms, cut away their stems, and cut the caps into halves at an angle, by inclining your knife toward the cutting board.

Bring a medium pot of water to a boil. Remove the pot from the heat, add the mung-bean noodles, and let them stand in the hot water for 6 minutes.

Drain the noodles, discarding the water. Cut the bundle of noodles in half.

In a large pot, bring the chicken broth to a boil. Add the mushrooms, carrot, long onion, cabbage, and noodles, and cook over medium heat for 5 minutes.

Add the dumplings, and cook for 10 minutes.

Flavor the soup with additional salt or *shoyu*, if needed. Add the remaining $1/4$ teaspoon white pepper. Serve the soup hot in individual bowls, garnished with coriander leaves.

• *Yields 4 servings*

JAPANESE POT-STICKERS IN HOT POT

Gyoza-nabe

Gyoza dumplings are an ideal ingredient for a hearty hot-pot dish. I cook the dumplings together with ample Chinese cabbage. This is a body-and-soul-warming dinner.

If you do not have a tabletop stove, do all the cooking in the kitchen.

> $1^1/_2$ *pounds Chinese cabbage or head cabbage leaves*
> *40 uncooked gyoza dumplings (page 443)*
> *7 ounces chrysanthemum leaves or spinach*
> *1 medium carrot, sliced thin crosswise*
> *6 cups dashi (fish stock)*
> $1/_2$ *cup sake (rice wine)*
> $1/_4$ *cup shoyu (soy sauce)*
> *Ponzu dressing (page 73)*
> *2 yuzu citrons, preferably, or limes, cut into wedges*
> *Ground black pepper*

In a large pot of boiling water, cook the cabbage leaves whole until tender but still firm, 1 to 2 minutes. Rinse the cabbage leaves under cold running water.

Make a cabbage roll: Lay three cabbage leaves lengthwise on a bamboo rolling mat, alternating them so that the thick part of the center leaf is toward you and the thick parts of the outer leaves are away from you. Overlap the leaves by one-third of their width. Roll them tightly together to make a cabbage roll about 5 inches long.

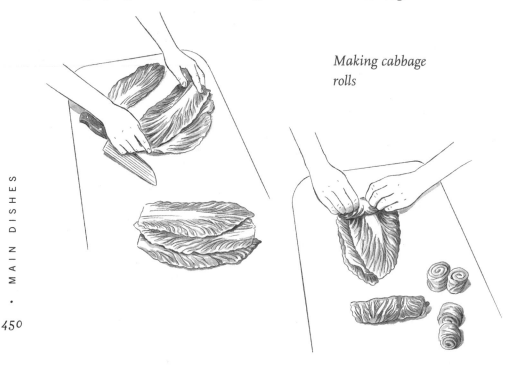

Making cabbage rolls

Cut the roll into quarters. Make more rolls, using three leaves at a time, until you have used all the cabbage. Place the cabbage rolls on a large platter, and place the dumplings next to the cabbage.

Cut the chrysanthemum leaves or spinach into 2-inch lengths, and place the pieces on the other side of the cabbage on the platter.

Bring a small saucepan of water to a boil. Cook the carrot slices for 2 minutes. Drain the carrot slices, and place them next to the chrysanthemum leaves or spinach.

Set a tabletop stove at the dining table (see page 9). In the kitchen, bring 5 cups *dashi* and the *sake* to a boil in a *donabe* earthenware pot or an enameled pot. Add the $1/4$ cup *shoyu*, and heat the broth briefly. Transfer the hot pot to the tabletop stove. Bring the platter with vegetables and dumplings to the dining table. Put the remaining 1 cup *dashi* into a glass or ceramic jar, and bring it to the table for refilling the cooking pot. Set individual bowls on the table, and summon the diners.

Put two to three dumplings per person into the broth, and cook for about 8 minutes. Add the Chinese cabbage, chrysanthemum or spinach leaves, and carrot slices, and cook for 2 minutes. Each diner should now transfer a portion of the dumplings and vegetables into his or her bowl, add a generous amount of ponzu dressing, and squeeze *yuzu* citron or lime over the dish for additional flavor.

Repeat the cooking process until all have had their fill, adding the reserved 1 cup *dashi* whenever the cooking broth has reduced too much.

After all of the dumplings and vegetables are cooked and eaten, a deliciously flavored broth will be left in the pot. Serve it in small cups or bowls with black pepper. If the broth is too concentrated, dilute it with hot water.

- *Yields 4 servings*

PORK *SHABU-SHABU*

Buta-Shabu

Shabu-shabu is a super-quick, delicious light meal in which very thinly sliced beef is quickly blanched in boiling liquid. This technique works just as well with thinly sliced pork. In this preparation, pork *shabu-shabu,* pork is served with grilled or broiled vegetables, fresh-cut fruit, and a spicy dipping sauce.

Ask your butcher to slice the pork for you.

DIPPING SAUCE
2 teaspoons sesame oil
1 to 1¹/₂ teaspoons toban jiang *(chile-bean sauce)*
¹/₄ cup shoyu *(soy sauce)*
2 tablespoons dashi *(fish stock)*
2 to 3 tablespoons sugar
2 tablespoons komezu *(rice vinegar)*
2 tablespoons minced naganegi *long onion or scallion*
1 tablespoon minced coriander

> *2 red bell peppers*
> *2 zucchini*
> *12 asparagus spears, tough ends and scales removed*
> *1 grapefruit, peeled and sectioned (remove all the*
>   *membranes and the white, inner rind)*
> *1 mango, peeled and sliced*
> *2 kiwis, peeled and cut into disks*
> *10 ounces boneless pork loin, sliced paper-thin*

In a small saucepan, heat the sesame oil until it is fragrant. Add the chile-bean sauce, and give several stirs. Add the *shoyu*, *dashi*, and sugar. Cook the mixture, stirring, until the sugar is dissolved.

Remove the saucepan from the heat, and add the *komezu*. Let the sauce cool to room temperature. Add the minced long onion or scallion and the coriander.

Broil or grill the red bell peppers until all sides are charred. Wrap the peppers in plastic wrap, and let them steam for 10 minutes.

Unwrap the peppers, and remove their skins, seeds, stems, and white ribs. Cut each pepper into strips.

Cut off the ends of the zucchini, and cut them each in half crosswise. Cut each half lengthwise into thin slices.

Brush the zucchini and asparagus with a little vegetable oil, sprinkle them with salt, and broil them, or grill them on top of aluminum foil, until they are slightly golden, turning them once.

Arrange the vegetables and fruit on a large platter, leaving space for the pork.

Bring a large pot of water to a boil. Have a bowl of ice water at hand. Using a pair of cooking chopsticks or tongs to hold the meat, cook the pork one slice at a time until it is done. As each piece is cooked, plunge it into ice water, then drain it in a colander.

Arrange the cooked pork on the platter next to the vegetables and fruits. Serve the dish with individual saucers of the dipping sauce.

• *Yields 4 servings*

COLD BEEF *SHABU-SHABU* WITH CREAMY SESAME DRESSING

Hiyashi-shabu

Shabu-shabu is a dish in which paper-thin slices of beef are cooked in simmering water at the dinner table by the diners. If you see beef cut for *shabu-shabu* in a Japanese market, you will be amazed at how highly marbled with fat the meat is. The better the quality of *shabu-shabu* beef, the more fat you will see scattered through the meat slices. This fat, which is partially melted away in the boiling water, determines the flavor and textural qualities of the beef. The more fat, the sweeter and more tender the meat is. Stories of feeding cattle beer to fatten them, and of massaging them to distribute the fat evenly in the meat, have been famous inside and outside Japan for years. If you know beef only as steak, roast, stew, or hamburger, *shabu-shabu* can be a revolutionary as well as a healthy way to enjoy the true flavor of beef.

In this hot-weather version of *shabu-shabu,* the beef is cooked in advance—in the kitchen, not at the table—and served cold. Although *shabu-shabu* is traditionally served with two dipping sauces, one based on *shoyu* and the other on sesame paste, this version has only one sauce, a sesame-*shoyu* blend.

If you can't buy sliced beef especially intended for *shabu-shabu,* ask your butcher to cut ordinary beef sirloin into paper-thin slices.

DRESSING
5 tablespoons sesame paste, preferably Japanese
$^1/_2$ cup dashi (fish stock)
$^1/_4$ cup mirin (sweet cooking wine)
$5^1/_2$ tablespoons shoyu (soy sauce)

Put the sesame paste into a *suribachi* or other mortar or bowl. Little by little, grind or stir in the *dashi*. Grind or stir in the *mirin*, and then the *shoyu*. Set the mixture aside.

Grill or broil the bell peppers until they are charred all over, and wrap them in plastic wrap. Let them stand in their steam for 10 minutes.

Remove the stems, seeds, and white ribs of the bell peppers. Cut the peppers into strips.

In a medium pot of boiling water, cook the asparagus spears for 1 minute. Cool them in ice water, drain them, and wipe them dry in a paper towel. Cut the asparagus into quarters crosswise.

Drain the onion or leek, and wipe it dry with a paper towel. Cut the mango into 3-inch-long strips.

Bring a large pot of water to a boil. Have ready a large bowl of ice water.

Just before serving time, pick up a slice of beef with a pair of chopsticks or tongs. Immerse the beef in the boiling water, shaking it swiftly, until it turns nearly white with a slightly pink tinge, about 10 seconds. Avoid overcooking the beef.

Immediately plunge the beef into the ice water to stop the cooking. Quickly pull the beef out, give it a shake, and lay it in a bamboo tray or colander. Cook all of the beef in the same way.

Mound the cooked beef in the center of a large platter. (If the day is very hot, mound the beef on top of ice cubes.) Arrange the vegetables and papaya side by side around the mound of beef.

Serve the dish with the sesame sauce in individual small cups. The beef, vegetables, and fruit should each be dipped in the sesame sauce before eating.

• *Yields 6 servings*

Shabu-shabu is an onomatopoeic word. It describes the sound made when you hold anything—such as clothes, vegetables, or beef—and "swish" it back and forth in a liquid. Now let's do an experiment: Hold one end of a thin beef slice with a pair of chopsticks. Plunge it into simmering water to blanch it. Quickly move the beef on the surface of the water from right to left several times, until the beef is faintly pink. During this operation, the water will bubble and splash, and you will hear the famous sound. Doesn't it sound like *shabu-shabu?* I think so!

By the way, Japanese people hear and reproduce many sounds in different ways from English speakers. Cats mew *nyaa-nyaa,* not *meow;* dogs bark *wan-wan,* not *bow-wow;* cows bellow *moh-moh,* not *moooo,* and sheep bleat *mee-mee,* not *baa-baa.* While enjoying a *shabu-shabu* dinner you can explore more of these linguistic differences with your family and friends.

POTATO AND BEEF CROQUETTES

Korokke

Korokke may have its origin in French croquettes. Many such Western preparations, which were introduced at the turn of the twentieth century, have been modified for the Japanese kitchen and Japanese tastes and are now deeply rooted in Japanese cuisine.

Japanese croquettes are made from mashed potato, ground beef, and onion. The mixture is shaped into patties and then cooked crisp with a coating of *panko* breadcrumbs.

Every butcher across Japan sells his own croquettes, and boasts that his are the best. The smell of just-cooked croquettes tempts passersby from all walks of life into the shop all day long. Biting into a steaming hot croquette is a treat.

You can vary this recipe in many ways. Form the mixture into 50 to 60 small balls (1¼ inches in diameter) for a delightful party appetizer. To make fish croquettes, replace the beef with canned salmon. For vegetarian croquettes, use canned corn and green peas. I often use sweet potato as a substitute for the white potato.

3 pounds (3 large) potatoes
2 to 3 tablespoons vegetable oil or butter
14 ounces (2 medium) onions, chopped
¹/₂ pound ground beef
2 tablespoons minced parsley
Salt and ground black pepper to taste
¹/₂ teaspoon ground nutmeg
1 teaspoon Worcestershire sauce
¹/₂ cup all-purpose flour
2 eggs, lightly beaten
2 to 3 cups panko breadcrumbs (see page 386)
Vegetable oil, for deep-frying (page 20)
Mixed salad greens
Tonkatsu *sauce (page 94)*

In a large pot of water, simmer the whole potatoes, with their skins, until the potatoes are soft.

Drain the potatoes, discarding the water. Peel them, and cut them into quarters. Return the potatoes to the empty pot, and dry-cook them over medium heat, shaking the pot back and forth, 1 to 2 minutes. This process removes excess water from the potatoes.

Transfer the potatoes to a bowl, and mash them with a potato masher or fork. Set the mashed potatoes aside.

Heat a skillet, and add the vegetable oil or butter. Add the onions to the skillet, and cook them over medium-low heat, stirring, until they are soft, 3 to 4 minutes.

Add the beef to the skillet, and cook over high heat until the liquid has evaporated, stirring continually to break the lumps into crumbles. Add the parsley, and give several stirs.

In a bowl, combine the potatoes with the onions and beef. Add the salt and pepper, nutmeg, and Worcestershire sauce. Let the mixture cool, and then refrigerate it, covered, for 20 minutes. Refrigeration makes the potato mixture firmer and easier to shape.

Divide the mixture into quarters and form each quarter into a thick log. Cut each log into five pieces. Shape each piece into an oblong, flat patty, about 3 inches by 4 inches. Make the remaining 19 patties.

Put the flour, beaten eggs, and breadcrumbs into three separate bowls. If some of the breadcrumbs are large, crush them between your hands.

Dredge each patty with flour. You can prepare the patties to this point one day in advance, and store them in the refrigerator, covered.

Dip each patty in egg. Pat the patty well with the breadcrumbs to cover every surface. At this point you can freeze the croquettes, well wrapped, for later use.

Heat 2 inches vegetable oil in a deep skillet to 370 degrees F. (The oil temperature should be very high because the patties require only quick browning, since the ingredients have already been cooked. If the oil temperature were too low, the patties would burst and absorb too much oil.) Cook several patties at a time until they are golden, about 2 minutes. If you are cooking frozen croquettes, put them straight from the freezer into the hot oil. Drain the patties on a rack without overlapping them.

Serve the hot croquettes over salad greens, with the *tonkatsu* sauce poured over or served in a saucer on the side.

- *Yields 5 to 8 servings*

PAN-FRIED BEEF WITH VEGETABLES

Gyuniku Gomayaki

In this popular recipe, thin-sliced beef is marinated and then simply pan-fried. Cooking the meat takes only a few minutes. During the cooking, I add vegetables to the skillet. When you want a quick beef dinner, this is it.

If possible, have the butcher slice the beef for you.

MARINADE
5 tablespoons white sesame seeds, toasted (page 100)
2¹/₂ tablespoons shoyu (soy sauce)
2 tablespoons sake (rice wine)
2 tablespoons mirin (sweet cooking wine)
1 tablespoon honey
3 garlic cloves, grated
1 teaspoon grated ginger
¹/₄ teaspoon paprika
1 tablespoon sesame oil

> 1 pound beef sirloin, cut across the grain
> into 16 to 20 slices
> 8 fresh shiitake mushrooms, preferably,
> or button mushrooms, stemmed
> 2 to 3 tablespoons vegetable oil
> 2 medium onions, cut into thin disks
> 8 asparagus spears, tough ends and scales removed,
> cut crosswise into halves
> 10 ounces soybean or mung-bean sprouts,
> rinsed and drained well
> Plain cooked white or brown rice

In a *suribachi,* preferably, or other mortar, grind the sesame seeds until they are roughly broken. Mix in the *shoyu, sake, mirin,* honey, garlic, ginger, paprika, and sesame oil. Marinate the beef in this mixture for 15 to 20 minutes.

Remove the beef from the marinade, leaving the sesame seeds that adhere to the surface of the meat. Discard the remaining marinade.

Briefly rinse the mushrooms under cold running water, and wipe them dry with a paper towel.

Heat a large skillet over medium heat, and coat the bottom with a thin layer of vegetable oil. When the oil is hot, add several slices of beef, leaving room for the vegetables. Put the mushrooms, onions, and asparagus into the unoccupied part of the skillet, and lightly salt the vegetables. Add more oil, if needed. Cook the beef, turning it once, until it is medium-done, or done to your taste. The vegetables should be ready at the same time.

Serve the beef and vegetables hot, with plain cooked white or brown rice.

• *Yields 4 servings*

JAPANESE-STYLE BEEF STEAK

Wafu Steak

Japanese-style steak is really just a variant of steak by any other name. Using well-marbled Japanese beef, such as Kobe, makes the steak Japanese. Slicing the steak before serving it, for ease of handling with chopsticks, and serving it with ponzu dressing and grated daikon makes the steak Japanese. In my recipe, additionally, the beef is tenderized in a marinade of *sake* (rice wine) and grated daikon, and served with crisply cooked sweet potato and lotus root disks. You might instead mash the sweet potato. Enjoy this change from your ordinary steak-and-potato meal.

> Salt and ground black pepper
> 1 pound well-marbled sirloin steak, cut in half,
>   excess fat cut off and reserved
> 2 tablespoons sake *(rice wine)*
> ¹/₂ cup grated daikon
> 1 Japanese sweet potato, preferably, or regular sweet
>   potato, soaked in salted water for 10 minutes
> 1 lotus root, sliced paper-thin and soaked in 2 cups
>   water and 2 teaspoons vinegar for 15 minutes
> Vegetable oil, for deep-frying
> 1 or 2 tablespoons butter
> 2 tablespoons brandy
> 2 tablespoons mirin *(sweet cooking wine)*
> 1 tablespoon shoyu *(soy sauce)*
> ¹/₂ to 1 teaspoon sugar

Salt and pepper the beef. In a dish, combine the *sake* and grated daikon. Marinate the beef in this mixture, covered, for 30 minutes.

Remove the beef from the marinade, and discard the marinade. Wipe the beef with a paper towel.

Drain the sweet potato and lotus root, and dry them with a kitchen cloth.

In a wok or skillet, heat 2 inches vegetable oil to 320 degrees F. Fry the vegetables over low heat, in small batches, until they are slightly golden and crisp. Drain the vegetables on a rack, and sprinkle them with a little salt.

Heat a skillet, and add the reserved beef fat or 1 tablespoon butter. Grease the entire inside surface of the skillet with the fat or butter. Add the beef, and cook it over medium heat until the bottom is browned. Reduce the heat somewhat, turn over the beef, and cook it until the other side is browned and the meat is done to your liking. The total cooking time for a medium-rare 1-inch-thick steak is about 10 minutes.

Remove the beef from the skillet, and set it aside, covered with aluminum foil.

Pour off the excess oil from the skillet and add $1/2$ cup water and the *mirin*. Deglaze the skillet. Add the brandy and light a flame in the skillet to cook away the alcohol. Add the *shoyu* and 1 tablespoon butter, cook the mixture briefly, and add the sugar. Remove the skillet from the heat. Cut the beef into bite-sized slices, and serve it with the sauce poured over and the fried vegetables on the side.

- *Yields 2 servings*

MISO-MARINATED BEEF STEAK

Gyuniku no Misozuke

As fish was once preserved in a miso marinade, so was beef. The technique of marinating beef was developed in the domain of Hikone, now Shiga Prefecture, during the Edo Era (1600 to 1868). Even then, Hikone was known for its excellent beef, *oumi-gyu*. To bring this top-quality beef as tribute to the Tokugawa shogunate in the city of Edo (now Tokyo) the people of Hikone used miso as a preservative.

Beef can be marinated in either sweet white miso or salty brown miso. I prefer brown miso, whose very rich flavor complements the robust flavor of beef.

Unlike in the Edo Era, the marination time today can be short, from five hours to overnight. Marinating meat longer dries it out and toughens it. When you remove the meat form the marinade, however, you don't have to cook it right away; it will keep for three days in the refrigerator, stored in a container with a tight-fitting lid.

Traditionally, the beef is served without sauce in Japan. But I always make a sauce of miso and *mirin*, and serve the sauce with stir-fried rice flavored with the excess fat cut from the steaks. The fat imparts a very delicious flavor to the rice.

7 ounces akamiso *(brown miso)*

¹/₂ cup mirin *(sweet cooking wine)*

¹/₄ cup sake *(rice wine)*

Four 6-ounce sirloin steaks, 1 inch thick,
   excess fat cut off and reserved

¹/₄ cup vegetable oil

¹/₄ cup brandy

STIR-FRIED RICE

One 1-inch cube beef suet, or 2 tablespoons butter

1 small onion, minced

3 garlic cloves, minced

4 cups day-old cooked short-grain white or brown rice

20 shiso leaves, roughly chopped

Salt, tamari, and fresh-ground black pepper to taste

In a medium bowl, combine the miso, ¹/₄ cup of the *mirin*, and the *sake* to make a soft paste. Spread one-third of the mixture in the bottom of a large pan in which the steaks can fit without overlapping. Place a tightly woven cotton cloth or two layers of cheesecloth over the miso mixture and place the steaks on top. Cover them with another tightly woven cloth, or two more layers of cheesecloth, and spread the remaining miso mixture over it. Cover the pan with plastic wrap, and let the beef stand for from 5 hours to overnight in the refrigerator.

Remove the cloth from the beef and the beef from the pan, reserving the marinade. If there is any miso residue on the surface of the beef, gently wipe it away with a paper towel. Do not rinse the beef in water.

Heat a large skillet, and add the vegetable oil. When the oil is hot, add the beef, and brown it on one side. Shake the pan from time to time to make sure that the meat is not sticking to the skillet. Reduce the heat to low, and cook the steaks for 3 minutes. Turn the steaks over, and brown them on the other side. Continue cooking them for 2 to 3 minutes longer.

Check the doneness by pressing the meat with your fingers. When it is resilient on the outside but feels softer as you press a little deeper, it is still rare. A 1-inch-thick steak takes 10 minutes to cook medium-rare.

Remove the beef from the skillet, transfer it to a warmed plate, and cover it. Pour off the excess oil from the skillet, and add ¹/₂ cup water and the remaining ¹/₄ cup *mirin*.

Deglaze the skillet. Add 2 tablespoons of the reserved miso marinade, and cook, stirring, over medium-low heat for 2 minutes.

Remove the skillet from the heat. Add the brandy, light it with a match, and burn away the alcohol. Strain the mixture through a sieve lined with a cotton cloth, and transfer the sauce to a small saucepan. Cook the sauce until it is slightly thickened.

If you will be serving stir-fried rice with the beef, start the preparation while you are cooking the beef. Heat a large skillet over medium heat, and grease it with the reserved beef fat and the additional suet or butter. Add the onion, and cook it over medium-low heat until it is soft, about 5 to 8 minutes.

Add the garlic, and cook for 30 seconds. Add the rice to the skillet, and break up any lumps with a wooden spatula. Cook the rice over medium-low heat, stirring all the time, 15 minutes. Stir in half the shiso, and season the rice with salt, tamari, and fresh-ground black pepper.

Cut the hot steaks into $1/3$- to $1/2$-inch slices. Serve the beef with the rice, drizzled with the sauce.

• *Yields 4 servings*

PAN-FRIED BEEF IN SWEET SOY-SAUCE BROTH

Sukiyaki

Sukiyaki is a popular dish all over Japan. There is a story behind this famous dish. In the past, when farmers and hunters were out in the mountains and fields, they would cook wild game that they caught on a scythe, *ski,* that they carried with them on their treks. Hence this dish was named *ski-yaki,* "scythe-cooking." When the Meiji government began promoting the consumption of beef in the late nineteenth century, the principal ingredient of sukiyaki switched from game to beef.

As beef for *shabu-shabu* is highly marbled with fat, so too is sukiyaki beef. For sukiyaki, the beef is cut slightly thicker than for *shabu-shabu.*

The sliced beef is sautéed in a lightly sweetened *shoyu*-based sauce at the table. Each diner is supplied with a medium bowl of beaten egg for dipping the piping-hot beef before eating it. The egg both cools the freshly cooked beef and adds a sweet, mellow flavor. If you feel uneasy about consuming raw egg, you may omit it, and eat the cooked beef as it is (don't burn your mouth!). But I advise you instead to find a reliable source for clean, fresh eggs so you can enjoy the true flavor of a sukiyaki dinner.

Highly marbled beef sirloin cut, sliced for sukiyaki, can be found at Japanese food stores in a refrigerator case. Have the butcher slice the beef very thin.

For this recipe, you will need the following items: a *tetsunabe* (see page 9) or other heavy-bottomed skillet or pot (not a *donabe*), a tabletop stove, and fuel for the stove. You will also need four small pitchers.

Unlike in *shabu-shabu* cooking, one person may serve as sukiyaki chef. Each diner can take a turn playing this role. When I was a child, my father, who never ever spent any time in the kitchen, was always the sukiyaki chef.

2 naganegi long onions, preferably, or young,
slender leeks, white parts only, cut into
1¹/₂-inch lengths
4 fresh shiitake mushrooms, rinsed and stemmed
1 bunch chrysanthemum leaves, cut into halves
7 ounces shirataki (taro gelatin noodles, available at
Japanese food stores), cut into 5-inch lengths
1 block (about 11 ounces) firm tofu, cut in half
lengthwise and then into 8 pieces crosswise
1¹/₂ to 2 pounds well-marbled beef sirloin, sliced very thin
One 2-inch cube beef suet
1 cup shoyu (soy sauce)
1 cup sake (rice wine)
6 tablespoons sugar
8 eggs

Arrange the vegetables, noodles, and tofu side by side on a large platter. Arrange the beef slices, partially overlapping one another, on another large platter, and place the beef suet in the center.

In a small pitcher, combine ¹/₂ cup of the *shoyu*, ¹/₂ cup of the *sake*, and the sugar. Into a second small pitcher put the remaining ¹/₂ cup *shoyu*; into a third put the remaining ¹/₂ cup *sake*; and into a fourth put 2 cups water. Break the eggs into a bowl.

Set a tabletop stove on the dining table. Place a heavy-bottomed deep skillet or shallow pot on the stove. Bring to the table the vegetable and beef platters, the four pitchers, and the bowl of eggs. Set four individual bowls on the table, and ask the diners to sit around the table.

Heat the skillet or pot over medium heat, and add the beef suet. Using a pair of chopsticks or tongs, grease the entire inside surface of the skillet with the suet. Add as many beef slices as there are diners. Cook the beef, without stirring or turning it, for 1 minute.

Add enough of the *shoyu-sake*-sugar mixture to barely submerge the beef. When the liquid begins to boil, turn over the beef, and cook it for 30 seconds.

As the beef cooks, each diner should break an egg into his or her bowl and beat it with a pair of chopsticks. When the beef is ready, each diner picks up a piece, dips it in raw egg, and eats it.

Add a portion of all the vegetables except the chrysanthemum leaves to the skillet or pot. Add a little of the water to submerge the ingredients by about $1/2$ inch. Cook the vegetables over medium-low heat for 5 minutes. Check the flavor as the vegetables cook, and, if you like, add more of the *shoyu-sake*-sugar mixture. Add the chrysanthemum leaves at the last minute, since they cook instantly.

Again, each diner picks out some of the ingredients, and dips them in egg before eating them.

Cook more beef, and then more vegetables, in the same way. Repeat the process until you have used all of the ingredients on the platters. While cooking, adjust the flavor by adding *shoyu*, *sake*, water, or the *shoyu-sake*-sugar mixture.

• *Yields 4 servings*

MOM'S POT-COOKED "ROAST BEEF"

"Rosuto-Bīfu!"

Until I reached late elementary school age we did not have an oven at home, so my mother cooked beef roast in her way, in a pot. She proudly called it *rosuto-bīfu*, "roast beef," although it had little relationship to real roast beef. Even after my mother obtained an oven, she continued cooking her beef in this way, until one day my sister came back from her Western cooking class with an authentic roast beef recipe. My mother was surely impressed with this new preparation.

Once in a while, however, I still enjoy my mother's version of *rosuto-bīfu*. She served the sliced beef with wasabi, grated daikon, and a delicious sauce made from the liquid left in the cooking pot.

Salt
Fresh-ground black pepper
1 1/2 pounds beef top round
3 garlic cloves, crushed
3 tablespoons vegetable oil
1 tablespoon sugar
1/2 cup sake (rice wine)
1/4 cup mirin (sweet cooking wine)
1/3 cup shoyu (soy sauce)
Top leaves from 2 bunches watercress
1 tablespoon wasabi
1 cup grated daikon

Salt and pepper the beef, and rub it with garlic. Let the beef rest for 15 minutes.

Heat a large skillet, and add the vegetable oil. When the oil is hot, add the beef, and cook it until the outside is lightly browned. Sprinkle the sugar over the beef, and turn the beef to caramelize all surfaces. Remove the beef from the skillet, and set it aside.

In a medium pot, combine the *sake* and *mirin*. Bring the mixture to a boil over medium heat. Turn the heat to low, add the beef, and cover the pot with a drop lid (see page 26). Cook the beef for 10 minutes.

Add the *shoyu*, and cook the beef for 5 to 8 minutes longer, turning it for even coloring and flavoring.

Remove the beef from the pot, and let the beef stand, covered, for 10 minutes. The beef will be quite rare.

Strain the remaining cooking liquid through a fine sieve into a small saucepan. Cook the sauce over low heat until it thickens.

Cut the beef into thin slices. Serve it on a large platter, garnished with watercress. Serve the sauce, the wasabi, and the daikon in separate small bowls on the side.

• *Yields 4 to 6 servings*

BRAISED BEEF IN JAPANESE STYLE

Gyuniku no Wafu-ni

Since in the past beef was expensive in Japan, few recipes were developed to use large pieces. My mother, who was raised in a nontraditional household with abundant chicken and meat, prepared this Japanese-style stewed beef dish from time to time in winter. Unlike in Western beef stew, the beef in this recipe is cooked alone until tender, when the vegetables are added. The beef and vegetables are then cooked together, and, at the end of the cooking, the broth is lightly thickened with potato starch. It is a simple and hearty dinner.

1 medium potato, cut rangiri-style (see page 28)
*   into 1¹/₂-inch pieces*
1 medium Japanese, preferably, or other sweet potato,
*   cut rangiri-style into 1¹/₂-inch pieces*
¹/₂ cup vegetable oil
1¹/₂ pounds boneless beef shoulder or rump, cut into
*   14 to 16 cubes, about 1¹/₂ ounces each*
1 large onion, cut rangiri-style into 1¹/₂-inch pieces
1 large carrot, cut rangiri-style into 1¹/₂-inch pieces
7 ounces daikon (about 8 inches of a medium root)
¹/₂ to 1 teaspoon salt
1 cup sake (rice wine)
1¹/₂ tablespoons sugar
¹/₄ cup shoyu (soy sauce)
¹/₂ broccoli head, broken into flowerets
Juice from 2 teaspoons grated ginger
¹/₂ teaspoon sansho pepper
1 tablespoon potato starch or cornstarch,
*   mixed with 1¹/₂ tablespoons water*
Plain cooked white or brown rice or country-style bread

In a bowl of cold salted water, soak the potato and sweet potato for 10 minutes.

Drain the potato and sweet potato, and wipe them dry with a paper towel. In a wok or skillet, heat the vegetable oil until it is medium-hot. Cook the potato and sweet potato, separately, until the outside of each piece is slightly golden, 2 to 3 minutes. Drain the potato and sweet potato, reserving the oil, and set them aside.

In a stew pot, heat 3 tablespoons of the oil from the wok or skillet. Cook the beef pieces over high heat until the outsides are browned. Transfer the beef to a platter, and set it aside. Add the onion, carrot, and daikon to the pot, salt the vegetables, and stir-fry them for 2 minutes. Remove the vegetables from the pot.

Return the beef to the pot, and add the *sake*. Add cold water to cover the beef by 1 inch. Bring the mixture to a boil over medium heat. Skim the foam until no more appears. Reduce the heat to low, and simmer the mixture, tightly covered, for about 40 minutes.

Add all of the vegetables except the broccoli, and simmer, uncovered, for 10 minutes.

Add the sugar, and simmer for 5 minutes.

Add the *shoyu*, and simmer for 10 minutes more.

While the stew cooks, bring plenty of water to a boil in another pot, and cook the broccoli for 1 minute. Drain the broccoli. Two minutes before the other ingredients have finished cooking, add the broccoli.

At the end of the cooking, add the grated ginger and *sansho* pepper to the stew pot. Reduce the heat to low, check the flavor, and add the potato-starch or cornstarch liquid to thicken the broth. To soak up all the delicious broth, serve the stew with plain cooked white or brown rice or country-style bread.

• *Yields 4 to 6 servings*

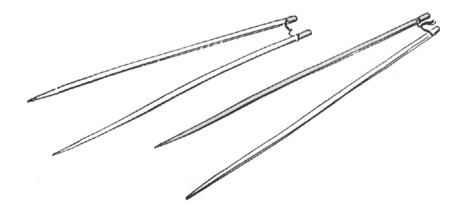

BRAISED BEEF AND NEW POTATOES

Shinjaga to Gyuniku no Nikomi

This is a version of the popular home-style dish called *niku-jaga,* meat and potato, in which beef, potato, and onion are cooked together until the three flavors completely mingle.

> 10 ounces beef sirloin, sliced thin across the grain
> 3 tablespoons vegetable oil
> 2 medium onions, one cut into thin disks
>   and one into thin wedges
> 1 pound small new potatoes
> 1 tablespoon sesame oil
> 1 cup dashi (fish stock), preferably, or water
> 2 tablespoons sake (rice wine)
> 2 tablespoons sugar
> $\frac{1}{4}$ cup shoyu (soy sauce)
> $\frac{1}{3}$ to $\frac{1}{2}$ cup fresh or frozen green peas

In a bowl, combine the beef, 1 tablespoon of the vegetable oil, and the onion disks. Marinate the beef for 30 minutes.

While the beef marinates, cook the potatoes in a large pot of boiling water for 8 minutes or until they are cooked through but still firm. Drain the potatoes, wipe them with a paper towel, and set them aside.

Heat a skillet and add the remaining 2 tablespoons vegetable oil. When the oil is hot, sauté the potatoes, rolling them in the skillet until they are golden all over. Remove the potatoes from the skillet, and set them aside.

In a medium pot, heat the sesame oil. Remove the beef from the marinade, discarding the onion. Add the beef to the pot, and cook it until it turns pale.

Add the potatoes and onion wedges to the beef, and give several large stirs. Add the *dashi* and *sake*, and bring the mixture to a boil. Cook the mixture over low heat, covered with a drop lid (see page 26), for 10 minutes.

Add the sugar, and cook for 5 minutes more. Add the *shoyu*, and cook the mixture until the liquid is almost all absorbed.

At the end of the cooking, add the green peas. Cook them just until they are heated through, and then serve the mixture hot.

• *Yields 4 servings*

MISO-MARINATED BEEF
IN AN EGG-WHITE JACKET

Gyuniku no Ranpaku-age

In this preparation, beef is marinated in miso, coated with egg white, and then deep-fried. An unusual presentation and flavor experience! Serve the beef with assorted salad greens on the side.

7 ounces Saikyo miso (sweet white miso)
3 tablespoons sake (rice wine)
2 tablespoons minced scallion
1 teaspoon toban jiang (chile-bean sauce)
1 pound beef sirloin, sliced ¹/₂ inch thick
4 egg whites
¹/₂ teaspoon salt
1 tablespoon potato starch or cornstarch
Vegetable oil, for deep-frying
Tosazu dressing (page 74)
Mixed salad greens

In a bowl, combine the miso, *sake*, scallion, and chile-bean sauce.

In a pan large enough to hold the beef in one layer, spread one-third of the miso mixture. Place two layers of cheesecloth on top of the miso mixture, and arrange the beef slices on the cloth without overlapping. Cover the beef with another thin, tightly woven cloth or two layers of cheesecloth, and spread the remaining miso mixture over the cloth. Marinate the beef in the refrigerator overnight.

Remove the beef from the marinade, wipe off any residue with a paper towel, and cut the beef into thin strips.

In a bowl, beat the egg whites until stiff peaks form. Beat in the salt and potato starch or cornstarch.

In a skillet, heat 2 inches vegetable oil to 320 degrees F. Dip each slice of beef in the egg white, and fry the beef slices a few at a time until the coating is fluffy, about 2 to 3 minutes.

Serve the beef hot, accompanied by the salad greens and, on the side, a small bowl of *tosazu* dressing.

• *Yields 4 servings*

HIROKO'S LAMB STEW

Ramu no Nikomi Hiroko-fu

In this variation on traditional Japanese meat stew, lamb is cooked in a broth with miso. The preparation illustrates how to produce a very flavorful dish by combining Japanese techniques and ingredients with a basic Western idea such as lamb stew. The Japanese contribution is the broth of Japanese ingredients—*sake*, *mirin*, *shoyu*, miso, and *kombu*—in which the meat is cooked. Western touches include the use of lamb, which has no traditional place in the Japanese kitchen, mirepoix (the sautéed vegetables on which the meat is placed) as a broth thickener, and balsamic vinegar, added to the broth at the end to balance the dish with extra sweetness and acidity. In this way a very classic Japanese meat stew has been transformed into a delightful "Western" lamb stew.

3 tablespoons vegetable oil
2 pounds lamb shoulder, with bones, trimmed of
excess fat and cut into 2-inch cubes,
bone reserved
1 tablespoon sugar
1 large carrot, sliced thin
1 medium onion, sliced thin
One 2-inch piece ginger, peeled and sliced
5 tablespoons sake *(rice wine)*
5 tablespoons mirin *(sweet cooking wine)*
One 3-inch square kombu *(kelp)*
1 tablespoon shoyu *(soy sauce)*
3 tablespoons mamemiso *(soybean miso)*
12 to 16 baby carrots
2 medium potatoes, cut into 12 to 16 potato pieces
the size of the carrots
1 spinach bunch
Balsamic vinegar to taste
Minced parsley or chervil

In a large skillet, heat the vegetable oil over medium heat. Add the lamb and bones, and cook, turning them, until all sides are browned. Add the sugar, and cook until the sugar caramelizes. Remove the meat and bones from the skillet, and set them aside.

Add the carrot, onion, and ginger to the skillet. Cook the mixture over medium-low heat until the vegetables are slightly golden and soft, 5 to 8 minutes, stirring occasionally.

Transfer the vegetables to a medium pot, and spread them to cover the bottom. Add the lamb and bones to the pot. Add enough water to cover the lamb, and the *sake*, *mirin*, and *kombu*. Bring the mixture to a boil over medium heat.

Remove and discard the *kombu*. Reduce the heat, cover the pot, and gently simmer the mixture for 2 hours. Or put the covered pot in an oven heated to 350 degrees F for 2 hours. After one hour of cooking, add the *shoyu* and miso.

While the meat cooks, parboil separately first the baby carrots, then the potato pieces, and finally the spinach in a medium pot of boiling water until the vegetables are tender but still firm. Cool the vegetables in ice water, and drain them. Cut the spinach into 2-inch lengths.

Remove the lamb and bones from the pot, transfer the meat to a large platter, and cover it with aluminum foil to keep it warm. Discard the bones.

Transfer the broth and the vegetables that have been simmering with the lamb to a food processor or blender, and purée them.

Return the mixture to the pot, and bring it to a boil over medium-low heat. Cook the mixture a little more to thicken it.

Return the lamb to the pot, add the parboiled carrots and potato, and cook for 5 minutes. Season the mixture with a few drops of balsamic vinegar.

Serve the lamb and vegetables drizzled with the broth from the pot and sprinkled with minced parsley. Either plain cooked rice or country-style bread goes very well with this dish.

• *Yields 6 to 8 servings*

SWEET AZUKI BEAN PASTE

Anko

The foundation of many Japanese sweets, *anko* has a sweet, chestnutlike flavor. Master the technique of making sweet azuki paste, and you can expand your sweets repertoire by preparing many Japanese desserts. Or use *anko* in Western desserts.

Sweetened cooked azuki beans, in either whole-bean or paste form, and unsweetened powdered azuki are available as a substitute for "the real thing," but, as is usually the case, there is no comparison between the made-from-scratch and shortcut products. Though a little time consuming, making sweet azuki paste is simple. I encourage you to try it—it's well worth the effort.

> *1 cup (7 ounces) dried azuki beans*
> *1 cup sugar*

In a medium pot, combine the dried beans and 4 cups water. Bring the mixture to a boil over moderate heat.

Drain the beans, discarding the water. Return the beans to the pot, and add 4 cups fresh water. Bring the mixture to a boil over moderate heat. Turn the heat to low, and cook the beans, uncovered, until they are tender, 60 minutes. During the cooking, add additional water if necessary. At the end of the cooking, the beans should be barely covered with cooking liquid.

In a food processor or blender, blend the beans with their cooking liquid to a smooth purée. Press the puréed beans through a fine sieve set over a bowl. You will get about 2¼ cups purée.

Place a large bowl in the sink, and fill it with cold water. Transfer the puréed beans to a tightly woven cotton cloth. Hold the top ends of the cloth closed, and grip tightly so that the puréed beans won't come out of the cloth. Plunge the cloth into the bowl of water, holding the top end of the cloth, and rinse the puréed beans by squeezing the cloth in the water.

Discard the water, add fresh cold water, and rinse the beans once more. Remove the puréed beans in the cloth from the water, and squeeze the cloth tightly to remove excess water.

In a medium pot, combine the puréed beans, the sugar, and $1/3$ cup water. Bring the mixture to a boil over medium-low heat. Cook, stirring with a wooden spatula, until the texture becomes like that of soft peanut butter, about 20 minutes. Cool the bean paste by scooping it with a wooden spatula, about $1/3$ cup at a time, and dropping it into a large pan.

Refrigerate the cooled bean paste, covered, for up to three days, or freeze it for later use.

• *Yields about 2 cups (19 ounces) sweet azuki paste*

INSTANT SWEET AZUKI BEAN PASTE

Sokuseki Anko

When you have no time to cook dried beans, use unsweetened azuki bean flour. This product, called *sarashi-an* or *koshi-an,* is available at Japanese stores. With it you can make sweet azuki paste in 20 minutes or so.

> *1 package (6.5 ounces)* sarashi-an *or* koshi-an
> *(azuki flour)*
> $1^1/_2$ *cups sugar*

In a medium pot, combine the azuki flour with 2 cups and 6 tablespoons water. Stir with a wooden spatula until the mixture is smooth. Add the sugar, and mix. Place the pot over medium heat, and bring the mixture to a boil. Reduce the heat to low, and cook, stirring with a wooden spatula, until the texture becomes like that of soft peanut butter, 20 minutes.

Cool the sweet azuki paste by scooping it with a wooden spatula, about $1/3$ cup at a time, and dropping it into a large pan.

• *Yields $2^3/_4$ cups (27 ounces) sweet azuki paste*

CHILLED AZUKI GELATIN

Mizu Yokan

In this summertime, teatime snack, sweet azuki bean paste is set in agar-agar gelatin. The gelatin is so smooth and slippery that it slides down your throat, leaving a cool feeling. To make the gelatin you can use agar-agar in either stick or string form. I prefer the latter type, which produces a much softer touch.

I sometimes add sweetened cooked chestnuts to the gelatin. They are available at Japanese food stores, but if you can't find them you can leave them out.

Look for dried bamboo leaves at Japanese or Asian food stores, too. When the gelatin is served on top of the leaves, they give it a refreshing flavor.

For this recipe you need a 6-inch-square steel, metal, glass, or plastic mold. A milk carton can also be a good mold for the gelatin.

> *¹/₃ ounce* ito kanten *(agar-agar strings), soaked in*
> *cold water overnight, or* 1 bo kanten
> *(agar-agar stick)*
> *5 tablespoons sugar*
> *1 cup (10 ounces) sweet azuki bean paste*
> *(page 472 or 473)*
> *3¹/₂ ounces kuri no kanroni (sweet chestnuts*
> *in syrup), cut into halves (optional)*
> *2 dried bamboo leaves, soaked in cold water*
> *for 5 hours (optional)*

If you are using an agar-agar stick, tear it into quarters, and soak the pieces in cold water for 5 minutes.

Drain either form of agar-agar, and squeeze it to remove excess water. Transfer the agar-agar to a medium pot, and add 2 cups water. Bring the mixture to a boil over moderate heat. Cook the mixture, stirring all the time with chopsticks, until the agar-agar is completely dissolved, 6 to 8 minutes.

Add the sugar to the pot, and cook, stirring, until the sugar is dissolved.

Strain the agar-agar liquid through a sieve set over a bowl. Return the strained liquid to the pot, and put the pot over moderate heat. Add the sweet azuki paste to the pot, and stir until smooth.

Transfer the azuki liquid to a clean bowl, and let the liquid cool to about 110 degrees F.

Wet a 6-inch-square mold with water, shake out the excess water, and quickly pour in the agar-agar and azuki paste liquid. When the liquid begins to set, gently place the chestnuts, if you are using them, on top of the gelatin (they should not sink down and disappear).

When the gelatin is completely set, cover the mold with plastic wrap, and chill the gelatin in the refrigerator.

Cut the gelatin into 2-inch squares, and serve them, if possible, on the bamboo leaves.

• *Yields 9 servings*

STEAMED AZUKI BEAN CAKE

Azuki no Mushigashi

Mushigashi is a steamed cake with a slightly moist, spongy texture. Egg whites raise the cake and make it very light. Sweet azuki paste, sweet white bean paste, and sweet white miso are favorite principal flavor ingredients for *mushigashi*.

In this preparation the cake is flavored with the sweet azuki paste that is so popular in Japan. Serve the cake with whipped cream or green-tea ice cream.

You need a 9- to 10-inch-diameter, 3-inch-deep cake pan lined with parchment paper.

1 cup cake flour
¹/₂ cup joshinko (rice flour)
²/₃ teaspoon plus a pinch salt
1 cup plus 6 tablespoons (14 ounces)
    sweet azuki bean paste (page 472 or 473)
6 eggs, separated
10 tablespoons sugar
3¹/₂ ounces kuri no kanroni (sweet chestnuts in
    syrup, available at Japanese food stores), cut
    into rough pieces and coated with a mixture of
    1 tablespoon cake flour and 1 tablespoon
    joshinko (rice flour)
1 tablespoon matcha (powdered green tea)
2 cups lightly whipped cream

Place a bamboo or metal steamer basket over plenty of water in a deep pot over high heat. In a medium bowl, sift the two flours and the salt. Line the side and bottom of a 9- or 10-inch cake pan with parchment paper.

Reserve 2 tablespoons of the sweet azuki paste. Put the remaining azuki paste into a bowl. In another bowl, beat the egg yolks with 3 tablespoons sugar until the yolks are slightly thickened and lemony yellow. Add the yolks to the azuki paste little by little, beating thoroughly.

In another bowl, beat the egg whites with 3 tablespoons sugar and a pinch of salt until fairly stiff, shiny peaks form. Add one-third of the egg whites to the mixture of yolks and azuki paste, and mix thoroughly. Fold in the remaining egg whites, gently but thoroughly.

Add the flour mixture to the egg-and-azuki mixture, and fold with a wooden spatula, trying not to deflate the egg white foam.

Fold in the chestnuts gently, and immediately transfer the mixture to the pan. Bang the pan lightly on the counter to eliminate large voids in the batter. With a spatula, make a slight depression in the center of the batter, since the center part will rise more than the surrounding area during steaming.

Transfer the pan to the hot steamer. If you are using a metal steamer, cover the underside of the lid with tightly woven cotton cloth to prevent condensed steam from dripping down onto the cake. Cook the cake over medium-high heat for 25 to 30 minutes.

Check for doneness by inserting a wooden skewer. When the skewer emerges dry, the cake is done. Carefully turn the cake out of the pan onto a rack, and cover the cake with a dry cotton cloth. Let the cake cool to room temperature. The cake can be served at room temperature or chilled.

In a small cup, combine the powdered green tea with 1 tablespoon boiling water, and stir until smooth. Put 1 cup whipped cream into each of two bowls. Stir the green-tea paste into one bowl of whipped cream, and the reserved azuki paste into the other. Serve the cake with both sauces.

- *Yields 12 servings*

STEAMED *KABOCHA* CAKE

Kabocha no Mushigashi

Cooked *kabocha* squash has the most pleasant natural sweetness and creamy texture. Enjoy it in a steamed cake. You need a 7-inch steel cake pan, preferably springform, lined with parchment paper.

> 3 ½ ounces steamed and skinned kabocha or
>   buttercup squash
> 2 ½ tablespoons cake flour
> ⅓ cup joshinko (rice flour)
> 3 eggs, separated
> 5 tablespoons sugar
> Pinch of salt
> ⅓ cup raisins, tossed with 1 tablespoon additional flour
> ⅓ cup walnuts, roughly chopped, and tossed with
>   1 tablespoon additional flour

Place a bamboo or metal steamer basket over plenty of water in a deep pot over high heat. Line a 7-inch cake pan with parchment paper. Press the *kabocha* through a fine sieve set over a large bowl, or mash the *kabocha* in a large bowl with a potato masher. You should have about 1 cup.

Into a medium bowl, sift the two flours.

In another bowl, beat the egg whites with the sugar and a pinch of salt until fairly stiff, shiny peaks form.

Add the egg yolks to the *kabocha* one at a time, stirring with a wooden spatula until the mixture is smooth. Stir in one-quarter of the egg whites to lighten the *kabocha* mixture. With the spatula, fold in the remaining egg whites. Mix thoroughly, but do not deflate the foam.

Add the flour mixture, and mix gently but thoroughly. Add the raisins and walnuts, and give a few more stirs. Immediately pour the mixture into the paper-lined cake pan. With a spatula, make a slight depression in the center of the batter, since the center part will rise more than the surrounding area during steaming. Transfer the pan to the steamer. If you are using a metal steamer, place a tightly woven cotton cloth on the underside of the lid to prevent condensed steam from dripping over the cake. Steam the cake over medium-high heat for 40 minutes.

Insert a wooden skewer into the cake to check the doneness. When the skewer emerges dry, the cake is done. Turn the cake out of the pan onto a rack, cover the cake with a dry cotton cloth, and let the cake cool.

Serve the cake at room temperature or chilled.

- *Yields 8 servings*

LIGHT AND DELIGHTFUL
STEAMED CHOCOLATE CAKE

Mushi Chokoreito Keiki

I developed this recipe for chocolate lovers. Steaming produces a very moist, rich chocolate cake without the use of butter or cream.

If you don't have time to make the sweetened orange strips that are added to the cake, use 2 to 3 tablespoons bitter orange marmalade instead, and add the orange liqueur along with the marmalade to the melted chocolate.

You will need a 9- to 10-inch-diameter, 3-inch-deep cake pan, preferably springform, lined with parchment paper.

SWEETENED ORANGE STRIPS
8 oranges
1²/₃ cups sugar
2 tablespoons orange liqueur

1 cup cake flour
¹/₂ cup joshinko *(rice flour)*
12 ounces bittersweet chocolate,
*   broken into rough pieces*
²/₃ teaspoon salt
6 eggs, separated

In a large pot of boiling water, blanch the whole oranges for 10 to 20 seconds. Drain the oranges, and rinse them under cold running water. Wipe them dry with paper towels. Remove the outer rinds in thin strips with a zester, or use a vegetable peeler to make wide strips. Slice the rind pieces into narrow strips. Reserve the oranges.

In a medium pot, bring 1 quart water to a boil over medium heat. Add the orange strips, and cook them until tender, 5 minutes.

Drain the orange strips in a colander, and cool them in a bowl of ice water. Drain them again, and wipe them dry with paper towels.

In a small saucepan, bring 1 cup of the sugar and 6 tablespoons water to a boil over medium heat. Cook the mixture, stirring, until the sugar is dissolved. Remove the saucepan from the heat, and add the orange strips and liqueur. Let the mixture stand for 30 minutes. You can refrigerate the orange strips in a covered container for up to a week before making the cake, or freeze them for later use.

Place a bamboo or metal steamer basket over plenty of water in a deep pot over high heat. Into a medium bowl, sift the two flours.

In the top of a double boiler over a medium pot of gently simmering water, combine the chocolate and 4 tablespoons water. Stir occasionally until the chocolate is melted. Add the orange strips and their syrup, about $1/4$ cup, and stir. Remove the mixture from the heat. Add the egg yolks to the chocolate mixture one at a time, mixing thoroughly after each addition.

In a bowl, beat the egg whites with the remaining $2/3$ cup sugar until fairly stiff, shiny peaks form.

Stir one-quarter of the egg whites into the chocolate mixture. With a wooden spatula, fold in the remaining egg whites, and mix gently but thoroughly. Fold in the flour mixture. Mix thoroughly, but do not deflate the egg-white foam. Immediately pour the chocolate mixture into the parchment-lined pan.

Transfer the pan to the hot steamer, and steam the cake for 45 minutes. Check for doneness by inserting a wooden skewer. The skewer will emerge a little wet when the cake is done.

Turn the cake out of the pan onto a rack, cover the cake with a dry cotton cloth, and let the cake cool. Chill it in the refrigerator.

Completely peel the oranges, and section them. Serve the cake with the orange sections and the remaining orange syrup in the saucer.

• *Yields 12 servings*

For a change, prepare half the recipe for *kabocha* cake batter (page 477) and half the recipe for chocolate cake batter and steam them together in layers in one pan. The resulting cake will have an attractive look and provide a two-flavor experience.

STEAMED DUMPLINGS
WITH SWEET AZUKI PASTE AND SESAME SEEDS

Goma-anko Manju

Manju is a popular kind of steamed dumpling, made of a thin layer of flour dough that is wrapped around sweet azuki paste, white bean paste, yam paste, or sweet miso paste. In this recipe, sweet azuki paste is flavored with black sesame seeds for an especially rich flavor.

> 1¹/₃ *cups (13 ounces)* anko
> *(sweet azuki bean paste, page 472 or 473)*
> 1¹/₂ *tablespoons black sesame seeds, toasted (page 100)*
> ³/₄ *cup plus 2 teaspoons cake flour*
> ¹/₂ *teaspoon baking powder*
> 4¹/₂ *tablespoons sugar*

In a medium pot, combine the sweet azuki paste and 4 tablespoons water. Cook over medium heat, stirring, until they are thoroughly mixed. Add the sesame seeds, and stir thoroughly. Transfer the mixture to a large pan, and let it cool to room temperature. Divide the bean paste into 12 portions.

Into a medium bowl, sift the flour and baking powder together.

In a small saucepan, combine 2 tablespoons water and the sugar, and cook the mixture over low heat, stirring, until the sugar is dissolved. Transfer the liquid to a large bowl, and let it cool to room temperature.

Add the flour mixture to the sugar liquid, and mix with a wooden spatula. Form the mixture into a ball, and let it stand, covered, for 30 minutes.

Line a bamboo or metal steamer basket with parchment paper, and place the steamer basket over plenty of water in a deep pot over high heat.

On a floured counter, knead the dough briefly, 10 to 20 times. The dough should be as soft to the touch as your earlobe. Roll the dough into a long, thin log, and cut the log into 12 pieces of equal size. Flatten one piece of dough with your palms into a 1-inch disk. Place the dough disk on one hand, pick up one portion of the bean paste with the other hand, and wrap the bean paste in the dough. Make 11 more dumplings in the same way.

Transfer the dumplings to the paper-lined steamer. Cook them over high heat for about 10 minutes.

Serve the dumplings with *ryokucha* green tea or *bancha* brown tea.

• *Yields 12 dumplings*

KABOSU GELATIN

Kabosu no Zeri

Kabosu is much like *yuzu* citron; both are acidic citrus fruits similar to lemons and limes. *Kabosu* juice is used in Japanese dressings and sauces. Unsweetened, the juice is available bottled at Japanese food stores.

Kabosu juice can produce a very refreshing, tart gelatin, perfect for serving on hot summer days. You'll need a 6-inch-square steel, metal, glass, or plastic mold. Or substitute a half-gallon milk carton, cut in half lengthwise to make a long, shallow container.

> *¹/₃ ounce ito kanten (agar-agar strings),*
> *soaked in cold water overnight*
> *¹/₂ cup sugar*
> *¹/₂ cup kabosu juice, preferably, or yuzu juice*
> *9 small mint leaves*
> *3 cups raspberries*

Drain the agar-agar, and squeeze it tightly to remove excess water.

In a pot, combine the agar-agar and 2 cups water. Bring the mixture to a boil over medium heat, and cook, stirring all the time, until the agar-agar is dissolved. Add the sugar, and stir to dissolve it. Continue cooking the mixture for 3 minutes more.

Strain the liquid through a sieve set over a bowl. Let the agar-agar mixture cool for 5 minutes.

Add the *kabosu* or *yuzu* juice to the agar-agar mixture, and stir. Wet a 6-inch-square mold with water, shake out the excess water, and quickly pour in the agar-agar mixture. Let the gelatin cool at room temperature until the surface is almost set.

Place nine mint leaves, evenly spaced, on the surface of the gelatin. Place a raspberry on top of each mint leaf. Cover the mold with plastic wrap, and chill the gelatin in the refrigerator.

Cut the gelatin into 9 square pieces, each with its own mint leaf and raspberry. Serve each square with additional raspberries.

• *Yields 9 servings*

SWEET POTATO CAKE

Yaki Satsuma-imo

When steamed or baked, Japanese sweet potato develops an intense sweetness and creamy texture. A little salt or butter enhances the flavor of this delightful vegetable.

In this preparation, steamed and mashed sweet potato is shaped like miniature sweet potatoes, brushed with egg, and baked in the oven until golden. Serve this sweet with apple jam as a satisfying autumn dessert.

APPLE JAM
4 Granny Smith or other tart, firm apples,
        peeled and quartered
$^2/_3$ cup sugar
Juice from $^1/_2$ lemon
2 tablespoons Calvados (apple brandy)

One 10-ounce Japanese sweet potato,
        steamed until soft, and peeled
5 large egg yolks
$^1/_4$ cup heavy cream
2 tablespoons sugar
Ground nutmeg to taste
Vegetable oil, for greasing your hands and the pan
$^1/_4$ cup black sesame seeds

GARNISH
20 mint leaves

Core each apple wedge, and cut it into thin fan-shaped slices. In a pot, combine the apple and $^1/_2$ cup water. Bring the mixture to a boil, turn the heat to medium-low, and cook, covered, for 10 minutes. Add $^2/_3$ cup sugar and the lemon juice, and cook for 5 minutes more. Add the Calvados. Chill the apple jam in the refrigerator.

Rub the sweet potato through a fine sieve into a bowl, or mash the sweet potato with a potato masher. Add four of the egg yolks, one at a time, mixing thoroughly after each addition. Stir in the cream, 2 tablespoons sugar, and ground nutmeg.

Grease a baking sheet and your hands with a little vegetable oil. Pick up about 3 tablespoons of the sweet-potato mixture, shape it like a miniature sweet potato, and place it on the platter. Use the rest of the mixture to make more mini–sweet potatoes.

Heat the oven to 375 degrees F. In a small cup, combine the remaining egg yolk and 1 tablespoon water, and mix until smooth. With a pastry brush, brush the egg liquid over the surface of the mini-potatoes. Sprinkle the black sesame seeds over the mini-potatoes.

Bake the miniature sweet potatoes until they are golden, about 15 minutes. Let the mini-potatoes cool at room temperature.

Serve the mini-potatoes with apple jam, garnished with a mint leaf on the side.

• *Yields 20 mini-potatoes, or 4 to 5 servings*

TEA-FLAVORED ROLLED CAKE

Ocha no Roru Keiki

This is a Western-style rolled cake with Japanese ingredients. Tea leaves baked in the sponge cake provide a delightfully different flavor and color. The success of this rolled cake is assured if you use the best-quality green tea leaves, known as *sencha*.

2 large eggs
6 tablespoons sugar
1 teaspoon matcha *(powdered green tea)*
2¹/₂ tablespoons sencha *tea leaves*
¹/₃ cup plus 1 tablespoon cake flour
Apricot jam
3 tablespoons apricot or other fruit liqueur
1 cup heavy cream
2 tablespoons sarashi-an *or* koshi-an *(azuki flour)*

Place a 10-by-12-inch sheet of parchment paper on a baking sheet. Beat the eggs in the top of a double-boiler, incorporating 3 tablespoons of the sugar little by little. Remove the egg mixture from the heat, and continue beating it until firm peaks develop.

Place the oven rack at the highest level in the oven. Preheat the oven to 375 degrees F.

Add the *matcha* and 2 tablespoons of the *sencha* tea leaves to the egg mixture, and mix thoroughly. Sift the cake flour, and stir it into the egg mixture. Spread the egg mixture on the parchment paper, forming an 11-by-9-inch rectangle. With a plastic spatula, flatten the surface. Bake the cake on the highest rack of the oven for 10 minutes.

Remove the pan from the oven. Lay a cold, wet towel on the counter. Place the cake, still on the parchment paper, on the wet towel. Carefully loosen the cake from the parchment paper.

In a small bowl, mix the apricot jam and the liqueur. With a pastry brush, brush the mixture over the entire surface of the cake.

In a bowl, whip the cream until it begins to form peaks, and gradually beat in the remaining 3 tablespoons sugar. Beat until firm peaks form. Put one-third of the whipped cream into another bowl. Add the azuki flour to the smaller portion of cream, and stir well.

With a spatula, spread the azuki-cream mixture over one-third of the cake surface along a long edge of the rectangle. Spread the unflavored whipped cream on the remaining two-thirds of the surface of the cake, leaving $1/2$ inch uncovered at the far end. Sprinkle the remaining $1/2$ tablespoon tea leaves over the whipped cream.

Roll the cake from the long edge nearest you, so that the whipped cream with azuki ends up in the center of the roll. Wrap the cake in clean parchment paper, and let the cake stand for 30 minutes.

Cut the cake into $3/4$-inch slices, and serve them with *matcha* green tea or *sencha* tea.

• *Yields 15 slices*

"*Natsumo chikazuku hachiju hachiya, no nimo yama nimo wakaba ga shigeru*": "At the approach of summer in May, rush-green color begins to cover every place, from the fields to the mountains. Now it is the time to harvest the first leaves of the tea plants." In Japan, people from all walks of life hum this song at the beginning of summer. This is an indication of the important role of tea in Japanese society.

The many varieties of teas found in the world today may be divided into three groups, according to how the leaves are processed. Tea may be unfermented, partially fermented, or fully fermented. Japanese tea is an unfermented type, also called green tea.

Drinking tea has many benefits. First of all, it refreshes the mouth. The fluoride naturally occurring in tea also helps to prevent tooth decay. And tea is rich in antioxidants, including vitamins A, C, and E. Recent medical reports have disclosed an additional benefit of green tea: One of its tannins, catechin, helps to lower blood cholesterol. Regardless of the health benefits of this age-old beverage, drinking a cup of delicious green tea is the natural conclusion of a good Japanese meal.

In Japan, fresh-picked tea leaves are steamed, quickly cooled, and rolled by hand or machine while hot air blows them dry. This process helps to preserve the leaves' maximum flavor, to be released when the tea is brewed.

Several types of Japanese tea are available at stores both in and out of Japan. This is how to choose and brew them.

1. **Sencha** is good-quality tea. The timing of the harvest determines its grade. The highest-quality *sencha* is made from the first harvest, in May. Later harvests produce three lower grades. *Sencha* is consumed on both formal and everyday occasions. It has a pleasant bitter flavor and a lovely light-green color.

To brew *sencha* for two, bring a kettle of water to a boil. Warm a teapot and two teacups by filling them with boiling water and then discarding the water. Add 1 tablespoon tea leaves to the pot, and, when the water in the kettle has cooled to 180 to 190 degrees F, pour about 1 cup of the hot water into the teapot. Cover the pot with the lid, and let the tea leaves stand in the hot water for two minutes.

2. **Gyokuro** is premium-quality tea, grown in the shade to prevent bitterness. *Gyokuro* tastes milder and smoother than *sencha,* and is served in smaller than ordinary cups. While an ordinary teacup holds $1/2$ cup tea, a *gyokuro* cup holds only about $1/4$ cup.

Brew *gyokuro* as you would *sencha*, but use only about $3/4$ cup hot water per tablespoon of tea leaves, and steep the leaves three minutes. This will make three servings.

3. **Bancha** is made from mature, tough tea leaves and twigs. It is often roasted, which gives the leaves a brown color. *Bancha* is an everyday, informal tea with a toasty, nonbitter taste that suits all occasions.

To make three servings of *bancha*, put 2 tablespoons tea leaves into a teapot. Add about $1^1/2$ cups boiling water, and let the tea steep for one minute.

4. **Matcha** is a bright green, powdered tea that is prepared and served at formal tea ceremonies. It is made thick or thin, with froth floating on top. The strong taste and pleasant bitterness of *matcha* makes it the most suitable accompaniment to Japanese sweets—like espresso after a rich, sweet dessert.

MATCHA MOUSSE

Matcha no Musu

I created this dessert while playing with agar-agar to see how far I could extend its useful-
ness. Among all forms of *kanten, ito kanten* (the string form) produces the most pleasant,
lightest mousse. Unlike ordinary mousse, this *kanten* mousse can sit at room temperature
for one hour or more without melting, a characteristic very useful for the chef or party host.

¹/₃ ounce ito kanten *(agar-agar strings),
soaked in cold water overnight*
¹/₃ cup sugar
²/₃ cup whole milk
Yolks of 4 large eggs
2 teaspoons matcha *(powdered green tea),
mixed with 2 teaspoons boiling water*
1 cup cream

GARNISH
1 tablespoon matcha *(powdered green tea), mixed with
1 tablespoon sugar and 1¹/₂ tablespoons
boiling water*
Shaved bittersweet chocolate (optional)

Drain the agar-agar, and squeeze it to remove excess water. Transfer the agar-agar to a pot,
and add ¹/₂ cup water. Bring the mixture to a boil, and cook over medium heat, stirring, until
the agar-agar dissolves. Stir in 1 tablespoon of the sugar.

Add the milk to the agar-agar, and bring the mixture almost to a boil. Transfer the mixture to a small bowl. Place a large bowl in the sink, and partially fill the bowl with cold
water. Cool the bowl containing the agar-agar–milk mixture in the cold water.

In a bowl, beat the egg yolks, and beat in the remaining sugar. Beat the egg mixture in
the top of a double-boiler over simmering water until the mixture thickens. Add the mixture
of 2 teaspoons *matcha* and boiling water to the egg mixture, and stir thoroughly.

When the agar-agar–milk mixture is no longer hot, add it to the egg mixture little by
little, beating thoroughly with a whisk. Beat the cream until soft peaks form. With a whisk,
beat the cream into the egg mixture. Transfer the mixture into individual glass dessert cups.
Cover each cup with plastic wrap, and chill the mousse in the refrigerator.

Serve the mousse garnished with the sauce of green tea, sugar, and hot water. Sprinkle shaved bitter chocolate on top, if you like.

• *Yields 10 servings*

JAPANESE GREEN PLUM JUICE

Umejusu

When the hot and humid summer months approached during my childhood, my mother was always busy redecorating each room in our house. Heavy wool curtains and cushions were replaced with light straw blinds and cotton cushions. Paintings of winter and autumn scenes were changed for ones illustrating summer subjects. Heaters were wiped thoroughly and stored away, and, in the days before air conditioning, electric fans were brought into each room.

After this arduous project, my mother, still bathed in sweat, would treat herself to her delicious homemade plum juice. In those times even hot and humid summer days were pleasant, because my mother magically changed our living conditions to suit a summer lifestyle, and frequently served us chilled, refreshing plum juice.

> *2 pounds* ume *(Japanese green plums; see page 50)*
> *Honey*

Rinse the green plums under cold running water, wipe them dry with paper towels, and remove the brown stems with a toothpick. Prick each green plum all over its skin with the toothpick.

Sterilize a large glass jar. Pack the green plums tightly in it. Pour in enough honey to cover the green plums completely.

Store the jar, covered, in a cool, dark, and dry place for 1 week, shaking the jar gently every day.

Refrigerate the jar for another 2 weeks.

Strain the juice through a sieve lined with a tightly woven cotton cloth. Refrigerate the plum juice in a bottle, covered. Serve it diluted with five parts cold plain or sparkling water to 1 to 2 parts juice.

MOM'S JAPANESE GREEN PLUM WINE

Umeshu

For me, one of the joys of plum wine preparation comes when I can taste the first sip of mature, year-old wine. Fresh *ume,* Japanese green plums, are unfortunately still hard to find outside Japan. Perhaps you may find them at some large Japanese supermarkets. If you or a friend is in Japan during plum season, and regulations permit, bring back several bags, or have your friend do so. Look for *ume* toward the end of May or the beginning of June.

Rock sugar is preferred for this preparation because it dissolves more slowly than granulated sugar, and so helps to extract more juice from the green plums. Both rock sugar and distilled white liquor are available everywhere in Japan.

> *2 pounds* ume *(Japanese green plums)*
> *1 to 1¹/₂ pounds rock sugar*
> *2 quarts distilled white liquor (30 percent alcohol)*
> *for making fruit liqueurs*

Rinse the green plums carefully in cold water, and wipe them dry with paper towels. Remove the stems with a toothpick. Sterilize a gallon glass jar by immersing it in boiling water for 15 minutes.

Place one-quarter of the green plums in the bottom of the jar, and cover them with one-quarter of the rock sugar. Repeat this layering process until all the green plums and sugar are used.

Pour the distilled liquor over the plums and sugar, and cover the jar tightly with a lid. Store the jar in a dark, cool place. Once or twice every month for the first three months, shake the jar gently to dissolve the sugar in the liquid.

After one year, when you are ready to prepare a new batch of plum wine for next year, it is time to filter the previous year's matured wine. Strain the plum wine through a sieve lined with a tightly woven cotton cloth, funnel the filtered wine into sterilized bottles, and cap them tightly. Refrigerate the "drunken" plums in a clean glass jar.

Serve plum wine on the rocks.

With its rich golden color and sweet, tart flavor, *umeshu*, "plum wine," welcomes our guests all year-round. *Umeshu* preparation and drinking is a continuous cycle of work and enjoyment. When Japanese green plums appear in vegetable markets and supermarkets in June, every liquor store and supermarket stocks kits for making plum wine. Each kit includes a large glass jar, a bag of rock sugar, and a carton of distilled white liquor, which contains about 30 percent alcohol. By this time of year a family will have consumed most of their store of two-year-old plum wine. (If not, they may let it mature for several years, which will improve the color and taste.) This is now the time to filter the one-year-old plum wine and store it in clean glass bottles for consumption over the next 12 months, and to prepare this year's batch of wine. As long as a family faithfully balances production and consumption, they can be assured of an unbroken supply of this delicious drink. The trick is to make sure to be in Japan during the few weeks every June when the plums are available. If one season is missed, one year later the family could face a year without plum wine—not a very pleasant prospect.

After the plum wine is made, liquor-soaked plums remain. These "drunken plums," as I call them, are delicious to nibble as they are, or they may be served with the drink (only to the most special guests, since the quantity is limited).

Factory-made *umeshu* is available at liquor stores and Japanese supermarkets, but unfortunately it is less tasty and much sweeter than the homemade variety.

SOURCES FOR
JAPANESE FOOD PRODUCTS

CALIFORNIA

Marukai Wholesale Mart
1740 West Artesia Boulevard
Gardena, California 90248
310-660-6300

Suruki Supermarket
71 East Fourth Avenue
San Mateo, California 94401
650-347-5288

Sakai K. Uoki Company
1656 Post Street
San Francisco, California 94115
415-921-0514

CONNECTICUT

Fuji Mart Corporation Greenwich
1212 East Putnum Avenue
Old Greenwich, Connecticut 06878
203-698-2107

MAINE

Johnny's Selected Seeds
Foss Hill Road
Albion, Maine 04910
207-437-4301
www.johnnyseeds.com

MARYLAND

Daruma
6931 Arlington Road
Suite E
Bethesda, Maryland 20814
301-654-8832

NEW JERSEY

Nippon Daido USA, Incorporated
1385 16th Street
Fort Lee, New Jersey 07024
201-944-0020

NEW YORK

Fish-One Seafood Center
7145 Yellowstone Boulevard
Forest Hills, New York 11375
800-544-5884
718-544-0942

Fuji Mart Corporation Scarsdale
816 White Plains Road
Scarsdale, New York 10583
914-472-1468

Katagiri
224 East 59th Street
New York, New York 10022
212-755-3566
www.katagiri.com

Nippon Daido USA, Incorporated
522 Mamaroneck Avenue
White Plains, New York 10605
914-683-6735

Sunrise Mart
4 Stuyvesant Street, 2nd Floor
New York, New York 10003
212-598-3040

OREGON

Nichols Garden Nursery
1190 Old Salem Road Northeast
Albany, Oregon 97321
541-928-9280
www.nicholsgardennursery.com

Uwajimaya
10500 Southwest Beaverton-Hillsdale Highway
Beverton, Oregon 97005
503-643-4512

TENNESSEE

Oriental Best Market
3588 Ridgeway
Memphis, Tennessee 38115
901-366-1570

TEXAS

Nippon Daido USA, Incorporated
11138 Westheimer Road
Houston, Texas 77042
713-785-0815

VIRGINIA

Naniwa Foods
6730 Curran Street
McLean, Virginia 22101
703-893-7209

WASHINGTON

Uwajimaya
519 Sixth Avenue
Seattle, Washington 98104
206-624-6248
www.uwajimaya.com

Uwajimaya
15555 24th Avenue Northeast
Bellevue, Washington 98007
425-747-9012

I N D E X

liver, skewered, 409

pan-fried flavored, 412

simmered with chestnuts,
422-424

simmered Chikuzen-style,
420-422

skewered, 404

skewered with long onion,
406-407

skewered, miso-marinated,
408

skewered with pickled
plum and *shiso*,
407-408

in spicy vinegar marinade,
415-416

steamed with *kimizu*
sauce, 425-426

steamed with *shiitake* and
long onion, 424-425

stir-fried rice and, 315

teriyaki with orange,
413-414

and vegetable miso soup,
223-224

wings, skewered,
409-410

chikin raisu (stir-fried rice
and chicken), 315

chikin-katsu (crisp chicken
cutlet), 417

chikuwa (fish cake cylinder),
126

chile-bean sauce, 54-55

chilled sesame squares,
179-180

Chinese cabbage, 38, 434

simmered with fried thin
tofu and mung-bean
noodles, 264

Chinese chives, 44-45

chirashizushi, 285

chocolate cake, steamed,
478-479

chopsticks, cooking, 15-16

chrysanthemum leaves, 49

chukasoba (Chinese-style
noodles), 157-158

chilled, 346-348

chilled, with spicy sesame
sauce, 348-349

crisp pan-fried with
vegetables and seafood,
344-345

stir-fried, for a party,
332-334

cinnamon, 53

citron, 33, 52, 73

clam and miso chowder,
Hiroko's, 226-227

clams

purging, 22

steamed in *sake*, 194

classic agar-agar gelatin in
syrup, 113-114

clear soup with soft egg
cake, 213-214

cloves, 53

consommé with duck
dumplings, 217-218

consommé with sardine
dumplings, 215-216

cooking implements, 9-19

cooking techniques, 20-32

cookstove, portable, 18

cornstarch, 114

creamy fish croquettes,
396-397

creamy sesame-vinegar
dressing with broccoli,
103

cubed vegetable miso soup,
222

cucumber

Japanese, 41

rolling in salt, 24

cutting techniques, 26-29

D

dai-ginjoshu (premier sake),
86

daikon, 33-34, 70

sprouts of, 40

daikon oroshi (grated
daikon), 22

daikon simmered with *yuzu-*
miso sauce, 253-254

daikon to sumoku sāmon-
sando kimizu-zoe
(*daikon* and smoked
salmon sandwiches with
kimizu sauce), 169-170

daizu (soybeans), 96-97,
98-99

daizu gohan (soybean rice),
98-99

daizu hamosu (soybean
hummus), 175

GAYLORD RG